ISLAM IN THE
AFRICAN-AMERICAN
EXPERIENCE

RICHARD BRENT TURNER

INDIANA
UNIVERSITY
PRESS
Bloomington & Indianapolis

The paper used in this publication meets the minimum
requirements of American National Standard for Information
Sciences—Permanence of Paper for Printed Library
Materials, ANSI Z39.48–1984.

Manufactured in the United States of America

Library of Congress Cataloging-in-Publication Data

Turner, Richard Brent.
Islam in the African-American experience / Richard Brent Turner.
p.   cm.
Includes bibliographical references (p.   ) and index.
ISBN 0–253–33238–9 (cl. : alk. paper). — ISBN 0–253–21104–2 (pbk. : alk. paper)
1. Islam—United States.   2. Afro-Americans—Religion.   I. Title.
BP67.U6T87   1997
297'.089'96073—dc21   96-52515

1   2   3   4   5   02   01   00   99   98   97

To the memory of my beloved cousin,
LAMONTE W. FOREMAN (1947–1994)

CONTENTS

ILLUSTRATIONS

PREFACE

The genesis of this book can be traced to the autumn of 1973, the beginning of my junior year at Boston University. I was studying the early history of African-American Islam in Gayraud Wilmore's course, "Black Sects and Cults." Although I had only recently declared a major in the Department of Religion, I knew there was something special about the fascinating but incomplete narratives of Noble Drew Ali and W. D. Fard that I was reading in C. Eric Lincoln, *The Black Muslims in America*; E. U. Essien-Udom, *Black Nationalism*; Arthur H. Fauset, *Black Gods of the Metropolis*; and Gayraud Wilmore, *Black Religion and Black Radicalism*.

I continued to think about the mysterious identities of Noble Drew Ali and W. D. Fard during my senior year in college and while pursuing an M.A. in the Afro-American Studies Program at Boston University. However, I did not develop a serious research plan to learn more about African-American Islam until 1980, when I began my Ph.D. work in the Department of Religion at Princeton University. For the next six years, Princeton's rich intellectual environment provided me with the training and the resources to write *Islam in the United States in the 1920s: The Quest for a New Vision in Afro-American Religion*, a ground-breaking dissertation on the Indian-based Ahmadiyya Movement in Islam, which I later recognized as a hidden key to the multi-racial dimension of African-American Islam. My initial inspiration for pursuing the Ahmadiyya lead came from Tony Martin's book *Race First*, which mentioned their journals, the *Muslim Sunrise* and *The Review of Religions*, in the context of Marcus Garvey's movement in the 1920s. Generous financial support from Princeton's Graduate School enabled me to spend the summer of 1983 researching these journals in the New York Public Library and to follow up on other leads related to the Ahmadiyya movement in Chicago.

During my years on the faculty of the University of California, Santa Barbara, I transformed my dissertation into this book. My travels have taken me across the United States to the Library of Congress and the F.B.I. archives in Washington, D.C., the Schomburg Center for Research in New York, the W. E. B. DuBois Institute and Widener Library at Harvard, and the homes and institutions of Muslims in Boston, Washington, D.C., Chicago, Los Angeles, and San Francisco. This study has truly been enriched by the information and insights that I have acquired during these travels.

Until recently, the history of the African-American Muslim community in the United States had been on a treadmill for several decades. Scholars repeated the same information in articles and books, shedding little light on either the developments in the community or its transformation. One of the special concerns of this book is to break new ground in our understanding of signification or identity formation among African Americans who chose to identify with Islam. I have tried to investigate new documents as well as to suggest new interpretations that I hope can be considered as providing a quantum leap in our knowledge of Islam in every period of African-American history.

I owe thanks to many people for their assistance in the conception and publication of this book. I wish to thank John Wilson and Albert Raboteau, who served as advisors for my doctoral work at Princeton. I am indebted to Cain Felder for his advice and encouragement during my Princeton years and beyond. Appreciation is also due to Randall Burkett, who made the resources of the W. E. B. DuBois Institute at Harvard available to me. I have truly been blessed to have had the support and guidance of Ernest Allen, Jr., Yvonne Haddad, and Sulayman Nyang, who read various drafts of my manuscript and praised my work when my spirit was low. I express my love and thanks to my colleagues in the Department of Black Studies at the University of California, who provided me with a haven in a storm during my last two years of writing. Cedric Robinson, my department chair, unselfishly read every chapter of the manuscript and suggested important critical insights, and Claudine Michel offered unwavering moral support during my battle to achieve social justice at the University of California, Santa Barbara. To Lindsey Reed and Carole Self, I express thanks for extraordinary editorial assistance. Special thanks are due to the Ahmadiyya Movement in Islam, a community that provided important interviews and information for this study. And finally, Robert Sloan, my sponsoring editor at Indiana University Press, and Jeff Ankrom, Assistant Managing Editor, enabled this project as well.

On the personal order, I wish to thank my mother and father, Mavis and James Turner, and my aunt, Kelsie Foreman, for providing me with love, education, and spiritual guidance during my childhood. As noted, this book is dedicated to the memory of my cousin, Lamonte W. Foreman, who supported me in my struggle to finish this project until his last day on earth, October 13, 1994. My dear friend and companion, J. B. Parker, provided me with countless cups of coffee and good humor as I worked on the various drafts of this book in the wee hours of the morning. And finally, thanks be to God.

Introduction

WHAT SHALL WE CALL HIM?

ISLAM AND AFRICAN-AMERICAN IDENTITY

The name means everything.   —Noble Drew Ali

Black tells you about skin color and what side
of town you live on. African-American evokes discussion of the world.   —The Reverend Jesse Jackson

Naming the African American has been a problematic issue in black
political and religious discourse. Jesse Jackson, for example, has recently
suggested that black people in the United States call themselves African-
American in order to emphasize "the African roots of American culture"
and "the link to Africa as a key to America's relations with the third
world."[1] Suggestions like this one have drawn mixed reactions from black
leaders. Arthur Ashe, the late tennis star, believed that " 'African-American' was much more appropriate than 'Afro-American' or 'black' or any
other alternative,"[2] while Bayard Rustin, the late civil-rights leader, said in
1971 that African Americans "should not be fooled by names or appearances. The real problems lie beneath the surface."[3] Clearly, the issue of
naming is crucial to the formation of black identity in North America.
Unlike white Americans, African Americans, who were involuntarily
taken away from their land of origin, have been stripped of their genealogy and their history. For these Americans to reclaim a cultural identity,
they must not only reject the names imposed on them by their former slave
masters or chosen from a European repertoire, but also create new names
that signify new identities. Since the colonial era, Islam has provided black
Americans with alternative names and identities. With this perspective in
mind, Noble Drew Ali, the charismatic and mysterious prophet of the

Moorish Science Temple of America, issued a universal message to his followers in the 1920s, entitled "What Shall We Call Him?" He proclaimed:

> So often our various journalists find trouble in selecting the proper name for the Moorish American. Some say "Negro," another will brand him "Race Man," still another will call him "Afro-American." . . . Is it that these people had no proper name when first brought to these shores in the early part of the seventeenth century? If so what was it? Did not the land from which they were forced have a name? . . . The matter of the various names given to these twenty-two million people with all of the colors of every race of the globe was an act of European psychology. They gave him a name, then defined it as something inferior to theirs.[4]

The questions that these words raise regarding black identity and names permeate the history of Islam in America from the eighteenth century to the present. This book is an attempt to look comprehensively at this history and to analyze the threads of signification that are woven in the ever-changing tapestry of a vibrant religious tradition that has profoundly influenced political consciousness, intellectual thought, economics, music, dress, diet, and family life in black America.

Signification (the issue of naming and identity) is not only the interpretative thread that runs through the historical narrative of Islam in black America, it is also the key to understanding that history in the context of global Islam. This book demonstrates how signification became a central aspect of Islam in West Africa and the Middle East before modernity. In these contexts, black peoples' signifying themselves as the people they wanted to be, through their embracing of Islam, was the result of the adaptation of the religion to local cultures that was integral to global Islam. In America, signification continued to be central in African-American Islam. There is a difference, of course, between a people who manage their own society and who themselves determine, on a selective basis, which aspects of an Arabian Islamic tradition they wish to practice and a religious organization of people, drawn from a numerical minority of a society who nominally declare themselves to be separate from that society. However, in both America and in West Africa, naming and renaming became controlling acts that documented black peoples' struggles to define themselves separately in the context of global Islam.

The concept of signification, as Charles H. Long has developed it in the context of religious studies, is the basic analytical tool used throughout this book, although it should be noted that I also draw upon the ideas of Michael Marony, Kenneth W. Harrow, Steven Barboza, R. Lawrence Moore, John Esposito, William Strickland, Vincent Cornell, Yohanan Friedman, Yvonne Haddad, Sulayman Nyang, Ernest Allen, C. Eric Lincoln, Lawrence Mamiya, and others. By signification, Long refers to the process by which names, signs, and stereotypes were given to non-European realities and peoples during the western conquest and exploration of the world, from Christopher Columbus's voyage in 1492 into the twentieth century. Signification was part of the ambiguous heritage of the Enlightenment. For on the one hand, people of color were categorized, stigmatized, and exploited for the purposes of economic and political hegemonies, but on the other, egalitarianism and the universality of humanity were affirmed by critical Enlightenment thinkers such as Thomas Jefferson and John Locke. The black American community was signified during this period as inferior to the dominant group in America. Since slavery, however, Islam has undercut this signification by offering black Americans the chance to signify themselves, giving them new names and new political and cultural identities.[5] Thus, signification was both imposed and self-affirmed.

In Long's work, signification is a thematic mode, as well as a concept. This book, however, develops signification into a concept for understanding the cultural strategies of the African-American community more generally and the black experience in global Islam. The most useful way to see this concept may be as self-signification—the counter-conception to the hegemonic discourse of an oppressive majority community; for it identifies an ideological fulcrum which has enabled this community to achieve independence from the dominant culture. There are two sources of meaning for the term, one derived from popular culture and the other from intellectual culture. In African-American popular culture, signifying is a clever verbal game that has a long, rich, and continuing tradition. More important for this study, however, is the intellectual meaning of signification, derived from Ferdinand de Saussure's work in structural linguistics, which posits that between truth and falsity is something else—an interface of meanings—signification. According to Saussure, language has a structure of its own—meanings and names are arbitrary. Thus, there are no absolute meanings. African slaves in the New World knew this when they received their European names. For the same names that Europeans gave to blacks were indications of another time, space, and meaning for black people. Signification thus involved double meanings. It was both a potent form of oppression and a potent form of resistance to oppression.[6]

The sharp and original angle of vision in Long's work is connected to other theoretical writings about hegemony and resistance, or what has sometimes been called "the infrapolitics of subordinate groups." There is a major discourse about what defines, and who gets to use, the space of a dissident culture. It has been highlighted, above all, by James C. Scott in *Domination and the Arts of Resistance*. (Scott himself, of course, acknowledges his indebtedness to his antecedents, such as the Subaltern Studies group, especially Ranajit Guha; Antonio Gramsci; and Barrington Moore, Jr.) In Scott's view, all relationships of domination and subordination are two-way. On the one hand, the dominators construct a public persona and offer a public transcript that makes their domination seem natural, even inevitable. But the subordinate, faced with their seeming powerlessness, devise strategies for creating their own social space, and they become proficient in the arts of political disguise, perpetuating an infrapolitics of resistance, a crucial element of which is the hidden transcript. Chapter 1 of the present volume draws on aspects of Scott's multiply staged analysis to develop the signification of naming and the politics of identity among African Muslim slaves in America. However, Charles Long's insider concept of signification remains the key to understanding the cultural strategies of the African-American community in the context of global Islam.[7]

In America, a black person preserved his or her Muslim name or took a new Muslim name to maintain or reclaim African cultural roots or to negate the power and meaning of the European name. The African-American adoption of a Muslim name, whether the person was a Muslim or not, always signified a radical change in political, cultural, and/or religious identity. This was positive; it represented intellectual resistance to racism. With this view in mind, although black Americans were signified outside the realm of mainstream structures, they were empirical others—they were not just the product of theory and imagination, but real others who had their own meanings and significations. Thus, naming and renaming, in the context of Islam, documented the struggle of people of African descent to define their communities of origin in the context of a global non-European religious tradition.

This study also analyzes how the signification of black people in Islam has been acted out in contemporary African-American culture. Islam has a double meaning in this context. On the one hand, the religion has a central spiritual, communal, and global meaning among African-American Muslims, based on a genuine conversion experience rooted in global Islam and divorced in some ways from American politics and public life. On the other hand, Islam has a political and cultural meaning in African-American popular culture. This latter meaning locates and utilizes the symbols of Islam outside the confines of the mosque and particular Muslim communities and asserts their life and meaning in a general understanding and articulation of African-American cultural and political identities. In African-American popular culture, then, the adoption of the symbols of Islam sometimes has little to do with religion.

Islam's double meaning for African Americans comes together in the theme of jihad—the Muslims' struggle for the truth in the way of God. I have imposed jihad as a conceptual construct in this book with the understanding that striving or struggling to defend and "extend the Islamic community through preaching, education and [self-transformation] . . . is [an] obligation incumbent on all Muslims." The signification and racial separatism of black people in Islam have varied as Muslims have interpreted jihad differently in different locations and periods of history. As Vincent J. Cornell has noted, "jihad has many meanings, from warfare against unbelievers to an inner struggle with the ego," which is the "greater jihad." The "greater jihad" and the "lesser jihad," which in the modern interpretation of the concept is the "jihad of words," connect themes of signification in twentieth-century African-American Islam to issues of global Islam as African-American Muslims have utilized this concept vis-a-vis signification.[8]

Islam in the African-American Experience has two parts: Part I, "Root Sources" and Part II, "Prophets of the City." Part I of the book roots twentieth-century African-American Islam in the themes, structures, and history of global Islam in the Middle East, West Africa, and antebellum America. Part II tells the stories of the "Prophets of the City"—the leaders of the new urban-based African-American Muslim movements in the twentieth century. These "prophets of the city" reinterpreted the global themes of African-American Islam in the context of the significant Pan-Africanist impulse in twentieth-century black America.

Some of the book's ideas may surprise the reader. The book takes the study of Islam as a world religion out of the realm of mythic racial harmony and positions it in a historical context of racial, ethnic, and political divisions that influenced the history of slavery in America. It offers evidence that racial separatism among Muslims in America in the twentieth century was not completely the result of black nationalism and was not a new phenomenon in Islam, but was, in fact, a normative pattern for black people in Islam that was established in Africa before the Atlantic slave trade. Thus, the pre-American situation of African Muslim slaves is important for understanding the history of Islam in America. This study attempts to move beyond the parochial and xenophobic nationalism that has characterized the social scientific construction of black American Islam in the twentieth century. It proposes that we counterbalance the weight accorded to black nationalism as the major force in shaping Islam in black America by examining the missionizing influences from India that have been prominent since the late nineteenth century. This will lead us to a discussion of the Ahmadiyya Movement in Islam, a missionary group from India which was a model for heterodoxy and continuous prophecy, and which provides one of the hidden keys to the history of Islam in America in the twentieth century. Although the Nation of Islam and its legacy are at the heart of this book, the Ahmadiyya movement functions as a kind of bridge between the saga of the Moorish Science Temple and that of Elijah Muhammad's movement by reading Ahmadiyya as integral to the development of an African-American Islam that possesses its own kind of continuity and integrity.

More important, the Ahmadiyya movement's missionary work among African Americans provided a model of multi-racial community experience. This experience is central to a significant theme of this book. From the early twentieth century to the present, there have been two racial dimensions in African-American Islam: racial-separatist Islam, as typified by the Nation of Islam, and multi-racial Islam, as typified, until recently, by the Ahmadiyya Movement in Islam.[9] Since the beginning of the Ahmadiyya mission to America in the 1920s, there has been dynamic tension between these two dimensions of African-American Islam; tension which is evident in the work of the two foremost African-American Muslim leaders today: Imam Warith Deen Mohammed who represents multi-racial Islam and Minister Louis Farrakhan who represents racial separatism. In Chapter 4 this book will explicate how the Ahmadiyya's jihad of words—expressed in its widespread distribution of the Quran and instructional materials on Muslim prayer rituals and doctrines—was groundbreaking in preparing African-American converts for other versions of Islam in America; and in Chapter 6, we will learn how the Ahmadis paved the way for Imam Warith Deen Mohammed's multi-racial Islamic mission today by working behind the scenes to influence him and by subtly persuading his late father, Elijah Muhammad, to understand the virtues of multi-racial Islam. All of this new information builds on the work of two pioneers in the study of Islam in America, Yvonne Haddad and C. Eric Lincoln. However, my analysis of the Ahmadiyya movement goes beyond their work and offers a fresh re-interpretation from the perspective of identity politics as it revises Haddad's typology of separatist "immigrant" and "indigenous" Muslim communities in the United States and Lincoln's single-minded emphasis on the racial-separatist dimension of African-American Islam.

Until recently, the history of Islam in America has been largely ignored by historians of American religions, despite the fact that Islam is today the second largest religion in the United States, surpassed only by Christianity. Informed observers believe that there could be almost eight million Muslims in the United States by the year 2000.[10] A major world religion and an arena for politics and cultural identification, Islam is at the center of current world events. Yet, one still looks in vain for a complete history of Islam in America.

Little enough has been written on the history of black Christianity in America. Much less is known about Islam in black America. Part of the problem has been the assumption that primary sources do not exist or that they were invented by overzealous, heritage-hungry black historians and writers. The popular novelist James A. Michener stated this presupposition in the *New York Times Book Review* in reaction to Alex Haley's novel *Roots*:

> To have Kunta Kinte, or one of his fellows praying to Allah while chained in the bottom of a Christian ship is an unjustified sop to contemporary developments rather than true reflection of the past.[11]

Studies by C. Eric Lincoln, Allan Austin, Clifton Marsh, Yvonne Haddad, Steven Barboza, and others have shown that Muslims did indeed leave a record of their experience in America.[12] In keeping with their efforts, I have attempted to analyze slave narratives, black autobiographies, journals of white observers and Muslims, missionary reports, twentieth-century African-American archival materials, and personal interviews to explore the rich religious experiences of black Muslims in America.

Part One

ROOT SOURCES

Chapter 1

MUSLIMS IN A STRANGE LAND

AFRICAN MUSLIM SLAVES IN AMERICA

To rob people or countries of their name is to set in
motion a psychic disturbance that can, in turn, create
a permanent crisis of identity.   —Jan R. Carew

In one of his novels, Daniel Panger dramatized the life of a man he called
"Black Ulysses":

> I am Estevan, a black man from Azemour in Morocco. And this is an
> account of my journey with Alvar Nuñez, called Cabeza de Vaca. And if there
> has been a like journey in all the long history of humankind, I have never heard
> of it. Even the tale of Jason and his courageous Argonauts, although magnifi-
> cent by any standards, is not its equal. But you be the judge.[1]

Estevan, the first identifiable Muslim in North America, was a black
Moroccan guide and interpreter who came to Florida from Spain in 1527
with the Panfilo de Narvaez expedition. For more than a decade, he
explored unknown areas of the southwest with Spaniards who were
commissioned by Emperor Charles V. In 1539, Estevan was the first non-
Indian to enter the fabled seven cities of Cibola, in what are presently the
states of New Mexico and Arizona. Shortly thereafter he was executed by
the Zuñi Indians.[2]

Estevan's story was not known to students of American history before
the twentieth century primarily because he was an African and a Muslim.
Three hundred years after Estevan's death, Noah Webster wrote authori-
tatively: "Of the wooly-haired Africans who constitute the principal part
of the inhabitants of Africa, there is no history and there can be none. That
race has remained in barbarism from the first ages of the world." Even if

some enlightened people in Webster's time discounted this statement because of its blatant racism, few of his contemporaries were aware that although Islam was a relatively rare phenomenon in the United States in the nineteenth century, there had been a subtle Muslim presence in America since the early 1500s.[3]

Primary sources indicate that Estevan was a slave in Spain and America; the cataclysmic Atlantic slave trade was already in operation during his time. The implications of this enterprise, which resulted in the enslavement of more than ten million Africans and the death of countless more, are still being studied. Allan Austin estimates that 7 to 8 percent of the West Africans enslaved in America from the seventeenth to the nineteenth centuries were Muslims.[4] These Muslims were a distinctive and resistant minority in the slave population. Their life stories are fascinating and extraordinary, for they tell us about African princes, teachers, soldiers, and scholars who were captured in their homelands and taken across the Atlantic Ocean to the "strange" Christian land called America, where they became the only known Muslims to maintain Islamic traditions during the antebellum period. Although their presence in America was noted for posterity only because they were objects of interest for orientalists, Christian missionaries, and curious journalists in America and England, these African Muslims were far more significant than anyone could have imagined in their time. They were the transmitters of a major world religion to the American continent. Later in this chapter, we will explore who they were, where they came from, what they did in America, and how their signification of themselves, which involved preservation of Muslim names and traditions and literacy in Arabic, constituted intellectual resistance to slavery. We will also examine why the "old Islam" of these original African Muslim slaves did not survive to the present day, but was replaced by a "new American Islam" on the eve of the twentieth century.

First, however, we must document the root sources of Islam in America, long before the twentieth-century saga of the Nation of Islam, and position this early history in a global Islamic context. The situation of African Muslim slaves prior to their arrival in America is important for understanding the history of Islam in America. The new religion that African Muslim slaves brought to America was born and shaped in West Africa and the Middle East, where Muslims had their own forms of signification and racial separatism before modernity. This last fact is important because it links the racial separation and signification of the Nation of Islam and related groups to a racial separatism and signification that was endemic to Islam throughout its history and that was connected to Islamic jihad or struggle for the truth. The starting point for this chapter, then, is the seventh century, when Islam was established as a world religion, for it is impossible to understand the significance of Islam in black America fully without examining briefly black Islam as it developed among Africans in the Muslim world and West Africa prior to the Atlantic slave trade.

PART I. THE MUSLIM WORLD AND WEST AFRICA

Black People in the Muslim World

From the seventh century until the beginning of the modern era, Islam used conquest, conversion, and trade to establish a global civilization that united Africans, Asians, and Europeans under a common religion, language, and rule. Indeed, the mingling and cohabitation of many different peoples under the domain of Islamic civilization produced new ethnic, racial, and political identities in the world. Important here is the interaction of North African Muslim conquerors, teachers, and traders with the native populations of sub-Saharan Africa, for West African Islam was born and shaped in these encounters.[5] West African Islam can be traced to the introduction of Islam in the Sudan in the eighth or ninth century. There began the central themes of signification, separatism, and identity for black people in Islam in premodern times. To understand this story, we must first examine briefly how Islam adapted to black people and other non-Arab peoples during the lifetime of the Prophet Muhammad and shortly thereafter.

From the beginning of the religion, slavery was a central issue for black people in the Islamic world. Although Arabs had enslaved black people and other peoples long before Muhammad's time, the issue for Muslims began with the model of the Prophet. For Muhammad was a slaveholder. Early in his career as Prophet and reformer of the Arabian peninsula, however, Muhammad freed his slaves and later established structures to regulate slavery in Islam. In 622 C.E., the revelations from Allah that Muhammad believed he had received in the mountains near his home and his attacks on polytheism and social injustice in Mecca were synthesized into a new religion and community when he and his followers fled Mecca to settle in Medina. Muhammad encouraged the emancipation of slaves and accepted black people as equals in his new religion and community. Bilal, a recently freed Abyssinian slave, became part of the inner circle of Islam and the first muezzin—the person who called Muslims to prayer in Medina. In 614 C.E., Muhammad had sent a group of his followers across the Red Sea to the black Christian kingdom of Abyssinia (Ethiopia) to escape persecution. This development undoubtedly contributed to his positive attitudes and actions toward black people, for there was not a hint of anti-black prejudice in the Quran.[6]

If Muhammad was able to purge notions of black inferiority from himself and his companions during the first generation of Islam, he was not able to eliminate this evil from the Bedouin tribal people who brought Islam to the conquered lands. Often their prejudices overlapped with anti-black prejudices embedded in some of the cultures of the lands that they conquered.[7]

The exact relation between black people and the institution of Islamic slavery is still an unresolved question that is textured with ambiguities about the inferiorization of black people in the Muslim world, which was complicated by the multi-racial nature of Islamic slavery and by the fact that slavery had been an integral aspect of African societies since the beginning of recorded time. Moreover, some black slaves and their descendants assumed specialized occupational roles in the Muslim world that further obscured the question of inferiorization. For some of the sons of African slaves became prominent leaders in North Africa, the Middle East, Spain, and Portugal. Typical of this trend were Yaqub al-Mansur, black ruler of Morocco and parts of Portugal and Spain in the twelfth century; Abu Hassan Ali, "the Black Sultan," who captured Castille and Gibraltar for Morocco in 1330; and Ibrahim al-Mahdi, ruler of Syria and caliph of Baghdad in the ninth century. Although we will return briefly to the question of black people in Islamic slavery later in this chapter, this issue is not a primary concern of this book and deserves more critical attention from Arabists and Africanists.[8]

Jihad was a dynamic principle of resistance that partially explained both Islam's rapid growth as a major world civilization and religion and the way that it adapted to the local cultures in Asia, Africa, and Europe. The essence of jihad as a religious obligation for all Muslims was the "struggle for truth in the way of God," which in Islam's history was expressed in different forms, from military force against nonbelievers to an inner struggle with one's self. The former interpretation of jihad came to be emphasized in some classical sources that contended that the basic political fact of the religion was that "Muslims ought to be ruled by Muslims." Eventually, some Muslims indirectly found Quranic sanction for aggressive jihad in verses that mentioned fighting (*qaatilu*): "Those who believe fight in the way of God; and those who do not, only fight for the powers of evil; so you should fight the allies of Satan; surely, the stratagem of Satan is feeble" (4:76).[9]

During Muhammad's lifetime, jihad emerged as a method of expanding Islam by military force as Muslims divided the known world into the "house of Islam" (*dar al-Islam*) and the "house of war" (*dar al-harb*). The first jihads occurred when Muhammad led his armies victoriously against the Jews in Medina and the polytheists in Mecca in 630 C.E. According to Arab Muslim oral tradition, Muhammad sent messages to the leaders of the Byzantine Christian and Persian empires and Ethiopia, asking them to accept Islam. Two years after Muhammad's death, his successor Abu Bakr unified Arabia under Islam and began the conquest of Syria, which was controlled by the Byzantine Christian empire. By 644 C.E., the Muslims controlled Syria, Egypt, Iran, and Iraq. During the next one hundred years they extended their power to India, the Mediterranean areas of Africa, and southern France. Eventually they established a series of culturally dynamic empires that challenged Europe until the colonial era.[10]

The Arabs were a ruling minority elite in much of the Islamic world. They "enjoyed the highest degree of prestige and honor, with non-Arab Muslims ranked below them, and 'unbelievers' at the bottom." The lands that the Arabs conquered, in turn, adopted their language and religion and eventually created an "international Arabic culture." Arabic culture reached its peak in Egypt, Baghdad, Persia, Turkey, Spain, and India—and each land contributed "its own values and practices."[11]

Although Sunni and Shia Islam emerged as the central sects of the religion, Islam adapted to the local cultures of Asia, North Africa, and Europe. This is an important point because it established the possibility of a separatist West African Islam once the religion penetrated the Sudan. From the beginning, the very nature of Islam as an all-encompassing way of life for Muslims encouraged adaptation of the religion to local cultures. In this context, Michael Morony's groundbreaking study of the Muslim conquest of Iraq in the seventh and eighth centuries will serve as a paradigm for understanding the construction of black identities in the Muslim world and West Africa. His work emphasizes "different and conflicting trends among Muslims, multidimensional explanations" and creative adaptation by individuals based on their different backgrounds and interests. Morony has demonstrated that both continuity and change occurred in the cultural contacts between North African Muslims and native populations and that the most important concern for the researcher is "to demonstrate the causes and means responsible for change or continuity and how or why either occurred." Here, it is not productive to understand Islamic civilization "as a monolithic whole," and "even a dialectic treatment of issues is an oversimplification."[12]

Kenneth W. Harrow's work in African literary criticism will also serve as a model for our analysis of how black Islamic identities were constructed in the Muslim world and West Africa. Like Morony, Harrow also discourages monolithic views of Islamic identity which "reduce Islam to an unchanging doctrine, and its multitudes of adherents to a single entity." On the contrary, Harrow's approach emphasizes that "Islam varies considerably with time, place, and text—reflecting the diversities of African Islamic culture. . . . Nonetheless, common features of history, and similar institutional patterns, allow us to postulate the existence of an African Islamic culture." With this approach in mind, the central issue presented in the next section of this chapter will be how West Africans "appropriated" Islam and "made it their own."[13]

Islam in the West African World

Mervyn Hiskett describes the Islamic lands of West Africa as

the area commonly referred to as "the west and central Sudan" . . . extending from the desert scrub in the "north" to the southern edge of savanna in the south. From west to east it extends across this scrub and savanna belt, from the Atlantic coast to the eastern shore of Lake Chad.[14]

Arab and Berber Muslims from Egypt and North Africa first established contact with this area in the eighth century through the caravan trade across the Sahara, which was inhabited by Berber nomads and black town dwellers. The merchants initially involved in this trade were interested mostly in gold, ivory, and slaves, not in proselytizing. By 990, however, the Arabic geographer al-Muhallabi reported that the West African city of Gao had a mosque and a Muslim ruler. In the tenth century, the desert trading city of Tadmakatt was also an important source of Islamic ideas for West Africa. During the same period, the empire of Ghana, which was the center of the gold trade, already had a separate Muslim district and employed Muslims in governmental affairs, even though its ruler was a Soninke polytheist. Al-Bakri's account of Ghana in the eleventh century indicates that the racial and cultural separatism characteristic of West African Islam was already evident in the capital city of this empire:

> The city of Ghana consists of two towns in a plain. One of these towns is inhabited by Muslims. It is large with a dozen mosques in one of which they assemble for the Friday prayer. There are salaried imams and muezzins, as well as jurists and scholars. . . .
> The king's town is six miles distant from this one and bears the name of Al-Ghaba. . . . In the king's town and not far from his court of justice, is a mosque where the Muslims who arrive at his court pray. Around the king's town are domed buildings and groves and thickets, where . . . men in charge of the religious cult live. In them too are their idols and tombs of their kings. . . . The king's interpreters, the official in charge of his treasury and the majority of his ministers are Muslims.[15]

Although the sources for a reconstruction of the history of Islam in Ghana are scarce and contradictory, many of the Soninke people of Ghana seem to have converted to Islam under the influence of non-black Muslim immigrants from North Africa who impressed them with their literacy, prayers, and spiritual powers. The praxis of African traditional religions remained strong in this empire, however. Clearly, the new non-black populations lived under the control of their native West African hosts.

In the eleventh century, Islam first became a major factor in West African history when the orthodox "Muslim militants"—the Almoravids, led by Abu Bakr, organized the Sanhaja Berbers in a holy war against non-Muslims in the western Sudan. The motivation for this jihad was economic as well as religious, for the Almoravids wanted to control the northern end of the desert caravan routes. Eventually they succeeded in making Islam the official religion of the empire of Ghana and Islamicized some of the black kingdoms and towns in the Sudan. Although historians dispute whether the Almoravids came to power in Ghana by military force or peaceful means, it is certain that they quickly lost their military and political advantages over the Soninke people and eventually became wandering scholars and preachers of Islam in the Sudan. Indeed, black Muslims in West Africa were not seriously affected by the military power of the Muslim world again until the Moroccan invasion of Songhay in the sixteenth century.[16]

The development of Islam in Ghana illustrates the mixed agenda of trading, proselytizing by scholars and clerics, political patronage, racial separatism, and urbanization that characterized Islam in West Africa before modernity. In this context, jihad, Islam's struggle for the truth, was acted out peacefully, as North African Muslims converted black West Africans to their religion as a result of their exemplary spiritual and intellectual qualities and trading interests. The Arab and Berber advance in West African societies often occurred in subtle stages over a long period of time. First, Muslims established contact with the Sudan as visiting merchants and craftspeople to obtain slaves and precious minerals. Eventually some of these merchants would settle in permanent trading outposts in West African towns and villages as African leaders began to perceive the advantages of economic ties with North Africa and the Middle East. These immigrant merchants and craftspeople were the first representatives of Islam in sub-Saharan Africa. Although they took no direct action to convert black people, their spiritual powers were impressive in crisis situations such as infertility and illness.[17]

These traders and craftspeople prepared the way for the wandering "teachers and messengers of Islam" who came after them, fanning out along the trade routes from the North to West Africa. These preachers, who included the Dyula/Wangara, Ineslemen/Zwaya, Muslim Fulani, and Shurafa, were often members of clerical classes. In West Africa, some of them set up Quranic schools where black children achieved basic literacy in Arabic; others established advanced schools where African Muslims prepared for the learned professions. Other clerics manufactured Muslim charms and impressed the West African elite with their powers in medicine and divination. The institutions of the clerical group were also part of the trading networks, for they were set up along the caravan routes which led African and Arab scholars and traders to Egypt for more advanced training, or to Mecca for the Pilgrimage (Hajj).[18]

Although the impression of these different Muslims influenced the West African black ruling elite and merchants to convert to Islam, they had little impact on the traditional religious praxis of West African peoples in rural areas before modernity.[19] The racial separatism of West African Islam resulted from the signification of black Muslim identities by rich and powerful black rulers who attempted to reconcile their new religion with African traditional religious and cultural praxis. Thus, as we shall see,

North African and Middle Eastern Muslims and blacks were deliberately segregated from each other in separate residential areas in West African cities and towns, to ensure that Islam would be used to the economic, political, and cultural advantage of black ruling elites. In the Muslim state of Takur (inhabited by the Tukolor people), the Jolof empire of the Wolof, the Senegambian villages and towns established by Mande traders, Mali, and Songhay, the issues of signification and separatism were played out in the context of West African Islam. In these locations West African Muslims attempted to define their identities both as Muslims and as ethnic people in light of the competition between their allegiance to the religions and cultures of their ethnic groups and the beliefs and practices of orthodox Islam from North Africa and the Middle East.[20]

West African Muslim Empires

No individual attracted North African and Middle Eastern Muslims to the potential and the riches of West Africa more than Mansa Musa, who ruled Mali from 1307 to 1332. The Arabic historian al-Umari described Musa's pilgrimage to Mecca in 1324:

> This sultan Musa during his stay in Egypt both before and after his journey to the Noble Hijaz, maintained a uniform attitude of worship and turning towards God. It was as though he were standing before Him because of His continual presence in his mind. He and all those with him behaved in the same manner and were well-dressed, grave, and dignified. He was noble and generous and performed many acts of charity and kindness. He had left his country with 100 loads of gold which he spent during his Pilgrimage in the tribes who lay along his route from his country to Egypt, while he was in Egypt, and again from Egypt to the Noble Hijaz and back. . . .
>
> He controls, of the land of the Sudan, that which [he] brought together by conquest and added to the domains of Islam. There he built ordinary and cathedral mosques and minarets, and established the Friday observances, and prayers in congregation, and the muezzin's call. He brought jurists of the Malikite school to his country and there continued as sultan of the Muslims and became a student of religious sciences.[21]

Forty years later, Mansa Musa's fame had spread to Europe as mapmakers put Mali on the Catalan map of West Africa and referred to its ruler as "Lord of the Negroes of Guinea." They described his country's gold as "so abundant . . . that he is the richest and most noble king in all the land."[22] Mansa Musa had inherited the mantle of leadership from a long line of black Muslim kings from the Keita clan of the Mandinka chiefdoms. This line included Sundiata (c. 1230–1255), a Mandinka Muslim convert who had built the vast empire of Mali on the ruins of Ghana, thus unifying the Mandinka people; Mansa Uli, the son of Sundiata, who was the first in his line to make the pilgrimage to Mecca (sometime between 1260 and 1277) and brought the famous cities Gao, Timbuktu, and Jenne under the control of Mali; Wati and Khalifa, brothers of Mansa Uli; Sakura, a usurper who made the pilgrimage to Mecca in 1298; Mansa Qu, son of Mansa Uli; and Mansa Muhammad, son of Mansa Qu.[23]

Although Mali borrowed ideas about government, economics, and religion from the central Islamic lands, culturally and politically it remained a black African kingdom. Here, West African Islam was the rule, as Mansa Musa controlled the signification of Mali's identity in the religion. Mansa Musa was willing to import ideas and people from the Islamic Middle East, but refused to give up African traditional political, economic, and cultural autonomy as a price for conversion to Islam. During Musa's reign and after, Mali remained a black African Muslim kingdom. This pattern of adaptation became firmly established in West African Islam during this golden age in West African history. Mansa Musa's reign institutionalized the royal pilgrimage as an important political event that connected West Africa with international politics, diplomacy, and trade in the Islamic world. In his time, as West African Muslims became more literate in Arabic, they were able to codify their laws, institutions, history, and knowledge in the great urban intellectual centers of West African Islam in Timbuktu and Jenne. In spite of the benefits in state building that came to Mali as a result of Islamization, these West Africans refused to give up their ethnic religion, which was the traditional basis of their culture. Instead they practiced a mixed form of Islam and chose to govern their country according to customary native African law.[24]

North African historian and world traveler Ibn Battuta (1304–1368) noted the racial particularity and mixed religious and cultural agenda of West African Islam when he visited Mali during the reign of Mansa Musa's successor, Mansa Sulaiman in 1352:

> I arrived at the city of Mali, the capital of the king of the blacks. I alighted by the graveyard and went to the quarter of the whites. I sought out Muhammad ibn al-Faqih and found he had rented a house for me opposite his own. . . .
>
> They do not interfere with the property of the white man who dies in their country even though it may consist of great wealth but rather they entrust it to the hand of someone dependable among the white men until it is taken by the rightful claimant. . . .
>
> Another of the good habits amongst them is the way they meticulously observe the times of the prayers and attendance at them. . . . When it is Friday, if a man does not come early to the mosque he will not find a place to pray because of the numbers of the crowd. . . .
>
> Among the bad things which they do—their serving women, slave women and little daughters appear before people naked. . . . I used to see many of them in this state in Ramadan. Another of their bad customs is their putting of dust

and ashes on their heads as a sign of respect. Another is the laughing matter I mentioned of their poetic recitals [by traditional griots]. And another is that many of them eat animals not ritually slaughtered, and dogs and donkeys.[25]

Although Arab Muslims had problems with the racial and cultural particularity of West African Islam in the Mali empire, when the Arab Muslim Leo Africanus visited the country in its early sixteenth-century years of decline, he still extolled its cultural virtues:

> The inhabitants are rich. . . . Here are great stores of temples, priests, and professors. . . . The people of this region excel all other Negroes in wit, civility and industry, and were the first that embraced the law of Muhammad.[26]

In the heyday of Leo Africanus, Songhay, a state that had been annexed by Mali in the thirteenth century, had already achieved prominence in the fickle world of West African political affairs. Sunni Ali, the first great king of Songhay, broke the power of the Mali empire when he conquered Timbuktu in 1468 and Jenne in 1473. Although Sunni Ali was Muslim, Songhay remained a black African culture under his reign, and he continued the pattern of cultural and racial particularism in Islam that his Malian predecessors had established. Sunni Ali was such an ardent adherent of African traditional religions that the religious authorities among the descendants of the Almoravids at Timbuktu began to challenge his authority as a Muslim ruler. As a result, he isolated and persecuted the Berber intellectuals and religious authorities at Timbuktu, and Jenne emerged as the intellectual center for West African Muslims who wished to control the signification of their identity in Islam and to preserve their "indigenous African cultural roots."[27]

Under the reign of Askiya Muhammad I (1493–1528), the cultural and political tensions between West African and North African Muslims in Songhay were superficially resolved. Like Mansa Musa, in 1497 Askiya Muhammad I made the pilgrimage to Mecca, where he was authorized as the caliph of the Sudan by the Abbasid caliph. Thus he officially brought West Africa into the cultural and diplomatic orbit of the Islamic world. As his empire grew through military force, he consulted North African Muslim scholars to decide how best to rule his kingdom along the path of Islam. In reality, however, through his connections with the Islamic world, Askiya Muhammad I was not able to completely eliminate the traditional belief system of Songhay. In the Songhay state, Askiya Muhammad I and his successors were faced with the co-existence of the two religious traditions. This was the only interpretation of Islam that West Africans would readily accept.[28]

The tradition of mixed Islam in Songhay continued on shaky political ground as Askiya Musa ousted his father, Askiya Muhammad I, and became ruler. The usurper remained in power until 1531, when he was overthrown by Askiya Benkan, who was abruptly replaced by Askiya Ismail in 1537. Political stability returned to Songhay from 1539 to 1591 under the rule of Askiya Iskaq I and Askiya Daud.[29] Some of the political tensions in sixteenth-century Songhay resulted from different rulers' efforts to reconcile Islam, the religion of the urban ruling elite, with the African cultural particularism of the traditional religions which were also practiced by the rulers and the peasants. This tension between orthodox Islam and African cultural particularism was at the heart of what made West African Islam a vibrant and distinctive religious tradition in the world of Islam. Although West African Muslims had signified themselves as the people they wanted to be through their embrace of Islam and separated themselves from the judgments of non-black Muslims from North Africa, they could not unite politically and militarily to sustain their powerful Islamic empires in the modern era. On the eve of modernity, Islam in West Africa was destined for radical changes, although its themes of racial and cultural particularism, signification, and jihad were destined to live on as a paradigm endemic to global Islam, and would later be utilized by black Muslims in America.

Black Islam and Modernity

In 1591, the Songhay empire fell when its supposed ally, Morocco, invaded the country to seize its salt mines. Although Songhay had carefully developed diplomatic and cultural ties with North Africa, the Moroccan sultan wanted complete control over the salt mines, gold, and slaves of the Sudan, which legally belonged, in part, to Songhay. This was a watershed event in West African history for several reasons. First, it signaled the end of the mighty economic and political power of the empires that had sustained West African Islam. Second, Timbuktu, the great West African city, declined as a black Muslim intellectual center. Third, the focus of West African Islam changed radically as Islam entered a period of decline which lasted until the nineteenth century. Fourth, the fall of Songhay signaled the beginning of modernity, during which cataclysmic changes in the institution of slavery were destined to change the fortunes of African peoples in the world.[30]

By the beginning of the sixteenth century, it became clear to informed observers that Arab Muslims had a separate and radical agenda for black Muslims in West Africa. They were enslaving them in record numbers under the banner of jihad and taking control of the rich mineral resources of their lands. This was clearly against the laws of Islam. The issue of the enslavement of West African Muslims by their Arab co-religionists had still not been resolved in 1614 when Ahmad Baba, a Muslim scholar from Timbuktu, wrote a legal interpretation of the issue:

Whoever is captured in a condition of non-belief, it is legal to own him, whosoever he may be, but not he who was converted to Islam voluntarily, from the start, to any nation he belongs, whether it is Bornu, Kano, Songhai, Katsinsa, Gobir, Mali and some of Zakzak. These are free Muslims, whose enslavement is not allowed in any way.[31]

Slavery was the chink in West African Islam, for Ghana, Songhay, Mali, Kanem, Bornu, Senegambia, the city states of the Hausas, and Yorubas, had been playing a dangerous game with North African Muslims for decades. They supplied the Arabs with black slaves in return for advantages that might consolidate their political and economic power in West Africa. Some of the West African kingdoms utilized slave labor in their own societies as well. These slaves, who were captives of war, adulterers, suspected criminals, sorcerers, debtors, or human substitutes for taxes, became soldiers, eunuchs, and concubines in the central Islamic lands. Although West African Muslim rulers probably believed that selling their enemies into slavery was a small price to pay for empire and state building, their vision was shortsighted. For their continent during Ahmad Baba's time had become so politically fragmented and unstable that no one leader was able "to consolidate huge areas into centralized states." As West African political and religious rivalries were perpetuated, slavery was transformed from a marginal institution to a primary means of connecting power-hungry and unscrupulous African Muslim leaders to political and economic power bases in North Africa.[32]

With the emergence of the Atlantic slave trade in the fifteenth century, the European market globalized West African slavery and transformed the institution into an industry and a mode of production that forever changed the political and economic structure of Africa and the Americas. This external trade for capitalist markets represented what Lovejoy called "a radical break in the history of Africa" because of its numbers, the brutal methods it employed, and the fact that it involved politicians and merchants in its bureaucracy. Over a period of four centuries, the Atlantic slave trade robbed Africa forever of more than ten million people—a large portion of its human resources.[33]

The first Portuguese traders and explorers who arrived on the coast of West Africa in the early 1400s were primarily interested in gold and integrated themselves into the existing Muslim trade routes in and around Senegambia and the Gold Coast. However, Christopher Columbus's exploration of the western world at the end of the fifteenth century began a period of European conquest in the West that stimulated the astounding growth of the Atlantic slave trade providing African slaves for agricultural work and mining in America. On the occasion of the 500th anniversary of his voyage, scholars and political activists in America debated his legacy. Was it the beginning of a "daring experiment in democracy" or the beginning of doom for non-white people in Africa and America? At any rate, his voyage marked the beginning of the modern era, a period of "conquest and cultural contact," "novelty and exploration," as Europeans first encountered the cultures of black and brown peoples in Africa and the Americas.

The seventeenth century also meant the beginning of a new kind of racial slavery that was more evil and destructive than anything African peoples had ever encountered. The Atlantic slave trade expanded with such tremendous ferocity that it had surpassed the Islamic slave trade in volume by 1600. Whereas the Muslim trade had stimulated moderate political instability in Africa, the new trans-Atlantic trade devastated the continent as it permanently displaced millions of people and dramatically transformed the economic and political structure of West Africa. Slavery became a major industry in which Portuguese, Spanish, French, Dutch, English, Arab, and West African peoples participated for profit. For Europeans, it signified the beginning of a new mercantile and capitalist system. But for the Africans, some of whom were Muslims who sold their own people into slavery in return for European goods, the slave trade ultimately meant the ruin of a mighty continent.[34]

PART II. AMERICA

Shuttles in the rocking loom of history
the dark ships move, the dark ships move,
their bright ironical names
like jests of kindness on a murderer's mouth;
plough through thrashing glister toward
fata morgana's lucent melting shore,
weave toward New World littorals that are
mirage and myth and actual shore.

Voyage through death,
    voyage whose chartings are unlove
   . . . .
Voyage through death
    to life upon these shores
   . . . .

    —Robert Hadyn, *Middle Passage*

Black Islam and Resistance

In the New World, African Muslim slaves were noteworthy for their sometimes violent resistance to the institution of slavery. In Brazil, hundreds of African Muslim slaves planned and executed a major slave uprising in Bahia in 1835, fighting soldiers and civilians in the streets of Salvador. Moreover, at least one African Muslim participated in the revolt on the Spanish slave ship the *Amistad* in the Caribbean in 1839. The slaves' knowledge of Arabic and of the religion of Islam were key factors in their identification as African Muslims. In other locations, African Muslims were noted for their bold efforts both to resist conversion to Christianity and to convert other Africans to Islam. Mohammed Sisei, an African Muslim in Trinidad in the early nineteenth century, noted that the Free Mandingo Society on the island was instrumental in converting a whole royal West Indian regiment of blacks to Islam. At the same time, prominent African Muslim slaves in Jamaica in the early 1800s circulated a letter urging other African Muslims in their communities to adhere to their religion. Muhammad, an African Muslim slave in Antigua, was manumitted by his master because of his stubborn adherence to Islam and returned to Africa in 1811.[35]

Resistance, then, was a global theme in New World black Islam in the eighteenth and nineteenth centuries.[36] In the United States, however, African Muslims practiced more subtle forms of resistance to slavery—some of them kept their African names, wrote in Arabic, and continued to practice their religion; some of them used the American Colonization Society to gain their freedom and return to Africa. All of this constituted intellectual resistance to slavery, as African Muslims, who had been members of the ruling elite in West Africa, used their literacy and professional skills to manipulate white Americans. This peculiar form of resistance accounts in part for the compelling and provocative nature of the life stories of the known African Muslim slaves in America.[37]

Even the slave community noted the compelling presence of African Muslims in its midst. Ex-slave Charles Ball, one of the first African Americans to publish an autobiography, was struck by the religious discipline and resistance to Christianity of a nineteenth-century African Muslim slave on a plantation in North Carolina. He wrote:

> At the time I first went to Carolina, there were a great many African slaves in the country. . . . I became intimately acquainted with some of these men. . . . I knew several, who must have been, from what I have since learned, Mohamedans; though at that time, I had never heard of the religion of Mohammed.
>
> There was one man on this plantation, who prayed five times every day always turning his face to the East, when in the performance of his devotions.[38]

Signification and jihad (the struggle for the truth in the way of God) are the analytical keys that explain resistance in the lives of the African Muslims noted above and in the biographical sketches that follow. For African Muslim slaves preserved their Islamic identities by refusing to internalize the Christian racist significations that justified the system of exploitation. These were profound acts of resistance to an institution that had set the terms for pre-twentieth-century racial discourse in America, attempting to eradicate all aspects of African heritage in the slave quarters by stripping slaves of their culture, leaving them powerless. As African Muslims signified themselves as the people they wanted to be in America, they transformed Islam to meet the demands of survival and resistance in the "strange Christian land." Their significations turned their history, religion, and genealogies into "an instrument of identity and transformation" in America.[39]

Related to signification was the African Muslim slaves' reinterpretation of jihad. For African Muslim slaves, the practice of jihad through armed warfare against unbelievers was not possible in America. Instead, they reinterpreted jihad as an "inner struggle with the ego," a resistance to oppression, and a struggle for justice in an unjust land. In this context, writing in Arabic, fasting, wearing Muslim clothing, and reciting and reflecting on the Quran were the keys to an inner struggle of liberation against Christian tyranny. Thus, for African Muslim slaves, the inner jihad became "the ultimate test of their faith" in America and a "paradigm for the liberation struggles" of other oppressed blacks in the New World. Their stories reveal that African slaves had ethnic and religious identities that could not be erased by the trauma of slavery.[40]

Fascinating portraits of a few influential African Muslim slaves exist in the historical literature. Some excerpts from their life stories follow.

Job Ben Solomon: "No Common Slave"

Signification and intellectual resistance were central in the fascinating story of Job Ben Solomon (c. 1700–1773). He was born Ayuba Suleiman Ibrahima Diallo in the kingdom of Futa (in Senegal) around 1700. The name Job Ben Solomon was an anglicization of part of his original name. Job came from a prominent Fulbe family of Muslim religious leaders; his grandfather had founded the town of Bondu, where Job was born. As a teenager, he was a companion to Sambo, the prince and heir to the throne of Futa, and studied the Quran and the Arabic language with him.[41]

In 1730, while on a trip to the coast to buy paper and to sell two of his father's slaves to English traders, Job was himself captured and sold into slavery by Mandingos, who were enemies of his people. He arrived in Annapolis, Maryland in the same slave ship to which he had planned to sell his father's slaves.[42] Job Ben Solomon worked on plantations in Maryland, where white children "would mock him and throw dirt in his face" as he attempted to recite his Muslim prayers in the woods. He escaped, but eventually was captured and imprisoned. In June 1731, while Job was in prison in Maryland, Thomas Bluett, an English minister, heard about him and arranged to meet him. In this initial meeting Bluett was impressed by Job's ability in Arabic and his devotion to Islam. He wrote:

> He was brought into the tavern to us, but could not speak one word of English. Upon our talking and making signs to him, he wrote a line or two before us, and when he read it, pronounced the words Allah and Mohammed;

by which and his refusing a glass of wine we offered him, we perceived he was a Mohametan. . . . For by his affable carriage, and the easy composure of his countenance, we could perceive he was no common slave.[43]

Due to Job Ben Solomon's inner struggle to maintain his religion in difficult circumstances, his refusal to alter his Muslim identity, and his intelligence as demonstrated in his command of oral and written Arabic, his plight became well known and arrangements were made for him to go to England in 1733. There his acquaintances included the royal family and Sir Hans Sloane, founder of the British Museum. Job wrote out several copies of the Quran from memory and translated other Arabic materials for the Royal Society. He also obtained the freedom of his friend and former servant Lamine Ray, who had come with him to America. In 1734, Thomas Bluett published Job's biography in London, and the Royal African Company arranged for his return to Africa, where they used him in their trade of slaves, gold, and rum. Job Ben Solomon eventually returned to Bondu, where he helped Melchour De Jaspas, an Arabic-speaking Armenian representative of the Royal African Company, with his explorations in Africa from 1738 to 1740. He kept in touch with his English friends until his death in 1773.[44]

Yarrow Mamout: "Man is no good unless his religion come from the heart"

In 1819, the white American artist Charles Wilson Peale (1741–1827) painted a striking portrait of an African Muslim named Yarrow Mamout in Georgetown. At the time of this work, Mamout was said to be more than one hundred years old. Although Yarrow Mamout was a popular local figure in the Virginia area, Peale's diary, which recorded his impressions of Mamout during his two-day sitting for the portrait, is the only document available on the life of this provocative Muslim.[45]

The biographical sketch that can be drawn from these short notes suggests the themes of signification and inner jihad. Yarrow Mamout's life in Africa was a mystery. We do know, however, that he was a slave for the Bell family in Georgetown and was eventually freed because of his industriousness. In 1819, Mamout owned his own house in Georgetown and had saved enough money to buy stock in the Columbia Bank, founded by Alexander Hamilton in 1771. Apparently, Mamout had successfully resisted conversion to Christianity and maintained his Muslim name and identity, for Peale noted that he "professes to be a Mahometan, and is often seen and heard in the streets singing praises to God—and conversing with him." Peale said "man is no good unless his religion come from the heart." Although there is no evidence that Yarrow Mamout wrote Arabic, he did dress in "Muslim style" and observed the dietary laws of his religion. According to Peale's diary, "the acquaintances of [the Muslim] often

YARROW MAMOUT, *an African Muslim and former slave, in 1819. Painting by Charles Wilson Peale.* From the collection of the Historical Society of Pennsylvania. Used by permission.

banter him about eating and drinking whiskey—but Yarrow say 'it is no good to eat hog—and drink whiskey is very bad.'" Finally, although the information about Yarrow Mamout is harder to come by than that of the other known African Muslim slaves in America, his life story deserves more recognition than it has received because he successfully struggled to maintain his Muslim name, identity, and praxis longer than any other known African Muslim slave of his time.[46]

A Prince in a Strange Land

I was born in the city of Timbo. . . . I moved to the country of Foota Jallo. . . . I lived there till I was twenty-five years old—I was taken prisoner in the war. . . . They took me to Dominique, took me to New Orleans—took me to

Natchez. I was sold to W. Thomas Foster. I lived there forty years. I got liberated last March—1828.[47]

These written words (originally in Arabic) of Abd al-Rahman Ibrahima (1762–1825) tell the remarkable story of a West African Muslim prince whose white captors called him a Moor. His story sheds further light on the central themes of global Islam, intellectual resistance, signification, and jihad, and shows how some African Muslim slaves used the American Colonization Society to gain their freedom and passage back to Africa.

Ibrahima was born in 1762 to Sori, the king of Timbo, which is in present-day Guinea. Sori was the leader of the Muslim Fulbe people, who had established a thriving Islamic community in the midst of various unfriendly polytheistic peoples. In Timbo during Ibrahima's time, Muslim boys were sent to the Quran schools at the age of seven to begin learning to read and write parts of the Holy Book. The young prince was very adept at his studies, and when he was twelve, his father sent him abroad to Jenne and Timbuktu to continue his studies.[48]

At seventeen, he returned to Futa Jallon to join his father's army, which was engaged in a series of jihads against various non-Muslim peoples. These military ventures eventually brought Sori to the height of political power in Futa Jallon. In 1781, Ibrahima became a military hero when he led his people victoriously against a Bambara army of several thousand soldiers and ended the campaign by beheading the Bambara leader with a sweep of his sword.[49]

The year 1781 also portended Ibrahima's life in America, for that is when the Fulbe first saw a white man. John Coates Cox was a one-eyed Irish ship surgeon who had accidentally been separated from his shipmates on the coast. When the Fulbe found him further inland, he was close to death from the bites of insects and a poisonous worm. Sori had him brought to Timbo, where he was cured and welcomed as a guest to stay as long as he wanted. Ibrahima became close friends with Dr. Cox and learned a little English from him. After six months, however, the Irishman became restless, and with Sori's assistance, found his way back to the ship in which he had arrived. But he never forgot the kindness of the Fulbe people or Abd al-Rahman Ibrahima.[50]

John Ormond of Liverpool was "a drunken, illiterate, . . . believer in witchcraft, . . . exceptionally notorious for his cruelty." As a boy, he had worked as an apprentice in a slave ship and in a slave factory on the coast of West Africa. In 1787, he operated the Portool, one of the largest and most lucrative slave ships on the Rio Pongas River. The Fulbe had established an active trade with him; he gave them guns and European goods and in return, the Muslims gave him gold, ivory, and slaves. However, some of the non-Muslim peoples who were enemies of the Fulbe held slavers like Ormond in deep contempt, ultimately raiding their ships in 1787. This set

ABD AL-RAHMAN IBRAHIMA *circa 1825. Crayon drawing by Henry Ihman.* Frontispiece of *Colonizationist and Journal of Freedom* (1834).

off a war between the Fulbe and the neighboring communities. Ibrahima later wrote, "at the age of twenty six, they sent me to fight the Hebohs because they destroyed the vessels that came to the coast and prevented our trade."[51]

As Ibrahima and an army of two thousand advanced into the land of the Hebohs, burning and attacking their towns, they were ambushed and defeated on a mountainside. Ibrahima's life was spared when a Heboh soldier realized from his clothing that he was a prince. His captors stripped him of his garments and ornaments and forced him to walk barefoot for one hundred miles to the Gambia River. There they sold him to the Mandinka slatees who were the middle-men for the European slave traders. Terry Alford described them as "black merchants [who] traveled great distances in the interior to buy prisoners of war and other goods to sell to Europeans. They were Muslims generally, people of influence and often of great wealth. These slatees from the Gambia River were those who would set in motion the irremediable slide to a distant part, sale to a slaver, shipment beyond the sea, and bondage or worse in a land from which no one returned." Ibrahima's fate was sealed. He was sold into slavery by fellow Africans for "two flasks of powder, a few trade muskets, eight hands of tobacco, and two bottles of rum." He later wrote, "My father came and burnt the country, but the slatees had already begun moving their new property North."[52]

The African prince made the Middle Passage across the Atlantic Ocean in a slave ship named the *Africa*. His first stop in the Americas was in Domenica, on the Windward Islands, where Christopher Columbus had landed on his second voyage. From there he proceeded to New Orleans and then to Natchez, Mississippi, where he was purchased by Thomas Foster, a tobacco and cotton farmer, on April 21, 1788.[53]

During the fifteen years that followed, Ibrahima ran away, but eventually resigned himself to slavery: he married a black woman named Isabella, had nine children, and was appointed overseer of Thomas Foster's lands. In 1807, Ibrahima accidentally came in contact with John Cox, the Irish ship's surgeon whom the prince's father had taken in years ago. Cox learned of his plight and tried unsuccessfully to gain his freedom.

Ibrahima never forgot his Muslim traditions and identity. In the final evaluation, it was through his knowledge of European stereotypes of Muslims and his manipulation of his Muslim identity that he gained his freedom and passage back to Africa.[54] In 1826, Colonel Marschalk, a Natchez newspaper editor, solicited an Arabic letter from Ibrahima, which included a passage from the Quran. At the same time, his letter was sent with a short note from the former to Thomas Mullowny, the American consul in Morocco. Marschalk's note read:

> Dear Sir,
>   The enclosed letter in Arabic was written in my presence by a venerable old slave named Prince. . . . He claims to belong to the royal family of Morocco, and the object of his letter, as he states it to me, is to make inquiry after his relations . . . with the hope of joining them. I have undertaken to endeavor to forward his letter for him and therefore beg leave to commit it to your care, with a request that you will lend your aid to the old man's wishes.[55]

Mullowny received the letter in March 1827 and immediately discussed Ibrahima's case with Abd al-Rahman II, the ruler of Morocco: "The intention of the letter appears to me to prove he is a Moor, as it is taken from the Quran to excite an exertion for his relief. The documents appear to be clear of deception." Although there was no evidence of Ibrahima's nationality in the letter, it was clear from his writing that he was a Muslim, and on this basis, Abd al-Rahman II requested his liberation. In return, the Moroccan ruler agreed to release Americans who were illegally taken in his empire.[56]

In February 1828, Ibrahima's master finally signed the African prince's manumission papers when Secretary of State Henry Clay interceded on his behalf. After he and his wife Isabella were freed, Ibrahima engaged in a lecture tour in the Northeast and earned enough money to free his children. Along the way, he met black notables such as John C. Murphy, a pioneer in the Black Baptist movement; Samuel Cornish, the founder of *Freedom's Journal*, the first black newspaper in America; John Russwurm, the first black American to receive a Bachelor of Arts degree from Bowdoin College; and David Walker, the political firebrand who would later publish his influential *Appeal* in Boston. In the course of his travels, Ibrahima wrote in Arabic when white people requested it, but his intellectual resistance never waned as he sometimes substituted passages from the Quran for Christian prayers.[57]

In order to get passage to Africa, however, he convinced important white leaders of the American Colonization Society that he would become a trader and a preacher of the Gospel there. This group included Thomas H. Gallaudet, who established deaf-mute education in the United States; Arthur Tappan, the brother of Charles and a wealthy importer of European and eastern goods; and John F. Schroeder, a minister at Trinity Church in Boston and an Arabist who certified that "Ibrahima read the Quran with correctness and fluency and writes it with neatness and rapidity." These men attempted to indoctrinate the African with their Christian beliefs, although Gallaudet expressed his doubts about a true conversion. "I hope that he is a Christian," he wrote, "but his means of religious instruction have been very limited."[58]

The American Colonization Society was established in 1816 as a means of "colonizing the free people of colour in the United States" in West Africa. Although free blacks in the north had begun planning to emigrate back to Africa as early as 1773 in Massachusetts, the majority of free black Americans vehemently opposed the American Colonization Society. Its real purpose, they believed, was to place free blacks in "white controlled" areas of West Africa such as Liberia in order to make slavery more secure in America. The basic issue of contention for black people was self-determination, for major black religious leaders such as Richard Allen, James Forten, and Peter Williams, although they were anti-colonizationists, endorsed schemes for emigration to Haiti and to other locations where ex-slaves could determine their own destinies. It may appear as if Abd al-Rahman Ibrahima and other African Muslim slaves allowed themselves to be used by racist colonizationists; in reality, the opposite often occurred. Ibrahima manipulated the American Colonization Society, per-

suading them that he had converted to Christianity and that he planned to
missionize for the religion.[59] Thomas Gallaudet endorsed the African
prince's repatriation in a public meeting in Boston on October 15, 1828:

> I would ask, then if humanity and patriotism do not urge us to render
> assistance to Prince for this hospitality afforded one of our countrymen. . . . We
> may be able to extend our commercial relations to the very heart of Africa, and
> the influence of our institutions also. As Christians, we must especially rejoice
> that an opportunity will be afforded for diffusing the blessings of Christianity
> to that dark and benighted region.[60]

The African prince set sail for Africa on February 7, 1829 and arrived in
Monrovia, Liberia, on March 18. Sadly, Ibrahima never made it back to his
homeland of Futa Jallon. He died from an extended illness on July 6, 1829
at the age of sixty-seven. In spite of his promises to his white benefactors,
he returned to the practice of Islam as soon as he arrived on the African
continent.[61]

Bilali and Salih Bilali: Muslims of the Georgia Sea Islands

Bilali and Salih Bilali were two of at least twenty black Muslims who
are reported to have lived and practiced their religion in Sapelo Island and
St. Simon's Island during the antebellum period. The Georgia Sea Islands
provided fertile ground for Islamic and other African retentions thanks to
their relative isolation from Euro-American influences. Both Bilali and
Salih Bilali remained steadfast in the struggle to maintain their Muslim
identities in America. Both men were noted for their devotion to their
religious obligations, for wearing Islamic clothing, and for their Muslim names—and one was noted for his ability to write and speak Arabic,
which he passed on to his children. Moreover, available evidence suggests that they might have been the leaders of a small black Muslim
community in the Georgia Sea Islands.[62]

Georgia Conrad, a white American resident of one of the Sea Islands,
met Bilali's family in the 1850s and was struck by their religion, dress, and
ability to speak Arabic. She wrote:

> On Sapelo Island near Darcen, I used to know a family of Negroes who
> worshipped Mohamet. They were tall and well-formed, with good features.
> They conversed with us in English, but in talking among themselves they used
> a foreign tongue that no one else understood. The head of the tribe was a very
> old man named Bi-la-li. He always wore a cap that resembled a Turkish fez.[63]

Bilali, who was also known as Belali Mahomet, Bu Allah, and Ben Ali,
was a Muslim slave on the Thomas Spaulding plantation on Sapelo Island,
Georgia from the early to the mid-1800s. His great-grandchildren told his

story to Works Progress Administration writers in Georgia in the 1930s. Bilali maintained his identity by giving his nineteen children Muslim names and teaching them Muslim traditions. When he died, he left an Arabic manuscript that he had composed and had his prayer rug and Quran placed in his coffin.[64]

Only a few facts are known about Bilali's pre-American history. Although his surname is unknown, we do know that his first name represents the West African Muslim fascination with Bilal, the Prophet Muhammad's black companion and the first muezzin. Bilali was born in Timbo, Futa Jallon. Like his Fulbe compatriot, Ibrahima, he was probably raised in a prominent scholarly family, for the Arabic manuscript that he composed in America was undoubtedly the product of someone who wrote and read Arabic at an advanced level. The manuscript was a compilation of pieces from the Malikite legal text, *ar-Risala,* which was originally written by Abu Muhammad Abdullah ibn Abi Zaid al-Qairawani. Bilali's work, "First Fruits of Happiness," attempted to reconcile the law of Islam with a wholesome daily life. It suggests that Bilali was struggling to uphold his faith in America.[65]

Bilali's leadership ability, reflecting his elite roots in West Africa, was legendary on Sapelo Island. He was the manager of his master's plantation, which included close to five hundred slaves. During the War of 1812, Bilali and approximately eighty slaves who had muskets prevented the British from invading their island. Some of these slaves were undoubtedly Muslim, since Bilali forewarned Thomas Spaulding that, if in a battle, "I will answer for every Negro of the true facts, but not for the Christian dogs you own." Moreover, in 1824, during a hurricane, Bilali saved the slaves on Sapelo Island by leading them into cotton and sugar shacks constructed of African tabby.[66]

Perhaps the most fascinating aspect of Bilali's Islamic legacy was that his descendants on Sapelo Island remembered him in the 1930s, when they were interviewed by the Savannah Unit of the Georgia Writer's Project. These interviews also brought to light other nineteenth-century blacks who practiced Islam on the Georgia Sea Islands. Although they have been criticized for inaccuracy and contextual problems, these interviews are an invaluable source of information on Bilali and his descendants.[67]

According to Shadrack Hall, who was Bilali's great-grandson, the African Muslim slave was brought to Georgia from the Bahamas with his wife Phoebe and maintained Islamic names and traditions in his family for at least three generations:

> Muh gran wuz Hestah, Belali's daughter. She tell me Belali wuz coal black, wid duh small feechuhs we hab, an he wuz very tall. . . . Belali hab plenty daughtahs, Medina, Yaruba, Fatima, Bentoo, Hestah, Magret, and Chaalut.
>
> Ole Belali Smith wuz muh uncle. His son wuz George Smith's gran. He wuz muh gran Hestuh's son an muh mudduh Sally's brudduh. Hestah an all

ub um sho pray on duh head. Dey weah duh string uh beads on duh neck. Dez
pray at sun-up and face duh sun on duh knees an bow tuh it tree times, kneelin'
on a lill mat.[68]

Finally, Katie Brown, another one of Belali's great-grandchildren, recalled her Muslim grandmother Margret, who wore a Muslim head dress
and made rice cakes for the children at the end of a fast day;

> Yes 'm, I membuh gran too. Belali he from Africa but muh gran she came
> by Bahamas. . . . .
> She ain tie uh head up lak I does, but she weah a loose wite clawt da she
> trow obuh uh head lak veil an it hang loose on uh shoulduh. I ain know wy she
> weah it dataway, but I tink she ain lak a tight ting roun uh head.
> She make funny flat cake she call "saraka." She make um same day ebry
> yeah, an it big day. Wen dey finish, she call us in, all duh chillun, an put in hans
> lill flat cake an we eats it. Yes'm, I membuh how she make it. She wash rice, an
> po off all duh watuh. She let wet rice sit all night, an in mawnin rice is all swell.
> She tak dat rice an put it in wooden mawtuh, an beat it tuh paste wid wooden
> pestle. She add honey, sometime shuguh, an make it in flat cake wid uh hans.
> "Saraka" she call um.[69]

* * * * *

James Hamilton Couper, a Georgia aristocrat who owned a plantation
on St. Simon's Island with several hundred slaves, contributed a paper to
the American Ethnological Society about one of his Muslim slaves, Salih
Bilali, also known as Tom:

> He is a strict Mahometan; abstains from spiritous liquors, and keeps the
> various fasts, particularly that of Rhamadan. He is singularly exempt from all
> feeling of superstition; and holds in great contempt the African belief in
> fetishes and evil spirits. He reads Arabic and has a Koran. . . . in that language
> but does not write it. . . . Mr. Spaulding of Sapelo, has, among his Negroes, one
> named Bul-Ali who writes Arabic and speaks the Fonlah language. Tom and
> himself are intimate friends. He is now old and feeble. Tom informs me that he
> is from Timboo.[70]

Salih Bilali, born in Massina in 1765, was probably a member of a
prominent Mandingo Fulbe clerical family. When he was twelve years old,
he was taken into slavery while he was returning home from Jenne, one of
the major black Muslim intellectual centers of West Africa. In his African
reminiscences, Salih Bilali remembered well the racial and cultural differences between the black Muslims in his land and the white Arab Muslim
traders who sold them goods in Jenne, Timbuktu, Kouna, and Sego.[71]
Salih Bilali's odyssey in the New World brought him first to the Baha-

mas, where he was purchased by the Couper family around 1800. By 1816, he had become the overseer of their St. Simon's plantation, which had more than four hundred slaves. By all accounts, Salih Bilali was an impressive figure in the Georgia Sea Islands. His religious steadfastness may have been the result of Islamic training under Bilali in the Bahamas and Georgia.[72] Together they formed the nucleus of a small Muslim community, of which the members can only be suggested by the interviews that the Georgia Writer's Project conducted with Salih Bilali's grandchildren on the Georgia Sea Islands in the 1930s.[73]

Salih Bilali's grandson, Ben Sullivan, remembered that his father had received his Arabic name—Bilali—from his own father. Bilali was the butler on another Couper plantation until the end of the Civil War, when he chose the surname Sullivan. Bilali Sullivan also made saraka (rice cakes) at certain times of the year. Ben Sullivan was one of several of Couper's slaves who practiced Islam. This group included Alex Boyd (his maternal grandfather), a light-skinned man named Daphne, and Israel: "Ole Israel he pray a lot wid a book he hab wit he hide, and he take a lill mat and he say he prayuhs on it. He pray wen duh sun go up an wen duh sun go down. . . . He alluz tie he head up in a wite clawt."[74]

At the same time, Rosa Grant, who may have been descended from Salih Bilali, recalled her Muslim grandmother who lived in Possum Point: "Muh gran came from Africa too. Huh name wuz Ryna. I membuh wen I wuz a chile see in muh gran Ryna pray. Ebry mawnin at sun-up she kned on duh flo in uh ruhm an bow abuh an tech uh head tuh duh fo tree time."[75]

Finally Grant remembered one more Muslim woman in Darien:

> Baker told us that many people in the section refused to eat certain foods, believing bad luck would follow if they ate them.
>
> Deah's lots dataway now. Lots uh folks dohn eat some food cuz ef dey did dey say it would bring bad luck on duh parents. Some dohn eat rice, some dohn eat egg, an some dohn eat chicken.
>
> Muh gran, she Rachel Grant, she use tuh tell me bout lot uh deze tings. I membuh she use tuh pray ebry day at sunrise, at middle day and den at sunset. She alluz face duh sun an wen she finish prayin she alluz bow tuh duh sun. She tell me bout duh slaves wut could fly too. Ef dey didn lak it on duh plantation, dey jus take wing an fly right back tuh Africa.[76]

In the biographical sketches of Bilali and Salih Bilali, there is fragmentary evidence of a small African Muslim slave community that attempted to preserve Muslim identities and traditions in the nineteenth century. In these sketches, we also have evidence of how African Muslim women were involved in the struggle to preserve Muslim identities in America. It appears that they played a significant role in this struggle, for their preparation of Muslim foods, their Muslim clothing, and their disciplined devotion to their religion deeply impressed their children and grandchildren. And their families' memories of their Muslim identities have influenced the significations of nineteenth-century Islam that African Americans have preserved in their folklore in the twentieth century. Finally, the stories of these Muslim women convey the theme of resistance through signification as strongly as the earlier examples that we have discussed.

Lamine Kaba: Scholar and Signifier

The issue of signification and resistance was central in the story of Lamine Kaba, who was also called Lamen Kebe and Paul. Kaba knew this when he said, "There are good men in America, but all are very ignorant of Africa" and told his biographer, Theodore Dwight, Jr., to

> write down what I tell you exactly as I say it, and be careful to distinguish between what I have seen and what I have only heard other people speak of. They may have made some mistakes; but if you put down exactly what I say, by and by, when good men go to Africa, they will say Paul told the truth.[77]

Making a commodity of this African Muslim's identity was important both to him and to certain groups of white Americans. In 1835, Kaba proclaimed before a group of white philanthropists that he wanted to return to Africa to reunite with his wife and children and to do Christian missionary work among his people. He claimed that he had experienced a sudden conversion to Christianity when his good Christian master manumitted him. Kaba ended his presentation by blessing America. All of this was part of an intelligently planned performance intended to ensure his passage back to Africa. Kaba also meant to defend the colonization movement, which was languishing at the time of his speech. Several months later, in New York, he made another bid to solicit money for colonization, which resulted in donations of two thousand dollars to aid black emigrants to Liberia. On this occasion, the American Colonization Society's magazine the *African Repository* reported:

> A coloured man was now presented to the audience, who expected shortly to go out as an emigrant to Liberia. The gentleman who presented him said that he was an educated man, that he spoke, read, and wrote the Arabic language very perfectly; and was a professed believer in Christ. He intended to act as a missionary to his race. He had been liberated by his master for this end; and had been waiting now for 90 days for an opportunity of going.[78]

Kaba finally arrived in Liberia in August 19, 1835, under the name of Paul A. Mandingo. Eventually he settled in Sierra Leone. During the year before his departure from the United States, Kaba told the story of his life to Theodore Dwight, Jr., a Yale graduate, linguist, editor, and officer of the American Ethnological Society. Although Dwight did not believe that his informant had been successfully converted to Christianity, he decided to use his story for two purposes: first, to learn about African Muslim education and, later, to inspire an educational campaign to utilize African literacy in Arabic by sending Arabic Bibles to Liberia. Although Dwight's essays on Kaba are biographically disappointing, they provide some useful information on West African Muslim educational methods.[79]

Lamine Kaba was born around 1780 in Futa Jallon to a Sereculeh family of rich and famous Jakhanké teacher-clerics. The Jakhanké—wandering teachers-clerics who were dedicated to Islam, historical accuracy, and the religious instruction of young people—made use of indigenous traditions along with ideas from the Muslim world. In the tradition of his family, Kaba received seven years of advanced education in theology, law, philology, linguistics, hadith, and scriptural exegesis. He began his teaching career at the age of twenty-one and taught for five years, until he was kidnapped and sold into slavery while he was looking for paper near the coast. He probably arrived in America in 1807 and served almost thirty years in slavery, in Georgia, South Carolina and Alabama, before his return to Africa in 1835.[80]

After Kaba returned to Africa, he kept in touch with an old African Muslim friend in America, Omar Ibn Said (whose life will be discussed in the next section), demonstrating that some black Muslims in West Africa and America maintained global connections during the nineteenth century. The following excerpt was the beginning of a letter in Arabic that Omar sent to Kaba in Africa in 1836:

> In the name of God The Compassionate, [etc.] I am not able to write my life. I have forgotten much of the language of the Arabs. I read not the grammatical, and but very little of the common dialect. I ask thee, O brother, to reproach me not, for my eyes are weak, and my body also.[81]

Omar Ibn Said: Signifying and Deceiving

My name is Omar-ben-Sayeed. The place of my birth is Footah Toro, between the two rivers. [Probably the Senegal and Gambia, or the Senegal and Niger, in their upper parts.] The teachers of Bundu-foota were a sheik, named Mohammed-Sayeed, my brother, and the sheik Soleyman Kimba, and the sheik Jebraeel-Abdel. I was teacher twenty-five years. There came a great army to my country. They killed many people. They took me to the sea, and sold me in the hands of the Christians, who bound me, and sent me on board of a great ship. And we sailed a month and half a month, when we came to a place called Charleston in the Christian language. Here they sold me to a small, weak, and wicked man named Johnson, a complete infidel, who had no fear of God at all. Now I am a small man, and not able to do hard work. So I fled from the hand of Johnson, and, after a month, came to a place where I saw some houses. On the new moon I went into a large house to pray; a lad saw me, and rode off to the place of his father, and informed him that he had seen a black man in the great house. A man named Handah, (Hunter,) and another man with him, on horseback, came, attended by a troop of dogs. They took me and made me go with them twelve miles, to a Place called Faydill, (Fayetteville,) where they put me in a great house, from which I could not go out. I continued in the great house, which in the Christian language they call *jail*, sixteen days and nights. One Friday the jailer came and opened the door, and I saw a great many men, all of them Christians, some of whom called out, What is your name? I did not understand their Christian language.

A man called Bob Mumford took me and led me out of the jail, and I was very well pleased to go with them to their place. I stayed at Mumford's four days and nights, and then a man named Jim Owen, son-in-law of Mumford, who married his daughter Betsy, asked me if I was willing to go to a place called Bladen. I said yes, I was willing. I went with them, and have remained on the place of Jim Owen until now.[82]

This narrative was written in Arabic by Omar Ibn Said (1770–1864) to his friend Lamine Kaba in 1836. He called it a "true reflection of his past." Perhaps it should serve as a correction to the deceptive signification that resulted in the legend of Omar Ibn Said. Omar was an outstanding example of how sophisticated African Muslims who "declared a conversion to Christianity" utilized intellectual resistance and inner jihad to manipulate their paths through slavery.[83] Omar was the most famous African Muslim slave in the antebellum period. Numerous articles about his life have been published from 1825 to the present, and some of his manuscripts and his portrait have been preserved. However, fact must be separated from fiction in the life story of this remarkable man. The legend of Omar Ibn Said depicts him as a fair Arabian "Prince Moro" who was captured and sold into slavery by his fellow Africans, whom he always hated. As a slave in Charleston, South Carolina, he is said to have loved his kind master but ran away from a cruel overseer. Eventually, according to legend, John Owen, a former governor of North Carolina, recognized Omar's noble qualities and helped him convert to Christianity. Thereafter, this African Muslim supposedly abandoned his interest in Africa and Islam and continued in a love of white Americans and Christianity.[84]

All of the above is a deliberate distortion of history intended to soothe American consciences and maintain, if not create, certain myths about the Old South. The real Omar Ibn Said was not an Arabian, but a Tukolor Fula who was clearly black. In Africa he was trained to be a scholar, teacher, and trader. Omar arrived in America in 1807, ran away from a cruel master, and was eventually bought by James Owen, the governor's brother. He presented himself to his new master as a frail, spiritual, and intellectual man and was somehow exempted from all hard labor. Although he convinced the Christian community of his religious assimilation, the fact that his Arabic Bible and all of his manuscripts include references to Muhammad challenges the assumption that he was successfully converted.[85]

Moreover, Omar Ibn Said's case demonstrates that when Islam is a major factor in a slave narrative, the historian must watch with extra care for "Christian crusading" and traces of orientalism in the accounts of white antebellum editors. For we know from Edward Said's eloquent and powerful work that scholars and imaginative writers created an intellectual tradition of orientalism during Omar Ibn Said's time. Thus, the "bloodstained Koran" and "Arabian prince" in white American treatments of Omar's story were familiar representations of Islam that defined it as exotic, mysterious, Arab, and inferior.[86]

Omar was still practicing Islam in 1819, when John Louis Taylor, an officer of the American Colonization Society in Raleigh, North Carolina, wrote Francis Scott Key (also a colonizationist), requesting an Arabic Bible for the Muslim slave. Although Omar attended church regularly and was said to have written Christian prayers in Arabic for white people, the evidence indicates that he used these occasions actually to write Mus-

OMAR IBN SAID (1770–1864), *African Muslim slave in North Carolina.* Courtesy of the Library of Davidson College. Used by permission.

lim inscriptions suggestive of inner jihad or the struggle within himself to maintain his faith in an alien environment. Omar's last known Arabic manuscript entitled "The Lord's Prayer" was actually a paraphrase of Surah 110 of the Quran, which speaks of the ultimate victory of Islam.[87]

Also, there is evidence that Omar may have used these passages from the Quran as magical protection against his enemies. The Arabic drawings and pentacles inscribed on several of his Arabic manuscripts are similar to those found on the amulets that African slaves in Brazil used in the Muslim insurrection of 1835 in Bahia. João Reis has noted that these amulets, which consisted of leather pouches in which were placed "pieces of paper containing passages from the Koran and powerful prayers[, had] great seductive power over Africans" in Brazil and West Africa, and that "the magic in the Islamic texts and drawings worked as protection against various threats." Thus for these black Muslims in the New World, the written word offered a potent means of resistance to domination.[88]

Two final notes remain regarding Omar Ibn Said's connections to global Islam. In 1858, Omar received a letter in Arabic from Yang, a Muslim in Canton, China. Yang had written to Omar in response to Reverend D. Ball, a missionary in Canton, who knew both of the Muslims and had previously shown an Arabic letter from Omar to Yang. Finally, one of Omar's letters was indirectly responsible for the initial fieldwork of the Pan-African scholar Edward Wilmot Blyden's initial field work among black Muslim communities in West Africa. In 1863, Timothy Dwight, Jr. told Daniel Bliss, head of the Syrian Protestant College, about the Arabic manuscripts of Omar Ibn Said. This information led Bliss to believe that there were many black Muslims literate in Arabic in the area of Omar's homeland. Thus, he arranged to have Arabic Bibles sent to Liberia and to be taken to Muslim areas further inland. Furthermore, Bliss required that each Bible contain a leaflet requesting information about black individuals and communities who were literate in Arabic. As a result of this plan in 1867, Karfae, a Mandingo Muslim in Liberia, sent a reply to the College of Liberia:

> We are of one religion and that is the religion of Mohammed: Whosoever believes in our prophet shall enter heaven, but whosoever does not believe in our prophet shall dwell in hellfire. [But] come to us with the books which are among you, and your paper and we will write to you.[89]

This letter helped to initiate contacts between Edward Wilmot Blyden, who was planning an Arabic studies department at the College of Liberia and black Muslim communities in West Africa. These contacts and their relationship to Islam in the African-American context will be discussed in chapter 2.[90]

Mahommah Gardo Baquaqua and Mohammed Ali Ben Said: African Muslim Slaves and World Travelers

The biographical sketches that remain describe two African Muslims who survived slavery in Brazil, the Middle East, and Europe and came to America as free men during the antebellum period. Mahommah Gardo Baquaqua and Mohammed Ali Ben Said told the stories of their impressive world travels to white American editors and writers who had various motives for publication, but unfortunately did not emphasize their Islamic origins. Only because of these two men's resistance to the overwhelming signifying power of Christianity—which they opposed for personal, if not religious reasons—did the truth about their Islamic roots come to light.

Drinking and carousing got Mahommah Gardo Baquaqua kidnapped from his native land, Benin, and sold into slavery. He led an adventurous life in which he was a slave in Brazil, a fugitive in the United States, a Christian convert in Haiti, and a student at Central College in New York. Baquaqua's biography was written and published as a pamphlet by Samuel Moore in 1854 to garner support for Mahommah Baquaqua's plans to be a Christian missionary in Africa. However, the biography shows that the African did not really have much interest in either Christian or Islamic religion.[91]

Born in the 1820s into a Muslim family that did not require him to adhere strictly to the rules of his religion, Baquaqua developed little interest in education, religion, or traditional middle-class occupations. His wanderings along the Islamic trade routes eventually brought him to Ghana, where he was a house servant until his master used his weakness for alcohol to trick him and sell him to a slave ship that was headed for Brazil.[92]

From 1845 to 1847, Baquaqua had three cruel masters in Brazil, but luckily his last one was a sea captain. The African escaped from slavery when his master's ship docked in New York harbor and was spotted by the New York City Vigilance Society, which was composed of free blacks. They helped Baquaqua escape to Boston. Eventually, he went to Haiti, where he met Rev. William Judd of the American Baptist Free Mission Society. Judd's written account of Baquaqua describes the latter's conversion to Christianity in hagiographic terms:

> His experience before the church was very affecting. Several persons present, not professors of religion, wept on hearing it. He is endowed by nature with a soul so noble that he grasps the whole world at a stroke, in the movement of his benevolent feelings. And the expression of such noble feelings, in a style so simple and broken as his, is truly affecting. He now seems filled with the most ardent desire to labor for the salvation of souls: talks much of Africa, and prays ardently that her people may receive the gospel. Dreams often of visiting Kachna, accompanied by a good white man, as he calls a

Missionary, and being kindly received by his mother. He had been asking for baptism a considerable time, when I felt that I could not refuse him any longer.[93]

In reality, Baquaqua's conversion was a stormy two-year affair that was hampered by his mistrust of white people and his penchant for alcohol. It also appears that partial motivation for this conversion was to solicit charitable contributions for his fare back to Africa. When this venture failed, this African Muslim used his conversion to Christianity to get an education.[94]

With the encouragement of his mentor, Baquaqua returned to America to enroll in New York Central College in McGrawville, New York. This institution, which was established by the abolitionist American Baptist Free Mission Society in 1848, was revolutionary in its time—it had black and female students as well as black professors. However the racism of the white students must have been too much for Baquaqua to bear indefinitely, as he moved to Canada after three years at Central College. His collaboration with the white pamphleteer Samuel Moore in the *Biography of Mahommah Baquaqua* in 1854 indicates that the former was disillusioned with white Christians and abolitionists.[95] Baquaqua consented to this second biography to solicit support for his plans to return to Africa as a missionary to his people. Unfortunately, Moore's pamphlet did not help his cause, and no further information is available about his life.[96]

Mohammed Ali Ben Said was also carousing (against the rules of his religion) when he was kidnapped in Bornu and "marched across the Sahara desert to Tripoli" to be sold into slavery.[97] Norwood P. Hallowell, a white editor and author, was dazzled by the linguistic skills of this Muslim ex-slave whose autobiography he edited for the *Atlantic Monthly* in 1867. He wrote:

> [Said] wrote and spoke fluently the English, French, German and Italian languages, while there is not doubt he was master of Kanouri (his vernacular), Mandara, Arabic, Turkish and Russian—a total of nine languages.[98]

Thanks to Hallowell's words, we have a window on a world that was long hidden from view. Mohammed Ali Ben Said, alias Nicholas Said, was born in 1831 in Bornu, West Africa. Said was well educated and came from an important Bornuese family. His father, Barca Gana, was a general and personal slave to Shehu el-Kanemy, who was the major military hero of Bornu. After Said was kidnapped into slavery in Africa, he looked for wealthy and cultivated masters who could furnish him with fine clothes, vacations, and interesting books to read. His adventures in slavery took him to Tripoli, Mecca, Alexandria, Cairo, St. Petersburg, Teheran, Warsaw, Vienna, Dresden, Munich, Zurich, Milan, Florence, Rome, Paris, London, and Liverpool. In Russia, Said became the servant and traveling companion of Prince Nicholas Trubetskoy, whose godfather was Czar Nicholas. This association facilitated the African Muslim's travels through Europe.[99]

Said's autobiography, which focused on his world travels, said very little about his religion except that he regretted that he had been baptized in Russia and renamed "Nicholas," because he had not been informed beforehand about the meaning of the ceremony. Although he probably was not very religious, it appears that he remained a Muslim in spite of his baptism. Said also regretted that he was not permitted to make the full pilgrimage when he accompanied his former master to Mecca. He wrote:

> I had not come of my own free will and for the express purpose of a pilgrimage and therefore I was not permitted to go to Daoud to the grave of the Prophet, and was obliged to content myself without the title of Hadji, which is one much respected among Mohammedans.[100]

In 1860, Said was liberated by Prince Nicholas, and given "two fifty pound bills" as a gift, when the latter realized that his faithful servant and friend was unhappy and had been grieving for his native land:

> About this time I began to think of the condition of Africa, my native country, how European attachments might be stopped and her nationalities united.... I cried many times at the ignorance of my people, exposed to foreign ambition, who . . . could not contend against superior weapons and tactics in the field. I prayed earnestly to do some good to my race.[101]

In Liverpool for two weeks, waiting for his ship back to Africa, Said met a man from Holland who persuaded him first to go to America. They left on January 1, 1860. Along the way, the pair stopped in the West Indies and Canada. When these fellow travelers reached a "village named Elmer" (probably in upstate New York), Said loaned his companion five hundred dollars, which was never fully paid back. Thus, the African Muslim was forced to remain in America to earn a living.[102]

For a short time in 1861, Said was a teacher in Detroit, Michigan. In 1863, he became a soldier in the 55th Regiment of the Massachusetts Colored Volunteers, where he achieved the rank of sergeant and was known as a storyteller. Finally, Said wrote the colorful story of his life for one of his military officers in 1865 or 1866. After that, nothing further is known about him, except that "like many a warrior before him, he fell captive to woman, married in the south."[103]

Names and Signification

What did these African Muslim slaves' retention of Muslim names and traditions signify in American racial discourse in the nineteenth century? We know that identity was important to this discourse for both blacks and whites. The act of taking away an African's name and religious traditions and assigning him a new name and a new religion in an alien land imposed on the black a rite of passage, an unholy confirmation—"branding a mark" into his consciousness that symbolized his depersonalization and his subordinate state in a new social order. These measures placed the slave in a state of permanent marginality, for his old identity was lost forever and he could not acquire a new one on his own. Therefore, he was positioned as an "acquired stranger" or a "non-person" in the structure of the racial discourse. In that discourse, only the master had the power to define who or what the African slave could signify. For a slave to retain Muslim names and traditions must have been perceived by some whites as an intolerable threat to the social order.[104]

For some whites, slaves had to remain "the unspoken invisible other" in the racial discourse. Who they were was not important. What they could signify, however, was. Therefore, some white Americans used the power of signification and characterized the Muslim slaves as "overly tanned" Arabs or referred to them as "Moors" instead of Africans.[105] For people of European descent, the term "Moor" signified their Muslim enemies wherever they encountered them in the world. Indeed the term "Moor" held complex and longstanding religious/political significations for European Americans. In the Middle Ages, Europe was significantly threatened by the political, military, and cultural power of the Moors from Morocco. It was not until the eve of the modern era that Spanish, Portuguese, and southern Italian Christians achieved a "reconquest" after centuries of domination by Muslims from Morocco; around the same time, Russian Christians conquered the Tatar Muslims who had ruled and/or threatened them for centuries. Partly because of the long-standing history of warfare between Christians and Muslims during the Crusades in the holy lands, other European peoples welcomed the Christian reconquest of Europe and connected it ideologically to the new voyages of discovery and exploitation in the New World. It was not until 1683, however, that the "Moorish" threat to Europe really ended. On September 12 of that year, Turkish Muslims finally withdrew from the outskirts of Vienna after a failed attempt to seize the city. In 1699, the Treaty of Carlowitz officially signaled the hegemony of the Habsburg empire over the Muslim Ottoman empire. Because of the history of conflict between Europe and North African Muslims, Europeans tended to generalize the use of their ethnic designation and then "continued to name all of their Muslim enemies 'Moors'."[106]

Although Europeans had finally surpassed global Islam in terms of technology and military power by the time of the antebellum period in America, the image of the "Moor" or the Muslim enemy was still a powerful signification for people of European descent everywhere. It explained the awe and respect that some African Muslim slaves received from some white Americans, as well as the repeated attempts on the part of whites to facilitate their return back to Africa, in order to rid America of Islam.[107]

According to Charles H. Long, encounters between the enslaver and the enslaved, the colonizer and the colonized, and the conqueror and conquered during this period produced during the modern period a "structure of experience" and an intellectual problem for both the signified and the signifier. The signifier created new intellectual categories, such as "race" and "Moor," to objectify people who were "novel" and "other." At the same time, they used these intellectual formulations to obscure their culture's real economic, political, and military objectives among black people. The signified had to cope with these new names and categories in order to survive in the context of European domination. However, especially in the nineteenth and early twentieth centuries, they began to reformulate their racial/cultural identities through "a signification upon this legitimated signifying."[108]

For blacks, both slave and free, slave names were an emblem of the cultural pain inflicted on Africans. The purpose of this pain was to destroy the African's ethnicity and to replace it with a racial identity in America, and that is one of the reasons that naming the African American was such a controversial issue for black political leaders and intellectuals in the nineteenth century. Some of those leaders were attempting to come to terms with their own slave names and to reconstruct their ethnicity. They proposed many names for their race: Free African, African, Children of Africa, Sons of Africa, Ethiopian, Negro, Colored American, Colored, people of color, free people of color, Afro-Saxon, African, Afro-American, Africo-American, African-American, Aframerican, and Afmerican.[109]

African Muslim slaves established a unique position in this discourse. They constituted the first Islamic group in America, and their original ethnic identities and names had remained intact in the eighteenth and nineteenth century. They were Songhai-Hausa, Manding, Fulani, Kanuri-Mandara, Sereculeh, and Tukolor. In Africa, most of them had been professionals: teachers, doctors, traders, translators, religious scholars, and military and political leaders. Their positions in the racial discourse of their time were complex, for their names, dietary laws, rituals, dress, literacy in Arabic, former social status, and ethnicity set them apart from the other slaves.[110]

Moreover, as the evidence has demonstrated, the very qualities that distinguished African Muslims from other slaves impressed their black compatriots, both slave and free, because they represented resistance, self-determination, and education. Vincent P. Franklin has shown that resistance, self-determination, and education were the "core values" of African-American culture from slavery to the present. Indeed, in the antebellum period, no other group of blacks in America had a religion that articulated these values more effectively than the African Muslims.

Aspects of global Islam—literacy in Arabic, signification, and jihad—equipped them with the tools for a liberation struggle in America that in many cases resulted ultimately in their emigration back to Africa. Furthermore, resistance, self-determination, and education connected the religion of the African Muslim slaves ideologically to the multi-ethnic Pan-Africanist impulse, binding slaves together and sustaining them under brutal oppression. This Pan-Africanist impulse, which became more pervasive and influential in black America as the nineteenth century progressed, was the ideological link between the "old Islam" of the original African Muslim slaves and the "new American Islam" that developed in America at the turn of the century.[111]

At the same time, by the eve of the Civil War, the old Islam of the original African Muslim slaves was, for all practical purposes, defunct—because these Muslims were not able to develop institutions to perpetuate their religion in nineteenth-century America. They were religious oddities and mavericks in America, because there was no community of believers for them to connect with outside the slave quarters. When they died, their version of Islam, which was private and individually oriented, disappeared. Unfortunately the historical record does not provide us with a holistic picture of their religious life. But they were important, nevertheless, because they brought the religion of Islam to America.

Pan-Africanism and black bitterness toward Christian racism were new seeds planted in the consciousness of nineteenth-century African Americans, seeds that in turn flowered into a new American Islam in the early twentieth century. This new American Islam in the African-American community was at once anti-Christian and multi-cultural, and it developed a distinct missionary and internationalist political agenda. It was also part of a new era in American religion, as Eastern religions began to flourish in the United States. Ironically, the new American Islam began with the ideas of a black Presbyterian minister named Edward Wilmot Blyden.

Chapter 2

PAN-AFRICANISM AND THE NEW AMERICAN ISLAM

EDWARD WILMOT BLYDEN AND MOHAMMED ALEXANDER RUSSELL WEBB

Mohamedanism in Africa has left the native master
of himself and of his home; but wherever Christianity has been able to establish itself . . . foreigners have
taken possession of the country, and, in some places,
rule the natives with oppressive rigour.
—Edward Wilmot Blyden

It is impossible to understand fully the transition between the "old Islam"
of the original African Muslim slaves and the "new American Islam" of the
early twentieth century without giving some attention to nineteenth-
century Pan-Africanism, which formed the ideological bridge between
these two phases of Islam in the United States. Moreover, the Pan-Africanist ideas of Edward Wilmot Blyden (1832–1912) are the key to understanding how and why the racial particularism and signification of black
American Islam became linked to a racial separatism and signification that
was endemic to global Islam in the nineteenth century. Blyden, who is
sometimes called the "father of Pan-Africanism," used the example of
Islam in West Africa as the paradigm for racial separatism and signification in his Pan-Africanist ideology and ultimately argued that as a global
religion for blacks, Islam was preferable to Christianity. These ideas were
destined to have a profound impact on black nationalist and Islamic
movements in America in the twentieth century.

EDWARD WILMOT BLYDEN:
ISLAM AND PAN-AFRICANISM

For our purposes, the significance of Edward Wilmot Blyden's story began in 1850 with the passage of the Fugitive Slave Law. John Hope Franklin and Wilson J. Moses have noted that the Fugitive Slave Law was a landmark in the "history of black nationalism." With it the South scored a decisive blow over anti-slavery, as federal agencies received "unlimited powers" to apprehend runaway slaves. The most frightening aspect of this law was that in its execution, free blacks were often seized as runaway slaves. This phenomenon inspired such panic, terror, and turmoil in the free black community that most African-American leaders at least contemplated the idea of emigration to Africa.[1]

In 1850, Edward Wilmot Blyden was a promising young West Indian candidate for the Presbyterian ministry who had just arrived in the United States to enroll in his pastor's alma mater, Rutgers Theological College. Being denied admission because of his race and suffering excruciating fear "of being seized for a slave" convinced him that he could not stay in the United States. In New York, he met John Pinney, Walter Lowrie, and William Coppinger, Presbyterian leaders of the American Colonization Society, an organization established in 1816 by white Americans including Henry Clay for the purpose of making an African homeland for free black Americans. Although their explicit rationale was humanitarian, in practice, white colonizationists tended not to speak out against racism and slavery in America, and thus, most free black Americans viewed them with suspicion. Moreover, since the late eighteenth century, Christian missionaries saw colonization as a means of bringing "Christian civilization" to the "dark continent" of Africa. In this regard, the British had first sent westernized blacks to establish the colony of Sierra Leone in 1787, and the Americans had done the same in Liberia, which became independent in 1847. Despite the mixed motives of his white Presbyterian mentors, Blyden cast his lot with the Colonization Society in order to bring Christianity and civilization to the "barbarous tribes" of Africa. He arrived in Monrovia, Liberia in January 1851.[2]

Edward Wilmot Blyden was destined to become one of the pioneers of the nineteenth-century Pan-African movement. His colleagues included Alexander Crummell, James Theodore Holly, Martin R. Delany, Henry McNeal Turner, and others. These men proposed and debated different "back to Africa" plans to solve the problem of racism and slavery in the western hemisphere. Although they frequently disagreed with each other about emigration plans and the best way to uplift and unite people of African descent worldwide, their objectives were concisely summed up in the Constitution of the African Civilization Society in 1858. Their goal was

the civilization and Christianization of Africa, of the descendants of African ancestors in any portion of the earth, wherever dispersed. Also, the destruction of the African slave trade, by the introduction of lawful commerce and trade into Africa . . . and generally, the elevation of the condition of the colored population of our country, and of other lands.[3]

In 1857, on the eve of the Civil War—as the Supreme Court's Dred Scott Decision dashed African-American hopes for a peaceful resolution of slavery by ruling that a slave's status could not be changed by residence in a free state—African-American interest in Africa increased, and Pan-Africanism grew, with more players using more complex strategies. Wilson J. Moses has called the period from 1850 to 1925 "the Golden Age of Black Nationalism" because "it was the locus of the most significant black nationalist movements and thinkers in history." According to Moses:

[Black nationalism] attempts to unify politically all [black] peoples whether they are residents of African territories or descendants of those Africans

EDWARD WILMOT BLYDEN (1832–1912), the father of Pan-Africanism. From the collections of the Library of Congress.

who were dispersed by the slave trade. . . . Black nationalism has sometimes, but not always, been concerned with the quest for a nation in the geographical sense. But often it has been nationalism only in the sense that it seeks to unite the entire black racial family, assuming the entire race has a collective destiny and message for humanity comparable to that of a nation. For this reason it is impossible to speak of black nationalism without simultaneously speaking of Pan-Africanism.[4]

Throughout most of African-American history, the Pan-Africanist vision has opposed and transcended the apparatus of the nation state (a political concept emphasizing the particular historical and political identities inherent in nationalism) and has envisioned a trans-national state for black people. For our purposes, Pan-Africanism is the most important analytical pole of black nationalism, with its focus on "a movement toward economic cooperation, cultural awareness, and international political solidarity among people of African descent." Perhaps Edward Wilmot Blyden's most significant contribution to Pan-Africanist discourse was his use of West African Islam as a paradigm for black cultural nationalism. Clifton E. Marsh has summed up the ideas and attitudes of cultural nationalism:

> Cultural nationalists feel blacks represent a distinct and separate culture from that of the white society. It is this cultural link with other blacks which forms a major portion of the ideology. Glorification of African art, literature, philosophy and history are essential to liberate the Afro-psyche from the traditions of Western Civilization. Also, the assertion of a distinct life-style and world view in such ways as assuming African or Arabic names, wearing African clothes, and speaking African languages is essential to becoming free.[5]

With these perspectives in mind, the important questions are (1) how and why Edward Wilmot Blyden linked Islam to Pan-Africanism and (2) how and why Pan-Africanism became the major political ideology of the new American Islam that arose among African Americans in the early twentieth century. To answer these questions, we must analyze Blyden's role as a scholar in the new field of Islamic studies, for he created and transmitted a particular representation of Islam that became one of the focal points in the political cultural discourse noticed by American literati in 1869, when he published an article on the black contribution to ancient Egypt in *The Methodist Quarterly Review*.[6] However, he made his mark with several articles on Christianity, Islam, and the black race which appeared in the 1870s in *Fraser's Magazine* in Great Britain.[7]

While European orientalists were busy creating negative and exotic representations of Islam "by which European culture was able to manage—and even produce the Orient politically, sociologically, militarily, ideologically, scientifically, and imaginatively during the post-Enlightenment period,"[8] Blyden was doing something quite different with the religion: he began with his positive impressions of the black Islamic experience.[9]

Edward Wilmot Blyden's interest in global Islam may have been initially sparked by some of Omar Ibn Said's Arabic manuscripts, which were sent to Daniel Bliss, president of the Syrian Protestant College, by Timothy Dwight, officer of the Ethnological Society of New York, in 1863. Omar's manuscripts convinced Bliss and other Christian missionaries in that part of the world that there were significant black Muslim populations in the area of the African Muslim slave's homeland. Thus, a plan was initiated to send Arabic Bibles to Liberia. Each Bible contained a note which requested information about particular black Muslim communities in the interior. Edward Blyden was undoubtedly aware of this plan, because in 1866 he spent the summer months in Syria, studying the Arabic language. At that time, he had already acquired a number of Arabic manuscripts from black Muslims in Liberia, which he brought to Syria for analysis.

In January 1867, Blyden traveled to Vonsua, a village outside Monrovia, to visit Karfae, a Mandingo Muslim cleric, who had received one of the Arabic Bibles from Syria and had responded to the request for information. Karfae gave Blyden an Arabic manuscript which described the mosque at Mecca. He then traveled to Liberia College with a delegation of learned Muslim dignitaries. Later in 1867, Blyden established the Arabic Studies Program at Liberia College to facilitate Christian missionary work and political contact with the black Muslim communities in the interior of Liberia.[10]

During numerous visits to Muslim areas in Liberia and Sierra Leone in the 1860s and 1870s, Blyden became deeply impressed by the level of learning among African Muslims and by Islam's ability to unify African peoples. Blyden interacted with Muslim scholars who could not only "reproduce from memory any chapter of the Koran, with its vowels, and dots and grammatical marks," but also discuss the Muslim classics in Arabic. He admired the social and political organization of these communities, which he attributed to the influence of Islam, and noted with favor the synthesis of Islam and indigenous structures that had occurred in West and Central Africa over the centuries. "While [Islam] brought [Africans] a great deal that was absolutely new, and inspired them with spiritual feelings to which they had been utter strangers," Blyden said, "it strengthened and hastened certain tendencies to independence and self-reliance which were already at work." He continued:

> Their local institutions were not destroyed by the Arab influence introduced. They only assumed new forms, and adapted themselves to the new teachings. In all thriving Mohammedan communities in the West and Central Africa, it may be noticed that the Arab superstructure has been superimposed on a permanent indigenous substructure; so that what really took place, when

the Arab met the Negro in his home was a healthy amalgamation, and not an absorption or an undue repression.[11]

Blyden's research had been inspired by the British Islamicist R. Bosworth Smith, who was fed up with Christian academics who attempted to "vilify and misrepresent" Islam and who offered a "sympathetic" view of the religion. Blyden's extensive fieldwork, however, distinguished his research from that of all of his predecessors. In the final evaluation, his observations in the field radicalized his political perspective on Islam. Although he was a Presbyterian minister, his experience in West Africa led him to believe that what he perceived as Islam's lack of racial prejudice and doctrine of brotherhood made it a more appropriate religion for people of African descent than Christianity. This is a recurring theme in his collection of essays entitled *Christianity, Islam, and the Negro Race.* Blyden went on to show in this volume that Christianity, in spite of its eastern origins, had become an exclusively European religion that debased African Americans and taught them to deny their own racial heritage. He noted that Christianity "came to the Negro as a slave, or at least as a subject in a foreign land" and that all of its images in art and literature exalted

the physical characteristics of a foreign race . . . and had only a depressing influence on the Negro. . . . While Mohammedanism and learning to the Muslim Negro were coeval . . . the Christian Negro came in contact with mental and physical proscription and the religion of Christ, contemporaneously.[12]

Although much of Blyden's work was tinged with a subtle Christian missionary agenda and a blatant disrespect for African traditional religions, the implication was not only that Islam might be a preferable religion for African Americans, but also a focal point for an internationalist perspective that would lead them to think of themselves, in concert with Africans and the darker races of the world, over and against white Europeans and Americans. This Pan-African internationalist perspective was very important because African-American Muslims in the twentieth century would use it to globalize their religious/political discourse. From Blyden's work we can see that the new American Islam's predominant political discourse—Pan-Africanism—was not only a product of America, it was an international phenomenon based on global connections. Although he did not to look deeply enough into Islamic affairs in Africa to notice the subtle latent racial and color distinctions and prejudices that existed among Muslims, he understood correctly that Islam was the only major world religion in which black people had historically been able to maintain social, cultural, political, and economic autonomy. Blyden and other black leaders observed positive racial, cultural and political separation among West African Muslims and used these characteristics in their Pan-

Africanist discourses as a paradigm for black community development. The important point for us is that this black community model—which was later utilized by black leaders of the new American Islamic movements in the early twentieth century—was an international Islamic paradigm, based on historic patterns of racial interaction among Muslims in West Africa and not on a parochial black nationalism in the United States.

Mudimbe has aptly characterized Edward Wilmot Blyden's Pan-Africanist discourse as "a sort of prophetism," in which the latter believed that the most compelling aspects of Islam and Christianity would eventually interface to create a new vision of religion for people of African descent:

> Where the light from the Cross ceases to stream upon the gloom, there the beams of the Crescent will give illumination; and, as the glorious orb of Christianity rises, the twilight of Islam will be lost in the greater light of the Sun of Righteousness. Then Isaac and Ishmael will be united.[13]

The emigration of selected African Americans and West Indians back to Africa was central to Blyden's prophetic vision of the redemption of Africa and the black race. In his own words, he envisioned "Ethiopia stretching out her hands unto God; or Africa's service to the world." Blyden's "interpretation of religions and political nationalisms" under the rubric of "Ethiopian mysticism" was typical of the understanding of history in "The Golden Age of Black Nationalism." Wilson J. Moses has noted that often the black nationalist "view of history is mystical, based on the prophesy that 'Ethiopia shall soon stretch forth her hands unto God,' that Africa's redemption will be accompanied by a decline of the West; that God will make a new covenant with black people." Aspects of this "mystical" view of history are important because they were appropriated by the African-American formulators of the new American Islam in the early twentieth century.[14]

Edward Wilmot Blyden was a complicated man. Although he laid the intellectual groundwork for what was to become Islam's great emotional appeal for African Americans in the twentieth century, some of his political activities and intellectual sources undercut the prophetic nature of some of his ideas. Like Henry Highland Garnet, Martin R. Delany, and Alexander Crummell, Blyden was a Christian civilizationist who despised Christianity's political and racial agenda. He did believe, however, that Christianized blacks in the western hemisphere were culturally superior to Africans and that the former had a divine mission to "lift the veil of darkness" and bring "modern civilization" to Africa. Thus, when the European "scramble for Africa" began with the Berlin conference in 1885, Blyden was in favor of "European imperialism in Africa" and had already launched a campaign to bring British rule to West Africa. When the British occupied Egypt in 1882, he was hopeful that they would put an end to the Arab slave trade in blacks from Egypt and the Sudan to the Middle East. For Blyden, European rule in Africa was a "necessary evil" which would bring modernity to Africans and Muslims.[15]

The emphasis on African civilization in Blyden's Pan-Africanist discourse originated from European sources of "romantic racialism" and nationalism. Moses has emphasized the conservative nature of nineteenth-century black nationalism in the context of its elitist and civilizationist attitudes. According to him,

> civilization as developed in the writings of such social thinkers as Guizot and Gobineau, came to imply the concept of progress. The idea was European not African. . . . Westernized Africans were exquisitely conscious of the differences between African societies and the self confident, civilized Anglo-Saxon culture. Thus, did they begin to advocate African civilization, which embodied a sense of obligation to aid in the uplifting of the continent and its "backward peoples" as an initial step in the elevation of black people everywhere.

Moreover, Pan-Africanists such as Edward Wilmot Blyden viewed the supposed "lack of civilization" in Africa as one of the causes of African slavery in the western hemisphere and saw the redemption of the black race in the destruction of the connection between "slavery and the blackness." He believed that this would be a result of African civilization.[16]

Blyden envisioned the establishment of African civilization through the unification of the black race. Implicit here was his understanding of races as "organic types of beings," each endowed with a specific type of personality and divine mission. In the latter respect he echoed Gobineau's idea of the black race as "sensual, emotional, and feminine" as opposed to the hardy, aggressive and "masculine" Anglo-Saxons. In the former respect Blyden was clearly in line with nineteenth-century German nationalist theorists such as Herder, Schleiermacher, von Treitschke, and Hegel, who also argued for organic racial unity based on "the divine plan in history." In Blyden's case, these ideas led to the belief in black genetic racial purity—a form of racial supremacy that was acted out in his vicious opposition to the mulatto elite in Liberia.[17]

Blyden's views on "Black personality" and racial purity had ramifications for the new American Islam in the early twentieth century. When European racial ideas were linked to the paradigm of racial separatism that Blyden appropriated from Islam in West Africa, the result was an extremely potent model for Pan-African racial separatism and supremacy that was later adopted and expanded by the leaders of the Universal Negro Improvement Association, the Nation of Islam, and other black American Muslim groups. Thus, in Blyden's Pan-Africanist discourse, we can trace the origins of racial supremacist ideas in twentieth-century black American Islam.

Edward Wilmot Blyden can be criticized for his lack of critical attention to one of the sources of West African Islam that he so admired in Liberia and Sierra Leone. In the nineteenth century, Islam spread in much of West and Central Africa by means of a series of jihads that pitted a "militant, universalist Islam" against African traditional religions and mixed Islam. Unlike the relatively peaceful spread of Islam and its accommodation to traditional customs in West Africa in the medieval period, this time, the religion spread by means of the sword and was intent on stamping out "local interpretations of faith." These jihads "were [an] intellectual as well as a military movement"; for in their wake, literacy in Arabic and West African languages increased scholarly activity, Sufism (Islamic mysticism) advanced, and new towns were established. Although these militant jihads resulted in some positive economic, political, and cultural changes in West Africa, they tended to denigrate African traditional practices. In this respect, the Islamic jihads were in line with Blyden's negative views of African traditional customs.[18]

The most negative consequence of these jihads is that they accelerated the Islamic slave trade among African peoples. Mudimbe has rightly criticized Blyden for his ignorance on this matter:

> The historical facts badly contradict Blyden's belief in the positive capabilities of Islam. Throughout the nineteenth century in Central Africa, Islamic factions represented an objective evil and practiced a shameful slave-trade. And here, again, we face an unbelievable inconsistency in Blyden's thought: his naive admiration for Islam led him to accept the enslavement of non-Muslim peoples![19]

Although Blyden did speak about the evils of the Muslim slave trade on at least one occasion, on several occasions he rationalized both the Muslim and the Atlantic slave trades as civilizing institutions for blacks. Moreover, if we believe that Blyden saw evidence of the Muslim slave trade in his frequent contacts with West African Muslim communities, it is all the more striking that there was no sustained critique of Islam in his writings. How can this critical void be explained? Edward Wilmot Blyden, like several other nineteenth-century Pan-Africanists, was so anxious to find a monotheistic alternative to the racism of Christianity that he was willing to forgive the racism of Islam in its slave trade. At least, he reasoned, it had not destroyed African identities and self-determination. In Blyden's Pan-Africanist discourse, the black Muslim community model was the global trade-off for the racism and slavery of Islam.

In his construction of a Pan-African Islamic model that ignored the racism of global Islam, Edward Wilmot Blyden created the first paradigm of what this book will call "the myth of a race-blind Islam," that Islam is a religion without racial prejudice or discrimination in its global history. "The myth of a race-blind Islam" refers to a discourse and to an intellectual tradition that have created and perpetuated ahistorical conceptions of

Islam and black nationalism. This myth was important because it would function as a major intellectual impediment to the analysis of the global and political implications of black nationalism in the twentieth century. As we shall see, Blyden's idea that Islam was a global religion without racial prejudice or discrimination was adopted and expanded by some black intellectuals and religious leaders in the twentieth century in order to discredit some African-American Islamic groups because of their focus on racial issues.[20]

A final question with regard to Edward Wilmot Blyden remains unresolved. Did he convert to Islam? Hollis R. Lynch believed that Blyden "never formally became a Muslim," although he was sympathetic to Islam, while Mudimbe wrote that "spiritually and politically, Blyden was, at least from 1900 on a Muslim." The evidence corroborates Mudimbe's assessment of Blyden, with a few modifications. In Blyden's correspondence from 1870 to 1910, Islam was the most persistent theme. The initial purpose of his extensive interaction with West African Muslim communities during this period was to use the Arabic language to train Christian missionaries and to establish an independent African Christian Church, based partly on the conversion of Muslims. However, his correspondence demonstrates that the West African Muslims had a more profound impact on Blyden's religious consciousness than he had on theirs.[21]

From 1871 to 1873, Blyden worked for the Church Missionary Society as an instructor in Arabic at Fourah Bay College in Sierra Leone. The evidence indicates that his conversion to Islam may have begun as early as 1871, for in that year he wrote, "I am in daily intercourse with the Mohammedans with whom I sometimes read the Arabic scriptures." Moreover, in September of that year, Blyden was visited in Freetown by a delegation of leading Muslims from "Fulah town." His account of that meeting indicates that the Muslims perceived him and he presented himself as a propagator of Islam as well as Christianity:

> They began their interview by offering a prayer for my long life, prosperity and usefulness in Sierra Leone. Then each of the men pronounced a series of blessings upon me in Arabic ending with bibarakat al-nabi (with the blessing of the Prophet). I then informed them of my object in coming to live in Sierra Leone, that my desire and the desire of all good men was that the word of God—His truth—should spread over all Africa—that good men in England had sent me to reside in Sierra Leone that I may teach the Arabic language to young men who are to be the future teachers and missionaries, that they may be able to understand the Moslem ulemas and carry the word of God to Futah, Jenne, Timbuctu in the Arabic language—the loghat-es-sherifat. That I hoped, by and by, to be able to go out myself and establish schools in the large Mohammedan towns in the interior. I then quoted several passages from the Koran showing the testimony which their own books bear to the divine origin of the Christian Scriptures. I further told them that all truth came from

God, who is the fountain of truth, and that, whatever is true in their Koran good and wise men would not ignore, and that whatever superiority they enjoyed over their pagan brethren was due entirely to whatever of truth was in their book.[22]

Although Blyden gave each of these Muslims an Arabic Bible during this meeting, they gave him two Muslim names, which he accepted. Indeed, these names signified a change in his religious status in the Muslim community, for the Muslims viewed him as a special spiritual person:

> The oldest man retaining his seat and holding in his hands his rosary, spoke up for the rest. He said that of all the missionaries, they had seen here, they had never seen one like me, and that they believe God had sent me to this colony—that the feelings of welcome which they had come to express were shared by all the people of their town, young and old: that they were poor, they had no money to give me, but in carrying out my work they would give me every possible assistance, that they would do whatever I said, and I must do what they advise. They said that they looked upon me as chosen of God and they would call me *Mukhtar*—the chosen one. The name given to me by the Mohammedans in the interior is *Abd-al-Kerim*.[23]

Did Blyden have a dual religious identity? There is no definite answer. The above evidence, however, makes a fairly strong case for this possibility. In light of the long history of mixed Islam (Islam combined with African traditional religion) in West Africa, a dual Islamic/Christian religious identity would not have been structurally unusual there. Also, if Blyden did begin his conversion to Islam as early as 1871, this would explain his reluctance to criticize the religion for its racism in his early writings.

If Edward Wilmot Blyden did convert to Islam, why didn't he make his conversion public knowledge in western circles? A large part of Blyden's income was derived from Christian sources. If he did convert to Islam, he could only have been open about his religious status in Muslim circles. His conversion would not have been acceptable to the various missionary boards or to the literary circles on which his professional reputation and income depended. Indeed, after the initial publication of his essay "Mohammedanism and the Negro Race" in 1875, John C. Lowrie, a member of the Presbyterian Board of Foreign Missions, expressed his reservations about Blyden's religious motives. In a letter that may have been a cover-up, Blyden responded:

> I beg to assure you that there are no grounds for the apprehensions you entertain with regard to my position in Mohammedanism. The religious papers, I notice, no doubt suppressed at the quarter from which the article proceeded, have misunderstood its tendency or aim and exaggerated its tone,

and some of them have uttered judgement without having ever seen the article, gathering the views at second hand.[24]

By 1886, there is evidence that Blyden had definitely moved spiritually away from Christianity and closer to Islam. In that year, he resigned from his clerical office in the Presbyterian Church and began to call himself a "minister of truth—not confined to places or offices." Around this time, Blyden became a fan of Samadu, a young Muslim jihadist from Konyan who for a short time established an Islamic theocracy in parts of Liberia and Sierra Leone and successfully challenged the French in western Sudan. The respect that Blyden received from this Muslim military leader indicates that politically he had also moved closer to the Muslim community. He wrote:

> I was visited yesterday by a messenger from the detachment of Samadu's troops near Sierra Leone. He came to express on behalf of the General Commander thanks for a Bible which I sent to Samadu and an Arabic note, and to invite me to visit the army at Samaya and to go and see Samadu. He assured me that my name is well and favorably known all through the interior tribes in town—Mandingo, Foulah, Seracoulee, Yoruba, etc.—have called upon me to beg me to remain permanently in Sierra Leone as their exponent to the Government. But my heart is in Liberia. The messenger from Samadu's army who came to see me yesterday says he was brought up near Musardu where I am well known.[25]

By 1888, Edward Wilmot Blyden's dual religious identity was very clear, as he became an open advocate for Muslim interests in West Africa and his adoption of Muslim names continued. In January 1889, he wrote to John Miller, a Princeton theologian, to propose a plan for a Muslim "literary centre" and mosque on "five hundred acres of land" in the hinterland of Sierra Leone. Blyden envisioned this as the Muslim "college corresponding to educational work at Princeton." He continued,

> The Mohammedans would not only be drawn to this place, but would assist us in pushing the work further out until we reach the highlands of Manding. I have travelled among them extensively in the interim, and from Sego on the Niger to Sierra Leone and Monrovia my name is known among them as "Tibabu More"—the Christian Muslim.

Around this time, Blyden's ideas came directly to America as he was sponsored by black church groups to give lectures in Chicago and the South in the 1890s.[26]

In 1901, Blyden resigned his professorship in Arabic at Liberia College because of his attachment to Islam and his support for polygamy. In his final years, his advocacy for Islam was unrelenting—he was "Director of

Mohammedan Education" in Sierra Leone from 1901 to 1906. During those years, he clearly preferred to be in the company of Muslims. He wrote, "It is with the Mohammedans and those who are least affected by the fringe of European civilization that I prefer to associate." At Blyden's funeral, in 1912, Muslims carried his coffin to the cemetery. Finally, the evidence is strong that he assumed a Muslim identity in West Africa. Whether he officially converted to Islam or not, however, his use of the religion in the construction of a black political and cultural identity constituted a new strand in the racial discourse of the nineteenth century and foreshadowed similar developments among African-American Muslims in the early twentieth century. Because of Edward Wilmot Blyden, Pan-Africanism— the cultural pole of black nationalism—became paradigmatically linked to the black cultures and politics of global Islam.[27]

HENRY McNEAL TURNER: BLACK
BITTERNESS TOWARD RACISM IN CHRISTIANITY

Black bitterness toward racism in Christianity was another important element in the creation of the new American Islam at the turn of the century. This bitterness was linked to the Pan-Africanism and multiple expressions of black nationalist ideologies which filled the air in late nineteenth-century black America. These ideologies were, in a sense, a response to the failure of Reconstruction. By the 1890s, it was clear that freed black slaves were not going to be full citizens in America. In the wake of legal disenfranchisement and segregation and lynch-mob terrorism in America, Pan-Africanism and black nationalism were alternative strategies for self-determination. They became a framework for asking questions about how to forge a separate base of power for African Americans. At the same time, numerous black church leaders criticized Christianity for its intimate links to the oppressive economic, political, and racial structures of America. This criticism is important because it opened the door for new religious alternatives in black America.

For our purposes, the most important figure in this critical response to racism in Christianity was Henry McNeal Turner (1834–1925). His ideas ultimately opened the door to Islam and pushed some black Christians to question Christianity. Bishop Henry McNeal Turner of the African Methodist Episcopal (A.M.E.) Church was a leader in the black missionary movement to Africa during this period. Through his efforts, the independent churches of South Africa attempted to affiliate with the A.M.E. Church, and some South Africans came to the United States to be educated at black colleges. Although Bishop Turner had been a representative to the Georgia legislature, a postmaster, and a customs official during the Reconstruction years, at the turn of the century he was best known for his complete disillusionment with the United States and white Christianity and for his assertion that "God is black." This was one of the primary beliefs that would shape the consciousness of the black Muslims in the twentieth century. For Turner, who believed that African Americans should emigrate to Africa to attain political and economic power, this belief was the cornerstone of black pride:

> We have so much right biblically and otherwise to believe that God is a Negro as you . . . white people have to believe that God is a fine looking, symmetrical and ornamental white man. . . . Every race of people since time began who have attempted to describe their God by words, or by paintings or by carvings, or any other form or figure, have conveyed the idea that the God who made them and shaped their destinies was symbolized in themselves, and why should not the Negro believe that he resembles God as much as other people? We do not believe that there is any hope for a race of people who do not believe that they look like God.[28]

As one of the leading African-American Pan-Africanists at the turn of the century, Turner traveled to Sierra Leone and Liberia in 1891. His letters from that trip indicate that like Edward Wilmot Blyden, his ideas about Pan-Africanism were influenced by the separatist community model of Islam in West Africa:

> These black Mohammedan priests, learned to kill, walking around here in their robes with so much dignity, majesty, and consciousness of their worth, are driving me into respect for them. Some came for hundreds of miles from the country—out of the bushes—better scholars than in America. What fools we are to suppose that these Africans are fools! . . .
> I verily believe that God is holding these Mohammedans intact, and that they will serve as the forerunners of evangelical Christianity; in short the Mohammedan religion is the morningstar to the sun of pure Christianity.[29]

John Henry Smyth (1844–1908), America's Consul General to Liberia in the 1880s, also criticized the racism of Christianity and praised the black communities of West African Islam. In his address to the "Congress of Africa" at the Cotton States and International Exposition in Atlanta in 1895, he described the various Muslim ethnic groups in Sierra Leone:

> Africans cannot be influenced by aliens, who, however Christian seek to subvert their manhood. . . . Of the foregoing races [of Sierra Leone] there has been no acceptance of anything of foreign influence. These races represent a very high and unique type of Mohammedanism and Arabic training. They have adopted the religion of the Prophet and made it conform to themselves. . . . They are not controlled by the Arab, the Persian, or the Turk, as to their conception of the Koran.[30]

Although Turner and Smyth were both African civilizationists with Christian missionary agendas, their rhetoric about Islam was undoubtedly important because it presented Islam in a positive light to black mainstream audiences. Furthermore, their rhetoric connected Islam to the Pan-Africanist ideals of racial separatism, self-determination, and the international solidarity of the black race. All of these ideas paved the way for the appeal of the new American Islam to black Americans in the early twentieth century.

At the same time, African-American leaders who did not talk about Islam contributed compelling indictments of Christianity's racism. John Edward Bruce, perhaps the leading African-American journalist at the turn of the century, was typical of this trend, when he wrote:

> [The] white church of America . . . preaches and perverts the Gospel [and] by indirection and evasion denies the brotherhood of man . . . makes the Black man who loves Jesus feel his inferiority and that he is a degree or two lower than the white Christian and a ward rather than an equal before God.[31]

Moreover, as Albert J. Raboteau has noted, late nineteenth-century African-American theologians such as James Theodore Holly and Theophilus Gould Steward, influenced by the reading of Psalms 68:31, prophesied a glorious new spiritual mission for black people in the next century:

> Steward, a minister of the A.M.E. Church, concluded in 1888 that the evidence of scripture and the signs of the times indicated that the end of the present age was near. The wave of Christian civilization had swept ever westward as far as it would go and now washed up, spent upon these American shores. Indeed an end to the militaristic and racist corruption of Christianity by the West had to come, if the pagan nations were ever to have the true gospel preached to them. Fratricidal warfare among "Christian nations" would end the present age and then a new and final age of a raceless and peaceful Christianity would begin in which the darker, non-Christian peoples of the world (Africans, Indians, Chinese) would hear and accept the pure gospel of Christ, undefiled by Anglo-Saxon prejudice.[32]

Psalms 68:31—"Princes shall come out of Egypt, and Ethiopia shall soon stretch forth her hands into God"—was the Biblical source for these millennial interpretations of history. If these ideas did not directly address the black community's movement toward Islam, they helped it, by depicting white Christianity as the work of the devil and predicting a new synthesis of religion in the redemption of Africans and African Americans in the twentieth century.

Finally, Smyth's praise of West African Islam and Turner's devastating indictment of white Christianity may serve as a useful summary of African-American intellectual thought on Pan-Africanist identity on the eve of the twentieth century. Blyden, Turner, and others undoubtedly influenced some black people to ask not only "What shall we call ourselves?" but also "Do we want to be Christians?" When these questions were rearticulated in the early twentieth century by black Pan-Africanist leaders, they opened the door to new religious alternatives, particularly Islam, in the African-American community. Some African-American Christians were predisposed toward Islam, first, as we have seen in the case of Blyden, because Islam was a "part of the baggage" of nineteenth-century Pan-Africanism which flowered in the early twentieth century.[33] Second, since African Americans were on the margins of white American mainstream culture, they had no political reason to share its deep hostility toward Islam. Pan-Africanism did not connect with a discrete religious tradition in America, however, until the 1890s at the World's Parliament of Religions.

THE WORLD'S PARLIAMENT OF RELIGIONS AND THE NEW AMERICAN ISLAM

In the 1890s Chicago was a thriving metropolis whose industries provided jobs for black and white people alike. The cosmopolitan vitality of this city shined brightly at the World's Columbian Exposition—the quadricentennial celebration of Christopher Columbus's landing in America, which was held there in 1893. This World's Fair drew almost 30 million people from more than 70 countries to Chicago. The World's Parliament of Religions was a part of this larger event, and it brought representatives of major religious traditions together to discuss their agenda for America in the twentieth century. Jamal Effendi, a Muslim muezzin, officiated at the opening ceremonies of the Parliament by reciting prayers to Allah while facing the east. Swami Vivekananda, a Hindu, and the Buddhists Angarika Dharmapala and Soyen Shaku, also addressed the Congress. Their exotic turbans and colorful garments were as striking to the audience as their new religious messages. Although the ideals of the Parliament were tolerance and freedom of religion, many of the American participants saw this as an opportunity to assimilate Asians to the values of Christian civilization. For the Asians who had been dealing with Christian missionaries in their own countries for decades, however, this was an opportunity to defend Eastern religions and to present them as viable alternatives to Christianity for twentieth-century Americans. Around the time of these meetings, representatives of Hinduism, Buddhism, Bahaism, and Islam established their first missions in the United States. The new American Islam, which would eventually focus on the African-American community in the early twentieth century, was at once anti-Christian and multi-cultural, and it developed a distinct missionary and internationalist political agenda. Most important, it was America's version of Islamic modernism, a movement which began in the Muslim world in the nineteenth century as a response to colonialism.[34]

Islamic modernism evolved during the nineteenth century as France, Great Britain, Holland, and Russia colonized large parts of the Muslim world in North Africa, the Middle East, south Asia, and southeast Asia.

After more than one thousand years of empire building, the Islamic world found itself for the first time under the political and cultural control of Christian Europe. According to John Esposito, this dilemma raised several important questions for Muslims:

> What had gone wrong in Islam? Was the success of the West due to the superiority of Christendom, the backwardness of Islam, or the faithlessness of the community? How could Muslims realize God's will in a state governed by non-Muslims and non-Muslim law? In which ways should Muslims respond to this challenge to Muslim identity and faith?[35]

As some Muslims adapted to Western secularism and others completely rejected the West, Islamic modernists responded to the challenge of European colonialism by initiating reform in their religion. They reinterpreted Islam and adapted the religion to particular aspects of western thought and technology that were relevant to their societies. Throughout the Islamic world, modernist movements emerged as Muslims tried to make Islam relevant to the modern world, reformulating their cultural and political identities. Moreover, the roots of a new American Islam can be traced to modernist reform in the Indian Ahmadiyya Movement in Islam. In the nineteenth century, the Ahmadis began to formulate plans to revitalize Islam as a world religion by missionizing the Western hemisphere. Although they did not formally begin their work in America until 1920, the spirit of their movement was embodied in the activities of a white American named Mohammed Alexander Russell Webb, primary representative for Islam at the World's Parliament of Religions.[36]

In Chicago, the audience booed as a thickly bearded white American wearing a turban attempted to discuss western misconceptions of polygamy on the platform of the World's Parliament of Religions. The audience finally settled down when Mohammed Alexander Russell Webb proceeded to another subject. However, he closed his presentation by saying:

> There is no system that has been so willfully and persistently misrepresented as Islam, both by writers of so-called history and by the newspapers and press. I feel that Americans . . . are disposed to go to the bottom facts . . . and when they have done so I feel that we shall have a universal system which will elevate our social system to the position where it belongs.[37]

Webb was fighting an uphill battle at the Parliament, for most Americans in attendance there had already judged Islam as a non-white, non-European phenomenon that was the flip side of Christianity—"mysterious, unchanging and ultimately inferior." The following comments of an American humorist who had observed Muslims praying at the meetings were typical of the overall insensitivity toward Islam there:

A lot a fellers was blacker than a pair o' shoes on Sunday morning. . . . You can't tell whether they're at prayer or a dog fight, but I suppose it's all the same in Arabia.[38]

Mohammed Alexander Russell Webb had been the United States consul to the Philippines from 1887 to 1892, and there he became the first known American convert to Islam. In 1892, Webb visited Bombay, India, where a group of wealthy Muslims designated him the main spokesman for a new organization for the propagation of Islam in America. It is rumored that the Ahmadis were the first Muslim group that shaped Webb's ideas about Islam in India. Moreover, with their financial backing and one third of the fortune of Abdulla Arab, a wealthy Arab merchant, he established the American Moslem Brotherhood on 30 East 23rd Street in New York City. In 1893, he founded the Moslem World Publishing Company, which published his short book, *Islam in America,* and about twenty-six volumes of *The Moslem World* and the *Voice of Islam.* Eventually Webb became the representative of the Turkish sultan Abdul-Hamid II and the Honorary Consul General for Turkey in New York City. Webb was also a theosophist, and he attempted to synthesize Islam and Indian philosophy. The important point here is that after his time, American Islam continued to be supported and shaped behind the scenes by Indian Muslims who were trailblazers in the movement to modernize their religion. Webb's primary contribution was the first step in the establishment in the United States of a missionary outpost for modern Islam. The religion did not develop into a real religious movement under his leadership. In his own words

The American Islamic propaganda is to be purely educational, although Mohammedan missionaries will come here and preach in various parts of the country when their services are required. But for the present the efforts of all engaged in the work will be to teach the intelligent masses who and what Mohammed was and what he really taught, and to overturn the fabric of falsehood and error that prejudiced and ignorant writers have been constructing and supporting for centuries against Islam.[39]

Webb was intent on refuting one of the primary errors about Islam—that it was "the religion of the sword." He attempted to demonstrate that in Muhammad's time, all of the militant jihads were actually humane and "defensive" wars and that Christianity had the most "horribly sanguinary record known to history." Having made this charge, Webb demonstrated that there were several dimensions to the meaning of jihad and that throughout most of Islamic history, Islam had been spread by means of a just struggle to uphold "piety, benevolence . . . and social virtues." To promote an understanding of Islam in America, Webb espoused a "jihad of words" by interpreting Surah 96 in the Quran:

MOHAMMED ALEXANDER RUSSELL WEBB, *the first known European American convert to Islam.* Frontispiece from *Islam in America.* Used by permission of the Watkinson Library, Trinity College.

Read! for thy Lord is the most beneficent,
Who hath taught the use of the pen;
Hath taught Man that which he knew not.

The "jihad of words" was to become the interpretation of jihad that African-American Muslims would utilize in the twentieth century.[40]

Webb's signification of his Islamic identity was also a model for some African-American Muslims in the early twentieth century. First, upon his conversion to Islam, he changed his name from Alexander Russell Webb to Mohammed Alexander Russell Webb. Second, he always wore Indian clothing, including a full white turban. Webb believed that western clothing signified western decadence and could ultimately lead to the moral corruption of Muslims. Thus, for him and for African-American Muslims in the twentieth century, Muslim clothing was an important aspect of resistance to western ideologies. The available sources are silent concerning the specifics of his work in New York City, but it is safe to assume that Webb's following was small. Webb also missionized briefly on the West Coast. He died in 1916.[41]

We do not know whether Webb had direct contacts with African Americans at the Congress, but we do know that a significant African-American presence there was important because of its anti-Christian rhetoric. It included African-American Methodist Episcopal and Colored Catholic Congresses and black leaders such as Frederick Douglass, Henry McNeal Turner, Daniel Payne, Benjamin William Arnett, Theophilus Gould Steward, and Ida B. Wells. The rhetoric at their meetings was fiery, for these black people used the Parliament as a forum to vent black America's intellectual and emotional ferment on the eve of *Plessy vs. Ferguson*. Just one generation after slavery, African Americans faced legal disfranchisement and segregation at the hands of the Supreme Court (*Plessy vs. Ferguson* formalized the Jim Crow era in 1896) and the possibility of genocide and random white mob violence by organized hate groups like the Klu Klux Klan. From 1889 to 1899, 1,240 black people were lynched in America. The dream of Reconstruction had been destroyed, and the United States was "standing at Armageddon" on the edge of a racial cataclysm. The basic message of the black clergymen at the Parliament was that Christianity, as a white clan religion "soaked in the pus of American racism," was unacceptable to black Americans. This idea was very important for the future shape of Islam in America: although these national leaders did not tell black people to abandon Christianity for Islam, their fiery Pan-Africanist rhetoric opened the door for that possibility when it became part of black popular culture in the early twentieth century.[42]

At the meetings, Benjamin William Arnett, a bishop of the African Methodist Episcopal Church, attacked the "false Christianity" of white America which, he said, had sanctioned the stealing of Africans from their native lands, the brutality of slavery, and the searching of the Bible to perpetuate slavery. Finally, the words of Frederick Douglass, ex-slave, writer, and celebrated black leader, sent a chill through the audience, as he said that he could not in good conscience tell foreigners at the Exposition

> that the American church and clergy . . . stand for the sentiment of universal brotherhood and that its Christianity is without partiality . . . that the souls of Negroes are held to be as precious in the sight of God as are the souls of whites.[43]

Clearly, the World's Parliament of Religions underlined the potential of global Islam for the African-American struggle for freedom. It revealed the political and cultural links between the anti-imperialist modernist reformers of the Muslim world and African-American nationalists who opposed the racism of white Christian civilization. With the World's Parliament of Religions, then, the religions of the East had come West, and a new era in American religion had begun. The message of the Muslim religion would be brought anew to black America by mysterious missionaries from the East and by self-styled black prophets in the northen cities. Moreover, the new American Islam was deeply influenced by racism in America, by the Pan-African political movements of African Americans in the early twentieth century, and by the historic patterns of racial separation in Islam. Indeed, to tell the full story of the flowering of Islam during this period, we must examine the racial-political landscape of black America in the early years of the twentieth century. This story begins with Noble Drew Ali's Moorish Science Temple of America and Marcus Garvey's Universal Negro Improvement Association.

PROPHETS OF THE CITY

Chapter 3

THE NAME MEANS EVERYTHING

NOBLE DREW ALI AND THE MOORISH SCIENCE TEMPLE OF AMERICA

I, the prophet was prepared by the Great God Allah
to warn my people to repent from their sinful ways.
. . . They are to claim their own free natural name and
religion.   —Noble Drew Ali

The official sources describe Noble Drew Ali as founder of the first black Islamic sect in America. In truth
he was less than this, for there were black Moslems
here before him; but he was more than this—he was
an American prophet. He could have stepped from
the pages of Melville or Ishmael Reed, "a thought of
Allah clothed in flesh," a fact, a poetic fact.
                            —Peter Lamborn Wilson

Booker T. Washington, an ex-slave and a conservative black leader at the
turn of the century, wrote that black people in the South generally agreed
upon two points when they were freed from slavery: "that they must
change their names and that they must leave the old plantations for at least
a few days or weeks in order that they might really feel sure they were
free." Thus in 1913, when Noble Drew Ali, the flamboyant prophet and
founder of the Moorish Science Temple of America, said "the name means
everything," his words surely echoed the sentiments of the ex-slaves.
Their children and grandchildren were part of the Great Migration of four
to five million blacks from the South to the northern and midwestern
industrial cities in the early twentieth century. Some of them were Drew
Ali's earliest followers.[1]

The Moorish Science Temple of America was the first mass religious movement in the history of Islam in America. It focused on the African-American community and embodied all the distinctive characteristics of this new religious tradition. It was urban, anti-Christian, and multicultural, and it developed a distinct missionary and Pan-Africanist political agenda. Its racial separation was due not only to black nationalism but also to the historic patterns of racial separatism in Islam; Arab and Eastern European Muslims in America probably considered the Moorish Science Temple an embarrassing, peculiar, non-Islamic movement (because it created its own Quran), and ignored it. As C. Eric Lincoln has noted, "the Muslims provided no more opportunity and even less incentive for black participation in the religion of Islam than the counterpart white church provided for a meaningful black involvement in Christianity."[2]

Noble Drew Ali was an intelligent and creative signifier, a self-styled prophet of the city who utilized eclectic religious, cultural, and political motifs to construct a new black American cultural and political identity that involved changes in name, nationality, religion, diet, and dress. His initial inspiration came from Islam as a global religious, political, and cultural phenomenon. Although he did not have Indian sponsors for his movement as Mohammad Alexander Russell Webb did, he was familiar with Indian philosophy and "central Quranic concepts such as justice, a purposeful creation of mankind, freedom of will, and humankind as the generator of personal action (both good and bad)." Thus the Indian subcontinent continued to be a source of information and inspiration for American Islam, as Drew Ali developed the tradition of the "jihad of words" by utilizing the written word to strive in the path of Allah. He also appropriated ideas and symbols about Islam from the black Freemason movement to which he belonged. His Pan-African political inspiration and rhetoric came from Marcus Garvey's Universal Negro Improvement Association, which began and declined in black America almost contemporaneously with the establishment and decline of the Moorish Science Temple. Marcus Garvey's movement and the Great Migration were two of the major social facts of black America during the interwar period, both of which had a profound impact on the political thought, worldview, and demographics of modern American Islam.[3]

Martin Marty's *The Noise of Conflict, 1919–1941,* focused on the word "America" as central to an understanding of the political and cultural identity of the Moorish Science Temple of America. Noble Drew Ali was an important voice in the "conflict between peoples and among people" about the shape of American religion in the interwar period. He described the "noise of conflict," which concerned public religious and political power and influence in the United States. At stake were "the shape and destiny of America, the role of various religions and peoples in the nation, and the part faiths should play in personal destinies." In this context, as Jewish, Catholic, European, and Asian immigrants came to America in unprecedented numbers, and as millions of black people moved into the cities, establishing scores of new religious and political movements, Anglo-Saxon Protestants who considered themselves "100 percent Americans" fought to maintain a racially homogeneous Christian America. Meanwhile, other Americans struggled to force their country to come to terms with its racial, cultural, political, and religious pluralism. Marty contends that because of its small numbers, Islam was "not in position to have public impact" in this conflict. But as we shall see, Noble Drew Ali, Mufti Muhammad Sadiq, W. D. Fard, Elijah Muhammad, and other Muslim leaders were all struggling to extend the political and cultural boundaries of white Protestant Christian America to include American Islam. Thus "conflict between whites and blacks" was a central issue in this "war" over religious and political hegemony in the cities of the United States.[4]

THE GREAT MIGRATION: URBANIZATION AS A PARADIGM FOR BLACK ISLAMIC IDENTITY

Urbanization, migration, and immigration were important factors that sensitized African Americans to Islam in the 1920s. What is especially significant for us is that the Great Migration of southern blacks to the northern and midwestern industrial cities from 1915 to 1930 resulted in new religious, political, economic, social, and psychological needs in the African-American community and thereby encouraged the growth of new urban religious and political movements. At the same time, the cultural history of the Great Migration is an important link to global Islam because urbanization is a context for understanding the theme of signification and identity in Islam in West Africa and black America. The causes of this mass movement of population were many and complex. The tense racial situation in the South was undeniably a contributing factor. The economic motives of northern industrialists and African-American southerners, however, were the primary factors behind the Great Migration.[5]

Foreign immigrants had supplied the main source of cheap labor for northern manufacturers before 1911. By the beginning of World War I, however, European immigration to the United States had declined so dramatically—from 1,200,000 in 1914 to only 110,000 in 1918—that northern industrialists began to look at southern blacks as a source of cheap labor. Many companies even sent labor agents to the southern states in order to persuade African Americans to migrate to the North. Most of the southern blacks, who had experienced the economic oppression of the tenant farm and crop-lien system along with the ravages of the boll weevil and natural disasters on their crops, were more than ready to accept free train tickets and new jobs in the North. Thus the Great Migration of millions of blacks to the northern cities was set in motion. The urbanization of these blacks is important because the rank and file memberships and social agenda of the first black Islamic movements originated in the cities.[6]

Kenneth Kusmer has emphasized that the African-American urban experience helps us to understand how "black urbanites responded [creatively] to their environment," as "poverty and discrimination . . . encouraged organization." In this context, American Islam can be viewed as a positive response to their new [urban] environment, for "the migrants 'remade it' both physically and cognitively to fit their needs." Kusmer provided an analytical framework for understanding the "three general forces" that have significantly influenced African-American urbanization. These include structural, "non-racial" forces in the urban setting (such as transportation, housing, and "economic structure"); external forces (for example, how white racial hostility and discrimination affected blacks); and internal forces (such as how African-American urbanites responded to their environment in terms of "the retention or creation of cultural values or institutions"). It should be emphasized that these structural forces were not independent phenomena but were acted out in concert with each other in the urban setting.[7] They are important for us because they set the stage for cultural exchanges that occurred between different groups of urban blacks; these cultural exchanges partially explain how Muslim identities were constructed in black American Islam.

The period between the Civil War and World War I marked the beginning of the noticeable residential segregation of African Americans in the northern cities. This phenomenon occurred because an era of growing racial hostility coincided with a period of dramatic transformation in American urban life. The number of residents in American cities increased from 6.2 million in 1860 to approximately 42 million fifty years later. From 1890 to 1930, the proportion of white Americans living in the cities rose from 39 percent to 58 percent. Among African Americans, the number went from 20 to 44 percent.[8]

Tightly organized urban centers emerged along with this increase in numbers. New forms of transportation—the elevated train and subway and the electric and steam-driven streetcar—allowed urban dwellers to segregate themselves according to ethnic, racial, or socioeconomic group. Thus, new transportation technology was a key structural factor in the ghettoization of blacks during World War I. Kenneth Kusmer has noted that the basic structures of nineteenth-century cities "inhibited ghettoization":

> Lack of adequate transportation systems, mixed patterns of land use, the rapid growth of cities, and the decentralization of work and residence led to the dispersal of both immigrant and black populations at the same time.[9]

Moreover, Howard Rabinowitz has demonstrated how transportation technology facilitated segregation at the turn of the century. In the 1870s and 1880s, transportation technology discouraged segregation because it was too costly to furnish separate cars and horses for blacks. However, at the turn of the century, the electric and steam streetcars had compartments large enough to segregate the races, as well as multiple cars, which also facilitated segregation.[10]

The forty years between 1890 and 1930 brought even more dramatic population shifts toward the major cities. New York City's black population increased by 51 percent, while Philadelphia's and Chicago's rose by 30 percent between 1900 and 1910. Between 1910 and 1920, the number of African Americans increased by 611 percent in New York, and 59 percent in Philadelphia. In the decade between 1920 and 1930, the black population in Detroit rose by 109 percent, in New York by 115 percent, in Chicago by 114 percent, and in Philadelphia by 64 percent. The black populations in Cincinnati, Gary, Pittsburgh, and Columbus, Ohio, also expanded dramatically at this time.[11]

External forces that indicated continuity with nineteenth-century patterns of urbanization in the North and the South reached a high point as white Americans responded with hostility and fear to this new wave of population. The Great Migration (not to mention the 14 million European immigrants who had come to the United States between 1860 and 1900) was too much for mainstream white city dwellers to bear. These African-American migrants and some of their Catholic immigrant counterparts were greeted with violent race riots in the northern and midwestern cities during and immediately after World War I. The two most vicious riots, in Chicago and East St. Louis, resulted in 85 deaths and over 1,000 people injured. These developments, combined with the resurgence of the Ku Klux Klan in 1915, culminated in the Red Summer of 1919, during which 26 race riots erupted in the northern cities.[12]

Moreover, the plight of the black migrants was part of general racism in America during this period. Racism was especially evident in the treatment of blacks in the military service during World War I. Intelligence testing—a new psychological technique during this period—was used to "prove" black inferiority and to justify the widespread belief that blacks were incompetent as combat soldiers. Consequently, only 40,000 of the 350,000 blacks who were drafted were used as fighting men. Also, black military men were segregated from their white counterparts during training and active duty. On the other hand, the respectful treatment African Americans received in Europe exacerbated racism in America. Black soldiers who were stationed in France enjoyed complete freedom for the first time in their lives. They were understandably bitter when they returned to their subordinate position in the United States at the end of the war. As we shall see, this situation encouraged urban blacks to redefine their racial identities in America, thus it is important for understanding the centrality of signification in black American Islam during this period.[13]

Nativism, with its extreme opposition to domestic minority groups on the basis of their foreign ties, also raged during this period. Although nativism was mainly directed against Catholic and Jewish immigrants, it was related to racist creeds that were influenced by social Darwinism, eugenics, and the Nordic superiority myth. Charles Carroll's *The Negro, a Beast*, Thomas Dixon, Jr.'s *The Clansmen*, Madison Grant's *The Passing of the Great Race*, and Lothrop Stoddard's *The Rising Tide of Color*, laid the intellectual foundation for what John Higham calls the "Tribal Twenties," when many white Americans believed the basic premises of the myth of Nordic superiority. According to Stoddard,

> The white man's salvation rested with the Nordics and the immigration of inferior white races would mongrelize Americans into a walking chaos, so consumed by their jarring heredities that they would be quite worthless.[14]

Various middle-class black leadership organizations attempted to cope with the plight of black urban dwellers in the 1920s. Most of these organizations appealed to the business and professional people of the black communities and had little to offer to the masses. The National Urban League, established in 1911 by a coalition of social workers, white philanthropists, and conservative blacks, sought to improve employment opportunities for African Americans in the cities. The Urban League used economic and moral appeals to persuade white employers to hire blacks. Unfortunately this approach was largely ineffective in changing the bleak situation for African-American workers in the 1920s. Negotiations with the racist AFL unions were unsuccessful, and African Americans continued to be excluded from membership in labor unions. Urban League officials sometimes sent black strike-breakers to plants during labor disputes. However, even those gains were usually temporary, and white workers got the jobs after the disputes were settled.[15]

The NAACP, founded in 1909, concerned itself primarily with fighting racism through the legal process. This multi-racial organization was very successful in defending the victims of race riots and in rallying public support against the large number of lynchings in the United States in the 1920s. Perhaps the NAACP's most significant contributions were its lengthy court battles to ensure the enforcement of the Fourteenth and Fifteenth Amendments. However, much of this litigation against disenfranchisement and segregation was not immediately successful, thus it had to be carried on over a period of several decades.[16]

From 1910 to 1934, the official publication of the NAACP, *The Crisis*, reached a peak circulation of 106,000, providing a militant voice of African-American protest for the black upper and middle classes and the black intelligentsia. *The Crisis* was edited by W. E. B. DuBois, who during World War I replaced Booker T. Washington as the foremost spokesperson for African Americans. Elliott M. Rudwick has characterized DuBois as a man whose thinking and propaganda could move in the direction of either integration or black nationalism. It is better to understand DuBois as an eclectic thinker who was not afraid to change his opinions as he learned new things about his own country and the world.[17]

DuBois represented a significant Pan-Africanist strain of black nationalism during this period. Black nationalist movements and ideas were a creative response to urbanization, paving the way for black American Islam by emphasizing the cultural values of self-determination, education, resistance, and internationalism, which were adumbrated in the new identities that black Muslims created in the cities. Internationalism was always at the center of the nationalist discourse because nationalism originated in the relationship of African Americans to Africa. Thus, nationalist movements became the ideological forum for discussions of African-American peoplehood, in the context of a global perspective. In 1905, DuBois, with William Monroe Trotter, founded the Niagara Movement in order to agitate publicly for black rights in the United States, providing one of the first mainstream alternatives to Booker T. Washington's strategy of avoiding overt political struggle. Fourteen years later, DuBois framed the black civil-rights struggle in an internationalist context when he convened the Pan-African Congress in Paris in the spring of 1919. This Congress—which was composed of fifty-seven delegates representing the United States, the West Indies, and various African countries—proposed several amendments to the League of Nations Charter. It asked for the elimination of servitude, guarantees for civil rights, African participation in colonial rule, and the establishment of Germany's African colonies as a League of Nations trust. The League gave the Pan-African Congress a victory by including this last request in its mandate system, which placed several African colonies under its supervision in order eventually to grant independence to some native African peoples. Other Pan-African Congresses were convened in 1921, 1922, 1929, and 1945. DuBois had a significant impact on the worldwide black civil-rights struggle in the 1920s, and he continued to be influential in black affairs until his death in 1963. However, during the decade under consideration, his esoteric internationalist perspective appealed primarily to well-educated middle-class blacks, who were a minority group in their race.[18]

V. P. Franklin has emphasized that while DuBois' "talented tenth" or black chosen elite was a significant factor in black advancement in America, in the final evaluation the masses determined

> the ebb and flow of Afro-American social and cultural history in their power to reject or ignore leaders whose programs and statements do not appear to be in the best interest of the "race" and . . . through their support of leaders who combine an awareness of Afro-American culture and traditions with a viable program for advancement.

Although DuBois had demonstrated in *The Souls of Black Folk* that he understood the "feelings and emotions" of black folk culture, his elitist Pan-Africanism was based on a nineteenth-century British model of "universal history" which emphasized the influence of "great men" rather than the organized social and political movements of the masses. Clearly, these ideas were out of touch with the creative self-deterministic values of the masses of urban blacks who needed self-empowering nationalist alternatives in politics and religion.[19] Although these Pan-Africanist ideologies did not animate the masses, they paved the way for the Muslim prophets of the city who created new black Islamic identities that emphasized the "core values" of African-American culture.

During the World War I era, black nationalism came from all sides of black urban communities. At the center, the National Baptist Convention and the African Methodist Episcopal Church were influenced by nationalism as well. At the same time, African-American club women, inspired by the leadership of Mary Church Terrell, organized the National Association of Colored Women to advance the race by advocating "racial uplift . . . institutional separation . . . , improvement of the Negro family" and the elimination of negative sexual images. Working along the same lines were the National Association of Afro-American Women and Ida B. Wells, who established an international campaign against the lynching of black men in America. To the Left, African-American socialists and Marxists (led by A. Philip Randolph and Cyril Briggs, respectively) formed coalitions with nationalist organizations. Black bibliophiles such as Arthur Alphonso Schomburg and black journalists such as T. Thomas Fortune and William Monroe Trotter utilized the printed word to espouse aspects of nationalism. Meanwhile, new religious movements that defied mainstream classifications (e.g., Father Divine's Peace Mission and various Black Jewish groups) articulated new formulations of religious nationalism. Black fraternal groups like the Prince Hall Masons and black college fraternities and sororities like Alpha Phi Alpha and Delta Sigma Theta imparted nationalist ideas to their initiates. Finally, one of the most spectacular instances of nationalism in this era was represented by Chief Alfred C. Sam, a West African who organized a migration company in Oklahoma to repatriate African Americans to the Gold Coast.[20] In their separatist redefinitions of African-American politics and culture, all of these nationalist organizations and movements adumbrated the theme of signification and identity that was central to black American Islam.

This widespread emphasis on nationalism in black urban communities was stimulated in part by World War I, which had brought a heightened political consciousness to black people throughout the world. As the leaders of West European civilization wasted human lives and destroyed nations, blacks in Africa, the Caribbean, and North America began to question the legitimacy of colonial rulers who could not maintain peace with one another. Furthermore, over one million black people from Africa, the Caribbean, and the United States "fought for democracy" in Africa, the Near East, and Europe. When they came home, they were ready to demand democracy for themselves.[21]

These people were the "New Negroes," militant young race leaders who were ready to obtain their human rights by means of Pan-Africanism or socialism. Many of them, like Marcus Garvey and W. E. B. DuBois, had traveled extensively and therefore had an international perspective on the race problem. The development of large urban black communities in the United States during this period gave these leaders a ready-made public forum for their organizations.[22]

The fact that the popularity of the new American Islam in black urban communities coincided with the appearance of the "New Negro" was not accidental. For the spirit of the "New Negro" movement helped to ignite mass movements like the Moorish Science Temple of America and the Universal Negro Improvement Association among black people in their cities, with an emphasis on the redefinition of cultural and political identities. Black nationalism in the nineteenth century had been primarily an elitist affair in which educated black leaders, who revered European ideas, saw the liberation of the African race in the civilization of the masses according to the standards of white institutions. Although (as we shall see) civilizationist ideas did not disappear completely from black nationalist ideologies during the World War I era, there was a new ambivalence toward this mode of thought in black urban settings—and this ambivalence was a result of the "New Negro" movement.[23]

In *The New Negro,* the "definitive text" and manifesto of the cultural side of the movement, Alain Locke (1886–1954) articulated the new attitude of mass racial solidarity in the cities:

> The challenge of the new intellectuals among [the black masses] is clear enough—the "race radical" and realists who have broken with the old epoch of philanthropic guidance, sentimental appeal and protest. . . . The answer is in the migrating peasant. . . . The clergyman following his errant flock, the physician or lawyer trailing his clients, supply the true clues. In a real sense it is the rank and file who are leading, and the leaders who are following. A transformed and transforming psychology permeates the masses.[24]

The most spectacular cultural outcome of the "New Negro" movement was the Harlem Renaissance, in which Langston Hughes and other creative writers abandoned the old civilizationist and assimilationist modes for the urban masses and began to romanticize the creative spirit of lower-class blacks in the cities. At the same time, in *The New Negro,* Locke linked cultural creativity in the arts, social sciences, and political life to the self-determination and the signification of the masses:

> The Old Negro had long become more of a myth than a man. . . . His shadow, so to speak has been more real to him than his personality. Through having had to appeal from the unjust stereotypes of his oppressors and traducers to those of his liberators, friends and benefactors he has had to subscribe to the traditional position from which his case has been viewed. Little true social or self understanding has or could come from such a situation.

... The Negro of to-day [must] be seen through other than through the dusty spectacles of past controversy. The day of "aunties," "uncles" and "mammies" is equally gone. . . . Uncle Tom and Sambo have passed on. . . . The popular melodrama has about played itself out, and it is time to scrap the fictions. . . . In the very process of being transplanted, the Negro is being transformed.[25]

To sum up, the "New Negro" movement helped the case of the new American Islam among blacks by defining the nationalistic spirit of the new black urban communities in terms of cultural creativity, mass self-determination, identity, and internationalism. At the same time, no mass movement in the World War I era expressed these ideals more creatively and effectively than Marcus Garvey's Universal Negro Improvement Association. Moreover, as we shall see, Garveyism was significantly influenced by and at times was linked politically and ideologically to the new American Islam's quest for identity.

MARCUS GARVEY AND ISLAM: SIGNIFICATION AND IDENTITY

More than any other leader, Marcus Garvey captured the imagination of millions of working-class black people around the world between 1914 and 1940. Garvey's concepts of Pan-Africanism, race pride, and self-help, as they were embodied in the Universal Negro Improvement Association (UNIA), led to the establishment of both the first extensive mass movement among black Americans and the largest international racial movement in the history of black culture.[26]

By 1920, the UNIA had almost 100,000 members in its eight hundred chapters in forty nations on several continents. Between 1920 and 1924, the Garvey movement attempted to achieve its economic and political goals. By 1925, however, black and white opposition in the United States had effectively stopped the UNIA's economic and political program, and in 1927, Marcus Garvey was deported from the United States after having served two years in the Atlanta Federal Penitentiary for mail fraud. Even after his deportation, however, the UNIA continued to be the largest mass movement for African Americans. Until the early 1930s, Garvey "dominated public consciousness" and challenged the political, cultural, racial, economic, and religious status quo of Anglo-Saxon Protestant America by offering alternatives for blacks.

The extraordinary power of Garvey's movement originated from his unification of the two aspects of black nationalism—the political concept of the nation, state, and the cultural concept of Pan-Africanism—into one international movement for black self-determination which emphasized the theme of signification and identity.[27] Although his alternative programs were not always successful, Garvey's rhetoric and public image inspired and attracted Muslim leaders who had the same goals. Noble

Drew Ali, Mufti Muhammad Sadiq, and Elijah Muhammad were all politically connected to Garveyism in different ways and mentioned Garvey frequently in their speeches and writings. At the same time, Garvey appropriated ideas from black Muslim leaders in Europe and the United States. These connections were part of a global Pan-Islamic movement that brought together Pan-Africanists from Asia, Africa, the United States, Europe, and the West Indies as they creatively reformulated black cultural and political identities around the issue of self-determination. Thus, significant cross-fertilization between the UNIA and black American Islam occurred during the World War I era, as the former became an important source for Islamic ideas in America.

In 1914 the Universal Negro Improvement Association and African Communities League put forth in its first manifesto a call to "all people of Negro or African parentage" to take part in a movement to

> establish a Universal Confraternity among the race; to promote the spirit of race pride and love; to reclaim the fallen of the race; to administer to and assist the needy; to assist in civilizing the backward tribes of Africa; to strengthen the imperialism of independent African states; to establish Commissionaries or Agencies in the principal countries of the world for the protection of all Negroes irrespective of nationality; to promote a conscientious Christian worship among the native tribes of Africa; to establish Universities, Colleges, and Secondary Schools for the further education and culture of the boys and girls of the race; to conduct a world-wide commercial and industrial intercourse.[28]

These ideas, partly inspired by the nineteenth-century Pan-Africanist thought of Edward Wilmot Blyden, were tailor-made for the political discourse of American Islam because of their emphasis on global connections and black identity. Moreover, wherever the UNIA had its branches, it always advocated the internationalist perspective, which led black people in diaspora to think of themselves in concert with Africans and the "darker races of the world"—instead of Europeans and white Americans. Of course, this message appealed to and attracted various American Muslims who were trying to reformulate their identities. The redemption of Africa was the focal point of the internationalist perspective and the universal goal of the Universal Negro Improvement Association. Indeed Africa functioned as an ontological symbol that connected the political, cultural, and spiritual aspirations of the black people whose consciousness had been shaped by the UNIA's internationalist perspective. Because Garvey understood the transcendent significance of Africa as the original homeland and universal symbol of the black race, he made Pan-Africanism and the establishment of a transnational black republic in Liberia the most important objectives of the UNIA. In his own words, "We may make progress in America, the West Indies and other foreign countries, but there will never be any real lasting progress until the Negro makes of Africa a strong and powerful Republic to lend protection to the success we make in foreign lands."[29]

Although Marcus Garvey was a Roman Catholic convert and his followers were predominantly Christians, this did not pose a problem for Muslims, who were attracted to the UNIA because of its multi-dimensional religious orientation. Indeed, Randall Burkett has argued convincingly that Garvey intended to establish a black civil religion with an ethos and a worldview drawn from the tradition of the black church yet charged with the self-consciousness of black nationalism. Although Burkett's interpretation is provocative, it does not suggest how the ethos and worldview of the UNIA were influenced by Islam's emphasis on signification and identity.[30]

Perhaps our analysis of the political and religious meaning of Garvey's movement should begin with his own thoughts on the subject. In Garvey's speeches in the West Indies and Central America in 1921, he advised his followers to search for "a new religion and new politics and to oppose the old-time order of things." In another speech in Washington D.C., he described "the larger purpose" of his movement:

> It is not a religious movement, purely. It is not a social movement, purely. It is not an industrial movement, purely. It is not a political movement, purely, but is a movement that includes all the wants and needs of the Negro. We are as much political as we are religious, we are as much religious as we are social, we are as much social as we are industrial.[31]

Clearly Garvey's ideas emphasized religion in his multi-dimensional Pan-Africanist movement; however they did not explicitly point to the white American concept of "civil religion," which was developed by Robert Bellah and focuses on the centrality of religious symbols and ideals in American political life.

E. Franklin Frazier gave one of the earliest and the best analyses of Garvey's unique appeal to the black masses and clarifies the religious meaning of his movement. His basic thesis is that Garveyism was a "crowd movement" distinct from other social phenomena among African Americans. According to Frazier, African Americans have historically looked to the church and fraternal orders for a definition of black consciousness. These organizations were unable to support the type of self-magnification that the white masses received as members of political organizations. In his sociological analysis of the ideals and symbols of the UNIA, Frazier remarked on Garvey's technique of oratory that created and controlled crowds. Indeed it was this technique which distinguished Garvey from black leaders who failed to attract the masses in the 1920s. Garvey was a dramatic speaker who idealized the black race and its homeland in Africa. He understood the tremendous religiosity of the black masses and therefore connected the redemption of Africa with the mystical rebirth of the human race. Garvey invented social distinctions and honors such as the African Legion, the Black Cross Nurses, and the Noble Order of the Knights of the Nile to honor African Americans. Finally, he provided the black masses with groups of people that could serve as objects of their hatred.[32]

The Episcopal priest George Alexander McGuire attempted to make his self-styled African Orthodox Church the official religion of the movement, and more than 250 black Protestant clergymen participated in the UNIA's activities in the 1920s, yet Garvey never abandoned his commitment to a nondenominational multi-dimensional movement. In 1924, the delegates at the Fourth International Convention of the Negroes of the World stated that "as there are Moslems and other non-Christians who are Garveyites, it was not wise to declare Christianity the state religion of the organization." Thus, it appears that the UNIA was favorably disposed toward Islam with its broader approach to signification and identity.[33]

Marcus Garvey was introduced to Islam in England as a young man. The Jamaican-born Garvey moved to London in 1912 to begin a program of study at Birkbeck College. However, he learned more in London's African intellectual circles than he did in the classroom. His mentor in Pan-Africanism was a Sudanese-Egyptian named Duse Mohammed Ali, a prominent member of London's Muslim community and one of the most significant figures in the international Pan-African movement during that time. In 1911, he began to receive public attention for his highly acclaimed book, *In the Land of the Pharaohs,* which analyzed the history of nineteenth-century Egypt in order to build a case for Egyptian home rule based on Islamic social and political traditions.[34]

However, it was his journal, *The African Times and Orient Review,* which was most influential for the Pan-African movement of those years. The journal had a wide circulation in the United States, the West Indies, Europe, East and West Africa, Egypt, Turkey, Japan, India, and Ceylon, and it was published almost continuously from 1912 to 1920. It contained high-quality book reviews, African and Asian advertisements, and many articles on Islam in the British Empire, particularly in India. At one point, the journal even had a section in Arabic. The rationale and the purpose of Duse Mohammed Ali's *African Times and Orient Review* was to make a case for the unification of Pan-Africanist and Pan-Islamic discourses in America, Europe, Africa, and Asia, and central to the journal's vision was the theme of signification and identity.

Early twentieth-century Pan-Africanism had African-American, West Indian, West African, Moroccan, Egyptian, Arab, Ethiopian, Turkish, and Indian components and advocates. Duse Mohammed Ali realized that after anti-imperialism, the cause that most united these diverse factions was that of global Islam as a form of resistance to Western domination. The inspiration for this vision of the journal began with the seminal meeting of Asian, African, and African-American nationalists with white people at the First Universal Races Congress at the University of London in 1911.

This Congress, which did for racial discourse what the World's Parliament of Religions did for religious discourse, "was the first such international gathering" to bring together races of the East and the West to discuss the issue of race in the context of international affairs.[35]

The important point here is that the Universal Races Congress and the *African Times and Orient Review* were instrumental in constructing a discourse that expanded the internationalism of Pan-Africanism to include the cases of the Egyptians, the Moroccans, and other African and Asiatic Muslim peoples. At the same time, this expanded global Pan-Africanist discourse influenced African-American Muslims, such as Noble Drew Ali, as they constructed their ideologies and imaginatively expanded the geographic referents of their political and religious identities in the World War I era. Moreover, Duse Mohammed Ali's journal was linked ideologically to Islamic modernism in his attempt to respond to the challenge of European colonialism by reformulating global Islamic identities and political coalitions to include Pan-Africanism. Central to this enterprise was Duse's "jihad of words" or his "use of the pen" in the defense and representation of the religion and its peoples. Typical of this trend, in the foreword of the first issue of the *African Times and Orient Review,* he wrote:

> The recent Universal Races Congress convened in the metropolis of the Anglo-Saxon world clearly demonstrated that there was ample need for an Oriental Pan-African journal at the seat of the British Empire which would lay the aims, desires and ambitions of the black, brown, and yellow races—within and without the Empire—at the throne of Caesar. For whereas, there is extensive Anglo-Saxon press devoted to the interests of the Anglo-Saxon, it is obvious that this vehicle of thought and information may only be used in a limited and restricted sense in its [communication] of African and Oriental aims. Hence the truth about African and Oriental conditions is rarely stated with precision and accuracy in the columns of European press. As a result of garbled and inaccurate statements . . . the voices of millions of Britain's enlightened dark races are never heard; their capacity underrated: discontent is fermented by reason of systematic injustice and misrepresentation.[36]

Indeed, the young Garvey learned much about African history and politics and Islam from Duse Mohammed Ali, and he contributed an article to *The African Times and Orient Review.* Moreover, he met future UNIA officials and race leaders through his association with the Egyptian Pan-Africanist. Some of them were William Ferris, a university professor and eventually a UNIA official; George O. Marke, an African graduate of Oxford and later a high-ranking Garveyite; James Yearwood, a leader of the workers of Panama and a future UNIA official; Casely Hayford, author of *Ethiopia Unbound*; and Hubert H. Harrison, Arthur Schomburg, John Bruce, and Richard B. Moore—the founders of the Schomburg Collection of African-American materials at the New York Public Library. During Garvey's stay in London, Duse Mohammed Ali's home was a center for

Asian, African, and African-American students and celebrities in England, and many of these were Muslims. At the same time, most likely, Garvey was introduced to the Ahmadiyya Movement in Islam, for Duse Mohammed Ali was associated with the Ahmadis' Woking Mosque, which was located outside the city.[37]

It is noteworthy that Duse Mohammed Ali was also involved with the political and religious activities of Muslim communities in West Africa. In the mode of Edward W. Blyden, in 1913 he had advocated the establishment of a University of Africa which would be accredited by the major universities in Great Britain. Robert A. Hill has emphasized the importance of Garvey's contact with "certain prominent West African figures" in London. For our purposes, Garvey's most important West African contact was J. E. Casely Hayford, whose work emphasized the theme of signification and identity.[38]

Hayford, born in the Gold Coast (Ghana) and educated in Sierra Leone by Edward Wilmot Blyden, was the most significant West African nationalist in the early twentieth century. His most important book, *Ethiopia Unbound*, was probably Garvey's source for Blyden's Islamic Pan-Africanist ideas, which he utilized in the Universal Negro Improvement Association. Garvey's thinking was so profoundly influenced by Blyden's emphasis on signification and identity that he quoted the latter's *Christianity, Islam, and the Negro Race* extensively in one of his earliest pamphlets and appropriated some of his civilizationist issues on racial uplift, improvement, and purity.[39]

It is appropriate to discuss briefly the scope of Hayford's book not only because of its influence on Garvey, but also because, independently, it may have been a source of Blyden's ideas for the budding African-American Muslim movement in the World War I era. *Ethiopia Unbound* is a fictional work which utilizes the rhetoric of its characters to articulate a Pan-Africanist discourse on black "race emancipation." Hill has noted that, before 1914, Pan-Africanism was described under the rubric of "Ethiopianism." This idea identified the redemption of the African race with the symbol of Ethiopia, the only African country that remained independent in the colonial era. As previously noted, Ethiopianism was also inspired by the Biblical passage in Psalms 68:31. Thus the idea of Ethiopianism became infused with religious "romanticism and myth."[40]

In Hayford's thinking, there was an ideological link between Ethiopianism and the title and substance of his book. He believed that with the global self-determination of people of African descent, Ethiopia (the African race) would become unbound or emancipated. In *Ethiopia Unbound*, Kwamankra (a fictive character) discussed in a series of lectures how this emancipation would occur. Elevating Edward Wilmot Blyden to prophetic status was central to race emancipation:

> The work of men like Booker T. Washington and W. E. Burghart DuBois is exclusive and provincial. The work of Edward Wilmot Blyden is universal,

covering the entire race and the entire race problem. . . . Edward Wilmot
Blyden is a leader among leaders of aboriginal thought and lest a prophet
should be without honour among his own kindred, I am happy in this occasion
also to have among others, the privilege and the opportunity of giving him the
recognition that is his due.[41]

Linked to Blyden's prophetic status is his paradigm for cultural nationalism, which focused on African nationality, racial separatism, and African
personality, with an emphasis on indigenous dress, language, names,
education, and religion. *Ethiopia Unbound* presented Europe as a cultural
and political "wilderness" for Africans and African Americans, thus bringing the issues of signification and identity to the forefront of African liberation in America:

How extraordinary is the spectacle of this huge race—millions of men
without land or language of their own, without traditions of the country they
came from, bearing the very names of the men that enslave them.[42]

Finally, *Ethiopia Unbound* discussed white Christianity as a racist and
inferior religion, especially in contrast to African religions. In this light,
Hayford offered a stunning critique of the Christian colonialist's role in the
destruction of African self-determination:

With the gin bottle in the one hand, and the Bible in the other, he urges
moral excellence, which in his heart of hearts, he knows to be impossible of
attainment by the African under the circumstance, and when the latter fails,
his benevolent protector makes such a failure a cause for dismembering his
tribe, alienating his lands, appropriating his goods, and sapping the foundations of his authority and institutions.[43]

Finally, just as the words of *Ethiopia Unbound* probably led Garvey to
study the Islamic Pan-African ideas of Edward Wilmot Blyden, they also
inspired him to contemplate his future as a race leader with divine
sanction:

The voice of the ancient universal God goes forth once more, who will go
for us, who will show us any good. May there be a full, free, and hearty
response from the sons of Ethiopia in the four quarters of the globe.[44]

When Garvey returned to Jamaica in 1914, his political thinking was
sharpened and international in scope, for his ideas had been deeply
influenced by London—a hotbed of Pan-Africanism—and by Islam, the
unifying religion of many African and Asian intellectuals and political
leaders in the early 1900s. Indeed, in the 1930s, old Garveyites in New York
City still noted that "Garvey was taught by a Muslim." Moreover, Duse

Mohammed Ali came to America in the early 1920s and worked for the UNIA's *Negro World* for a short time. Undoubtedly, he continued to disseminate his Pan-African Islamic message of signification and identity to African-American audiences in 1921 and 1922, as he lectured in Washington, D.C., Boston, and New York City. Finally, Duse (who, like Noble Drew Ali, was "fascinated by the mysteries and secret lore of ancient Egypt") established the Universal Islamic Society and America-Asia Society in Detroit in 1926 and 1927.[45]

Together, Garvey and the African intellectuals whom he met in London carried global Islam's message of signification and identity from Europe to America in the World War I era. When this message was combined with the work of the black American Muslim movements already in existence and the Pan-Africanist ideas that filled the air in the cities, the time was ripe for the dramatic introduction of a new interpretation of Islam on the American scene, in the context of the UNIA.

* * * * *

A high point of the Garvey movement—and one that undoubtedly impressed Islamic leaders in America with its global potential—was the second International Convention of the Negro Peoples of the World, which began on August 2, 1920. The pomp, pageantry, and flamboyance of the UNIA was evident as thousands of people lined the streets of Harlem to greet Garvey, who was chauffeured in an open car to the opening session at Madison Square Garden. When he arrived downtown, 25,000 people from four continents and twenty-five nations were assembled at the Garden to hear his opening address. The theme of signification and identity was underlined, as this delegation was religiously and politically diverse, with Protestants, Catholics, Jews, Hindus, Muslims, socialists, Marxists and blacks in electoral politics. The most outstanding achievement of this convention was the "Declaration of Rights for the Negro Peoples of the World." This document presented fifty-four demands for "social and political separatism and the recognition of the UNIA as sovereign representative of the race." Garvey demanded civil rights for blacks living in white-ruled societies. He also called for "Africa for Africans at home and abroad," which connected Pan-Africanism to the wars for national independence in Africa, and was to become the UNIA slogan. At the end of the convention, Garvey was declared the "President General" and "Provisional President" of Africa. Although these titles lacked any concrete connection to an African nation, they nonetheless provided a public symbol of black political power in America and thus inspired Pan-African pride and consciousness among the black masses.[46]

As Garvey began to negotiate with Liberia for territory for his Pan-African state and launched his ill-fated Black Star Shipping Line, his dominant position in African-American public discourse on race and international politics was apparent both to friend and foe. Therefore it was no surprise when a group of Muslim delegates at the 1922 UNIA meeting attempted to tap into this power by proposing that the organization take Islam as its official religion because, in their view, it was the only indigenous religion of the black race. Garvey's commitment to a nondenominational religious status for his organization caused him to reject this plan. He did not disapprove of Islam, however, and began to incorporate it into the religious and political rhetoric of the UNIA. And as the symbols of American Islam infused the rhetoric of the UNIA, so the symbols of the UNIA were infused by the rhetoric of American Islam.[47] The themes of signification and identity were central in all of these cultural exchanges.

The appropriation of Islamic referents by Garveyism was articulated in the rhetoric of the UNIA. First, the religion became part of the language of the UNIA as some black publications during this period couched the need for black leadership in Islamic terms. A March 1917 editorial in *Champion Magazine* affirmed: "The Negro is crying for a Mohammed to come forth and give him the Koran of economic and intellectual welfare. Where is he?" Meanwhile, the journalists for the *Negro World* compared Garvey to the Prophet Muhammad:

> The prophet of Allah, concentrating his inexhaustible incandescent energy on the spiritual-material liberation of his people and the Herald of the New Dawn, Garvey stressing with equal zeal the material-spiritual redemption of his race.

Another writer called Garvey "a child of Allah." And Garvey himself evidently agreed, comparing himself to the Prophet Muhammad in one of his speeches. "Mohammed suffered many defeats at certain times," he said, "but Mohammed stuck to his faith and ultimately triumphed and Mohammedanism was given to the world. And as Mohammed did in the religious world, so in the political arena we have had men who have paid the price for leading the people toward the great light of liberty."[48]

Arnold Josiah Ford, the musical director of the UNIA, utilized the symbols of Islam in several of his musical compositions for the organization. "Allah-Hu-Akbar" was the title of one of his hymns. Other pieces made similar references: "May he our rights proclaim, In that most sacred Name Allah—one God, one Aim, one Destiny"; "Father of all creation, *Allah* Ominipotent, Supreme o'er every Nation, God Bless our President"; "From murd'rous Cain whose vengeful mood, A doctrine curs'd preferr'ed, to spill or drink his brother's blood, When Love is in *Allah's* word." As a leader of the Black Jewish movement in the 1920s, Ford was particularly sensitive to the issue of signification and alternative religious identities in the UNIA. At the same point, he had studied Hebrew with a Jewish immigrant teacher and acquired some knowledge of Talmudic Judaism. By 1924, Arnold Ford was the rabbi of the black Jewish congregation Beth B'nai Abraham in Harlem.[49]

The *Negro World's* coverage of Islam in international affairs led to its further incorporation into the rhetoric of Garveyism. Appointed to the staff of the *Negro World* in March 1921, Duse Muhammad Ali offered the readers of the paper a preview of the style of news coverage that would follow in the 1920s with an emphasis on global politics, signification, and identity:

> India, Asia, and Africa—the strongholds of the darker races are in the throes of a violent proletarian revolt. Nationalism in India despite Mr. Gandhi's arrest is proceeding. . . . On top of all this, the Moslems in Turkey are adding coals to the smoldering flames of Mohammedanism. Black workers in the gold fields of Johannesburg are defying the government and insisting on the rights of working men. All over the world the awakening of the darker races is the sore spot of international intrigue. . . . For the benefit of the readers and the whole black world in general the *Negro World* takes pleasure in announcing that beginning with this number his excellency, Duse Muhammad, Ali Effendi, the famous Egyptian journalist, will conduct on this page a department devoted to foreign affairs.[50]

In September 1921, thousands of Spanish soldiers were killed and captured by Moroccan Muslims in a rebellion that began when a Spanish general kicked and punched a Moroccan sheikh, Abdel Krim. This victory of a Third World people over a European power was such an inspiration to the Pan-Africanists and anti-imperialists of the UNIA that they began to speculate in the *Negro World* about the role of Islam in redeeming of Africa:

> With the stirring events in India and elsewhere, Mohammedanism, dormant for centuries, is suddenly seizing the center of the stage in world politics. . . . Britain faces serious trouble with its Mohammedans in Egypt . . . and the Spaniards have met disaster in a fresh uprising in Morocco. All these things are part of a great Pan-Islamic movement intended to restore Mohammedan power.[51]

The words of one reporter for the *Negro World* were typical:

> From the west coast [of Africa] also comes news that the natives are exhibiting signs of dissatisfaction with things as they are and are raising the slogan "Africa for blacks." The teachings of the Universal Negro Improvement Association are taking firm hold and the front page of *Negro World* containing Garvey's weekly message to the Negroes of the world is translated into Arabic and circulated throughout Nigeria and adjacent countries. The awakening of

the black man is widespread and the desire to learn more of what is being done by Negroes outside of Africa for the redemption of Africa has been thoroughly aroused.[52]

Eventually this rhetoric began to echo Edward W. Blyden's ideas about the appropriate religious identity for blacks, and one Garveyite after another debated in the pages of the *Negro World* the virtues of Christianity or Islam as the best religion for people of African descent. In September 1923, John Edward Bruce, a prominent Garveyite and columnist for the *Negro World*, delivered to the Boston division a speech entitled, "Islam and the Redemption of Africa." This address denounced the racism of white Christian missionaries in Africa and suggested Islam as a preferable religion for Africans because of its practice of brotherhood and lack of racism. Bruce went on to suggest that future missionary work in Africa should be the exclusive responsibility of those African Americans who "think black" and have not been corrupted by European culture.[53] The issue of the role of European culture in the construction of black political, ethnic, and religious identities in Garvey's time was also a central question for Noble Drew Ali. His Moorish Science Temple of America, which reached its height during the heyday of the UNIA, owed some of its success to Pan-Africanist rhetoric of Garveyism.

NOBLE DREW ALI AND THE MOORISH SCIENCE TEMPLE OF AMERICA: ASIATIC IDENTITY

In these modern days there came a forerunner, who was divinely prepared by the great God-Allah and his name is Marcus Garvey, who did teach and warn the nations of the earth to prepare to meet the coming Prophet, who was to bring the true and divine Creed of Islam, and his name is Noble Drew Ali.[54]

These words from Noble Drew Ali's *Holy Koran* indicate the importance of Marcus Garvey in the symbolism of Drew Ali's movement. Noble Drew Ali, the first self-styled prophet of modern American Islam, appropriated ideas and symbols not only from Garveyism but also from the global religion of Islam, Freemasonry, Theosophy, and nineteenth-century Pan-Africanism. And although he lacked a formal education, he was a clever signifier who constructed an Asiatic racial-separatist identity for his followers.

Noble Drew Ali, whose birth name was Timothy Drew, was born in North Carolina on January 8, 1886. Diverse legends have developed around his identity and activities before 1913. Some of his first followers claimed that "he was a child of ex-slaves raised among the Cherokee Indians." Another hypothesis claimed that he was a descendant of "Bilali Mohammet," the famous African Muslim slave who inhabited Sapelo Island in the nineteenth century. He spent his early childhood as an or-

NOBLE DREW ALI, *founder of the Moorish Science Temple of America.* From the collection of Sheila Harris-El. Used by permission.

phan, wandering with a gypsy group, until he was spotted at the age of sixteen by a gypsy woman who took him to Egypt, where he studied in the Essene Schools. When he was a young man about sixteen years old, he returned to America, where he became a merchant seaman based in Newark, New Jersey. Another legend claimed that Ali went back to Egypt in the early twentieth century and met the last priest of an ancient cult of high magic. He proved that he was a prophet by finding his way out of the pyramids. He was also thought to have traveled to Morocco and Saudi Arabia, where he obtained a charter from the sheikhs to teach Islam in America and received the name Ali from Sultan Abdul Ibn Said in Mecca. In 1910, he returned to the United States, where he worked as a train expressman and joined the Prince Hall Masons. The final legend concerning his early years was that Noble Drew Ali went to Washington, D.C., in 1912 to ask President Woodrow Wilson for the authority to teach his people Islam, the religion of their "ancient forefathers." He also asked that the nationality, "Moorish American," and the names "Ali, Bey, and El," and the flag of Morocco, which were taken away from his people in the colonial era, be given back. Perhaps closer to the truth than these legends is the Associated Negro Press's report that "he [Ali] was accompanying a Hindu fakir in circus shows when he decided to start a little order of his own."[55]

In 1913 Noble Drew Ali with the advice of Dr. Suliman founded an order—the first "Moorish community," in Newark, New Jersey—which he initially called the "Canaanite Temple." He called himself the second prophet of Islam. Over the next decade, his movement grew to an estimated membership of about 30,000, and he established temples in Detroit, Pittsburgh, Chicago, Milwaukee, Philadelphia, Lansing, Cleveland, Youngstown (Ohio), Charleston (West Virginia), Richmond, Petersburg (Virginia), Pine Bluff (Arkansas), and Baltimore. In 1914, Ali's leadership was unsuccessfully challenged in Newark by Abdul Wali Farad Muhammad Ali, a mysterious teacher of Islam from the East. Little is known about that man and the early years of his Newark mission. Two years later, factionalism in the Moorish community culminated as one faction stayed in Newark and named itself "Holy Moabite Temple of the World." In 1923 Drew Ali moved to Chicago, where he set up the permanent headquarters of his movement, naming it the Moorish Holy Temple of Science.[56] In 1928, he changed the name of his community to the Moorish Science Temple of America and finally organized all of his temples under the name of the Moorish Divine and National Movement of North America, Inc.

In their quest for an alternate signification and identity, the Moorish Americans wore black fezzes and white turbans. They carried nationality cards and used as their symbol a red flag with a five-pointed star in the center, recalling the flag of Morocco. They claimed that they were not Negroes, blacks, or colored people, but instead an olive-skinned Asiatic people who were the descendants of Moroccans. According to their teachings, the Moorish Science Temple of America had been founded so that the prophet Noble Drew Ali could lift the fallen "Asiatic nation of North America" by teaching its members their true religion (Islam), their true nationality, and their true genealogy. Noble Drew Ali taught his followers that they could trace their genealogy directly to Jesus, who was a descendant of "the ancient Canaanites, the Moabites, and the inhabitants of Africa." The sacred text of the Moorish Science Temple of America, the *Holy Koran,* also called *Circle Seven Koran,* was written by Ali in 1927. He wrote several versions of the sixty-four page book and compiled his information from four sources: the Quran, the Bible, *The Aquarian Gospels of Jesus Christ* (an occult version of the New Testament), and *Unto Thee I Grant* (literature of the Rosicrucian Brotherhood, a Masonic order which was influenced by lore concerning the Egyptian mystery schools).[57]

The primary theme of the *Holy Koran* was the "genealogy of Jesus," and it focused on his supposed life and work in India, Europe, and Africa. Although the book glorified Jesus as a forebear of the Moorish Americans, it still insisted that Christianity was a religion for Europeans and that Islam was the religion of the Asiatics, the final message of the text being that civilization was in the hands of the descendants of the Asiatic nations. Noble Drew Ali maintained that a series of peoples were the descendants of Canaan and Ham and therefore the original Asiatic nations. Among them he numbered the Egyptians, the Arabians, the Japanese, the Chinese, the Indians, the people of South America and Central America, the Turks, and the African Americans.[58]

Here, we can discern Noble Drew Ali's ideological connections to the global Pan-Africanist and Pan-Islamic movements in the early twentieth century. In the style of Duse Mohammed Ali, Noble Drew Ali formulated a version of Pan-Africanism that expanded the original geographic referents of the ideology to include and unite people of color in Africa, Asia, and America. Noble Drew Ali's Pan-Africanism was also a form of Pan-Islamic thought in its attempt to unite "the descendants of the Asiatic nations" under the banner of Islam. The emphasis on "civilization" in his *Koran* and other texts linked him to the civilizationist agenda of nineteenth-century Pan-Africanists such as Edward Wilmot Blyden. At the same time, the concept of jihad, though not spelled out explicitly in the Moorish Science Temple, was central to Noble Drew Ali's efforts to signify black people in his movement, as his basic message was a struggle for the truth in the context of his opposition to the cultural and racial imperialism of white Christianity.

Moreover, Noble Drew Ali's emphasis on the lore of the ancient Egyptians and his mixing of eastern and western religious ideas indicate the influences of the eclectic occult religious movement of Theosophy, which its adherents view as a "spiritual pilgrimage of discovery to the East." Clearly, some of Noble Drew Ali's ideas were "theosophical lore without historical foundation." The Theosophical Society was one of the first organizations to introduce Eastern religious thought to America, and Mohammed Alexander Russell Webb, the first known American convert to Islam, was a theosophist. Moreover, Levi H. Dowling's *The Aquarian Gospel of Jesus Christ*, which inspired Drew Ali's *Holy Koran*, or *Circle Seven Koran* was also "mystical—Theosophical—gnostic in tone." Sufism was possibly another eastern religious influence for Noble Drew Ali. In 1910, Hazrat Inazat Khan, an Indian musician and Sufi came to the United States teaching a form of Sufism that emphasized mysticism, "the unity of the world's major religions and the unifying power of love." These esoteric ideas were also evident in Drew Ali's movement, which emphasized "love, truth, peace, freedom, and justice" as a path to Islam and synthesized ideas from several religions and cultural traditions, creating a new religious identity for his followers. Perhaps Noble Drew Ali's *Circle Seven Koran* and his esoteric ideas were partly inspired by the teachings of the Ismailis or Seveners "who have predicted all cosmic and historical developments on the number seven . . . and argue that one must look beyond the manifestations of expressed words [of the Quran] and seek the inner meaning of the verses."[59]

These ideas—the basic teachings of the Moorish Science Temple of America—were the product of a shrewd leader of the black masses in the 1920s. Noble Drew Ali cared little about the authority of orthodox Islam. However, he understood that the name and some of the symbols of the religion and some Quranic principles could be appropriated to subvert the racism and the ethnocentrism of American Christianity and to construct a new genealogy and ethnic identity for black Americans. He emphasized the dietary laws of Islam in order to stop his people from eating pork—a meat that they were forced to eat in slavery and therefore a dietary symbol of their oppression. He appropriated some of the symbols of Freemasonry, such as the fez, turban, crescent and star, circle seven, all-seeing eye, clasped hands, Sphinx of Giza, and pyramids for his movement. As Ali knew, black Freemasonry was a cultural conduit for eastern religious ideas and rituals and for Pan-Africanist thought, and it was packaged in a form that appealed to the black masses.

These links between Islam and Freemasonry are rooted in global Islam. Idries Shah[60] has noted that Freemasonry originated in the context of Sufism, the mystical teaching of Islam, and that Muslim architects from Africa brought Freemasonry from the Iberian peninsula in the ninth century. Thereafter, Freemasonry spread to England and Scotland, where its original roots were obscured by its European Christian practitioners. In America, the Islamic Asiatic roots of Freemasonry were resurrected in 1877, when Scottish Rite Masons established the Shriners, also known as the Ancient Arabic Order of Nobles of the Mystic Shrine, in New York. According to Peter Lamburn Wilson, the Shriners' signification of Islamic identity was similar to Noble Drew Ali's ideas:

They concocted a legend claiming initiations from a Grand Shaykh of Mecca, honors from the Ottoman sultan Selim III . . . and links with the Bektashi Sufi Order. They bestowed the titles "Noble" on themselves, wore fezzes, displayed a crescent moon and star with Egyptian ornament (including the Great Pyramid) and founded lodges called "Mecca," "Medina," and "Al Koran"; etc. Later Shriners found this esoteric mishmash embarrassing, repudiated the legend, dissolved the organization into a charitable fraternity, and saved their fezzes for parades and costume balls.[61]

The African-American signification of Shriner symbols began at the Columbian Exposition in Chicago in 1893. At this event, which was also the site of the first World's Parliament of Religions, a group of blacks said that they had been initiated by "visiting Moslem dignitaries" and established the Ancient Egyptian Arabic Order of Nobles of the Shrine and the Daughters of Isis.[62]

Noble Drew Ali was probably a Freemason (there are photographs of him in "Egyptian Shriner" garb), and his association with this organization partly explains the "eclectic religious motif" of his movement. In April 1922, the *Negro World* reported that

> there was a notable gathering of prominent Masons in . . . Garvey's well known hostelry, 102 130th St. . . . to meet Dr. Abdul Hamid of Khartoum, Egypt, a 96 degree Mason and a Shriner at a dinner. . . . Among others in the party were Arthur Schomburg, Duse Muhammad Ali Effendi, a friend of the guest of honor; John Edward Bruce, contributing editor of the *Negro World* and editor of the *Mason Quarterly Review*.

This report provides evidence for connections between Muslims, Egyptian Freemasons, and American Pan-Africanist Freemasons. At the same time, Drew Ali's appropriation of Freemasonic symbols has roots in late-nineteenth-century American middle-class culture that often "subverted the forms and ideologies of capitalist social organizations." Because Masonry generated profits that approached a billion dollars a year, "the writing of rituals" became a major industry. Carnes tells us that "self-styled ritualists used the Bible, ancient mythology, and even contemporary fiction for materials" and that they were not concerned with historical accuracy.[63] Thus, the cultural exchanges that were involved in Noble Drew Ali's quest for an Asiatic identity were part and parcel of a similar trend in white American middle-class culture.

Drew Ali's inquiries into the origins of western civilization and his construction of genealogy and a new identity were not new processes in the history of political ideas. Judith N. Shklar has noted that politically disaffected individuals, from Hesiod in antiquity to Rousseau and Nietzsche in modern times, have used myths of creation and genealogy to express their utter contempt for society. All of these writers utilized the political device of subversive genealogy, the search for the origins of a particular people or an institution, to question and possibly threaten the foundation of the established order of society. Such genealogical myths, as Shklar says, have been "typical forms of questioning and condemning the established order, divine and human, ethical and political."[64]

Noble Drew Ali also utilized an oppositional cultural strategy. He transformed the black American's marginality by reconstructing the forgotten Islamic identity of the slaves. His building blocks were fragments taken from four sources of African-American popular culture—Biblical imagery, Pan-Africanism, Theosophy, and fraternal groups such as the Freemasons. Ultimately, Drew Ali attempted to invert the religious values of American culture by presenting Christianity as an inferior European religion which had been surpassed by Islam, the "true religion" of African Americans.

Noble Drew Ali chose to connect his movement to Morocco, connecting it to the first African Muslim slaves in America. Abdal-Rahman Ibrahima—the extraordinary "Moorish Prince" from Futa Jallon whose story was told in Chapter 1—had used a pretended connection to Morocco to gain his freedom. If this strategy for liberation worked in the nineteenth century, Drew Ali probably reasoned that it might also work for black people in the twentieth century.

How did Noble Drew Ali's construction of a Moorish American ethnic identity position his group in the racial discourses of the early twentieth century? "Moorish American" signified an ethnicization or deconstruction of race. This shift from the racial category (black) to the ethnic category (Moorish American) was not only a psychic escape from racism, but also a shrewd if unrealistic political move. Cedric Robinson has correctly stated that black is the "pre-eminent category of racial discourse" and that there is a "dialectic between race and ethnicity" in America. When black leaders concentrate on ethnicity and construct new ethnic names for their race, they throw water on the coals of racial discourse, thereby making themselves and their constituencies more acceptable to the white American mainstream. Thus, by distancing themselves from their culture, these leaders hope to receive preferential treatment from white mainstream America. Ultimately, however, this strategy may retard black political progress, since everyone is ethnic, and only black Americans depend on the category of race for their cultural and political identity and survival.[65]

Nonetheless, when Noble Drew Ali said, "The name means everything," he was convinced that he could change the political and economic fate of African Americans in the Jim Crow era by ethnicizing the name of the race and by changing the names of his followers, thereby erasing the stigma of slavery and distancing them from ordinary Negroes who were not respected as Americans. After all, thousands of South, East, and

Central European immigrants had been able to assimilate into American society in the early twentieth century by changing their surnames, dress, and customs. This kind of assimilation was encouraged by white Americans of northwestern European heritage in order to generate loyalty to the United States. The immigration officials at Ellis Island had even aided the process when, unable to spell the names of these immigrants, they gave them new names as they entered America.[66] Although the European immigrants adopted what they took to be genuine American names, dress, and customs and the Moorish Americans were headed in the opposite direction, the ultimate objective of both groups was the same: to erase the stigma of their minority-group status in order to be accepted as genuine Americans by the prevailing culture.

But Noble Drew Ali misread the politics of assimilation in the United States in the 1920s. Assimilation was not a possibility for blacks; their physiognomy and white society's discriminatory practices against them prevented that. Although new white immigrants also faced prejudice and discrimination, that prejudice was based more on cultural identity than on race. Eventually, their crusade for assimilation and equality was welcomed as America came to be known as the "great melting pot." Unfortunately, Noble Drew Ali did not understand that the melting pot was closed to black people in the 1920s.[67]

THEORY AND SIGNIFICATION

Yvonne Haddad and Jane Smith have analyzed Noble Drew Ali and his religious movement in the context of "the sectarian challenge in Islam." Their basic point is that since the beginning of Islam, there have been theological and political tensions between the "dominant body of worshipers, those who . . . have identified themselves as 'orthodox' and opposition groups that have tended to be viewed by the orthodox as sectarian deviations." At the same time, the central question posed by sectarianism for these authors is "by whose authority and by what standards are persons and groups deemed to be true members of the faith?" Although this is a useful approach which situates black American Muslim groups in the context of global Islam, it does not begin to answer the complex question of signification in these groups.[68]

Approaches to Islam that have recently been developed by scholars of African literature are more useful in the analysis of signification in black American Islam and thus inform this analysis of Noble Drew Ali. These approaches are suggested by the case of black Islam in West Africa and therefore provide another probable link between the Moorish Science Temple of America and global Islam. Kenneth W. Harrow, a leader in this group of literary theorists, has posed the central issue and process that elucidates signification in West African Islam, as the way in which [blacks] appropriated the new religion and made it their own. . . . What occurred was a series of adaptations in which Islam came to occupy increasingly important spaces in the lives of various people—*psychological spaces, governing first the territory of the mind,* at times motivated by economic or other self-interested concerns and then larger, external spaces of an increasingly political and social nature. This process could be termed Africa's appropriation of Islam and . . . could be compared with the similar process that Islam underwent everywhere; cutting across geographic and temporal boundaries.[69]

With this perspective in mind, we can understand more clearly how Noble Drew Ali was influenced by the paradigm of Islam that was probably transmitted to him in the context of Pan-Africanism in his time. As in West Africa, Drew Ali's version of Islam was mutually connected to the interests of merchants and traders in its emphasis on small independent businesses in the black community. Along the same lines, the Moorish Science Temple of America was primarily an urban phenomenon emphasizing missionary activity. Typical of black Islam in West Africa, Noble Drew Ali's version of a new American Islam utilized the indigenous religious traditions of African-American culture as its base for signification. Thus, this movement mixed Islam, Christianity, Freemasonry, and Pan-Africanism.

David Robinson's work sheds light on why this kind of cultural mixing in West Africa (and by extension in black America) has been viewed as un-Islamic by some scholars. He notes that "Orientalist approaches" have obscured knowledge of "different Islamic realities" among black people. According to him, "these different Islamic realities—and their validity—have not been appreciated in the historical literature." Moreover, this literature has opposed the authenticity of black Islam, by advocating that all "genuine" manifestations of the religion be linked to the Arabian peninsula and the Arabic language. Although this view of Islam acknowledges "historical change or mixing," it blames these elements for the impurity of the "indigenous form" of the religion in the black context.[70] To counteract this approach to the study of Islam among black people, Robinson asserts that the historical change and mixing that occurred in black Islam was "the natural and inevitable dynamic of an ongoing [global] religious/cultural process" rather than the result of a pure Islam "resisting the infiltration" of foreign elements.[71]

COMPETITION FOR IDENTITY:
THE DECLINE OF THE ORIGINAL LEADERSHIP BASE
OF THE MOORISH SCIENCE TEMPLE OF AMERICA

Unfortunately, there was a downside to the creative religious consciousness of the African-American community in Noble Drew Ali's time.

Energies and resources that might have been invested in the development of separate secular economic, political, educational, and technical institutions under the leadership of experts in these respective fields had instead been placed since slavery in the hands of black religious leaders. These men, no matter how well-intentioned, could not possibly have expertise in all of these diverse and complex areas. Encouraging blacks to invest their resources and energies only in religious institutions was an overt strategy of institutional racism. The result was that African-American economic, political, and educational advances did not keep pace with those of a religious nature. The proliferation of so many different black denominations, churches, and religious movements sometimes resulted in fanaticism among lay people and economic exploitation and self-aggrandizing competition as different leaders offered diverse alternatives for black signification and identity. All of these factors eventually contributed to the decline of the original leadership base of the Moorish Science Temple.

Converts to the religion were given a free "national name"—El or Bey, both of which signified African heritage—and a nationality card with a message from the prophet:

> This is your nationality and identification card for the Moorish Science Temple of America and birthright for the Moorish Americans. We honor all the divine prophets, Jesus, Mohammad, Buddha, and Confucius. "I am a citizen of the U.S.A."

While the movement was at its height of influence in the late 1920s, some of its members began to flash their nationality cards boldly at white people in the streets of Chicago, telling them that Noble Drew Ali had liberated black people from the curse of European influence. The Moorish Americans believed that these actions would somehow magically eliminate racial discrimination. Recalling the persecution of other Pan-African movements at that time, Noble Drew Ali issued a proclamation to his followers:

> I hereby warn all Moors that they must cease from all radical or agitating speeches while on their jobs, or in their homes, or on the streets. Stop flashing your cards before Europeans as this only causes confusion. We did not come to cause confusion, our work is to uplift the nation.

Although Drew Ali preached loyalty to the American government, many of his followers became convinced that the destruction of white Americans was close at hand. This situation sometimes led to racial disturbances in Chicago, where the Moors became a problem for the police department.[72]

During this period, Noble Drew Ali also began to realize that his lack of education was a disadvantage in business. Therefore, he offered leadership positions to several men who were eager to exploit his movement. These new and better-educated leaders became rich by selling Asiatic charms, pictures, relics, herbal preparations, and literature to the masses in the context of the Moorish Manufacturing Corporation. They did not have a sincere commitment to the original theme of signification and identity that Noble Drew Ali had emphasized. Eventually, some of these individuals decided to do away with Noble Drew Ali in order to gain control of the movement's small businesses and its fortune, which had increased to an estimated $36,000 in its best year.[73]

The end of the prophet's reign began on March 15, 1929, when one of his opponents for leadership, Sheik Claude Greene, was shot and stabbed to death at the Unity Club in Chicago. Noble Drew Ali was arrested and jailed for the murder and died several weeks later while he was released on bond. His death has been variously attributed to Greene's supporters and the Chicago police department. However, according to Ernest Allen, Jr., he died on July 20, 1929, of tuberculosis. He was laid to rest at Burr Oak Cemetery in Chicago.[74] The coroner's inquest into Greene's murder revealed a picture of the Moorish Science Temple that was more like a melodrama than a religious movement. An investigation of Drew Ali's life showed that he was simultaneously involved romantically with three young women in his movement, respectively aged fourteen, sixteen, and in her twenties. Apparently he had married the two youngest girls in Moorish American ceremonies, but there were no legal records of the marriages. Since the youngest was pregnant at fourteen, Ali was guilty of statutory rape under Illinois law. At the same time, an alleged connection to Greene's murder came to light with rumors of an affair between him and Pearl, Noble Drew Ali's third wife, who is still alive and resides in Chicago.[75] After Noble Drew Ali's death, his attorney, Aaron Payne, tried unsuccessfully to unify the Moorish movement. Meanwhile, several of the late prophet's disciples—John Givens-El (his chauffeur), Ira Johnson Bey (a leader from Pittsburgh, Pennsylvania), Edward Mealy El, R. German Ali, and Kirkman Bey—fought each other for leadership positions. Steven Gibbons and Ira Johnson claimed that the dead prophet's spirit had entered their bodies. Eventually, a gun battle occurred at the Moorish Science Temple branch headquarters in which one Moorish American and two policemen died. The police department arrested sixty-three Moorish Americans, and Ira Johnson was sent to federal penitentiary for life. Soon after Drew Ali's death, Kirkman Bey was voted in as the president of the Moorish Science Temple Corporation and Grand Sheik, and Drew Ali's chauffeur, John Givens-El, proclaimed himself a "Brother Prophet" or reincarnation of the founder. Steven Gibbons was committed to the State Hospital but gained his release several years later. By 1941, he had founded a new Moorish Temple in Chicago on East 40th Street. Gibbons, along with six other Moorish leaders, still insisted that he was the Grand Sheik of the Moorish Science Temple of America. R. German Ali was the leader of a branch of the movement that recognized only Noble Drew Ali as prophet.

THE NAME MEANS EVERYTHING / 101

And a succession of "Brother Prophets" (reincarnated prophets) also vied for leadership. The quest for identity resumed, and the Moorish Science Temple movement continued to grow after Noble Drew Ali's death. According to Federal Bureau of Investigation records, there were at least fifty temples in more than twenty-five major American cities in the mid-1940s, and all of them were under surveillance for possible Japanese connections.[76]

THE 1940s AND BEYOND: THE FBI AND THE MOORISH SCIENCE TEMPLE OF AMERICA

The Federal Bureau of Investigation's deliberate campaign to break the Moorish Science Temple of America and other related black Muslim groups is an untold story that began in the 1930s and continues to the present. This story is important to our discussion, because it underlines the global identity of the Moorish American movement. As we shall see, its global identity was viewed by the Department of Justice as a significant threat to America's internal security during World War II. Moreover, the Department of Justice's distorted view of the Moorish Science Temple of America was an aspect of the signification of black Muslims because this distorted stereotype of the East against the West became the American public's substitute for critical and dispassionate information about Islam in the world.

In the 1940s, the FBI classified all black Muslim groups under the heading of "Extremist Muslim Groups and Violence." The basic fear was that these groups were "part of a worldwide organization" and were developing plans with various Japanese organizations in America to unite "the dark races" in order to "take over" the country while white soldiers were away fighting in World War II. Thus, the global identity of the Moorish Americans and their alleged plans to act in cooperation with the Japanese were considered a threat to American security. An excerpt from the field report of a FBI agent in St. Paul, Minnesota sheds light on the FBI's paranoia:

> From 1933 through 1936, it is known that Japanese organizers came to the United States to develop racial sympathy for the Japanese race and the Negroes. They found a fertile field for their activities which resulted in the formation of several national organizations among the Negroes which are listed as follows: The Pacific Movement of the Eastern World, the Allah Temple of Islam [Nation of Islam], the Triumph Church of God, the Development of Our Own. These and similar organizations flourished in the cities of Chicago, Detroit, and St. Louis and one by one, they were broken up or handicapped in their movements by the United States Government until only the MSTA [Moorish Science Temple of America] remains as the largest national organization of this group.[77]

During World War II, the FBI investigated all of the above organizations for sedition, based on their alleged pro-Japanese propaganda. The Pacific Movement of the Eastern World, like the Moorish Science Temple, was on the FBI's list of seditious movements because of its internationalist perspective. At the same time, its philosophy and objectives were remarkably similar to those of the Moorish Science Temple of America. Its motto was "Asia for the Asians, Africa for Africans at home and abroad," and its objectives included "cultivation of the spirit of love for the ancestral home of dark peoples; [and] the encouragement of the return of those peoples who find no opportunity for development in the United States, and the establishment of a government of their own in the land of their fathers." The Pacific Movement of the Eastern World was based in St. Louis until 1940 (and in East St. Louis thereafter) and was indicted for espionage in 1942.[78]

On July 30, 1942, the FBI arrested Mimo De Guzman because of his "sponsorship of various pro-Japanese organizations among the American Negroes." De Guzman admitted his Japanese sympathies but revealed that a Japanese national, Satokata Takahashi, was the real power behind such groups as the Pacific Movement of the Eastern World, the Onward Movement of America, and the Ethiopian Pacific Movement. Although he acknowledged that the Moorish Science Temple of America "was identical in philosophy and purpose with such pro-Japanese groups, he admitted that there were no direct organizational links between them.[79]

Mimo De Guzman's assessment of the Moorish Science Temple of America was accurate. Some of the rhetoric and philosophy of the Moorish American movement was sympathetic to the Japanese position, as is evident in the following excerpt from one of their publications:

> It is significant that many years ago when Japan won freedom from mental slavery, we gained physical freedom, and when Japan won her first battle over the Europeans, we won our first mental battle, and gained the right to become a National Unit through our Prophet Noble Drew Ali. Now Japan has reached the position where she can hold her own with all European nations, say and do when and what she pleases, and our people are aroused to the need of sticking together.[80]

These ideas were based on the Moorish Americans' affinity to the Japanese as an "Asiatic race," and pro-Japanese sympathies that were widespread in black nationalist organizations in the 1940s, however, and not on the former's involvement in an official Japanese plot to overthrow the United States government. Although there is new evidence that Takahashi had direct personal ties with at least two leaders of the Moorish Science Temple, it must be emphasized that the author's perusal of more than a thousand pages of FBI records on the Moorish Science Temple uncovered no evidence of violent or seditious behavior in the official activities of the organization. Despite the absence of hard evidence of sedition, however, local law-enforcement officers raided the Holmas County, Mississippi branch of the Moorish Science Temple in 1942, and the state grand jury indicted several prominent members for allegedly teaching that "the Japanese are fighting a war of liberation for the Asiatic race of which Negroes are members, [and] that the Japanese army will invade the United States and that the Negro members in good standing [will] cooperate with the Japanese." The FBI campaign against the Moorish Americans in Mississippi in the 1940s was probably based in part on their agitation for equitable treatment in the public facilities of that state. In 1942, several Moorish Americans in Belzoni, Mississippi were arrested for refusing to ride in the back of a bus. In the FBI report on this incident, the Moorish Americans were classified as an "internal security" risk.[81]

Although the FBI's investigation of alleged Moorish American involvement in Japanese and Pan-Islamic plots continued during the 1940s, as World War II progressed, the Department of Justice shifted its focus to some of the black Muslims' Selective Service violations. By this time, the FBI's signification of black Muslims as conspirators in a global Islamic plot constituted a threatening reality for most Americans. Thus, the mass arrest of Moorish Americans proceeded without significant public outcry. Typical of this trend, in 1942, fifteen members of the Moorish Science Temple in Kansas City, Missouri were arrested by federal officials for failing to register for Selective Service. These arrests were part of the federal government's campaign to "break up" the black Muslim groups in America.[82]

Apparently, the different factions of the Moorish Science Temple of America had different policies regarding Selective Service registration. An FBI report on the Detroit temples in 1943 noted two factions of the movement after Noble Drew Ali's death, each with different histories of Selective Service registration:

> The majority of [the] temples followed Kirkman Bey and the minority attached themselves to a headquarters of the Moorish Science Temple of America in Chicago . . . Temple 4 . . . Detroit, Michigan, in latter group. This temple was purely religious with no pro-Japanese or other subversive teachings. All members this temple registered for Selective Service except four members. Two now held for Grand Jury for failure to register.[83]

At the same time, C. Kirkman Bey, the leader of the major faction of the Moorish American movement from 1929 to 1959, was the subject of a federal case involving "internal security-custodial detention [and] sedition" in 1943. His activities were a major subject of FBI memos and reports in the 1940s. The FBI and Selective Service harassment of Moorish American men continued into the 1950s as the latter agency continued to make it difficult for black Muslims to attain conscientious-objector status.[84]

The factionalism of the Moorish American movement in the World War

II era created the ideal circumstances for the FBI to infiltrate various temples with informants who supplied them with detailed information about the plans and activities of the movement. For example, in 1943, seven Moorish-American Temples in New Jersey split into two antagonistic branches—one observed the dietary laws of Islam and required its men to grow beards and wear fezzes; the other did not require these things. This kind of inside information about the Moorish American movement provided the FBI with a factual basis for their exaggerated significations of black American Muslims as global conspirators. During this period, the FBI was busy investigating Moorish American Temples for sedition in Jackson, Mississippi; Pulaski and Chicago, Illinois; Detroit and Flint, Michigan; Chattanooga, Tennessee; Louisville, Kentucky; Kansas City, Missouri; Birmingham, Alabama; Woodstock, Connecticut; Becket, Massachusetts; Orangeburg, South Carolina; and Prince George County, Virginia.[85]

In the midst of this campaign of harassment, H. Peter Bey, the leader of the New Haven Temple, wrote a letter to President Franklin D. Roosevelt, which attempted to reconcile the Moorish American movement and the federal government:

> I have . . . received several visits from the "Justice Department" representatives concerning our movement. . . . At this time [I] ask an interview [with] you and cabinet [to] bring you a proof "picture" of who the so-called negro really is, this knowledge will acquaint all with the real meaning of the oft repeated "Brotherhood of Man." . . . I am enclosing a photo of myself with fingerprints (taken by myself) for your approval and to be handed over to the Justice Department FBI. I wish to be known only as a leader . . . interested primarily in assisting my people in their endeavor for justice and economic equality by teaching them their true identity.[86]

This letter was ultimately received by the FBI and placed in its files. It did little to improve relations between the Moorish Americans and the federal government, and the FBI continued in its persecution and negative significations of black American Muslims.

As the male membership of the Moorish American Science Temple of America was negatively affected by numerous arrests for Selective Service violations and sedition, the movement continued to maintain its activities in the 1940s under the leadership of its women. In this era, black women assumed multiple roles in the black Muslim movement. Behind the scenes they nurtured and supported their families, they cooked the meals required by the dietary laws of their religion, and they made much of the Moorish American clothing. In their local tight-knit communities, they joined informal voluntary and self-help networks which provided food, shelter, clothing, and health care for those in need. Their emphasis on economic uplift, modesty, cleanliness, and propriety countered the negative sexual images of black women prevalent in American society.[87]

At the same time, Moorish American women had their own national organization, the Sisters National Auxiliary, which was based in Indianapolis. In connection with this group, Noble Drew Ali had declared December 17 as "National Holiday for Sisters" in the 1920s; this holiday continued in the 1940s and beyond.

In the pages of the *Moorish Voice,* the official monthly magazine of the Moorish Science Temple of America, articles written by articulate black women predominated. This publication provided the national membership with news about births and deaths, and local, regional, and national events of the movement. The list of regular female contributors to the *Moorish Voice* in the 1940s included Sister H. Holden Bey, Sister E. Cook Bey, and Sister M. Groom El in New York; Sister A. Moss Bey, Sister S. Bradley El, and Sister A. Moses Bey in Flint, Michigan; Sister M. Porter El in Louisville; Sister L. Donald El in Toledo; Sister B. Stroyer Bey in Milwaukee; Sister E. Jones Bey in Trenton, New Jersey; and Sister M. A. Walker Bey in Kansas City. Moreover, women were governors or heads of Moorish American Temples in Chicago, Toledo, Steubenville (Ohio), Brooklyn, Troy (New York), Atlanta, and Chattanooga. Black women's leadership skills were also taken seriously on the national level, as Sister Mary Clift Bey was appointed grand governess of Kentucky in 1941, and Sister P. Reynolds El was the national chairperson of the Sisters Auxiliary.[88]

Undoubtedly, the significant roles that black women played in the Moorish American movement in the 1940s reflected similar roles that black women assumed in the black family, religion, social reform, work, and women's organizations elsewhere in America. These roles underlined the complex connections between gender, race, and class in America as Moorish American women resisted gender oppression and united with their men to battle racial and class discrimination. At the same time, these prominent roles for women in the Moorish Science Temple of America were in line with the thinking of some Islamic modernists, such as Qasim Amin, an Egyptian who had "argued for the equality of the sexes in Islam ... [and] linked the emancipation of women to the nationalist cause" early in the twentieth century. Although these ideas were not at the center of Islamic modernism, they did inspire some Egyptian female intellectuals early in the century and created a useful paradigm for the roles of women in Islam.[89]

In spite of the FBI campaign of persecution in the World War II era, the economic ventures of the Moorish Science Temple of America continued to thrive. In 1942, the organization established its national home in Prince George County, Virginia, an independent compound of homes and farm land that was populated by fifty members of the organization who appeared to be financially well endowed. In 1944, the Moorish Americans purchased a farmhouse in Becket, Massachusetts, in the Berkshires. Here, they maintained their links to their global African-Asiatic identity, hosting a visit from Princess Tamanya of the Ethiopian royal family. Finally, the organization purchased a 167-acre farm in Woodstock, Connecticut that was under constant surveillance by the FBI in the 1940s. However, as a result of their farms and other businesses, the Moorish Americans were able to establish a "Food for Freedom Program" in 1943 to feed poor people.[90]

The FBI's harassment of the Moorish Science Temple of America continued into the 1970s, when the organization filed a 43-million-dollar suit against the federal government for discrimination. At the end of that decade, the FBI was still investigating reports of informants who said that the Moorish Americans were involved in "criminal activity" and "plans for internal warfare."[91] However, at that moment, the attention and resources of the FBI had already begun to shift to other Muslim groups and organizations as global Islam was in militant ascendancy and challenged the skills of many investigators. Thus America's perception of a global Islamic threat shifted to Iran and the Middle East, which became new sources for the federal government's negative signification of Islam.

By the 1980s, the Moorish Science Temple of America had established programs in many of the federal prisons in the United States and had resumed publication of the *Moorish Guide,* a newspaper that was founded in 1928 by Noble Drew Ali. Other Moorish newspapers published from the 1960s to the 1990s included *Moorish Science Monitor, Moorish Review, Moorish Scribe, Moorish Voice,* and *Moorish American Voice.* The revived *Moorish Guide* contained all the usual information about the links between a healthy diet, spiritual purity, and Moorish herbal remedies. At the same time, the newspaper adumbrated the theme of Moorish American identity with a particular focus on college students:

> While you are working toward your undergraduate and graduate degrees, you should also work toward an understanding of who you are, what is your name and nationality. . . . If you do not you shall join thousands of Brothers and Sisters as the butt of a very cruel joke.[92]

In the 1980s, the headquarters of one faction of the Moorish American movement was in Baltimore, Maryland under the leadership of National Grand Sheik Dr. German-Bey, who was one of Noble Drew Ali's original disciples. Also in Baltimore, Richardson Dingle-El declared himself a reincarnation of Noble Drew Ali and started an organization at Morgan State University. Robert Love El was the leader of another faction of the movement with its headquarters in Chicago, Illinois. An event in 1986 underlined the legitimacy of the Moorish American claim to a Moroccan identity. In that year, the Moroccan ambassador to America, Maati Jorco, sent the following message to the movement:

[I am] well aware of your devotion to strengthening the ties linking the Moorish American community to Morocco. Morocco, for its part, welcomes your interest, and your work for better understanding between us. . . . Your initiative is to be both respected and encouraged. As to us, we in turn have every intention of doing all possible to make our relationship a vibrant and a special one.[93]

This development emphasized the power of signification as Noble Drew Ali's quest for an Asiatic identity and name was finally successfully resolved after more than fifty years of governmental persecution, ridicule, and negative signification.

One final question remains concerning Noble Drew Ali, the first self-styled urban prophet of black American Islam. What was his legacy for American Islam in the 1920s and beyond? We know that in his time he was ignored by black leaders and immigrant Muslims alike. In 1927, Leonard Smith of the Detroit UNIA reported to Marcus Garvey that "Ali was using Garvey's name" to recruit UNIA members for his movement. Garvey responded, "I know nothing of the man referred to. . . . I have spoken and written enough for the people of Detroit to understand [the] purpose of organization and not allow strangers to decoy and exploit them by calling on or using my name." Although Garvey had a cordial relationship with some Muslims such as those in the Ahmadiyya movement, the Moorish Science Temple of America was not on his list of preferred Muslim groups.[94]

As we shall see in Chapter 4, orthodox Muslim communities existed in the Midwest during Noble Drew Ali's time, but these "white Muslims" who "were more a spasm than an outpost in Islam" ignored black Muslim groups like the Moorish Science Temple of America, preferring to practice the religion of Islam in their Arab and East European ethnic language communities. Black people were excluded from these versions of American Islam that originated from "the fact of belonging to an ethnic or national group in the old country or a foreign geographic area." With these Muslims from the old country, East had truly come West, as the historic patterns of racial and ethnic separation in Islam were acted out on the American scene. Although Noble Drew Ali and his Moorish Americans did not wish "to amalgamate or marry into the families of pale skin nations of Europe," they probably would have welcomed other relationships with orthodox Muslims from the old country.[95]

Without a legitimizing connection to the international Muslim community, Noble Drew Ali created one in his mass Islamic movement for black Americans, and the initiative, independence, and creativity involved in this enterprise were his major contributions to American Islam. No matter how bizarre his ideas may appear in retrospect, he introduced thousands of black people to Islam early in the twentieth century. Because of his ideas, black Americans developed a global perspective on race and politics in the context of his version of Islam. Drew Ali's religious imagination was boundless, and his esoteric vision of Islam brought the religion from the elite international circles of Mohammed Alexander Russell Webb into American popular culture, where it would eventually thrive in spite of harassment by the federal government. Ironically, globalizing and popularizing Islam also Americanized it. The global part of the equation provided a political orientation for viewing the religion in the context of the Pan-African movement that was popular among black Americans, while the popular aspect opened the door for viewing Islam in a context of mainstream African-American movements and concerns. This dual process of globalizing and popularizing American Islam continued with the groundbreaking work of the Ahmadiyya Movement in Islam in the 1920s. These Asian Indians were important because they were the first people who attempted to break down the racial and ethnic barriers between different communities of Muslims in America to develop a multi-racial version of Islam in the United States.

Chapter 4

THE AHMADIYYA MISSION
TO AMERICA

A MULTI-RACIAL MODEL
FOR AMERICAN ISLAM

"Say, if you love Allah, follow me; then will Allah
love you."   —Al-Imran

Harlem's Moslems run into several thousands. . . . Since they have no
mosque, the faithful worship in private homes and hired halls, where on
Saturday mornings their children study the Koran. They live quietly in
Harlem, but during their festivals they don rich robes, shawls, turbans and
fezzes of their native land, and the women wear gorgeous brocades and heavy
decorative jewelry. Ordinarily, Moslems wear American dress, for most of
them have lived in the United States more than twenty years. . . . They possess
a religious fervor that is expressed in much missionary work among American
Negroes . . . whether they are African, Arabs, Tartars, or American Negroes,
Moors, Persians or whites, Moslems intermarry. The racial flow back and forth
defies classification.[1]

This is how Roi Ottley, an eminent African-American journalist, author,
and reporter for the *New York Amsterdam Star News*, described the cultural
richness that he observed in Harlem's Muslim community in 1943. Ottley's
observations are important not only for what they tell us about the ethos
of American Islam in the twentieth century, but also for what they say
about the relationship between African Americans and immigrant Muslim culture. During the 1920s positive social and religious interaction
between Muslims of different racial and ethnic groups was encouraged
by the Indian missionaries of the Ahmadiyya Movement in Islam. The

Ahmadiyya was unquestionably one of the most significant movements in the history of Islam in the United States in the twentieth century, providing as it did the *first multi-racial* model for American Islam. The Ahmadis disseminated Islamic literature and converted black and white Americans. They attacked the distortions of Islam in the media, established mosques and reading rooms, and translated the Quran into English. They also constituted the link between the immigrant Muslims (whose numbers included Arabs, Persians, Africans, Tartars, Turks, Albanians, and Yugo-slavians) and black Muslim groups such as the Nation of Islam and the Moorish Science Temple of America. Thus, their goal was to alter perma-nently the historic patterns of racial and ethnic separation that existed among Muslims in America. Before we can understand the American paths of the Ahmadiyya movement more completely, however, we must first understand its origins in nineteenth-century India.

THE AHMADIYYA MOVEMENT IN INDIA: HETERODOXY AND MUSLIM IDENTITY

Rubies, sapphires, delicate silks in deep hues of magenta and gold, turbans emblazoned with dazzling jewels, Bengal tigers with black, white, and orange stripes, and the elegant white marble of the Taj Mahal caused nineteenth-century India to be called "the jewel of the crown" of the British empire. But India had more than rich natural resources. If Roi Ottley could have traveled there in the late 1800s, he would have been deeply im-pressed by India's cultural richness, by its diverse and dynamic religious traditions—Hinduism, Buddhism, Christianity, Bahaism, Sikhism, and Is-lam. Indeed, India during this period was a "spiritual hothouse" in which new interpretations of ancient religions arose quickly in response to the political, social, and economic turmoil created by British colonial rule.

In the nineteenth century, Europe systematically conquered much of the Muslim world for the first time in history. The colonial era began for Muslims as Napoleon invaded Egypt in 1798. Before the nineteenth cen-tury ended, Russia, Holland, Britain, and France ruled many of the peoples of Islam in Asia, Africa, and the Mediterranean. As the Muslims of the Indian subcontinent "stood defeated, powerless, and demoralized" after the 1857 mutiny that established British rule in India, Islamic modernists in different locations and points in time attempted to reinterpret their religion and identity in light of the political and philosophical realities of the western invasion.[2]

The Ahmadiyya movement, which began among the Muslims of the Punjab in the 1880s, offered a new interpretation of Islam that in its worldwide missionary outreach contributed significantly to a rethinking of the religion for the modern age. Its founder, Ghulam Ahmad (1835?–1908), the son of a middle-class Muslim landowner, was born in the village of Qadiyan, Punjab, sometime between 1835 and 1839. Tradition has it that

HAZARAT MIRZA GHULAM AHMAD. From *The Moslem Sunrise*. Used by permission of the Ahmadiyya Movement in Islam, Inc., USA.

Ahmad was a dreamer who led a life of studious seclusion until he began to receive revelation in 1879 and became convinced that it was his obligation to spread his message throughout the world.[3]

Ahmad's public life began in 1880 with the publication of his first book, *Al-Barahin-al-Ahmadiyya*, in which he sought to rejuvenate Islam by arguing for the validity of its principles in the context of the increasing threat posed by the Hindu majority and the Christian missionaries in the Punjab. Ghulam Ahmad soon began to engage in fierce and controversial public debates with both Christians and orthodox Muslims. At first, his message deviated little from the tenets of orthodox Islam. However, the ideas that slowly unfolded in his public pronouncements and his books threatened many Christians and orthodox Muslims in India. In *Fath-i Islam, Izala-y*

Awham, and *Tawzih-i Maram,* which were published in 1890 and 1891, Ahmad claimed that he was the Mahdi of Islam, a prophet of Islam, the Promised Messiah of Christianity and Islam, and an avatar of Krishna for the Hindus. As we shall see, issues of signification and identity were central in this synthesis of religious ideas. Finally, in *Masih Hindustan Men* in 1899, Ahmad said that Jesus had not died on the cross, but instead had gone to India, died there, and had ascended physically into heaven. Fierce opposition from the orthodox Muslim community and serious controversy with Hindus and Christians began in 1891 with his declarations of messiahship, and these tensions continued until his death in 1908.[4]

To understand why the orthodox (Sunni) Muslim community violently opposed the Ahmadiyya movement, we must first examine briefly the religious meaning of Islam for orthodox Muslims. Muslims believe that Muhammad, the founder of their religion, was a prophet of God in the line of Abraham, Moses, and Jesus. However, they do not regard him as divine. Muhammad preached a message of radical monotheism and charity to the people of Mecca and eventually distinguished himself not only as a prophet but also as a social, economic, and political reformer in Medina. Studying the life of Muhammad and also his revelations, which are collected in the Quran, Muslims established not only a special way to worship God but also a way of life which encompassed communal solidarity and a distinct culture, with the Arabic language as the universal medium of expression.[5]

Iman—expression of faith—is a fundamental principle of Islam. It embraces the basic tenets of the religion: the unity of Allah, the acceptance of Muhammad as his messenger, the Quran as the word of God, belief in angels, commitment to commandments for behavior, and belief in the final judgment and bodily resurrection. The Five Pillars of Islam fall under the heading of *Ibadat,* the ceremonial duties of the religion. They are the following: (1) the basic confession of faith, "There is no God but Allah and Muhammad is His Prophet"; (2) prayer five times a day while facing Mecca; (3) fasting during the month of Ramadan; (4) almsgiving ; and (5) the pilgrimage to the sacred city of Mecca.[6]

Although the Ahmadiyya movement considered itself to be "the true Islam" and conformed to most of the fundamental tenets of the religion, its conception of prophecy as a process that continued after Muhammad, was controversial and potentially heretical. Orthodox Muslims believed that Muhammad was the final prophet and that he sealed Islamic revelation with the transmission of the Quran, which was thought to be the perfection of the Jewish and Christian messages. The idea of "the seal of the prophets" is so essential to Islamic identity that many Muslims believe "that a person who does not believe that Muhammad was the last prophet is not a believer."[7]

It is important to note, however, that the Ahmadiyya idea of "continuous prophecy" became a paradigm for black Islamic movements as new urban prophets called on this idea to support their creative signification of

Islamic identity for their black followers in the United States in the twentieth century. Moreover, with Indian Muslims as their first role models from the Islamic world, heterodoxy and synthesis became the rule rather than the exception for the black American Muslims. Two other aspects of Ahmadi heterodoxy that later influenced Islam in black America were the interpretations of *mujadid* and *jihad*.

Mizra Ghulam Ahmad claimed to be a *mujadid* or renewer—a special individual whom God sends at the beginning of each Islamic century in order to revive the faith. This notion was associated later with the Muslim concept of Mahdi or guide. In 1891, Ahmad declared that he was *masih maw'ud* or the Promised Messiah of Islam. The Sunnis regarded both of these claims as heretical. According to orthodox Muslim belief, the Mahdi and the Promised Messiah are two separate individuals, each of whom will lead Muslims in *jihad* or bloody battle against unbelievers or *kafirs*.[8]

Ahmad went further against the grain of orthodoxy by declaring himself a peaceful Mahdi and messiah who would conduct a jihad of words rather than blood. He believed that war in a physical sense was justifiable only for self-defense. For the Ahmadis, jihad was interpreted as "a spiritual war" which involved prayer duels and "arguments about faith." The orthodox claimed that the Ahmadis adopted this stance to accommodate British rule in India, for the British were ready to protect the persecuted Ahmadis from violence as long as they renounced a jihad of blood.[9] In America, the Ahmadiyya "jihad of words" was a model for the publications and speeches of the new urban prophets of Islam who used their words to support their unusual significations of Islamic identity.

Finally, the Ahmadis' heterodox ideas about Jesus established a paradigm for reinterpretations of Jesus Christ in the mythic histories of some black American Islamic movements in the twentieth century. Reinterpretations of Jesus Christ were central in the synthesis of Christianity and Islam that was often prominent in the signification of these movements. Traditional Islamic belief held that Jesus was not crucified but rather had ascended physically into heaven, from which he would have a second advent. The Ahmadiyya movement did not accept this view, holding instead that Quranic passages about Jesus were meant to be interpreted metaphorically; for example, that a messiah would appear "in the likeness of Jesus." Ahmad utilized the Quran, hadith, the Bible, and historical works to support the assertion that he himself was that person. This claim also made it necessary for him to prove that Jesus did not die on the cross. In *Masih Hindustan Men*, Ghulam Ahmad disproved the resurrection of Jesus. His evidence showed that Jesus was removed from the cross while he was still in an unconscious state and that his wounds were healed by a special ointment called *marham-i-'isa*. According to Ahmad, Jesus eventually left the sepulcher alive and traveled to Kashmir, where he taught the lost tribe of Israel until his death at the age of 120. Finally, Ahmad claimed to have discovered Jesus' tomb on Khan Yar Street in Sringar, Kashmir.[10]

The Ahmadiyya movement in India was formally established on November 4, 1900. Several years earlier, Ghulam Ahmad had set the following goals for his religion:

> To propagate Islam; to think out ways and means of promoting the welfare of new converts to Islam in Europe and America; to further the cause of righteousness, purity, piety and moral excellence throughout the world, to eradicate evil habits and customs; to appreciate with gratitude the good work of the British government.[11]

In 1901 the Ahmadiyya movement chose to separate itself from Sunni Islam after two years of persecution by the orthodox Muslim community in India. After Ghulam Ahmad's death in 1908, two factions of leadership developed within the movement. Khawajah Kamal-ud-Din and Muhammad Ali of Lahore led a more intellectual faction that wanted to reunite the Ahmadiyya movement with orthodox Islam, while the Qadians, a more conservative faction of professionals, businessmen, and landowners, remained loyal to the original teachings and the separatism of Ghulam Ahmad.[12] Finally in 1914, the Lahoris, led by Muhammad Ali, split from the Qadian group over the kafir of non-Ahmadis and the power of the caliph. The more powerful Qadian group, led by Khalifa-Masih II Mizra Bashir-ud-din Mahmud Ahmad, separated itself totally from Sunni Islam and escalated the conflicts within the Muslim community in India during the first two decades of the twentieth century. Ahmadis were not allowed to pray under the guidance of other Muslim imams; neither were they permitted to marry other Muslims or to attend non-Ahmadiyya funeral services. Hence by 1916, the Qadian Ahmadis had begun to suffer serious persecution in India.[13]

Before the Ahmadiyya movement split into permanent factions, however, it had already laid the groundwork for its missionary work to the English-speaking world in Great Britain. In 1913, Khawajah Kamal-ud-Din made an Irish baron, Lord Headley, the first English convert to Ahmadi Islam in their mosque at Woking, a suburb of London. The conversion of Lord Headley, who took the Muslim name of Saifurrah Shaikh Rahmatullah Faruq, caused a stir in the English press, as the English public was fascinated by Headley's dramatic changes in name and identity. Khawajah Kamal-ud-Din devoted the remainder of his life to missionary work in England, and in 1920 the Qadianis sent their first Indian missionary to America. His name was Mufti Muhammad Sadiq.[14]

THE AHMADIYYA'S EARLY DAYS IN AMERICA

On January 24, 1920, as daybreak settled over London's streets, an elderly, light-brown-complexioned man with spectacles boarded the S. S. Haverford bound for America. His dark green and gold turban and his amiable but mysterious manner attracted the attention of several Chinese

MUFTI MUHAMMAD SADIQ, *the first Ahmadiyya
missionary to America, in 1923.* From *The Moslem
Sunrise.* Used by permission of the Ahmadiyya
Movement in Islam, Inc., USA.

passengers, to whom he introduced himself as "Mufti Muhammad Sadiq,
missionary for the Ahmadiyya Movement in Islam." Each day at sea,
several passengers were eager to learn more about this exotic stranger's
religion and his plans for a Muslim mission in America. They were
mystified by his stories about the life of the Prophet Muhammad and the
teachings of the Promised Messiah Ghulam Ahmad, which he told in
English, interspersed with Arabic and Urdu phrases. "Say, if you love
Allah, follow me; then will Allah love you," he said. "There is no God but
Allah, and Muhammad is a Messenger of God." Before the end of the
voyage, Sadiq had converted four Chinese men, one American, one Syrian, and one Yugoslavian to Islam.[15]

The S. S. Haverford arrived in Philadelphia on February 15, 1920. The
United States immigration authorities seized Mufti Muhammad Sadiq
and took him into custody before he could leave the ship, although he
assured them that "he had not come here to teach plurality of wives. A
Muslim will be committing a sin against his religion." After they had
interrogated him for several hours and had established that he was a
citizen of India and a representative of a religious group that practiced
polygamy, the authorities asked him to leave the United States on the ship
in which he had just arrived. Sadiq refused to do so and requested an

appeal to the Secretariat in Washington, D.C. He was confined to the Philadelphia Detention House in Gloucester, New Jersey, until a favorable decision of the appeal was handed down several weeks later.[16]

Many men in the Detention House were impressed with Sadiq's passion and devotion to his multi-racial religion, which offered dramatic changes in name and identity, and they converted. "Under curious circumstances, we got acquainted in the closed walls of the Detention House," Sadiq said of his first convert in America, R. J. H. Rochford. "Watching me praying and reciting the Holy Book, Mr. Rochford inquired of my religion, which I explained to him and I gave him some books to study. Very soon he was convinced of the truth of our religion and being converted was named Hamid."[17] Although Rochford was eventually sent back to England by the immigration authorities, during those weeks of confinement Sadiq made nineteen other converts to Islam. These men were from Jamaica, British Guyana, Azores, Poland, Russia, Germany, Belgium, Portugal, Italy, and France. Thus, Sadiq's mission was at first generalized and only later focused almost exclusively on African Americans.[18]

Sadiq's tone during his confinement was conciliatory, as he attempted to convince the federal authorities that he could preach Islam in the United States without preaching polygamy.[19] To do so, Sadiq made a distinction between commandments and permissions in Islam. Muslims must follow the commandments of their religion, he explained, but might avoid the permissions. For instance, no government could persuade a Muslim to worship more than one God, since the worship of one God was a commandment of Islamic religion. However, polygamy was permitted only in countries whose laws sanctioned its practice. In countries that prohibited polygamy, permission for its practice was disallowed under the commandment that all Muslims must obey the laws of the country in which they lived.[20]

But if Sadiq was conciliatory, others were not so sanguine. The Ahmadiyya Movement in Islam expressed its outrage over Sadiq's detention, an outrage which Sadiq would share by the end of 1921. It cited in *The Review of Religions* the gap between America's ideas of freedom, justice, and equality and the nation's actual practice. Sher Ali proposed that if Sadiq could not preach Islam in the United States, then "American missionaries should be expelled from India." Finally, Ali warned the United States that Islam would soon spread throughout the world, with or without its cooperation.[21] After two months of confinement, Sadiq was finally allowed to enter the United States in April of 1920 on the condition that he would not preach polygamy.[22]

Apparently the Ahmadis had not been aware up to that time of the discrimination against Muslim and Indian immigrants in the United States in the early 1900s. Before Sadiq's ordeal, many Muslim immigrants from the Middle East had already been refused entry by the immigration authorities at Ellis Island. An initial court decision that was eventually overruled said that they could not become citizens of the United States "because they were neither Caucasian nor African."[23] This is important to our discussion because of the centrality of Indian racial identity to the Ahmadis' signification of Islamic identity—a signification that appealed to African-American converts in the 1920s.

In 1907, several "anti-Hindoo" riots erupted on the West Coast. These racially oriented uprisings were directed against immigrants from the Punjab, who were perceived as an economic threat to local workers in the smaller towns. Although some of these immigrants were Sikhs and Muslims, all Indians were viewed by white Americans as "Hindoos" or "ragheads" (because they wore turbans). Typical of the reaction, Agnes Foster Buchanan wrote:

> The Hindus and the Hindu invasion is the latest racial problem with which we in the West have to deal. . . . This is the propitious moment for the State Department to adopt an amendment to the Vedas and to tell our brothers of the East that while the earth is large enough for us all, there is no part of it that will comfortably accommodate both branches of the Aryan family.[24]

In 1917, widespread hostility against Asians in the United States resulted in the passage of the Oriental Exclusion Act, which excluded all laborers from the "Asiatic Barred Zone" (Arabia, Afghanistan, India, Indochina, the East Indies, and other Asian nations). The Johnson Act of 1921 established strict annual quotas for Asian immigrants, and finally the Johnson-Reed Act of 1924 closed the door to most non-European immigrants by setting up a "national origins system" that gave North and West Europeans a huge advantage over other groups.[25]

For a while, some Indians became American citizens by persuading the courts that their racial classification was "Caucasian" and that they were "white." However, when Bhagat Singh Thind brought his case for citizenship to the Supreme Court in 1923, the doors were closed to Indian immigrants, and they were not reopened until the 1960s. In the *United States vs. Bhagat Singh Thind*, Justice George Sunderland ruled that not all Caucasians were legally accepted as "white people in the United States," since immigration legislation in 1870 had ruled that only Europeans were white people. Indian immigrants therefore were not eligible for naturalization under a 1790 statute that limited naturalization to free white people. Because of these pressures, which reached a peak in the early 1920s, many Indians left the United States around the time of Mufti Muhammad Sadiq's arrival, and as we shall see, many of those who remained adopted a militant Third World racial identity that connected them politically and racially to oppressed people of color in the United States and abroad.[26]

The American press covered Sadiq's arrival in America with headlines such as "Picturesque Sadiq," "Hopes to Convert U.S.," "Speaks Seven

Tongues," "Optimistic in Detention," and "East Indian Here with New Religion."[27] *Press*, a Philadelphia newspaper, probably gave the most accurate account of Mufti Muhammad Sadiq's ordeal and his intentions in America:

> While many religious sects in the United States are spending many thousands of dollars and sending hundreds of philosophers and teachers to the wilds of Tibet, the far reaches of Arabia and Hindustan and to the unexplored regions of Africa and China, Mufti Muhammad Sadiq, after traveling thousands of miles, alone and friendless, hopes to begin his crusade to convert Americans to the doctrines taught by the prophet Ahmad, of whom he is the principal disciple.[28]

In the 1920s, New York had already acquired a reputation as a city of unparalleled opportunity for newcomers. The humorist Ogden Nash called it a city where "poor girls with nothing to their names but a letter or two can get rich and joyous,"[29] while Roi Ottley named it the "Black Mecca" because of its rich black culture and many job opportunities for African Americans.[30] Perhaps Mufti Muhammad Sadiq was also attracted by New York's reputation when he decided to settle there after his release from detention in April 1920. He set up his headquarters on Madison Avenue, and he was moderately successful in the city. By the end of May, he had made twelve new converts to the Ahmadiyya movement—six from the Christian community and six from Islam. Two of these, Dr. George Baker and Ahmad Anderson, were among the first white Muslim converts in the United States in the early 1900s.[31]

Sadiq missionized through lecturing and writing. By May 1920, he had contributed twenty articles on Islam to various American periodicals and newspapers, among them the *New York Times*.[32] During his first year of missionary work in the United States, he delivered fifty public lectures on a variety of subjects in American cities, including Chicago, New York, Detroit, and Grand Havens, Michigan. Although Sadiq's outward style was quiet, unassuming, and almost passive, he was a confident lecturer, well suited for his role as preacher, writer, and public speaker for the Ahmadiyya movement in the United States.[33] He had acquired valuable practical experience as a missionary in England, where the Ahmadis had been active since 1912.[34] A learned man, he was a graduate of the University of London, a philologist of international repute, and an expert in Arabic and Hebrew whose work had been published in *Philomath*. Indeed, before Sadiq's departure for the United States in 1920, H. M. Leon, Secretary of the International Society of Philology, Sciences and Fine Arts, had presented the farewell speech at his going-away party in London.[35]

Sadiq's missionary work for the Ahamadiyya Movement in Islam came from a deep spiritual commitment. He had been a close companion of Ghulam Ahmad, the founder of the movement, and believed that the latter had been "favored with the divine gift of prophecy." Mufti Sadiq also believed in the mystical power of dreams. While he was still in England, Sadiq had a dream about an American female convert. When S. W. Sobolewski walked into his headquarters in New York, he considered her the fulfillment of his dream. Sobolewski eventually converted to the Ahmadiyya movement, and Sadiq named her Fatima Mustafa. She was the first white American woman to join the religion.[36]

Sadiq's most active female convert and proselytizer in New York, however, was Madame Rahatullah, an African American who, according to Sadiq, "secured one American convert and one Muslim to the Ahmadia order" in 1921. She also wrote a poem entitled "The Beauties of Islam" to express enthusiasm about her new faith.[37]

THE AHMADDIYYA'S EFFORTS TO UNIFY BLACK AND NON-BLACK MUSLIMS

In October 1920, Sadiq moved the headquarters of the Ahmadiyya mission to Chicago because of its central location, which he claimed was more convenient for his work than New York.[38] In this new location, he cultivated multi-racial relations with various communities of "white" Muslims. Illinois had attracted small but significant waves of Muslim immigrants from Syria, Lebanon, Jordan, and Palestine from 1875 to 1912 and from 1918 to 1922.[39] These Arab Muslims, who came to the United States because of economic downturns in the Middle East, were mostly uneducated and worked as peddlers and industrial laborers.[40] Their eagerness to escape the immigration restrictions of the 1920s and to achieve financial success led many of the later arrivals to assimilate and to change their Arabic names to American ones.[41] It is important to note that with a few exceptions these white Muslims remained separate from black Muslims in America before the 1920s. Apparently, the former brought Islam's historic patterns of racial separatism to America from their old countries. Working against these separatist traditions, the Ahmadiyya movement struggled to bring together Muslims of different racial and ethnic groups in the 1920s.

Some Arab immigrants, conservative Muslims or Sunnis, organized a community in Ross, North Dakota, in 1900; in 1920, they established a mosque there. Before 1914, approximately ten Lebanese Muslims worked at the Huskel Railroad Company in Michigan City, Indiana. In 1914, many Arab Muslims were attracted to the good pay at the Ford Highland Park Plant in Detroit, and they established a community in Highland Park. Two years later, employment at the Ford Rouge Plant provided impetus for the establishment of an Arab Muslim community in South Dearborn, Michigan.[42] Muslim associations were established in Highland Park, Michigan, in 1919, and in Detroit in 1922. The Young Men's Muslim Association was founded in Brooklyn in 1923,[43] and the Rose of Fraternity Lodge in Cedar

Rapids, Iowa, in 1925.[44] There was also a significant Sunni community in Toledo, Ohio.[45] And the Shia immigrated to the United States around the same time.[46]

Still more communities of Muslim immigrants had arrived from eastern Europe during this period. They included Bosnian Muslims who came to the United States from Bosnia-Herzegovina, Yugoslavia, around 1900. These Muslim immigrants worked in the construction industry in Chicago and established their community on the Near North Side. Their social life focused on several coffee houses and a lodge, Dzemijetul Hajrije (Beneficiant Society), which was established in 1906. There were also smaller Bosnian Muslim communities in Gary, Indiana, and in Butte, Montana.[47] A very small number of Turkish Muslims had immigrated to America between 1820 and 1860. And by the early 1900s, larger numbers of Turks had immigrated to the United States and settled in New York City, Chicago, Detroit, Philadelphia, and San Francisco. Most of these early Turkish Muslims maintained their language and their religious tradition in the United States.[48] Albanian Muslims had settled in the United States by the early 1900s and established their first organization in Biddeford, Maine, in 1915. Finally, influenced by the Muslim immigrant community, by Muslim sailors from Yemen, Somalia, and Madagascar, and by the Ahmadiyya translation of the Quran, Shaykh Daoud Ahmed Faisal established an African-American Sunni group in New York City in 1924. His Islamic Mission of America, also called the State Street Mosque or Islamic Brotherhood, believed as the Moorish Science Temple did that black Americans "were not Negroes but were originally Muslims." Shayhk Daoud's groups spread Sunni practices among black Muslims on the East Coast in the 1920s and 1930s and continued to be significant to African-American Muslims for the remainder of the twentieth century.[49]

Although the Ahmadis were heterodox, they maintained a civil relationship with these conservative Muslims in America in the 1920s. Mufti Muhammad Sadiq spoke Arabic and encouraged Arab nationalism as well as relations between Persians, Arabs, and Turks in America. He was highly respected by all Muslims in the United States in the 1920s.[50]

In "My Advice to the Muhammadans in America," Sadiq mentioned that the thousands of Muslims in the United States came from many lands. However, he said, most of these people were "Muslims in name only" because Islam had ceased to play a practical role in their daily lives. Sadiq continued to say that the United States was a good country for millions of dispersed Muslims to settle in. To preserve their culture, however, they must (1) retain their Muslim names; (2) say their daily prayers; (3) read, write, and speak Arabic—the common language of Islam; (4) teach their children to be good Muslims; (5) donate the interest gained from their bank accounts to the propagation of Islam; (6) build mosques in every town; (7) promulgate Islam in America; and (8) join the Ahmadiyya movement.[51]

In the fall of 1920, Sadiq collaborated with Mohni, the editor of the

Arabic newspaper *Alserat*, to bring the orthodox and heterodox communities together to form a multi-racial society for the protection of Islam in the United States. Sadiq was elected president, and Mohni was elected the secretary of this society.[52] Also, in that year, Sadiq moved the American headquarters of the Ahmadiyya movement to Highland Park, a suburb of Detroit. This was the location of Karoub House, one of the first mosques in the United States, which was built at the cost of $55,000 by Hussain Karoub (a Syrian Muslim with real-estate holdings in Highland Park and Detroit), who became the imam of the mosque. Because Karoub House was utilized by Muslims from different ethnic groups, the building of this mosque inspired the Ahmadiyya movement in its efforts to link varied Muslim communities.[53]

THE MOSLEM SUNRISE, THE "JIHAD OF WORDS," AND PROTESTANT RESISTANCE TO SADIQ'S MULTI-RACIAL MISSION

In July 1921, Mufti Muhammad Sadiq published the first issue of *The Moslem Sunrise*. The journal, which appeared every three months, was established for the primary purpose of refuting the misrepresentations of Islam that appeared in the American press. Indeed, this activity was one of the Ahmadis' most significant efforts for the American Muslim community. Thus, *The Moslem Sunrise* brought the Ahmadis' jihad of words to the forefront of Islamic identity in America. As we shall see, the jihad of words was destined to exercise a profound influence on the signification that black Americans formed for themselves in Islam. Plans for this publication had been in the works since October 1920.[54] Significantly, the cover of each issue pictured a sunrise over North America, which symbolized the rising sun of Islam in the United States. Mirza Mahmud Ahmad, the leader of the Ahmadiyya Movement in Islam, compared the mission in the United States to that of the original American pioneers, and he called his missionaries in America "pioneers in the spiritual colonization of the western world." Multi-racial missionary work, then, would be a primary thrust of *The Moslem Sunrise*.[55]

During the first quarter of the journal's publication, from July through October 1921, the movement received 646 communications and sent out 2,000 pieces of mail, including the journal. Five hundred letters about Islam were mailed to Masonic lodges in the United States, along with copies of *The Moslem Sunrise*. Also, one thousand pieces of Ahmadi literature were sent to major libraries in the United States. The Ahmadiyya movement also mailed literature to many celebrities in the United States and abroad, among them Thomas Edison, Henry Ford, and President Warren Harding. These efforts resulted in thirty-one new converts during this period.[56]

Several articles published in *The Moslem Sunrise* during 1921 defended

Islam against erroneous information published by the American press. The *New York Herald*, for instance, had criticized the Quran for teaching Muslims "to hate and kill unbelievers."[57] And several newspaper articles criticized Islam in light of the Turkish atrocities in Europe, since the Greek Christians were fighting against the Turks in the early 1920s.[58] Convinced that American Christians were threatened by the infidel, editors of the *Syracuse Sunday Herald* took note:

> To the millions of American Christians who have so long looked eagerly forward to the time the cross shall be supreme in every land and the people of the whole world shall have become followers of Christ, the plan to win this continent to the path of the "infidel Turk" will seem a thing unbelievable. But there is no doubt about its being pressed with all the fanatical zeal for which the Mohammedans are noted.[59]

Ever alert to attacks on or gross misrepresentations of Islam, Sadiq exposed the biases of such stories, citing the programs in the Ukraine in which Christians had killed 140,000 Jews from February to June of 1921. Europeans and Americans should show as much concern for this massacre, he pointed out, as for the one perpetrated against the Armenians by the Turks.[60] Finally, Sadiq defended Islam by citing the race problem in the United States and the multi-racial agenda of global Islam:

> What sad news we came across . . . about the conflict between the Blacks and the Whites in this country. It is a pity that no preaching of equality or Christian charity has so far been able to do away with this evil. In the East we never hear of such things occurring between the peoples. There are people fairer than North Europeans living friendly and amiably with those of the darkest skin in India, Arabia and other Asiatic and African countries. . . . In Islam no church has ever had seats reserved for anybody and if a Negro enters first and takes the front seat even the Sultan if he happens to come after him never thinks of removing him from the seat.[61]

It is noteworthy that Sadiq's view of equality in Islam did not reconcile with the history of racism in the Muslim world. However, the Indian missionary's idealized view of his religion was not unusual, since few Muslims have dealt critically with the issue of racism in Islam.

In another article, Sadiq commented on his exclusion from preaching in Detroit churches:

> If the Detroit churches are not open for me to preach in I do not care a bit. No Moslem here cares to see me preach in the churches. Moreover the churches are not suitably furnished for our services. My challenge was to the broad-mindedness of the Christian pastors in comparison with that shown by our

Holy Prophet. I was sure that the Christian "Love your enemies" was only to preach and not to practice. But I wanted to get it out of their mouths and I have got it.[62]

Sadiq's indictment of racism in the churches also led him finally to express his bitterness about his ordeal with the immigration authorities. Rhetorically asking what would happen "if Jesus Christ comes to America and applies for admission to the United States under the immigration laws," Sadiq answered that the immigration authorities would decide "that Jesus would not be allowed to enter this country because (1) he comes from a land which is out of the permitted zone; (2) he has no money with him; (3) he is not decently dressed; (4) he has no credentials to show that he is an authorized preacher."[63]

By the second year of its mission in the United States, then, the Ahmadiyya movement had developed an adversarial relationship with the American media and with mainstream Christianity. Moreover, Mufti Muhammad Sadiq's negative experiences with the immigration authorities, the white Protestant churches, and the media had resulted in some significant changes in his personality and his attitude toward America. By 1921, he was no longer a humble saintly martyr, but instead a bitter and angry opponent of white mainstream Christianity and racism in America. He had been fooled by the United States' outward image as a place of freedom and equality, in a decade when both Protestant and Catholic churches "failed largely to abandon racism either at the altar or through their secular policies."[64]

The history of the Ahmadiyya movement reveals much about American religion during the early twentieth century, particularly the relationship between its Protestant center and those traditions outside it. Obviously, the "assimilationist" or "the melting pot" model in American history did not include the Ahmadis, for these Muslims were ultimately unwilling to abandon their old culture to embrace the new. Hardened by their encounters with racism, and by the contrast between their experience and that of other immigrant groups, they were intent on transforming the host culture by conversion to a multi-racial version of Islam and the signification of Indian cultural identity, not on being assimilated into it.

Originally, Mufti Muhammad Sadiq had envisioned an ecumenical movement of multi-racial cooperation and increased understanding between Protestants and Muslims in America. If this movement had succeeded, it could have resulted in partial acculturation along class lines rather than the complete alienation of American Muslims in the 1920s. After all, Sadiq was well-educated and had been accepted in middle- and upper-class circles in England. However, as we have seen, most white Protestants were unwilling to work toward an ecumenical multi-racial goal because of their racism and their deeply entrenched fear of Islam. As

C. Eric Lincoln put it, "Being 'American' presupposes the Judeo-Christian heritage of experience . . . and the religion of Islam is not in any substantial way a part of the critically valued American experience."[65]

As it became clear that the negative tensions with the host society were irresolvable, the Ahmadis began to focus their conversion efforts in the United States less on white people and more on blacks. For a short time, this new racial emphasis led to a new vision of a global Pan-Islamic alliance in which Indian nationalism and Pan-Africanism were linked in a potent multi-racial synthesis of anti-imperialist and anti-Christian religious and political ideas.

A MULTI-RACIAL MISSION TO BLACK AMERICA

"Asalaam Alaikum!" said Mufti Muhammad Sadiq, as he surveyed the small group of mostly black and brown worshippers gathered at the mosque on Wabash Avenue in Chicago. A young and strong-looking Russian man with fair skin and sandy hair stood out in the audience this Sunday evening in August 1922. He was seated next to a strikingly handsome Indian from Calcutta, a dental student at the State University in Iowa. Sadiq folded his arms across his green full-length jacket with a military collar and a scarlet-colored lining, as a black man named Abdul Hakeem sang "Allah Be Praised" in a rich baritone voice. Mufti Muhammad Sadiq's skullcap, his large, clear brown eyes, and his prominent nose gave him the appearance of a "brown skinned Jew," while his white mustache, sideburns, and flowing beard gave him a "gospel likeness." He looked and spoke like a biblical prophet, and this was an important aspect of the appeal of Sadiq's exotic Indian identity to his black American followers. Carefully he closed his leather-bound Quran and began his sermon:

> "There is but one God," he said. "All others are mere prophets, including Jesus. Muhammad was the last and the equal of the others. None is to be worshiped, not even Jesus or Muhammad. The Trinity is an illusion—the word is not found in the Christian Bible and its principle cannot be sustained. God created all races, all colors. Islam makes no difference between race and class." At the end of the service, worshippers rehearsed their new Arabic names and Sadiq blessed them: "Bismillah in the name of Allah."[66]

From 1921 to 1925, the Ahmadis made 1,025 American converts whose names and places of residence were listed in the pages of *The Moslem Sunrise*.[67] Many of the Ahmadiyya converts were black residents of Chicago and Detroit. These two cities, and to a lesser extent, Gary, Indiana, and St. Louis, Missouri, were hotbeds of Ahmadiyya activity in the 1920s. In 1922, Sadiq moved the American headquarters of the movement from

Early members of the U.S. Ahmadiyya Community with missionaries Sufi Mutiur Rahman Bengalee and Dr. Khalil Ahmad Nasir (sitting on the 4th and 5th chairs from the left). From The Moslem Sunrise. Used by permission of the Ahmadiyya Movement in Islam, Inc., USA.

Highland Park, Michigan, to Wabash Avenue on the southside of Chicago. A converted house served as a mosque and mission house from which *The Moslem Sunrise* was published. Outside, the Ahmadis erected a small dome or minaret to signal their commitments. Much of the financing for the mosque came from donations from Ahmadis in India.[68] Muhammad Yaqoob (Andrew Jacob), Ghulam Rasul (Mrs. Elias Russel), and James Sodick—a Russian Tartar—were key figures in the Ahmadiyya work in Chicago in the 1920s.[69]

Meanwhile, Sadiq continued to deliver lectures throughout the midwestern and eastern sections of the United States. Most of these lectures, which were delivered at schools, civic clubs, and lodges, were well received. For example, Sadiq noted with regard to a trip to Minnesota:

> In Crookston, Minnesota, I was invited by the superintendent of the State Farm School to give a talk on Islam in the school hall. I spoke for an hour ... and the chairman thanking me for the speech said: "All I knew of Muhammadanism before this was that the Muhammadans worship Muhammad and kill the Christians, but today I have learned the real facts and I am thankful for it."[70]

Although these lecture trips resulted in several new white converts for the Ahmadiyya movement, news of African-American converts continued to dominate the pages of *The Moslem Sunrise*. Several of these African Americans became prominent missionaries for the Ahmadiyya movement after their conversion. In 1922, *The Moslem Sunrise* first featured a picture and a short report about a recent black convert, Sheik Ahmad Din (P. Nathaniel Johnson), "a zealous worker for Islam," who had just been appointed as a missionary in St. Louis, Missouri.[71] Here Ahmad Din led a group of devout Muslims that included blacks, Turks, and a small number of whites.[72] In one of his pictures he wore a fez, which suggests that Din may have been a Freemason or a former member of Noble Drew Ali's Moorish Science Temple movement.

An article about Din in the St. Louis *Post Dispatch* reports that he had acquired one hundred converts during the first six months of his mission in St. Louis.[73] Another black convert—Brother Omar (William M. Patton) of the Lamarsary Shop—was also cited for his proselytizing efforts in St. Louis,[74] and Sister Noor (Ophelia Avant) was one of the most enthusiastic black female converts in the St. Louis area.[75]

Photographs of four other black women—Sister Khairat (Thomas), Sister Zeineb (Watts), Sister Ahmadea (Robinson), and Sister Ayesha (Clark)—were also featured in *The Moslem Sunrise*. It is noteworthy that all of these women wore traditional Muslim veils to cover their faces, and long dresses and long sleeves to cover their bodies. New clothing was a significant aspect of the conversion experience for these blacks. Although conversion was not a new phenomenon in African-American culture and African Americans had experienced "profoundly emotional new births" in the context of evangelical Protestantism since the eighteenth century,[76] Muslim clothing and Arabic names added a new dimension to this experience. The new clothes—veils, long dresses, skullcaps, turbans, fezzes, and robes, like the shadbelly coats and the dove-colored bonnets of the nineteenth-century Quakers[77]—differentiated the Muslims from their Christian neighbors and signaled their new religious commitment. For some of the black Muslims, the new clothes were undoubtedly a symbol of alienation and ethnic differentiation from the mainstream white culture. For others, they were probably a medium of creative, artistic expression. The converts' new Arabic names could be understood in the same way. Indeed a subtle interface between creative stylistic expression and genuine religious motivation might have attracted some blacks to the symbols of American Islam in the 1920s. Such cultural exchanges exemplify the black community's concern with signifying and identifying themselves as distinct from white culture.

Some of the black converts to the Ahmadiyya movement were Protestant ministers who were probably drawn to a multi-racial religious community with new opportunities for leadership not available in segregated evangelical Protestant contexts. For example, Brother Hakim (Dr. J. H.

Humphries) came to the United States from the Congo Free State (the Belgian Congo) at the age of seventeen. He studied for the ministry at Tuskegee Institute for five years, after which he was ordained and became a Christian missionary. After listening to one of Sheik Ahmad Din's lectures on Islam, Hakim became disillusioned with Christianity and converted to Islam. Soon he was a zealous missionary for the Ahmadiyya movement, and was thought to possess extraordinary healing powers.[78] He was a tall, handsome, distinguished-looking man, whom Ahmad Din praised without reservation, calling him a man of "great spiritual powers" and a "magnetic healer of extraordinary ability."[79]

Brother Hakim and Ahmad Din—articulate, well-educated, and middle-class—were well-suited for Mufti Muhammad Sadiq's sophisticated style of instruction in Islam. Much of the instruction occurred through public lectures. Other media included the Ahmadiyya Public Library. *The Moslem Sunrise* featured detailed articles on the writing and pronunciation of the Arabic language and the performance of *salat*—the Muslim mode of worship. There were also many articles on Islamic history and on the progress of Ahmadiyya missions in Europe, Africa, and Asia. After their instruction, all new converts to the Ahmadiyya movement signed the "Bismillah," signifying their commitment to a new religion that involved the particular beliefs and duties of Islam.

Although the Ahmadiyya Movement in Islam secured some white American converts, there were few white American proselytizers in the early 1920s.[80] Because of the leadership roles that it gave to its black participants, however, the movement began to attract members of the Universal Negro Improvement Association. Brother Abdullah (James Conwell), a prominent convert in Chicago, was a Garveyite. There were at least six other Garveyites in the Chicago mission, and they wore their Garvey uniforms to the Ahmadi religious services and meetings. In 1923, Sadiq gave five lectures at the UNIA meetings in Detroit. Eventually he converted forty Garveyites to Islam. "Out of the converts there, an intelligent and enthusiastic young man, Rev. Sutton, has been appointed as the leader of the congregation with his Moslem name as Sheik Abdus Salaam," he wrote. "Another zealous member of ours is Mrs. Wright (Sister Nazeefa), who together with her little children is studiously learning the Arabic language."[81]

Thus there was a direct relationship between the Universal Negro Improvement Association and the Ahmadiyya Movement in Islam. But the connection between the two groups occurred on a more subtle level as well, a fact that is significant to African-American religious history and that suggests a main concern here. The Ahmadis were Indians—one of the "darker races of the world"—who were seeking their independence from the British. The Garvey movement stressed the internationalist perspective that led African Americans to think of themselves in concert with Africans and the "darker races of the world" against white Europeans and

Americans. In the 1920s, this internationalist identity, which had been growing among blacks since the late nineteenth century, began to extend to their religious consciousness as well. Christianity was increasingly criticized as a "clan religion" for whites that needed to be revised by blacks or abandoned for another religion, such as Islam. The attraction of both the Garvey movement and the Ahmadiyya Movement in Islam was that they offered a new religious identity to African Americans who had been awakened to this perspective. Just as the UNIA was the *Universal* Negro Improvement Association with universality in the political sphere, the Ahmadis connected the faithful to a worldwide, multi-racial, but "non-white" religion.

Moreover, as we have seen, Garveyism and the Islamic movements in the 1920s were forms of political religion. David Apter has argued that, especially in Third World nations, the sacred is used to legitimate political ends and to mobilize the community for political goals. In this context, political doctrine becomes "in effect, a political religion" which gives "continuity, meaning and purpose" to a people's life.[82] With this perspective in mind, one could say there were three historical strands in the development of Islam in the United States in the 1920s. The first, the conservative Sunni Islam of the Muslim immigrants from the Middle East and the Islamic Mission of America, were orthodox, universalist, and also politically conservative. The second, the Moorish Science Temple movement, was heterodox, a racial-separatist interpretation of Islam, and Pan-Africanist with a "Moroccan" cultural base. Third, and important here, the Ahmadiyya Movement in Islam was heterodox, multi-racial, and politically mixed—the Ahmadis were advocates of both Pan-Islam and Indian nationalism. Ahmadis knew that the Garvey movement was sympathetic to both of these issues; they saw the parallels between the two movements and Pan-Africanism; and to a certain extent they identified with black people as fellow victims of European colonization and imperialism.

Pan-Islam was not a new issue for Marcus Garvey or for the UNIA. In Chapter 3, we examined Garvey's relationship with Duse Mohammed Ali, the Egyptian journalist who was also an advocate of this principle, as well as of Egyptian nationalism and Pan-African business ventures. He may have influenced Garvey to allow Sadiq to give the aforementioned lectures at the UNIA meeting in Detroit in 1923.[83]

Some people in the UNIA were undoubtedly familiar with the issue of Indian nationalism prior to any contact with the Ahmadis. On February 11, 1922, Ganesh Rao sent a letter to the editor of the *Negro World*, which dealt with this issue in the context of the internationalist perspective:

> I am sailing from that distant charming land of perpetual sunshine—India. I am one of those millions that are being oppressed by the imperialistic English government. My interest, my responsibility, my duty, has thus impelled me to study the tragic tales of other oppressed peoples, e.g., the Negro, and his

future. From my humble study so far I have confidently felt that the UNIA is doing the real work for the uplift of the Negro, and the U stands for, in word as in action—Universal. . . . India is in her birth-throes; she soon shall be free. Ethiopia, self conscious, is working for her independent and unhindered progress. Peace shall not dawn on this world until Asia and Africa and their ancient peoples are free and enjoy all human rights. Oppressed peoples of the world, unite. Lose no time![84]

In this context, in 1923 some of Sadiq's articles in *The Moslem Sunrise* took on a new militant internationalist tone, suggesting that Islam and the Arabic language could facilitate the primary political goal of Garveyism, the worldwide unification of all people of African descent. The basic message here was that Islam could be used to legitimize the internationalist perspective—a political end—and to mobilize the Garveyites and other African Americans for this political goal. In this situation Islam would, in effect, function as "political religion." Sadiq's article "Crescent or Cross?" was addressed specifically to the UNIA and indicated that Sadiq was no longer concealing his anger and bitterness toward Christianity and the Western world. He suggested that Garvey expand his motto of "One God, One Aim, One Destiny" to include "One language which would be Arabic." Finally, Sadiq mentioned that "all the white powers fear Mohammedanism" and that black people could find millions of "valuable [multiracial] allies" among the Muslims in China, Arabia, Afghanistan, Turkey, Persia, and India.[85]

This militant internationalist tone continued in another short piece.

My Dear American Negro . . . the Christian profiteers brought you out of your native lands of Africa and in Christianizing you made you forsake the religion and language of your forefathers—which were Islam and Arabic. You have experienced Christianity for so many years and it has proved to be no good. It is a failure. Christianity cannot bring real brotherhood to the nations. Now leave it alone. And join Islam, the real faith of Universal Brotherhood which at once does away with all distinctions of race, color and creed.[86]

The Nation of Islam used this kind of propaganda, which raised issues of signification and identity, to attract thousands of black converts in the 1930s. Such propaganda aimed to instill bitter resentment toward the white race that would result in complete rejection of Christianity and white culture. Black people influenced by this propaganda often converted to Islam, which they believed was the religion of their ancestors before slavery. Apparently through their connection with Garvey's global Pan-Africanist perspective, the Ahmadis had begun to acquire a keen understanding of the psychology of the ordinary black person that enabled them to connect Islam with Pan-Africanism and race pride and to create programs that they believed reflected the real situation of black people in America in the 1920s.[87] At the same time, although the Ahmad-iyya movement was indigenous to India, it had missions in Nigeria, Ghana, and the Ivory Coast in the 1920s. Thus, its global perspective was as expansive as Garvey's and almost as radical in its strategies for the liberation of people of color.

Garveyism and the internationalist perspective, however, were of no interest to the Ahmadiyya Movement in Islam during the years of the UNIA's decline. Unfortunately, we do not know how the Ahmadiyya movement reacted to Garvey's downfall. *The Moslem Sunrise* suspended publication from 1924 to 1930—the years of Garvey's trial, imprisonment, and deportation—probably due to financial difficulties. Also, since the Ahmadis had drawn some of their American converts and leaders from the ranks of the UNIA, it is probable that there was a shortage of new members and of vital services. Perhaps the Ahmadiyya movement saw the handwriting on the wall—that the mid-1920s saw the suppression of radicalism in the United States and that foreign leaders of radical move-ments were in particular danger of deportation. Garvey's ordeal was a lesson for all alien leaders in the 1920s.[88]

In September 1923, Mufti Muhammad Sadiq concluded his work in America and returned to India, where he was reunited with his wife and children after years of separation. His successor, Maulvi Muhammad Din, had been headmaster of a high school in India and editor of the Ahmadi journal *The Review of Religions*. A few months before his departure, Sadiq enthusiastically presented Din to the readers of *The Moslem Sunrise*. He wrote:

> He has been living at the headquarters of the Ahmadia movement and studying and practicing the sacred knowledge under the direction of the Promised Messiah and his successors for more than twenty years.[89]

During his three years in America, Mufti Muhammad Sadiq converted over seven hundred Americans to Islam. His impact on American religion during this period, however, cannot be adequately measured by numbers: he provided the first model of multi-racial community experience for African-American Muslims, and the Ahmadiyya community published the first Muslim newspaper and the first Quran in English in America—and most of the Islamic literature that would be available to African-American Muslims until the 1960s. Although Sadiq's bitter personal expe-riences in the United States led him to place the Muslim community in a defensive and alienated position, he was still determined to make Islam a permanent part of the American cultural fabric. In spite of his antipathy for "the West," Sadiq's independent spirit, his original ecumenical goal, his boundless energy, his appetite for new endeavors, his fierce pursuit of success, and his passion for social justice were also American qualities.

The American Muslim community in the 1920s likewise embodied these American qualities, although due to its religious outsidership and peculiarity, it was never incorporated into the mainstream culture. This paradox means that the assimilation/melting pot model in American history must be bracketed in the case of American Islam. In fact, the history of the Ahmadiyya Movement in Islam lends credence to R. Laurence Moore's work on religious outsidership, which emphasizes the importance of "unstable pluralism," "conflict," "contention," and "creation of a consciousness of difference" in American religious history. The social fact of this peculiar religious outsider group points to Moore's reading of Will Herberg that "American society is most dynamic when it encourages people to preserve . . . their genuine religious peculiarities."[90] In other words, the mainstream viewpoint represented only one way of being American and not necessarily the most vital way.

In the 1920s, the Ahmadiyya Movement in Islam had offered African Americans a multi-racial Muslim identity which involved the signification of Indian cultural and political elements with aspects of Pan-Africanist identity. In this context, African-American converts were trained by Indian teachers from the East who had a global agenda that was separate and different from the Moroccan emphasis of the Moorish Science Temple of America. Thus African-American Muslims were not united but had different visions of Islamic identity and signification that involved different syntheses of religion, politics, and culture. These different visions of signification and identity multiplied in the 1930s and contributed to several decades of transition in the multi-racial mission of the Ahmadiyya Movement in Islam.

YEARS OF TRANSITION: 1930–1950

The two decades between 1930 and 1950 were years of transition for the Ahmadiyya mission to America. First, during these years the Ahmadiyya movement came to terms with its failure to achieve its initial objective in the United States in the 1920s, which was to bring about a permanent departure from the historic patterns of racism and ethnic separation that existed among Muslims in America and to create a widespread multiracial movement in the United States. Second, the movement of the Indian missionaries was challenged slightly by the black nationalist missions of the Moorish Science Temple of America and the Nation of Islam, which will be discussed in the next chapter. Although the latter group displaced the Ahmadiyya movement as the most prominent and popular Islamic movement among black Americans in the 1950s, in the 1930s and 1940s it was still a private and obscure religious movement with a small following. Also Shaykh Daoud's Sunni Islamic Mission of America was also influential among some blacks on the east coast during this period. Third, in light of these developments, the Ahmadiyya movement began to broaden its agenda to appeal to a multicultural learned audience interested in comparative religions. At the same time, the internationalist identity of American Ahmadis broadened as their movement focused on the partition of India and the establishment of Pakistan, the creation of a Jewish homeland in Palestine, and communism in the Muslim world in the late 1940s and the 1950s. Although their "jihad of words" continued and rhetoric about racial equality in America remained an important aspect of their mission, the Ahmadis toned down their former radical emphasis on global Pan-Islamic coalitions to resist Western imperialism. Perhaps this was a wise transition in light of the FBI's campaign to break up American Muslim groups on suspicion of sedition. In spite of these reservations, the Ahmadiyya remained one of the most important Muslim groups in America, with the majority of the converts in the black communities during this period.

The *Chicago Herald Examiner* reported that the Ahmadiyya community in Chicago had its first meeting in three years on November 3, 1929 in order to plan for a new mosque. *The Moslem Sunrise,* which had ceased publication in 1924, resumed its work in 1930. At that time, the Ahmadiyya mission moved its headquarters from South Wabash Avenue to East Congress Street in Chicago. Sufi Mutiur Rahman Bengalee was the new Ahmadi missionary and the editor of *The Moslem Sunrise.*[91] Mufti Muhammad Sadiq's immediate successor, Maulvi Muhammad, had not been politically astute. The political consciousness of the Ahmadiyya movement in America resumed, however, under the leadership of Sufi Bengalee. Bengalee resumed the Ahmadiyya tradition of giving public lectures on Islam. In 1929 and 1930 he gave more than seventy of these talks to groups of "cultured people," a target group for the Ahmadiyya missionary efforts in the 1930s. Some of these presentations were facilitated by the multiracial Fellowship of Faiths (an ecumenical organization). They were often delivered to large audiences that ranged from 500 to 2500 people, in the Chicago Temple, the First Congregational Church, the Sinai Temple Men's Club, and the People's Church.[92]

Bengalee also gave several talks on the life of Muhammad at Northwestern University and the University of Chicago. Martin Sprengling, Professor of Semitic Languages and Literature at the University of Chicago, and Charles Braden, Professor of Comparative Religion at Northwestern University, also gave oral presentations on these occasions. During this same period, Bengalee was invited by the Liberal Science Institute of Chicago to take part in a series of debates on comparative religion.[93]

Some of these events were covered by important Chicago newspapers such as *The Chicago Daily Tribune* and *The Chicago Daily News.* The Ahmadiyya movement attributed this publicity to "their broadening character and their emphasis upon human understanding." Although such presentations carried a universalist emphasis, the Ahmadiyya movement had not forgotten the issue of race prejudice. Bengalee continued to focus on the civil rights of African Americans. Thus the Ahmadiyya movement resumed its emphasis on black identity with a new twist that toned down the radical rhetoric of the 1920s and appealed to mainstream multi-racial audiences. In a public lecture at the People's Church, Bengalee addressed the issue of racism in the United States:

> Treat the colored people in a truly democratic spirit. Do not shut the doors of your churches, hotels, schools, and homes against them. Let them enjoy all the privileges which you possess. If they are poor, help them. If they are backward, uplift them, but for heaven's sake, do not despise them.[94]

Bengalee was originally from Bengal, India. He had studied at the University of Calcutta and the University of Punjab, where he earned a master's degree in 1927. Since his first days as an Ahmadi missionary in America in August 1928, he had attracted the attention of the World Fellowship of Faiths, which, as was mentioned earlier, sponsored numerous Ahmadiyya programs in the late 1920s and the 1930s. One of the most outstanding of these programs was entitled "How Can We Overcome Color and Race Prejudice?" This discussion drew more than 2,000 people to the Washington Boulevard Temple in Chicago in November 1931. The speakers included representatives of several religions and races. The most prominent speakers were the Dean of the University of Chicago and the attorney Clarence Darrow, who began the forum by stating that Christianity was not going to overcome racism in the United States. The Christian ministers who were present agreed with him.[95]

In another conference on the same topic on September 1, 1935, Bengalee introduced a black Ahmadi convert, Omar Khan, and a white Muslim, Muhammad Ahmad, who spoke on the virtues of Islam as regards race relations. Charles F. Weller, the head of the World Fellowship of Faiths, gave a short presentation on this occasion. Harlan Tarbell, a Chicago-area psychologist, wrote an article on the meeting in *The Moslem Sunrise*.[96]

The final noteworthy event for the Ahmadiyya movement in the 1930s was its participation in the World Fellowship of Faiths Convention in August and September 1932. This meeting opened in Chicago with a cabled message from Hazrat Mirza Bashir-ud-Din Mahmud Ahmad, the head of the Ahmadiyya movement. Chaudhry Zafarulla Khan, a lawyer and the former president of the All-India Muslim League, gave a presentation entitled "Islam, Promoting World Unity, Peace and Progress," and M. Yousuf Khan and Bengalee of the Ahmadiyya movement gave speeches on racial prejudice and world problems.[97]

Although the event was impressive, it may have posed a minor problem for the African-American identity of black Ahmadis, for it showed that their movement's focus periodically changed, leaving America's interest

New converts to the Ahmadiyya movement. From *The Moslem Sunrise.* Used by permission of the Ahmadiyya Movement in Islam, Inc., USA.

behind as an international agenda developed. In this context, the issue of African-American Ahmadi identity was sometimes obscured by the tension between the political and cultural concerns of the East and the West. For although African-American Ahmadis were part of a religious organization with an East Indian political and cultural agenda, they were at the same time part of the black community in America, which had its own specific political and cultural concerns.

By 1940, the Ahmadiyya movement had almost two million followers worldwide and somewhere between 5,000 and 10,000 members in the United States. Their primary missions in America were located in Chicago, Cleveland, Kansas City (Missouri), Washington, D.C., and Pittsburgh. The Ahmadi missionaries were beginning to see signs that their movement's twenty years of work in America had begun to pay off in their converts' close adherence to the rituals and duties of Islam. The Chicago community was particularly impressive in its adherence to the fast during the month of Ramadan and in its celebration of Id al-Adha in 1940. Although the Ahmadiyya was a multi-racial community, the majority of its American converts were black, and it was one of the oldest and most important Muslim organizations among black Americans in the 1930s and 1940s. Wali Akram was noteworthy among the African Americans who were involved in and influenced by the Ahmadiyya community during this period. Akram was the leader of the Ahmadis in Cleveland from 1934 to

1937. He started a ten-year plan for savings for that community. In the 1940s, Akram's work resulted in there being 200 people in the Cleveland community. Although the community was still dominated by African Americans, there were frequent inter-ethnic and inter-racial marriages among these Ahmadis. Yusef Khan, an Ahmadi teacher, directed the education of an African-American splinter group from the Moorish Science Temple in Pittsburgh in early 1930s. Although most of this group abandoned Khan by 1935, they later became the nucleus of the first mosque of Pittsburgh in 1945 and continued to be guided "by the fundamentals of Islam given in the classes by Dr. Khan."[98]

The Moslem Sunrise continued to cover the racial situation in the United States during the 1940s and 1950s. In 1943, the magazine discussed the Detroit race riots which had occurred in that year. It cited bad housing, overcrowding in public facilities, the presence of "thousands of newcomers," and racism as the underlying causes of the unrest. Ultimately, the Ahmadis condemned the riots, lamenting that

the Detroit riots have smeared a dark blot on this country's good name. . . . Now the news goes all over the world, to North Africa, among the dark skinned peoples of India and the South Pacific Islands, among the yellow-skinned peoples of Malaya, Indochina, Thailand, China and Korea, that black-skinned people are killing and being killed by white-skinned people in free America.[99]

Segregation in the Protestant churches in the United States was one of the focal points of The Moslem Sunrise during these years. In "Segregation in the Christian Churches," the Ahmadi editors used information from the Christian Century (April 14, 1948) to show that the churches were "the most segregated institutions in America." To support their case, they cited statistics indicating that less than one half of one percent of the black Protestants in America worshiped in integrated churches. In the mid-1950s, the editors of The Muslim Sunrise (the journal changed the spelling of its name in the 1950s) expressed disappointment that most of the recent changes in the race situation in America had occurred outside the Christian churches and that in some cases those effecting these changes had to deal with direct opposition from the Christian clergy. The editors published a survey of 13,597 predominantly white Presbyterian, Unitarian, Lutheran, and Congregational churches which showed that only 1,331 of them had some nonwhite members. They were shocked to learn that segregation was prevalent in both the Northern and Southern churches. Finally, The Muslim Sunrise printed an excerpt from Newsweek which estimated that most of the delegates to the World Council of Churches in 1954 would return home to segregated churches.[100]

The Ahmadis did not limit their examination of racism in Christianity to the churches in the United States. They noted that color prejudice was also a problem in the Christian missions in Africa. One writer summarized the African situation by declaring that "the white missionary has no true brotherhood to offer the negro except at best those of teacher with taught, master with servant, grown man with child." He attributed the large number of independent churches in Africa to the fact that the Africans resented white control in their religious life. In his opinion, even the government officials treated the Africans better than the missionaries did.[101]

Finally, the Ahmadiyya movement's universalist emphasis led its leaders to present Islam as a better worldwide religion for blacks than Christianity. Although it was hardly the case, the Ahmadis stated that Islam had abolished racism and caste and color prejudice among its own people and that it could help to solve America's race problems. And there were more black Ahmadi leaders. The most prominent of them in the 1940s was Omar Cleveland, who published several articles on the brotherhood and culture of Islam in *The Muslim Sunrise*. Cleveland had been raised in the Methodist Episcopal Church, but he became attracted to the "simplicity of Islam" and the earnestness of its followers. In "The Democracy of Islam," he commented on race relations in the religion:

> Across the threshold of the mosque, in the fold of Islam, all are held to be equal. No distinction is made between men, regardless of race, class or position. The prince and the pauper meet on common ground. Here the irony of fate is refuted. The inequality of wealth and opportunity, which makes life so cruel ceases. All are children of Allah.[102]

The late 1940s brought a dramatic shift in the character and strategy of some segments of the Ahmadiyya movement, as the political situation in Pakistan demanded that the movement focus some of its primary resources there. During this period, British rule ended, and India achieved independence. When they left India, however, the nation was partitioned along religious lines. Hindus and Sikhs resided in the new India, and Muslims took up residence in the newly created "Islamic Republic of Pakistan." These developments ultimately resulted in the relocation and the persecution of the entire Ahmadiyya community in the Punjab.[103]

The date for the partition plan was made public in June 1947. In August 1947 100,000 Muslims were massacred in Patiala, a Sikh state in East Punjab. By the end of the summer, the violence against the Islamic community had escalated to the point that 650,000 Muslims were missing in East Punjab and more than 5 million Muslims were forced to migrate to Pakistan. By 1948, the population of Pakistan was 70 million people, of whom three quarters were Muslims.[104]

The Ahmadiyya community made Rabwah in Islamic Pakistan its new headquarters. However, the orthodox Islamic majority in Pakistan considered the movement to be a heretical form of Islam because of its belief that prophethood did not end with Muhammad but rather continued in the person of Ghulam Ahmad, the founder of the movement. In 1953, the mass persecution of the Ahmadis began when orthodox scholars demanded that the Pakistani government brand the Ahmadis as a "non-Muslim minority." This situation signaled a stormy future for the Ahmadiyya movement in the Islamic theocracy of Pakistan.[105]

The Jewish homeland in Palestine was another international concern for the Ahmadiyya press in the United States during the late 1940s and the 1950s. Sufi Bengalee, the Ahmadi missionary in Chicago, believed that the British government had reneged on its promise to the Muslims when it founded a homeland for the Jews in Palestine. He cited the fact that Palestine was also a holy land for the Muslims and that the British had promised to establish an Arab state there in return for the support that they received from the Muslims against Turkey in 1915.[106]

The Palestine issue reflected the Ahmadis' identification with the concerns of the worldwide community of Islam, which were sometimes as significant for their movement as the race problem in the United States. In the 1950s, they supported United Nations resolutions regarding Arab refugees in Israel which called for their repatriation and indemnification and the internationalization of Israel. A *Muslim Sunrise* editorial even addressed the problem of racism against Asian and African Jews in Israel by focusing on a group of Indian Jews who had moved to Israel and had subsequently returned to India because of the racist treatment that they had received from the European Jews there.[107]

A final international issue faced the Ahmadiyya movement. The question of communism in the Islamic countries of the Middle East and North Africa was a constant topic of discussion in *The Muslim Sunrise* during the 1950s. The Ahmadiyya movement opposed communism because they believed that it espoused atheism and limited religious and political freedom. In the 1950s, however, the Soviet Union sought to create revolutions in several Islamic countries of the Middle East and North Africa: Iran, Egypt, Tunisia, Algeria, and Morocco. In response to this situation, *The Muslim Sunrise* printed excerpts from an address entitled "Democracy's First Line of Defense: Islam" by Congressman John T. Wood of Idaho to the House of Representatives in February 1952. Congressman Wood suggested that the "resource-rich" Islamic countries of the Middle East, the Far East, and North Africa could form "a buffer zone against communism" and that Christians and Muslims should "collaborate to stop atheistic communism dead in its tracks." Then in 1953, *The Muslim Sunrise* published excerpts from a speech by Stephen Penrose, the president of the American University in Beirut, which also emphasized the importance of friendly relations between the United States and the Islamic countries in the Middle East for the economic and political stability of the Western world.[108]

YEARS OF CHALLENGES AND
CONSOLIDATION: 1950s–1990s

The years between the 1950s and the 1990s were a dynamic period of challenges and consolidation for the Ahmadiyya Movement in Islam. Until the mid-1950s, the Ahmadiyya was arguably the most influential community in African-American Islam. Then the dramatic success of the Nation of Islam's missionary work in the prisons and its access to the media catapulted this racial-separatist faction of Islam to a predominant position in black America. In the early 1960s, the position of the Ahmadiyya community among African Americans was challenged again by the influence of a new wave of Muslim immigrants from the Middle East who attempted to propagate Sunni Islam among black Americans.

In light of the changes in the position of the Ahmadiyya community among black Americans that resulted from these challenges, a superficial reading of the source materials during this period could lead to its dismissal as a failed movement in America after 1950. In fact, these challenges led to a consolidation of the Ahmadiyya movement's multi-racial agenda among the African-American members who remained in its ranks. They were an extraordinary group of dedicated Muslims who profoundly influenced Islam in America, educating the numerous African Americans who passed through their ranks to become members of other Muslim communities. Also, as we shall see in Chapter 6, the Lahore branch of the Ahmadiyya movement continued to cultivate the goal of multi-racial Islam among black Americans in the 1960s, working behind the scenes to influence two important leaders of the Nation of Islam: Elijah Muhammad and Warith Deen Mohammed. Thus, the Ahmadiyya movement played a pivotal role in keeping the option of multi-racial Islam alive in black America until the 1960s, when African American interest and participation in Sunni Islam challenged its position and came to provide the most popular multi-racial community experience in the religion.

Before discussing these challenges, it is important to note that in the 1950s, many African Americans—most notably, black jazz musicians—converted to Islam and came to dominate the Ahmadiyya community. Beverly Aminah McCloud writes about these developments:

> The membership of the Ahmadiyya community during the years 1917–1960 was predominantly African American. The "mission houses" (mosque-activity centers) were headed by African Americans in African-American areas of various cities. A significant number of African-American jazz musicians were members of this community . . . these musicians were major propagators of Islam in the world of jazz even though the subject of music was often a source of debate with the subcontinent Ahmadis. Some even developed their own jargon—a unique blend of bebop and Arabic. There also developed a merchant class of men in the community (comprised mainly of

vendors) due to lack of opportunities for formal education. Self employment became a way to earn a living while at the same time maintaining the freedom to propagate Islam, and to say prayer five times daily and the Jumah prayer on Friday with ease.[109]

The numerous jazz musicians who were associated with the Ahmadiyya movement in the 1950s included Ahmad Jamal in Chicago; Yusef Lateef in Detroit and New York City; Art Blakey; Fard Daleel, a trumpeter in New York City; Nuh Alahi, a drummer in Cincinnati who later became a vice-president for the Ahmadiyya community in Los Angeles; McCoy Tyner; Sahib Shihab; and the vocalist Dakota Staton (who changed her name to Aliya Rabia) and her husband Talib Daoud in Philadelphia.[110]

C. O. Simpkins explains the dynamic influence that the Ahmadiyya movement had on black jazz musicians, such as saxophonist John Coltrane, during the 1950s and beyond:

> Islam was a force which directly opposed the deterioration of the mind and body through either spiritual or physical deterrents. Among musicians the religion began to grow when Art Blakey, Talib Daoud, Yusef Lateef, Ahmad Jamal, Sahib Shihab and other musicians raised money to bring Moslem teachers of the Ahmadiyya movement from Pakistan to the United States to show musicians the way. . . . Many musicians were searching for a foundation in life. Islam taught that one should keep his body clean and healthy. It elevated the mind from the morass of American oppression and myths about Blacks.
>
> When singer Aliyah Rabia (Dakota Staton) and her husband, drummer Talib Daoud, moved to Philadelphia, the religion began to blossom there. Other groups such as the Moorish-Americans, and Elijah Muhammad's Muslims were also in Philadelphia but none was as popular as the Ahmadiyya movement. An advanced piano player, Hasan was a friend of John's [Coltrane]. They would discuss Islam as well as exchange musical ideas. John's exposure to Islam may have played a role in his struggle with drugs.
>
> In Philadelphia, Islam was a positive force. . . . Nasseridine, a drummer loved John. Nasseridine had progressed greatly in the religion, studying it from a theoretical as well as from a spiritual basis. He was advanced musically, spiritually, and intellectually. . . . He was a devout Moslem who carried his prayer rug wherever he went, and prayed dutifully five times a day, regardless of where he was. While praying nothing distracted him. Friends would pass by, and he wouldn't see them, sometimes seeming to look right through them.
>
> One night he stayed up praying continuously at John's house. The next day on the way to his sister's house, he stopped to pray under a tree. Two policemen came by and saw him kneeling nearby motionless. . . . An argument ensued. According to the police, Nasseridine either threatened them with scissors or began throwing rocks. They beat him savagely. He spent four days in the hospital and died on the last day. Nasseridine's loss sent a shudder through the music community. John, who loved Nasseridine, was hurt. . . .

McCoy [Tyner] was a devoted and faithful Moslem. He entered the religion when he was seventeen, the year that he first met John and Naima, as well as his wife Aisha, whom Naima had known since she was a small child. Aisha encouraged McCoy to enter the faith. He changed his name to Sulieman Saud. Uniquely, Saud was a man whose personal beliefs were in complete agreement with his personal practices, regarding family, friends, acquaintances and the Creator. John considered him an anchor that gave strength. For him Saud was a spiritual as well a musical influence.[111]

The Dayton, Ohio community was another important indication of the consolidation of African Americans in the Ahmadiyya movement. This community was almost one hundred percent black in the 1950s, and African Americans planned, funded, and built the Ahmadi mosque there in 1955. This was probably the first mosque built in America exclusively by African-American converts. Also in Ohio, Wali Akram, a black Ahmadi, led another African-American Muslim community that flourished in Cleveland in the 1950s. This mosque of more than two hundred Ahmadis maintained extensive records of its members and was noted for its "interethnic marriages." The Ahmadiyya movement also shaped the religious ideas of an African-American group of Sunni Muslims in Lincoln Heights, Ohio during these years.[112]

Thus, a dynamic group of African-American Ahmadi leaders developed in the 1950s, including Mursil Shafeek, president of the Dayton community, who was fluent in Arabic, though limited in formal education; Muhammad Sadiq, a jazz trombone player in the 1940s who became president of the New York City and New Jersey communities; Bashir Afzal, a New York City leader in the 1950s who died a few years ago; and Rashied Ahmed, who went to Pakistan to prepare for missionary work in the late 1940s and became an important Ahmadi figure in St. Louis, Chicago, Milwaukee, and New York in the 1950s.[113]

However, as the 1950s progressed, gradually a split occurred in the Ahmadiyya movement as many black people passed through its ranks because they did not want to seriously study Islam and became disenchanted with its multi-racial agenda. Some of these African Americans went to Sunni groups because they wanted to Arabize their identities to escape the stigma of their blackness. Others went to the Nation of Islam because they were attracted to its nationalist agenda.[114]

Aminah Beverly McCloud provides a different reading of this split in the Ahmadiyya community:

As the twentieth century progressed, the direct personal influence of the Ahmadi missionaries declined. Early members left the movement for a variety of reasons. Dissension arose due to the fact the African Americans were never appointed as missionaries. The title of shaykh acknowledged their accomplishments in Islamic studies, but did not give them any authority over communities. Surviving original members of this community complained that the effects of colonialism also came with the missionaries, who insisted on Indian customs and interpretations, rather than seeing African American culture as having something to offer American Islam. Islamic study also raised questions over the Ahmadi notion of prophethood, prompting others to leave the community.[115]

In spite of these different interpretations of this split, the transformations of the Nation of Islam into a mainstream Muslim movement among African Americans in the 1950s and 1960s certainly had a lot to do with the challenged positions of the Ahmadiyya movement. According to Rashid Ahmed, a black Ahmadi leader:

> In the mid 1950s, the Nation of Islam grew by leaps and bounds because of its conversions in the prisons. Working in the bakery, grocery store, and fisheries after they got out, kept the Nation of Islam members out of the prisons. The Nation of Islam gave the prisoners the color consciousness that they wanted and the regimentation. But as a religion they didn't have that at all. By the late 1950s, the Nation of Islam was getting more converts than we were. *Life Magazine,* the media, built the Nation of Islam up with white man as a devil doctrine. The media made them; they were not made because of their teachings.[116]

Muzaffar Ahmad Zafr also emphasized the role of the media in the transformation of the Nation of Islam and the new challenges to the Ahmadiyya community: "The American press or media found it more controversial to highlight Elijah Muhammad rather than the Ahmadis who were conducting a multi-racial movement that America was not ready to deal with."[117]

In the 1960s, the Ahmadiyya movement faced another challenge to its position among African Americans—from a new wave of immigrant Muslims in the United States. McCloud sketches the impact that these immigrants had on black American Islam:

> During the 1960s the Oriental Exclusion Act was repealed and large numbers of foreign Muslims began to immigrate to the United States. In 1963 the Muslim Students Association was organized by students at the University of Illinois and quickly spread to campuses all over the United States. This organization which publishes several magazines and disseminates Islamic literature was also a major influence on African American Muslim communities. Foreign Muslim students were frequent visitors in these communities sometimes providing classes in various Islamic disciplines. . . . The 1960s also witnessed a surge in the actual building of masjid in the United States.
> During this time, the embassies of several Muslim countries such as Saudi Arabia, Pakistan, Egypt, Libya, and the Sudan made available free copies of

Yusef Ali's translation of the Holy Quran and vast amounts of Islamic literature and pamphlets to the American public, a large number of African American communities also had English-speaking Egyptian or Pakistani imams in
residence and had frequent visits from traveling jama'ats (groups or communities of educators) more popularly known as tablighi jama'ats. . . . It is
significant . . . to recognize that the literature that made its way to the African
American communities was primarily from Pakistan and Egypt.[118]

Thus, a multi-faceted mosaic of Islamic identities and communities
flourished among African-American Muslims in the 1960s, as a result of
the black nationalist significations of the Nation of Islam and the various
foreign ethnic significations of this new wave of Muslim immigrants. In
the context of this "explosion of Muslim communities in the United States"
and the competition between various versions of Islamic identities that
ensued, the multi-racial Ahmadiyya movement continued to offer a stable
and politically noncontroversial option to its African-American converts.
Although its predominance was challenged by the ascendancy of other
communities, its black membership was consolidated as new African-
American converts turned to the Ahmadis as a pathway or bridge between
the various black nationalist and foreign ethnic significations that influenced African Americans in Muslim America. A key to the Ahmadiyya's
appeal to a diminished but significant segment of the African-American
Muslim community was its emphasis on the study of Islam over and
against some of the overt political concerns in the black nationalist and
immigrant Muslim communities. Perhaps the following personal religious portrait of Maneer Hamid may serve as a paradigm for understanding how and why some African-American Muslim converts continued to
choose the religious path of the Ahmadiyya movement in spite of attraction to and tensions from other more politically or nationally based
significations of Islamic identity in the 1950s and 1960s:

> My first introduction was around 1954 or 1955. My sister was in the singing
> group called the Capris. She met Len Hope, and he was a Sunni Muslim and a
> saxophone player who was very well known and had several albums out. He
> would wear a turban and say "a salaam alaikam." He had some moral quali-
> ties the other musicians didn't have. I became interested and started to read as
> much literature as I could. I was fifteen years old. I met a friend. Instead of
> hustling money, he gave me a book to read, *Our Promised Messiah*. He was
> having a meeting in his house in West Philadelphia on Hobart Avenue. The
> Ahmadi missionaries, Nur Haq-Anwar and Muhammad Sadiq were teaching
> a bunch of brothers in Philadelphia. The rituals made an impression on me so
> that when I went home I decided to become Muslim. But I hesitated.
>
> In Washington, D.C., I was stationed on Andrews Air Force Base. Khalil
> Ahmad Nasir, the Ahmadi missionary, invited me to come out for Friday
> Jumah, 1955—I was sixteen. I converted then. When I got to the mosque in

Washington, D.C., Islam in America was dominated by African Americans—thirty people in D.C. were Ahmadiyya—twenty-five were black. I was fortunate to hook up with some brothers. Dr. Bashiruddin Usma, he was going to Howard University at that time studying to be a dentist. He introduced me to E. Franklin Frazier. At that time the Sunni mosque on Massachusetts Avenue was about to open up.

I was still attached to the U.S. Service and I really wasn't practicing Islam as it was taught in the Quran. One of my friends who was Sunni in the service and a black African, Ali, discouraged me from the Ahmadiyya. I hesitated to sign the Baiyat. But the more I read the literature I saw that what he was saying wasn't true. But our group was the only group that was not saying negative things about the other groups in its literature. I was raised Baptist. I didn't pursue being a Sunni anymore.

In 1956, I got an assignment to go overseas to Japan. My roommate in the service had gotten his orders the next day to go to Turkey. We switched. So I went to Turkey to experience a Muslim country. I was stationed in Turkey for three years in the southern part, a small town about 3,000 people. I was able to blend in and practice my Islam. When my time in the service was up, they sent me to Greece for a while—six months; North Africa, Libya—six months.

They let me out in 1960. I went back to the D.C. Mosque on 2141 Leroy Place. I was going to study to be a missionary, but I was an amateur musician. I was caught sneaking out of the mosque to gig in the bar. The rigidity didn't work out.

In 1961, I went back to Philadelphia. The largest group was Elijah Muhammad's group. The most militant Muslims were on the east coast. We didn't give into negativism with them. We just remained aloof from them. Most of the people in Ahmadiyya were all from the 1920s, 1930s. They were not involved in nationalism. Loyal to America. But I was younger, involved in the Black Panthers and all that nationalism. We like to say that Elijah Muhammad was influenced by Mufti Muhammad Sadiq. There is a photograph that exists of Elijah Muhammad and Mufti Muhammad Sadiq sitting together on the stage with Noble Drew Ali and Marcus Garvey.

Bilal Sunni Ali played with Gil Scott Heron, saxophonist and flutist, and was with Panther 21 in New York when they got busted. He belonged with the Ahmadiyya movement along with me. The Ahmadiyya leaders didn't know about this. No one brought the nationalists to the meetings. We had one foot in that world and one foot in Islam. Other Muslim Sunnis were doing it, straddling the line. A lot of jazz musicians were Muslims. Charlie Parker, they said, was Muslim—Abdul Karim. Out there in the big world, a lot of people were Muslims. In the 1920s, 1930s, to be Muslim allowed you to pose as an Egyptian—a foreigner. You could avoid the segregation.

In the 1960s, African-American heritage though—it was really a unique time. A lot of people dressed like Muslims. There was really no conflict because Malcolm was moving in the same direction as Rap Brown. A lot of people were inclined toward Islam but black pride was the main thing. These were the most exciting days for Islam in America. A lot of closeness and brotherhood as far as the street was concerned.

Brothers started going overseas to train in Islam, Egypt, Saudi Arabia, etc. A lot of people were getting deeper in the religion. The relationships between the Nation of Islam and Ahmadiyya were behind the scenes with individual members. But most of the brothers acknowledged that their introduction came from the Ahmadiyya movement. Why should I claim to be an Ahmadi and be ostracized in Islam? A lot of brothers did not want this strike against them. The brotherhood thing glued and held us together—all the Muslims.

All the mosques were run by militant imams in the 1960s. Brothers who were carrying a piece. Everybody had a gun.

Now there's more separatism among the Muslims than there was in my time coming up. When the foreigners came over, they introduced the separatism. In their country they had this. When Wallace Muhammad started going overseas, Wallace's leaning was toward the people in the East. We needed a stamp of approval. So brothers hesitated in learning about Islam because of these people and their foreign tongues in Arabic. End of the seventies, they came over to revive us. But in the Ahmadiyya movement we never had that problem. We grew African American through propagation, missionary work.[119]

In the 1970s and 1980s, the Ahmadiyya Movement in Islam continued to attract a small but significant number of African-American converts to its community. During this period, the black Ahmadis' mentoring relationships behind the scenes continued, as did their ideological tensions with African-American Muslims who were members of racial-separatist communities. However, at a time when issues of multiculturalism and diversity and assumptions of ethnic and racial superiority were often at odds with one another and threatened to divide segments of African-American and immigrant Muslim communities in the United States, the long-term impact of the Ahmadiyya mission was evident as the community remained the most effective model of multi-racial community experience in American Islam. These developments and trends were central to the signification of African-American Muslim identity that Dhul Waqar Yacub constructed in the context of the Ahmadiyya community in the 1970s, 1980s, and 1990s. His fascinating personal religious history follows. It offers a composite portrait of the kind of intellectually and spiritually sophisticated African Americans who continued to convert to the Ahmadiyya Movement in Islam during this period:

My conversion began in 1969. I was going to college in Troy, Ohio, picked up *The Philosophy of the Teachings of Islam* in Dayton. The address of the mosque was in the book. I went to the mosque. I was raised Roman Catholic. I wasn't interested in joining at the time.

Ahmadi missionaries came to my house in Troy. After they left, it was impressed in my mind that I should go a step further. My wife at this time used to be a member of the Nation of Islam. When I joined the Ahmadiyya movement, we had to reconcile a lot of things from the Nation of Islam by reading the Holy Quran. We understood that the philosophy that Elijah Muhammad taught was not the "true Islam." We found that the Islam that he was teaching was designed by his own mind for the lost sheep in the West. His philosophy was that African Americans were at such a low spiritual state that they could not accept Islam straight but had to go through steps. The universal concept of Islam was taught by the Ahmadiyya movement. These things allowed my wife to gain some perspective.

I performed the Hajj in 1973, 1974. By performing the Hajj, it was difficult to come back to America and focus on Islam only for a specific group of people. When I accepted Islam, I didn't completely accept the Ahmadiyya movement. It was not until the Hajj that I began to accept what I was as an Ahmadi. On the tour we were in, there were four Ahmadis-including Yusef Lateef and his wife. We encountered these Muslims from New York and Philadelphia who were black, some Russian Muslims and Muslims from Pakistan. The blacks made me take off the Ahmadi ring because they said that the ring distinguished me from other people on the Hajj. The African Americans were involved not in the Hajj but nationalism. On the Plain of Arafat . . . these brothers were arguing about who knew Betty Shabazz. They were from Dar-al-Islam. It occurred also that they didn't understand the significance of the Hajj. They relied on us to give them insight into the different rites you would perform on the Hajj. We went to Medina. . . . We received an invitation of dinner from a professor who was engaged in a translation of some hadith into English. The questions that African Americans from Dar-al-Islam were asking were childish questions about dress, etc. This was my first encounter with non-Ahmadi Muslims. I found that the Muslims in the Middle East were backwards, had a lot of form, but no substance, leaderless.

I went to Africa in 1980. This brought a different dimension because we have a large Ahmadiyya community there. This was in Ghana. I had the idea of going there to stay. I wanted my children to be educated there because we have a lot of schools. The community was about 500,000. The people were at a very high moral and spiritual state. Everyone knew that the Ahmadis had contributed so much to the health and education of their country. I lived in the state of Ashanti. Kumasi is the capital of the state. The Ahmadi secondary school had a mosque there. There was a coup in 1979. I was there as a technician in a university. So I returned to the United States, 1979–1980.

I used to be in charge of Moral Reformation and Education for the Organization for Young Men under forty. I relocated to Chicago and joined the community. I was the vice-president in Chicago from 1980–1985; financial secretary for six years; president for three years. There were one hundred fifty people in the Chicago Ahmadi community in the 1980s. Fifty African Americans and the rest from Ghana, Pakistan, and India.

There are three hundred people in Chicago now. Recent converts have all reached a point where they were saturated with nationalism and saturated with striking out at the white man, but they still wanted Islam. The Ahmadiyya movement does not have nationalistic goals. Our goals are moral and spiritual in the United States. In the 1990s, more people have been interested because of our activities, building mosques. We have really good relations with the Nation of Islam. One of their writers Kabril Muhammad was at an Arab conference on the finality of prophethood in Chicago, five years ago. Arabs made a statement that they felt the Ahmadis should be killed. We made written rebuttals to this. Kabril Muhammad wrote an article in defense of the Ahmadiyya's right to exist in the United States in *The Final Call.* Minister Louis Farrakhan then received a copy of our five-volume copy of the commentary of the Quran and thanked us.

Ben Chavis had a meeting yesterday with the Ahmadis and Farrakhan in Chicago to formulate a national agenda for the African-American community. Nowadays, the Ahmadiyya community is more involved in the affairs of blacks. Mirza Tahir Ahmad, our khalifa, has said that if black Americans are not saved, America is doomed. He has a plan to present to African-American leaders to help the community. This has been on his agenda for about five years.[120]

The preceding composite religious portrait demonstrates the considerable influence that the Ahmadiyya Movement in Islam continues to have among a certain segment of the African-American Muslim community today. The internationalist identities of its African-American members are extraordinary; they "are probably the most widely traveled"[121] among black American Muslims. Although the Ahmadiyya movement is not attracting as many African-American converts as it did in the past, partly because of the ascendancy of Sunni Islam in the United States in the 1990s, its impact on the history of African-American Islam is significant. It was the first and continues to be the most effective model of a multi-racial community experience for black people in the religion.

But now it is time to turn to the saga of the Nation of Islam, which became a model for racial-separatist identity for African-American Muslims. This religious movement began in the black community of Detroit, Michigan in 1930 with the work of a mysterious street peddler, W. D. Fard.

Chapter 5

MISSIONIZING AND SIGNIFYING

W. D. FARD AND THE EARLY HISTORY OF THE NATION OF ISLAM

I am W. D. Fard and I came from the Holy City of
Mecca. . . . You have not seen me yet in my royal
robes.   —W. D. Fard

Scapularies and rosaries, beads and prayer books are almost hidden from
view by boxes of cheap cologne and ornamental shellwork. . . . Silks and satin
lacework, embroideries follow each other in rapid succession until the eyes are
reveling in a bewildering range of gorgeous, fantastic and beautiful colors.
. . . Pick up a filmy gossamer web of silken lace with a line from the Koran
running around its border and in your ear is whispered the magic word,
"Baghdad." . . . And in the midst of all this riot of the beautiful and odd stands
the dealer, the natural gravity of his features relaxed into a smile of satisfaction
at the wonder and delight expressed by his American visitor.[1]

This is how a reporter for the *New York Tribune* described the goods of a
New York Middle Eastern trading bazaar that supplied hundreds of Arab
immigrant peddlers in the United States at the turn of the century. In the
early 1900s, thousands of Arab peddlers stuffed their suitcases with mer-
chandise from New York suppliers and traveled across America selling
their wares. Initially, Arab Christians traded religious items—scriptures,
icons, crosses, and rosaries—for their American customers believed that
these holy items were blessed and "viewed everything the peddlers had
related to the Holy Land." These early immigrants earned good money
and received an intimate introduction to American life as they went from
house to house peddling their goods.[2] These peddlers are important not
only for what they reveal about the assimilation process of Arabic-speak-

ing immigrants, but also because they represent a unique way of transmitting new religious ideas.

In 1930, W. D. Fard, a mysterious Muslim missionary to America, began his work among poor black people in Detroit. Assuming the guise of an Arab street peddler, Fard established the Nation of Islam. In a global context, his occupation connected him to the original Arab trading and missionary networks that had brought Islam to black people in West Africa several hundred years earlier. It also conveyed the sense of strangeness and mystery that attracted some Americans to Eastern religions and cultures. *Street peddler, dope peddler, missionary, prophet, convict, charlatan, fraud, social reformer, Allah and leader of the "Voodoo Cult"* were some of the epithets used to describe Fard, who was to become one of the most important—and most mysterious—figures in the history of American Islam in the early twentieth century. Fard's "jihad of words," which was central to his mission, adumbrated several themes of Islamic modernism. Under the leadership of Elijah Muhammad, Fard's most trusted disciple, the Nation of Islam evolved from a local movement to the most powerful Islamic organization in America, establishing connections with Garveyism and espousing a unique model of racial separatism in the process. Although Chapter 5 sheds critical light on all of these issues, the question of W. D. Fard's identity is still not answered. The many mysteries surrounding this enigmatic figure are still at the heart of the enduring question: Who was the founder of the Nation of Islam?

THE STRANGE PEDDLER

Late in the summer of 1930, a door-to-door peddler of silks and of Asian and African wares appeared in "Paradise Valley," a predominantly black community in Detroit. Although his racial and ethnic identity is still a mystery, many of the ghetto dwellers believed him to be an Arab or Palestinian. This strange, yellow-complexioned man was known alternately as Mr. Farrad Mohammad, Mr. F. M. Ali, Professor Fard, and Mr. Wali Farrad. He called himself Wallace D. Fard and signed his name as W. D. Fard or W. F. Muhammad in the third year of his ministry.[3] One of his earliest disciples quotes him as having said, "I am W. D. Fard and I came from the Holy City of Mecca. More about myself I will not tell you yet, for the time has not yet come. I am your brother. You have not seen me yet in my royal robes."[4]

Fard soon became a frequent and welcome visitor in the homes of many lower-class blacks who were anxious to buy his goods and hear his stories. He told his customers about the rich history of their homeland in the East and warned them against consuming certain foods that were bad for their health:

> He came first to our houses selling raincoats, and then afterwards silks. In this way he could get into the people's houses, for every woman was eager to

see the nice things the peddler had for sale. He told us that the silks he carried were the same kind that our people used in their home country and that he had come from there. So we all asked him to tell us about our own country. If we asked him to eat with us, he would eat whatever we had on the table, but after the meal he began to talk: "Now don't eat this food. It is poison for you. The people in your own country do not eat it. Since they eat the right kind of food they have the best health all the time. If you would live just like the people in your home country, you would never be sick any more." So we all wanted him to tell us more about ourselves and about our home country and about how we could be free from rheumatism, aches, and pains.[5]

Eventually, Fard acquired many followers and began conducting regular meetings throughout Paradise Valley. His followers, who were used to the cottage prayer meetings of the Black Baptist and Methodist churches in the South, encouraged informal sessions in their homes.[6] The 1926 report of the Detroit Bureau of Governmental Research indicates that almost three-quarters of the black church members in Detroit belonged to the Baptist denomination, with the African Methodist Episcopal church being the second most popular denomination. The report also tells us that African Americans in Detroit were already accustomed to new religious movements (mostly Pentecostal) that were founded by individual ministers who had left the larger churches. These preachers set up independent religious groups whose practices were based on their own ideas. In some cases, these groups were founded by "eccentrics" like Fard, who were eager to be regarded as prophets by the black community.[7] As we shall see, the prophetic messages of religious leaders like Fard spoke to the black community's quest for new ways to signify themselves as a distinct, racial-separatist cultural group.

As he got closer to the black people in Detroit, Fard began to warn them about their vices—such as adultery and alcohol consumption (which are forbidden by religious law) and smoking and dancing (which are prohibited among some Muslims). He encouraged women and men to work hard, to be thrifty, to put their families first, to respect authority, and to conduct their business affairs with honesty and dignity. People listened to this peddler's advice because they believed he told them the truth. His manner was kind and wise, and they believed he offered solutions to their problems.[8]

Sometime during the early part of his mission, W. D. Fard revealed himself as a "prophet who had a startling message of African-American identity and destiny." Citing the Bible, he taught the black people of Detroit about the great religion of their brothers and sisters in Africa and Asia. He understood that the Bible was the religious book best known to his followers and cleverly utilized it to verify his description of the black people's history and the white people's doom. Fard's teachings openly and vehemently attacked the white race, Christianity, and the teachings of the Bible.[9] Using the Book of Revelation, he told the black community about the impending War of Armageddon, a battle between the forces of good and evil, that would be fought in "Har-Magedon in the plains of Esdraelon." When people asked Fard where these places were, he replied that the valley of Esdraelon was "the wilderness of North America" and Har-Magedon, "the United States." According to Fard, the War of Armageddon would be the final conflict between black and white people. The only hope for black people to win this war was to convert to their "natural religion [Islam] and to reclaim their original identity as Muslims."[10]

As a result of these teachings, some of his followers left his side, but many were suddenly and emotionally converted:

> The very first time I went to a meeting I heard him say: "The Bible tells you that the sun rises and sets. That is not so. The sun stands still. All your lives you have been thinking that the earth never moved. Stand and look toward the sun and know that it is the earth you are standing on which is moving." Up to that day I always went to the Baptist church. After I heard that sermon from the prophet, I was turned around completely. When I went home and heard that dinner was ready, I said, "I don't want to eat dinner, I just want to go back to the meetings." I wouldn't eat my meals but I goes back that night and I goes to every meeting after that. Just to think that the sun above me never moved at all and the earth we are on was doing all the moving. That changed everything about me.[11]

Although W. D. Fard said that he was a "prophet of Allah from the holy city of Mecca," he consciously portrayed himself as a Christ-like figure "to displace the old Christ that Christianity gave black people." To make this image believable, he sometimes performed tricks that his followers perceived as miracles. For instance, a group of Muslims put strands of their hair together in a circle, and Fard lifted their pile of hairs with a strand of his own hair. Some of his adherents believed that this was the sign of a Messiah, who said, "lift me up and I will draw all men unto me." Fard neither confirmed nor denied this interpretation. On another occasion, some of his people, who were already mesmerized by his revelations and the mystery of his identity, claimed that he was a Messiah because one day he appeared at their meetings with gray hair and the next day his hair was completely black.[12] These kinds of tricks, which are a familiar part of the baggage of leaders of new religious movements, reinforced the aura of mystery surrounding Fard's identity. They were an important aspect of the religious interaction between him and his followers in the first months of his mission.

News spread fast in the overcrowded black section of Detroit. Before long, the name of the mysterious peddler, whose self-styled mission was to teach Islam to black people, spread far and wide in Paradise Valley. The people who heard Fard's message at the first meetings returned with their friends and relatives. Soon these gatherings were so well attended that it became necessary to hire a hall, which became the first Temple of Islam. The people in attendance were the first members of the Nation of Islam.

One evening in August 1931, W. D. Fard spoke to a gathering of several hundred followers at the former Universal Negro Improvement Association Hall on West Lake Street in Detroit. Black people were crowded in the hall and outside to hear the prophet's message. He preached that the word "negro" was a misnomer for the people of the black African diaspora; this name was created by the white race to separate African Americans from their original Asiatic roots. Fard declared that the blacks of North America "were not Americans but Asiatics" whose ancestors had been taken from the African-Asiatic world by European slave traders in the name of Christianity four hundred years earlier.[13] His personality captured the imagination of his audience as he continued to tell them about their "real" name, history, and destiny. According to his captivating story, black Americans were the "lost-found members of the tribe of Shabazz."

> The black men in North America are not Negroes, but members of the lost tribe of Shabazz, stolen by traders from the Holy City of Mecca 379 years ago. The Prophet came to America to find and bring back to life his long lost brethren, from whom the Caucasians had taken away their language, their nation, and their religion. Here in America they were living other than themselves. They must learn that they are the original people, noblest of the nations of the earth. The Caucasians are the colored people, since they lost their original color. The original people must regain their religion, which is Islam, their language, which is Arabic, and their culture, which is astronomy and higher mathematics, especially calculus. They must live according to the law of Allah, avoiding all meat of "poison animals," hogs, ducks, geese, possums, and catfish. They must give up completely the use of stimulants, especially liquor. They must clean themselves up—both their bodies and their houses. If in this way they obeyed Allah, he would take them back to the Paradise from which they had been stolen—the Holy City of Mecca.[14]

FROM ELIJAH POOLE TO ELIJAH MUHAMMAD

Elijah Poole was one of the people in the audience that night. When he was introduced to Fard after the meeting, he declared, "I know who you are, you're God himself." Fard replied, "That's right, but don't tell it now. It is not yet time for me to be known."[15] Poole soon became the prophet's most enthusiastic student of Islam. Fard gave him the name Elijah Karriem, and later he took the name Elijah Muhammad. Eventually, he became W. D. Fard's chief minister of Islam and his successor.[16]

Elijah Muhammad, the son of a Baptist preacher, was born in Bolds Springs, Georgia, on October 7, 1897. Grown to adulthood and married, he and his wife, Clara, had eight children—Emmanual, Nathaniel, Herbert, Elijah II, Wallace, Akbar, Ethel, and Lotta. The Muhammads were destined

THE HONORABLE ELIJAH MUHAMMAD *and his son, Wallace (Imam Warith Deen Mohammed), posing beneath a painting of W. D. Fard, the mysterious founder and prophet of the Nation of Islam. Circa early 1960s.* Used by permission of the Photographs and Prints Division, Schomberg Center for Research in Black Culture, New York Public Library, Astor, Lenox, and Tilden Foundations.

to become the most remarkable family in the history of Islam in modern America. They became a ruling dynasty in the Nation of Islam. They understood their mission as the re-establishment of Islam as a permanent religious alternative in the United States in the twentieth century, and in this mission they succeeded.[17] Their achievements will be discussed in detail in Chapter 6. Here, though, a brief analysis of Elijah Muhammad's life at the time of his conversion to the Nation of Islam may serve as a paradigm for understanding how and why black people converted to this racial-separatist religious movement in the 1930s and how and why dramatic changes in name and identity were connected to this conversion experience. The basic social fact predisposing blacks to conversion to the Nation of Islam during this formative period was the Great Migration (1915–1930), during which great numbers of blacks left the South to find work in the cities of the North. The Great Migration set the stage for the cultural exchanges between different groups of people and for black economic exploitation in the North, both of which help explain the dramatic changes in name and identity that occurred among the black Muslims.

Black migrants traveled hundreds of miles and gave up their property, their businesses, and in some cases their families in the South to settle in northern industrial cities like New York, Chicago, Pittsburgh, and Detroit. Although they perceived their exodus as a movement to a Promised Land of opportunity and equality in the North, ultimately the Great Migration was a dismal failure for African Americans, resulting in permanent poverty in northern ghettos. Until recently, the starting point for understanding the "economic displacement, political disfranchisement, and social isolation" of the Great Migration was the failure of so-called black Southern "rural peasants" to adjust to urban living in the North. As Carole Marks has so convincingly demonstrated, however, the majority of the Southern migrants were actually skilled and semiskilled urban artisans with fairly high rates of literacy. Their failure in the North was not their own personal failure but was due to large structural factors. Black workers became part of a new economic system in the North that profited from a "supply of cheap labor that was both substitutable and disposable." Although the black migrants were a "highly selective population," there was no room for their upward mobility in this new system, in which they were forced to take and keep jobs that white people did not want.[18] Ironically, their movement from the South and their exploitation in the North had been planned in the boardrooms of northern businesses in order to benefit "American economic development." Unlike the European immigrants before them, however, they were not assimilated into the mainstream culture—their racial difference precluded that. They did not return home because their movement from the South had devastated its economy. In short, they had no structural advantages available to them to cushion their permanent exploitation.[19]

As we saw in Chapter 3, members of Noble Drew Ali's Moorish Science Temple movement in the 1920s were part of the first wave of the Great Migration. They identified themselves as Americans, albeit "Moorish Americans," despite their separatist ideology, because they still had some hope of structural assimilation into the mainstream of American culture. The black converts to the Ahmadiyya movement felt that association with middle-class, educated Muslims from the old country would facilitate this assimilation. However, Elijah Muhammad and his fellow converts to the Nation of Islam were a part of the last wave of the Great Migration. Hopes of assimilation or of structural means to offset their exploitation by the mainstream in the North died quickly as they struggled to maintain employment and housing during the first years of the Great Depression. This is important for understanding why black people chose W. D. Fard's Nation of Islam instead of religious and political alternatives in the 1930s. Elijah Poole's story is a paradigm for understanding the process of conversion, signification, and racial-separatist identity in this movement.

Elijah Poole moved to Detroit from Georgia at the age of twenty-two. Like thousands of other black people in the 1920s, he had heard about Marcus Garvey, the remarkable orator and leader of the black masses. Soon after Poole's arrival in Detroit, he traveled to Chicago with a friend to hear Garvey speak. "Awake you sons and daughters of Africa on the continent and in the lands of exile. Up, you mighty race! Man can accomplish what you will," Garvey proclaimed to his captivated audience. Poole was profoundly moved by what he felt was "the great truth" about the black race that Marcus Garvey had articulated that night. Garvey's message focused on the redemption of Africa, racial identity, pride and solidarity, and black economic independence. Poole joined the Universal Negro Improvement Association and became a corporal in the Chicago UNIA.[20]

For Poole, the UNIA was a model Pan-African movement for the black masses for several reasons. First, Garvey was a common man who lacked formal education but who could electrify and persuade an audience with his speaking ability and his focus on black identity. Second, the UNIA was an international movement, with branches on several continents. Third, the *Negro World*, its weekly newspaper, was written in the language of the ordinary black person and was widely read by black people in every section of the United States. It used the written word as a weapon to mold a black global identity and to resist racism. Fourth, the businesses of the UNIA offered hope for blacks who were unemployed. Finally, although the UNIA was not a religious movement, its serious attention to religion made it a good model for the political structure of a Pan-Africanist religious movement. Poole later used some of the political ideas and techniques of the Garvey movement as a model for the Nation of Islam. Unlike Garvey, however, Poole believed that migration to Africa would not solve the problems of black people in America. Only a dramatic change in black American destiny and identity would provide the solution. "We have as much right to this soil as the white man," said Poole. "Why should we claim the land of our black brother in Africa for which he has given his life and labor? It belongs to him. Our destiny is right here in America."[21]

Elijah Poole's fascination with the Garvey movement, however, was short-lived. He was stunned, as were millions of other black people around the world, when Marcus Garvey was deported from the United States in 1927 as a result of his mail fraud conviction. Although the UNIA continued in America, it was never the same after Garvey's deportation. Two years later, Noble Drew Ali, the outspoken leader of the Moorish Science Temple movement, died. And the Ahmadiyya movement in 1930 began a strange period of silence regarding militant black issues. Thus by 1930 no dynamic leaders and no religious or political movements in America were articulating Pan-Africanist issues for the black masses. Moreover, when the stock market crashed on October 24, 1929, militant Pan-Africanism was not on the list of priorities of most black churches, which displayed a "relative quietism and apparent vacuum of church leadership." Thus, the Nation of Islam was destined to fill a critical void in the African-American quest for a Pan-Africanist identity in the depression years.[22]

Elijah Poole was a skilled laborer. He had been a foreman for the Cherokee Brick Company in Macon, Georgia, in 1919, and in Detroit he had worked in the Chevrolet Auto Plant for six years. When the Great Depression began, however, Poole lost his job and was forced to accept relief for two years. He was not alone; Detroit blacks experienced massive unemployment in the 1930s.[23] The situation was probably worse than in other major cities because Detroit had been the fastest growing city in the United States during the mid-1920s. From 1920 to 1930, its population had increased from 993,678 to 1,568,662 people. During the same period, Detroit had a greater percentage of increase in black population than any other American city with over 5,500 black people. In the 1920s—a period of general economic prosperity—Detroit had been a "working-age city." Black migrants and European immigrants had come there to work. Indeed, it had more than its fair share of working-age people. As David Levine notes, "in 1920, when the percentage of the total United States population between the ages of 25 and 44 was 29.6 percent, nearly 40 percent of Detroit's total population and more than 50 percent of its black population was of that age."[24]

In 1930, the second year of the Great Depression, competition between black migrants and European immigrants for jobs, housing, and food was keen. The black people of Detroit became more bitter toward white people in all walks of life—the foreigners with whom they competed for menial jobs, policemen, welfare workers,[25] and most of all the Ku Klux Klan. Membership in the Detroit Chapter of the Klan increased from 3,000 in 1921 to 22,000 a year and a half later. The Detroit Klansmen overtly terrorized blacks and even entered politics on the mayoral level in 1924.[26]

Nationally, black people suffered the most during the Great Depression but benefitted less than white people from the public works and relief programs of the Roosevelt administration's New Deal. All of these changes produced despair in the black community of Detroit, so that "the words of Fard began to make more sense than ever."[27]

Migration, economic depression, and the demise of Garvey transformed the Pan-Africanist aspiration of a small but significant group of black people in Detroit so radically that political organization alone was not enough. The dynamics of the forces that led to conversion in the Nation of Islam are still not completely understood, but certain aspects are clear. First, signification was at the center of the conversion experience for members of this movement. No other black religious or political group up to this time had talked so explicitly and convincingly about the psychological damage that slavery had done to black Americans. Converts were taught that they were the descendants of the "original black nation of Asia, the Tribe of Shabazz" and that they had lost their original religion, Islam, and nationality, African Asiatic, in slavery. According to these ideas, the Asiatics were the "original" human beings, whose ancient civilization included the Nile Valley and the holy city of Mecca, while the slavemasters were the descendants of blue-eyed mutants who had been developed from black people by a mad black scientist named Yacub. Following this genetic experiment, the white race had enslaved the Asiatics for six thousand years.[28]

For the black Muslims, the slave name was the central symbol in this process of black debasement, since the signification associated with slavery "constituted a subordinate relationship of power expressed through custom and legal structures." Therefore, when W. D. Fard undercut this signification by another act of signification[29] that gave new names and new political and cultural identities to his converts, he empowered them "to a level of dignity and self-appreciation from which new informed choices about religion could be made."[30] Eventually, Elijah Muhammad required all converts to change their surnames to X in order to eradicate their slave names. The X signified the original identity that was lost when black people were taken from Africa by their enslavers. When the converts received their X, a new world of opportunities was thought to open up for them. Black Muslim leaders told them that "freedom, justice, equality, happiness, peace of mind, contentment, money, good jobs, decent homes— all these can be yours if you accept your God, Allah, now and return to His (and your original) religion, Islam."[31] Thus, signification was an important process that in some cases probably provided the rationale for conversion. For Elijah Poole, the change in status that his new-found signification symbolized was dramatic. When he became Elijah Karriem and eventually Elijah Muhammad, he was no longer a down-and-out unemployed Negro laborer on relief, but instead a dignified black Asiatic Chief Minister of Islam.

Sulayman Nyang believes that converts to the Nation of Islam chose the new religion for "utilitarian considerations." This is certainly one way of understanding their conversion. They viewed "Islam as a political weapon, a strategy for physical and spiritual survival and a way of life that could be effectively appropriated in their struggle for racial justice and ethnic freedom." The converts were understood as "simulationists," who simulated only the aspects of Muslim identity that served their own political "self-definition." According to Nyang, simulationists adopted Muslim names, Muslim dress codes, and heterodox Muslim worldviews. However, these converts redefined their black American identity in a manner that set them apart from the Muslim community and from the black Americans who were not Muslims.[32]

The idea that separated the Nation of Islam almost irrevocably from the larger Muslim community and other black American political and religious groups was the "hidden truth" that W. D. Fard taught Elijah Muhammad, positing the notion that black and white people did not come from the same God.[33] According to this idea, blacks and whites were "fundamentally different" in nature: black people were "righteous and divine" and white people were wicked "blond blue-eyed devils." "America is under Divine Judgement to destroy her for the evils done to Allah's people in slavery."[34] Although this aspect of black Muslim identity was intrinsically racist, on another level it was a part of the "ethnic therapy" of signification.[35] Before Fard could restore his converts' knowledge of their "true" names, history, religion, and ethnicity, he had to destroy that aspect of the white race's invincibility that made black inferiority and self-hatred possible on a deep psychological level. The idea of Nordic racial supremacy that placed blond blue-eyed northern Europeans at the top of a racial hierarchy and black people at the bottom was the most powerful and deep-seated model in Western racial thinking. The Nordic racial myth was at the root of the eugenics movement, the Ku Klux Klan, immigration restrictions, some aspects of anthropology, and Nazism in Europe and America.[36]

In the 1930s, Nazi groups like the Black Legion, Silver Legion, and German American Bund acquired thousands of members in the United States who wanted "to unite with all Americans defending the Aryan culture and the code of ethics upon which this nation was founded." Although Martin Marty tells us that "the American Nazi movement . . . did not amount to much" in the 1930s, a coalition between this movement and the insidious Ku Klux Klan must have been a frightening and ever-present possibility for politically aware black people in that decade.[37] In this context W. D. Fard's "hidden truth" could be understood as a deconstruction of the Nordic racial myth for the purpose of black political mobilization and self-defense against the possibility of genocide. This possibility was no doubt a significant part of the psychological baggage of black people whose parents and grandparents had been slaves in America in the nineteenth century. At the same time, these were black people who had experienced the brutality of racially motivated rapes and lynchings in the South in the twentieth century.

Although the Nation of Islam was not an integrated Islamic movement, it was not as racist a group as some scholars have contended. Unlike white supremacist groups in America and Europe in the 1930s, the black racial-separatist Muslims did not develop programs of genocide for racial outsiders. Instead, the latter's racial supremacy was a defensive stance to counter racial discrimination and atrocities against black Americans. Basically, the Nation of Islam wanted to be left alone. Thus, W. D. Fard and Elijah Muhammad did not allow white Americans to become members of the Nation of Islam and "discouraged fraternization with immigrant Muslims," for they considered white American converts to Islam to be "Muslim Sons" who "could not be Muslims completely."[38] Given that the Ahmadis had failed to unify American Muslims of different racial and ethnic groups, Fard's strategy was only a reflection of the historic patterns of racial and ethnic separation in Islam. Also, it is significant that these patterns were set in motion in America not by a black but by an Asian Muslim. According to Muhammad Abdullah, the leader of Lahori Ahmadis in California and a close friend, confidant, and mentor of Elijah Muhammad, "Elijah followed the real Islam, but he thought that if he taught the real Islam, black people would not follow him. Elijah thought that he should push certain things to arouse curiosity so he and Fard invented this story [the hidden truth]."[39]

C. Eric Lincoln correctly notes that Fard and Elijah "cut the cloak to fit the cloth." Their methods for teaching Islam to the "black victims of a new technocratic urban order" were imaginative, "controversial and sometimes ad hoc . . . but they were always addressed to the realities of the situation rather than to an abstract theory whose relevance to [their] peculiar task had nowhere been demonstrated." Religious orthodoxy was not the goal of this movement. Instead, Elijah Muhammad and W. D. Fard wanted to reconstruct African-American cultural, political, and religious identity and "make Americans aware of Islam, its power and potential." In this they succeeded.[40]

The theme of signification and identity was acted out differently in the Nation of Islam than it was in the Muslim organizations that black Americans had joined before its existence. In all of these organizations, there was a definite tension between East and West in the cultural and political identities that black Muslims assumed. This tension was apparent in the significations that black American Muslims formed for themselves in the different Muslim groups. In both the Moorish Science Temple of America and the Ahmadiyya Movement in Islam, eastern Islamic traditions were primary. Although both traditions were heterodox interpretations of Islam, the names, dress, politics, and worldview of their black converts focused respectively on Morocco and the Indian subcontinent. Thus, the African-American situation was sometimes secondary to the foreign ties that each of these organizations either had or imagined. This is why some observers have tagged the signification in these groups as a "psychic escape" from racism in America. However, in the Nation of Islam, from the beginning, the roots of African-American history and heritage were primary for understanding Islam. This was clearly illustrated in the naming process of the organization which underlined the slave heritage of African Americans. Although the Islamic tradition from the East was acknowledged in the deification and signification of W. D. Fard, the use of Arabic teachers from the Arab world in their schools, and financial support from North Africa, Elijah Muhammad refused to compromise the Western orientation of the Nation of Islam. Like the medieval West African Muslim rulers described in Chapter 1, Elijah mixed aspects of Islam with the indigenous (Christian) religious and cultural practices of his people. At the same time, he refused to allow his political authority to be compromised by the Islamic establishment from the East. As a result of these variations, critics have accused the Nation of Islam of being "un-Islamic" and "impure." Louis Lomax even branded Elijah Muhammad a product of racist America. A more accurate interpretation is that Elijah Muhammad's identity was a product of global Islamic, black American, and white American influences. And, as we have seen, impurity, heterodoxy, and racial separatism were more the rule than the exception for black identity in global Islam.[41]

Finally, although most historians of the period have routinely dismissed the Nation of Islam as an interesting but irrelevant movement, it may have been the most important Pan-Africanist organization in America in the 1930s. With the demise of Garveyism in the United States during the Depression years, the Nation of Islam became the predominant Pan-Africanist voice for black Americans. Its political ideology focused on the political, economic, social, and technological uplift of African Americans, making them aware of their cultural and historical connections to Africa and the effects of Western imperialism and colonialism on all the areas of the world in which people of color lived. Indeed, this message was a significant part of the appeal of the movement to converts and its general influence on the black Christian community. The latter issue is very important, for the significance of Pan-Africanist organizations in African-American life cannot be measured in terms of membership rolls but rather must be seen in terms of subtle influence on identity. The majority of black people in the 1920s and 1930s were not members of these organizations. Nonetheless, some of Marcus Garvey's and Elijah Muhammad's ideas about politics and race relations probably made sense to most black people on an intuitive level. Pan-Africanist ideologies during this period cut across social class lines in the black community and set forth ideas about internationalism and race that many black people believed but were afraid to articulate openly.

This is why Judith Stein's study of Garveyism, with its assumption that

Pan-African "solutions to the problems of race and racism were the product of class experiences and were best suited to the redress of elite ills," is problematic. Stein's class framework for understanding Pan-Africanism contends that "Afro-American history transcends race and racism," therefore in the black community "racial politics does not originate inevitably in an immediate experience of racial discrimination or oppression." This kind of thinking ignores continuities between Pan-African leaders, organizations, and ideologies in the 1920s and 1930s, asserting that Pan-Africanist organizations "disappeared in the 1930s" because black racial politics during that era were changed by the new strategies of the labor movement. But this is simply not the case. The Nation of Islam demonstrates that at least one major Pan-Africanist organization was alive and well during the Depression years. In fact, its impact on the Pan-African movement was so disturbing that in 1934 Charles James, the leader of the Gary, Indiana, UNIA, complained that "simple-minded Negroes were turning Moors, Arabs, Abyssinians. . . . They were growing beards and refusing to cut their hair . . . and have even gone to the length of changing their names."[42]

SIGNIFICATION AND IDENTITY: THE MYSTERY OF W. D. FARD

While the head of the Gary UNIA was disturbed by the phenomenon of ordinary black people who were changing their names, something even more disquieting had happened among the leadership of the Nation of Islam. The mystery of W. D. Fard's identity had become a web of significations, each of which revealed both the arbitrary nature of signifying and the "intrinsic relationship" between the signified and the signifier. Charles Long has commented that "signifying is a very clever language game, and one has to be adept in the verbal arts either to signify or to keep from being signified. . . . It is precisely the arbitrariness of signification that makes it so frustrating." With this perspective in mind, an analysis of Fard's various names and identities can elucidate the political and religious connections between him and various individuals and groups who signified him. For each new name and identity revealed the significations which different groups, including the black Muslims themselves, formed for the Nation of Islam.[43]

First, it is clear that W. D. Fard developed a litany of cryptic names for himself in order to create an aura of mystery, spirituality, and divinity for his movement. Originally he chose the name Wallace D. Fard, but in 1933 he began to identify himself as W. D. Fard. He was also known as Farad Mohammad, F. Mohammad Ali, Professor Fard, Abdul Wali Farad Muhammad Ali, and Wali Farrad. These various names were tied to a few words in Arabic. *Farada* means "to be simple, to be alone, to be unique." *Al-farīḍa* is "an obligatory religious duty." *Faraḍa* means "to decree" or "to ordain." Wali Farad is translated as the "unique man of God" and Fard Mohammad means "the unique praised one." Wali Fard Muhammad has been explained as a Persian construction meaning "unique guardian." This pattern of alternate names for the most important religious figures is deeply embedded in Islamic tradition, as there are scores of Arabic names with different spiritual connotations for Allah and the Prophet Muhammad in Islam.[44]

During the 1930s, many diverse legends surrounded the identity of W. D. Fard. Some of his first followers claimed that Mecca was his birthplace and that his parents were wealthy members of the "Tribe of Koreish," the tribe of the Prophet Muhammad. They also believed that Fard was a blood relative of the kings of Hejaz, who traced their origin to "the dynasty of the Hashimide sherifs of Mecca." Others said that Fard was educated at an English university as a diplomat for the kingdom of Hejaz, but that he gave up his career to liberate the black people of North America. Sister Carrie Mohammad, an early convert, maintained that Fard graduated from the University of Southern California. Some of his followers described Fard as "a black Jamaican whose father was a Syrian Moslem" or as a Palestinian who had been involved in racial disturbances in South Africa, India, and London before settling in Detroit. A Chicago newspaper called Fard "a Turkish-born Nazi agent [who] worked for Hitler."[45]

The Nation of Islam's official doctrine formed its signification of W. D. Fard's identity from the Quran, the Bible, African-American popular culture, Fard's ideas, and Elijah Muhammad's interpretation of Fard's ideas. According to these sources W. D. Fard was born on February 26, 1877 in Mecca, Arabia, "a member of the family of the original black man." His coming was foretold in the Bible: "For as the light cometh out of the East, and shineth even unto the West, so shall also the coming of the Son of Man be" (Matthew 24:27). According to this official doctrine, when Elijah Muhammad asked W. D. Fard who he was, he replied: "I am the one that the world had been expecting for the past 2,000 years. . . . My name is Mahdi; I am God." At the same time the Nation of Islam believed that W. D. Fard was born of black and white parentage. "He came to us out of the world of the white man to teach a new world order for the black man. . . . he would know the nature of the two people because he was from both races." Moreover, the black Muslims taught that Fard was both an Arab and a light-skinned black man and that the latter identity helped his mission, playing as it did into the color consciousness of the black community: "he was greatly accepted among blacks because of his light skin and wavy hair."[46]

For several important reasons, both Fard and his followers made the symbols of his identity pro-Arab. First, although black people in the 1930s knew that Arabians were not Africans, "the fact that they were 'non-white' and had a history of cultural connections with Africa gave them a special place in the ideological thought of African Americans." Some black writers at the turn of the century even chose the Prophet Muhammad as one of the "great black heroes of the world." These ideas predated the rise of Pan-Africanist Islamic movements among black Americans. Second, the pro-Arab symbols of Fard's identity were a significant aspect of "the politics of representing Islam and Muslims in American cultural and political discourse." Here, the "'otherness' of Islam" and Arab culture in "western representations" functioned as a form of ethnocentric self-identification for the black Muslims who sought to separate themselves racially, geographically, historically, and spiritually from Western culture. In this process, pro-Arab symbols were part of the

> mystification [of] the organization, its leaders and . . . names of persons. [For] Islam . . . best represented absolute otherness with American culture. It was a mysterious religion that was absolutely alien to American experience and history and belonged to an equally mysterious and alien culture.

Finally, the leaders of the Nation of Islam were aware of the presence of Arab orthodox Muslims in America. However, as C. Eric Lincoln has said, the Arab Muslims were more a "spasm" than an "outpost" for Islam in America. For the most part, they did not encourage relations with the black Muslims during this period and viewed them as an embarrassing non-Islamic group. In this situation, black Muslim leaders, for their part, ensured the legitimation of their form of Islam by appropriating pro-Arab symbols.[47]

Elijah Muhammad's pro-Arab signification of W. D. Fard's identity, also echoed the old civilizationist ideas of the late nineteenth-century Pan-Africanists. Along with Muhammad's emphasis on racial uplift and ancient black Islamic civilizations in his significations, he also asserted that present-day African traditional cultures and religions were backwards and in need of civilization:

> I have been preaching to the Black man in America that we should accept our own; and instead of the Black man going to the decent side of his own, he goes back seeking traditional Africa, and the way they did in jungle life and the way you see in some parts of uncivilized Africa today. They are not using barber's tools, shears and razors to keep themselves looking dignified as a civilized people should look. The Black man in America accepts the jungle life, thinking that they would get the love of Black Africa. Black Brother and Black Sister, wearing savage dress and hair-styles will not get you the love of Africa. The dignified people of Africa are either Muslim or educated Christians. But Africa today does not want Christianity.[48]

Dennis Hickey and Kenneth C. Wylie are right in noting that Elijah Muhammad's signification of black Muslim identity was influenced by his black Baptist background, for his basic assumptions about Africa were

remarkably similar to those of black American clergy who were his primary ideological rivals. Moreover, Muhammad's pro-Arab signification of
W. D. Fard's identity was influenced by Edward Wilmot Blyden's views on
"black personality" and racial purity. These ideas were partly the inspiration for Muhammad's construction of black racial supremacy. At the same
time, Muhammad's significations (like Blyden's) were based on "the myth
of a race-blind Islam" that was discussed in Chapter 2. This myth presented Islam as a religion without racial prejudice or discrimination in its
global history. Indirectly, however, the Nation of Islam's racial separatism
acknowledged racial tensions between black and nonblack Muslims. Elijah
Muhammad's glorification of Arab Muslim identity in W. D. Fard and his
denigration of African traditional religious values contributed to a conception of black Islamic identity that did not celebrate non-Muslim African
roots and did not critique the enslavement of black people in the Muslim
world. It should be noted that in the 1970s, the Nation of Islam began to
look more critically at these issues.[49]

Scholarly representations of W. D. Fard's identity are also an aspect of
his signification. Until the mid-1980s, most scholars had probably assumed that Fard was of Arab ethnic origin, although no one had done new
research on his identity since 1938, when a white American sociologist,
Erdmann D. Beynon (1892–1943), wrote the first scholarly treatment of the
Nation of Islam. Although his work was based on groundbreaking interviews with more than 200 Muslim families, it was sensationalistic, as is
indicated by its title, "The Voodoo Cult," which was the Detroit police
department's nickname for the Nation of Islam. In Benyon's work, Fard
was signified as a slick and mysterious "cult" leader who exploited the
weaknesses of recent black migrants from the South and led them to
practice human sacrifice. Beynon's only reference to the global Islamic
roots of Fard's identity was that the latter "introduced [the Quran] as the
most authoritative of all the texts for the study of the new faith . . . [and]
used only the Arabic text which he translated and explained to the believers."[50] FBI documents in 1957 and 1958 noted that Benyon and Louis Wirth,
a professor of sociology at the University of Chicago, were both interested
in the Nation of Islam in 1937 and consulted with each other. At the same
time, Benyon and "a detective from the Detroit Police Department who
was in charge of the investigation of the group conferred with each other
quite frequently and swapped information concerning the group." Thus,
Benyon began a tradition of scholarly representations of the Nation of
Islam that accepted local and national law-enforcement agencies' signification of the organization as a cult. This kind of scholarship on Islam in
black America expanded "the myth of a race-blind Islam" to include the
idea that black American Muslim groups were un-Islamic, pathological
cults based on a distorted version of black nationalism. In this context, the
Nation of Islam and W. D. Fard's identity were viewed in socio-political
rather than religious terms. In Chapter 6, we will examine how all of these

ideas resonated in C. Eric Lincoln and E. U. Essien-Udom's sociologically and politically oriented studies of the Nation of Islam in the 1960s, and how their ideas about Fard duplicated aspects of Benyon's research.[51]

No one had seriously looked at the religious significance of the Nation of Islam or Fard's identity until 1981, when a Pakistani scholar, Z. I. Ansari, published a pathbreaking article on "Black Muslim Theology." In the mid-1980s, Ansari did a sequel article, "Religious Doctrines of the Black Muslims," which posited that W. D. Fard "was still alive . . . that he was from the Indian subcontinent . . . a person of Qadiyani background . . . and was a man called Abdullah, an imam in one of the black Muslim mosques in Northern California." Ansari claimed that he had received this new information from Warith Deen Mohammed, Elijah Muhammad's son and successor.[52]

Muhammad Abdullah, the man whom Ansari claims is Fard, lives in Hayward, California, and is an imam for the San Francisco Bay Area. Abdullah is a missionary for the Lahore branch of the Ahmadiyya movement, and his son, Zafar, is the national president for the group and the editor of its magazine, *The Islamic Review*. The Lahoris consider Ghulam Ahmad to be a reformer, but not a prophet as the Qadianis do. Born in 1905 in India, Muhammad Abdullah came to the United States in 1959 from the Fiji Islands, where he was a teacher and a missionary. He learned about Elijah Muhammad from the newspapers and was a close friend and advisor, in constant contact with him by mail and in person until Elijah Muhammad's death in 1975. From 1961 to 1963, Abdullah was a teacher for Elijah's son, Warith, in Philadelphia. They were both members of the International Muslim Brotherhood, and Abdullah tutored Warith in Arabic, Urdu, and the Quran. Because of this relationship, Abdullah said, "It is all right to say I am Fard Muhammad for Wallace (Warith) D. Mohammed. I taught him some lessons. But I am not the same person who taught Elijah Muhammad, and I am not God." In 1976, Warith was at a Muslim meeting in Los Angeles where Abdullah read a paper. He started a rumor when he said that he suspected Abdullah of being W. D. Fard. Abdullah still contends, however, that

> Elijah Muhammad was a sincere and good Muslim, so he created the story of W. D. Fard to attract the western mind to Islam. It's the nature of a movement to add to the magnitude of a figure. However, Fard was a real person actually incarcerated. He came from the Middle East knowledgeable in multiple languages. He was light complexioned.

Additional evidence concerning W. D. Fard's ethnic origin coincides with aspects of Abdullah's description of him. Akbar Muhammad, who is also one of Elijah Muhammad's sons and a professor of history at the State University of New York at Binghamton, claimed in a paper that he read at the Muslim Media Conference in 1985 that Fard was "Turko-Persian culturally."[53] This is the version of Fard's identity that I assume to be the most valid one because of Muhammad's status, both as a researcher and an insider in the early years of the Nation of Islam.

The FBI did more than any other non-Muslim agency to cultivate an aura of mystery around W. D. Fard's identity. The significations that they formed for him and for the Nation of Islam revealed their paranoid views that African-American Islam was an "internal security risk" and a global menace. The FBI's intensive investigation of W. D. Fard began in the early 1940s and continued into the 1960s. The federal government was convinced that Fard was still alive and was the key to breaking the black Muslim movement in America during this period. According to the FBI files, Fard had more than fifty aliases and was born either in Portland, Oregon, in 1811; Mecca, Saudi Arabia in 1873, 1877 or 1900; or New Zealand in 1894. His race was listed alternately as white and black and his parents were allegedly Zared and Beatrice Fard, "both born in Hawaii."[54]

The FBI's investigation presented Fard as Wallace Dodd Ford, an unstable wanderer who came to the United States from New Zealand in 1913. Dodd's first marriage to Pearl Allen ended in a bitter separation, and he abandoned his infant son in Portland, Oregon. Thereafter, he moved briefly to Seattle, where he took the name Fred Dodd. Dodd changed his name to Wallace D. Ford in Los Angeles, where he was involved in a second common-law marriage to Hazel Barton between 1920 and 1926 and fathered another son, Wallace Dodd Ford, Jr. (1920–1942), who later changed his name to Wallace Max Ford. Wallace D. Ford was allegedly a petty criminal who had a record with the Los Angeles Police Department from 1918 to 1926 for assault with a deadly weapon and possession and sale of bootleg alcohol. In these years, Ford was also supposedly the owner of a restaurant on South Flower Street in Los Angeles. This is where he was arrested for selling narcotics "over his restaurant counter," on June 12, 1926. Thereafter he served a three-year term in San Quentin Federal Penitentiary. To prove his criminality, the FBI correlated prison mug shots, fingerprints, and identification records for Wallace D. Ford (San Quentin number 42314), with W. D. Fard's Detroit Police Department file and fingerprints from the 1930s (Detroit Police Department number 45138). The latter file reports that its subject was "arrested three times in Detroit prior to May 26, 1933 for teaching Islam." He is referred to as "chief of the Voodoos."[55]

In the late 1950s and early 1960s, the FBI COINTELPRO (counter intelligence programs against domestic threats) waged a public campaign in American newspapers and magazines to discredit W. D. Fard's status as a prophet and god in the Nation of Islam. Karl Evanzz believes that the intelligence community released "information on Fard ... to the media [to] disrupt and curb the growth of the Nation of Islam." In this context, major newspapers and magazines such as the *New Crusader, The Boston Record American, The Los Angeles Herald Examiner, Time,* and *U. S. News and World*

Report claimed that Fard was really a white man and a criminal whose main purpose was to exploit his black followers. In the furor that resulted from these accusations, Elijah Muhammad used his column in the *Los Angeles Herald Dispatch* to launch a "jihad of words" to defend the honor of W. D. Fard's identity. Later, he offered an award of $100,000 to anyone who could produce evidence to substantiate the media's claims about Fard. On August 8, 1963, Hazel Evelsizer wrote to Muhammad to collect the reward; she claimed that she was Wallace Fard's second wife. Evelsizer was "discovered" by the FBI on January 17, 1958 at the Sun Crest Trailer Park in Key West, Florida. In an interview with an FBI agent, she claimed that she had lived in a common-law marriage with Fard from 1919 to 1922 in Los Angeles and that she had borne a son for him named Wallace Dodd Ford "after its father." Evelsizer alleged that one day "she found a letter in [her husband's] trunk which was addressed to Fred Dodd, and although she never discussed it with him, she took it for granted that he had used the name Fred Dodd prior to his coming to Los Angeles." When Ford left for Detroit and Chicago he supposedly sent money to her for his son, on a regular basis. Finally, Evelsizer stated that in the summer of 1932 or 1933, Dodd "showed up at her place" and "said he was on his way to New Zealand." This was the last time she heard from her "husband." Elijah Muhammad refused to pay the $100,000 reward to Hazel Evelsizer. He refused to believe or admit that Wallace Dodd Ford and W. D. Fard were the same person. In the final evaluation, Evelsizer's version of her husband's identity was just another story in the saga of signification perpetuating the enigma of W. D. Fard's identity.[56]

FROM ELIJAH MUHAMMAD TO GULAM BOGANS AND MUHAMMAD RASSOUL: DISSENSION IN THE NATION OF ISLAM

Certain of W. D. Fard's ideas led to dissension in the Nation of Islam and persecution and exploitation from the outside. Fard taught his followers that they were not a part of the United States but instead were citizens of Mecca and owed allegiance solely to the Muslim flag. All Muslims, he argued, should take their children out of the public schools and send them to the University of Islam to study Arabic, the Quran, black history, astronomy, and higher mathematics. At the same time, Fard established the Moslem Girls Training and Civilization Classes for women and the Fruit of Islam, a paramilitary organization for men. In rebellion against these demands, Abdul Mohammed, one of the first officials in the movement, withdrew from the Nation and established his own Islamic group, which was loyal to the American Constitution and flag. An attempt by the Board of Education and the police to arrest Muslim teachers and close the University of Islam resulted in an uprising in which the Muslims tried to take over the Detroit police headquarters by force. After this incident, the court officials became so fearful of further racial confrontations that they suspended the sentences of most of the Muslims.[57]

Greater dissension in the movement occurred because of rumors of human sacrifice among the black Muslims. Although it is difficult to judge the veracity of these rumors, they first came to public attention in Detroit on November 21, 1932 when it was reported that

> a prominent member, Robert Harris, renamed Robert Karriem, erected an altar in his home at 1249 Dubois Street and invited his roomer, John J. Smith, to present himself as a human sacrifice, so that he might become, as Harris said, "The Savior of the world." Smith agreed, and at the hour appointed for the sacrifice—9:00 a.m.—Harris plunged a knife into Smith's heart.[58]

In 1932, W. D. Fard was arrested and sent to jail in connection with the Nation of Islam's alleged sacrificial murders. He was forced to leave Detroit, Michigan, on May 26, 1933. The prophet then went to Chicago, where he was again arrested and imprisoned. Sometime during 1933, Elijah Muhammad offered Fard refuge in Chicago, and the former was designated the Minister of Islam. In 1934, W. D. Fard vanished completely; to this day there are no substantive clues regarding his whereabouts, although there are several undocumented reports. Some say that he was seen on a ship traveling to Europe. Others hint at foul play on the part of the police or Elijah Muhammad.[59]

After Fard's disappearance, Elijah Muhammad became the leader of the Allah Temple of Islam. He left the Detroit group and set up headquarters in Chicago, where he had founded Temple No. 2 for W. D. Fard. Muhammad then deified W. D. Fard and called himself the Prophet of Allah. Muhammad's brother, Kallat Muhammad, challenged his authority and formed his own Muslim organization in Chicago in 1935. Augustus Muhammad, assistant minister in Elijah's Chicago headquarters, returned to Detroit to lead a pro-Japanese African-American organization called Development of Our Own.[60]

Angered by Elijah Muhammad's new claims to prophecy and leadership, some of his rivals vowed that they would "eat a grain of rice a day until Elijah was dead." Forced to leave his family behind in Chicago in order to save his life, Muhammad traveled mysteriously along the east coast for the next seven years, as an itinerant preacher for his movement. Like his teacher W. D. Fard, he assumed many names and identities to cover his tracks. During these shadowy years, Elijah Muhammad was known as Elijah Karriem, Elijah Evans, Gulam Bogans, Mr. Muckmuck, and Muhammad Rassoul. Washington, D.C., was a frequent resting place for Muhammad in this period. He sometimes rented a room in the home of Benjamin X, where he became known for communal dinners during which he used the Bible and the Quran to preach his version of African-American Asiatic Islamic identity.[61] In 1935, both of Muhammad's aforementioned rivals died, and he used their deaths to proclaim a jihad of words which supported his prophetic identity:

> God has closed the door and does not hear the prayers of the hypocrites when He sends chastisement upon them. . . . We actually witnessed this type of chastisement that fell upon those hypocrites in 1935. One of the hypocrites was my brother, and another was a minister by the name of Augustus Muhammad, my top assistant at that time in Chicago Mosque No. 2.[62]

The Asiatic identity and global ties of the black Muslim movement were accentuated in the 1930s and early 1940s by two outside political groups that tried to incorporate the Nation of Islam. In 1932, the Communists made an unsuccessful attempt to infiltrate the movement. Then Satokata Takahashi, a Japanese national, was successful in recruiting a small number of Muslims for his organization, Development of Our Own. Under Takahashi's leadership, Development of Our Own became the major organization in black America for the dissemination of pro-Japanese propaganda, which sought to connect the African-American economic and political struggle against Western imperialism with that of the darker races in Asia. Ernest Allen, Jr. has noted that both Abdul Muhammad and Elijah Muhammad were friends with Takahashi and admired his work. Although Elijah Muhammad never became a member of Takahashi's organization, the Allah Temple of Islam became a significant source of "pro-Japanese sentiment" among black Americans during the World War II era. Moreover, it is noteworthy that Takahashi's wife, Pearl Sherrod, was a former member of the Nation of Islam. Other pro-Japanese African-American organizations that influenced the Asiatic identity of Elijah Muhammad's followers were the Pacific Movement of the Eastern World, the Onward Movement of America, the Peace Movement of Ethiopia, the Ethiopian Pacific Movement, and the Original Independent Benevolent Afro-Pacific Movement of the World.[63]

In the context of these pro-Japanese connections, Elijah Muhammad's various names were also intended to help him elude the federal authorities who were monitoring the black Muslim movement for sedition and Selective Service violations. Beginning in 1942, the FBI carried out a series of raids on black Muslim homes and mosques in Detroit, Chicago, Milwaukee, and New Jersey. Even Elijah Muhammad's thirteen-year-old son Wallace was under surveillance by the FBI. Finally on May 8, 1942 in Washington, D.C. and in September 1942 in Chicago, Muhammad was arrested for refusing to register for the draft and for influencing his followers not to register. His son Emmanuel was also arrested around this time. The two men were convicted in Chicago and incarcerated in the federal penitentiary in Milan, Michigan, from 1942 to 1946, where they conducted weekly services and converted many prisoners to Islam. According to Ernest Allen, Jr., the Muhammads' arrests were part of a federal sweep of African-American pro-Japanese organizations that resulted in the arrest of more than eighty black people in 1942 and early 1943.[64]

Elijah's wife, Clara Muhammad, became the supreme secretary of the Nation of Islam while her husband was in prison. During this time, she was the movement's cohesive force and passed down Elijah Muhammad's orders from the prison to the ministers and captains. Clara Muhammad had a longstanding connection to the movement. She was the moving force behind the establishment of the University of Islam in 1934 in Detroit, which was a pioneering institution in its emphasis on teaching Arabic to its students. She had also been one of the first black people to hear W. D. Fard's message and is said thereafter to have encouraged her husband to attend one of the prophet's meetings. Sister Clara was a model for black Muslim women in the 1940s, who worked to financially support their movement and their families while their men were in prison for sedition and Selective Service violations. These women not only worked behind the scenes to keep their movement on track, but also frequently appeared en masse in courtrooms in Chicago and Detroit to monitor the federal trials of black Muslim men. And the black Muslim women were not afraid of the police or court officers. In a highly publicized 1935 courtroom battle in Detroit that involved Rosetta Hassan and other unarmed black Muslims and armed police, thirteen policemen and seven court officers were injured. Even more than the Muslim men who wore "red crescent headed fezzes," the Muslim women, with their long dresses and their white headdresses draped over their shoulders, presented a striking and modest appearance that signaled the Nation of Islam's Asiatic identity.[65]

In 1946, Elijah Muhammad was released from prison. His incarceration made him look like a martyr to the black Muslims, and it helped to establish him as the absolute leader of his movement when he went back to Chicago. When he resumed active leadership of the black Muslims in the late 1940s, there were four temples in the United States—in Chicago, Detroit, Milwaukee, and Washington, D.C.[66]

During the 1950s, the Nation of Islam expanded its operations throughout the United States—dramatically increasing its membership and becoming the major voice for Islam in America. These changes occurred in the aftermath of World War II, as African Americans made the first "decisive cracks in the citadel of white supremacy" and laid the groundwork for the black revolution of the 1950s and 1960s. Black people around the world began to redefine their identities as European colonial regimes began to fall in Asia and Africa. Also in the 1940s, a second great wave of millions of Southern blacks began to enter the so-called "Promised Land" of the Northern cities in the United States. This demographic factor is important because it brought to the Northern ghettos people who would become major actors in American Islam and the black protest movement in the 1960s. In the context of these dramatic changes, which will be analyzed in Chapter 6, American Islam became an important aspect of "the growing diversity and complexity of African-American cultural production" that occurred in America. However, here there remains a final important note regarding the mysterious missionary W. D. Fard and his contributions to American Islam.[67]

LEGACY OF W. D. FARD

Sydney Ahlstrom has described the period between World War I and World War II as the time of "the crumbling of the Protestant establishment and the emergence of a more general pluralism" in America. Although historians of African-American religion are still debating whether the mainline black denominations were co-victims in the decline of historic Protestantism or beneficiaries of the new pluralism, everyone agrees that there was a dramatic growth of new religious movements in the black community in these years. They ran the gamut from "storefront churches and new Holiness and Pentecostal denominations to Father Divine's Peace Mission" and black Jewish groups. Moreover, in the context of the world-wide human tragedy of the Depression era, new and bizarre religious and political movements that reflected the rise of fascism in Europe also became a part of the fabric of white American public life. Martin Marty notes that:

> On both the religious and political right and left in America there were a number of movements, each of which attracted thousands or even millions of citizens. . . . Only one or two of these threatened to prevail, which here means to alter the basic terms of American religious and political life. The rest are important because they illustrate the instability of American existence in the Depression era, the legacy of disturbances in the twenties, and the desires of many religious citizens to experiment, to reach out into experiences borrowed from elsewhere, or from nowhere, which is what Utopia means.[68]

Historians writing of W. D. Fard in the 1930s have tended to place him in the context of either the "exotic cults in the [black] urban environment" or "the extremist experiments" of the Depression years. Both approaches are inadequate and ignore the real significance of this man. W. D. Fard was one of the most important figures in American Islamic history because he formulated the structures of political and racial discourse that enabled the religion to move into the 1950s and 1960s with dramatic vitality under the leadership of Elijah Muhammad and Malcolm X. Furthermore, Fard's legacy for American Islam must be taken out of the realm of exotica and cult and viewed as an important aspect of the agenda of a world religion. For Fard was an Islamic modernist, missionary, and important voice in the "noise of conflict" about the boundaries of American religion and identity.[69]

W. D. Fard was one of a group of foreign Muslim missionaries in his time who viewed America, especially black America, as the last hope for Islam to regain its political prominence in the modern world. These Muslims from India, Turkey, and Egypt were anti-imperialists and Islamic modernists whose cultures had been ravaged by European colonialism and Christian missionizing in the nineteenth and twentieth centuries. In response to the dual challenges of Western imperialism and modern technology, these modernists became "trailblazers" who began "to chart [their religion's] future direction through a reinterpretation of Islam in light of modern realities. They were pioneers who planted the seeds for the acceptance of change." Both in the Islamic world and America, the modernists "claimed the right and necessity to formulate new regulations," which alienated the "religious establishment" of Islam. However, these modern Muslim missionaries to America also called on the traditional structures of Islam for inspiration. For daʿwa, the Arabic concept for missionary activity, has its roots in Surah 16:125 of the Quran which says: "Call unto the way of thy Lord with wisdom and fair exhortation, and reason with them in the better way." From the beginning, American Islam focused on missionary activity and thus these modern redefinitions of Islam were a global phenomenon and not only part of a more narrow rubric of black American nationalism.[70]

W. D. Fard's gift as a missionary and modernist was his ability to read correctly the racial and political discourses of African Americans, Muslim immigrants in America, and Muslims in the Islamic world. His predecessors did not share this gift. Mohammed Alexander Russell Webb, the white American Muslim convert who represented Indian Muslims, was not more successful in his missionary work in the 1890s because he appealed to the wrong audience—white elites, instead of African Americans. The Ahmadis initially made the same mistake, but later underestimated the ethnocentrism of American Muslims from the "old country" and their resistance to real integration with African-American converts to Islam. As what Akbar Muhammad called a "culturally" "Turko-Persian" Muslim, Fard knew that there were historic patterns of racial separation in Islam that came to America with Asian, Arab, and East European Muslim immigrants and that "these patterns would ultimately alienate African-American converts." Therefore in his movement, "he restricted membership to African Americans and discouraged fraternization with immigrant Muslims." This is an important point that needs emphasis—the racial-separatist model of African Americans in Islam was initiated not by a black nationalist but by a non-black Muslim from the "old country." Larry A. Posten notes that most of the early Muslim immigrants had a "defensive-pacifist" orientation to missionary activity in America; they were interested only in maintaining their own ethnic and religious identity and not in changing the "non-Muslim society." These Muslims "quickly adopted the spirit of individualism so characteristic of other Americans and this enabled them to blend easily into society." For them, close associations with African-American converts would have interfered with their agenda of assimilation into mainstream America.[71]

Although W. D. Fard chose racial separation for the Nation of Islam in the 1930s, he did not close the door to integration in American Islam in the future. The calculated significations of his identity pointed to Arab, Turkish, Persian, and African-American symbols and thus provided an interpretive strategy for underlining the global nature of Islam and the positive cultural and political connections between Muslims of different ethnic and racial groups. Moreover, as we shall see, behind the scenes the Nation of Islam "welcomed and maintained personal and organizational relations with some immigrant Turks, Pakistanis, Indians, Egyptians and Jordanians (Palestinians)."[72]

As a sharp political thinker, Fard recognized the connections between Pan-Africanism and Pan-Islam. Since the time of Edward W. Blyden, some Pan-Africanists had favored Islam. The political discourses of the movements were similar—both sought to make sense of the cultures of non-white peoples who had been subjected to colonialism and slavery and formulated international coalitions to oppose Western imperialism and to empower Africans and Asians. The signification of Europeans as the other—"blond blue-eyed devils" with a separate God and destiny—was the most controversial teaching of the Nation of Islam and has been attributed incorrectly to the xenophobia of black nationalist Muslims. W. D. Fard was the source for this idea, which was very much a part of the mindset of some Muslims in the Islamic world in the nineteenth and twentieth centuries, who for the first time since the Crusades had to tolerate European conquerors in their native lands. When Napoleon invaded Egypt at the Battle of the Pyramids in 1798, and when British, Dutch, and Russian colonial initiatives among Muslims followed in the nineteenth century, Islam's most basic response was a rejection of the West as a corrupt and dangerous threat to its culture and faith. This idea never disappeared completely, even among the modernists who attempted to make the best of the European era. The European was the enemy, and this was a primal reaction that came from Islamic tradition which divided the world into the land of Islamic rule (*dar al-Islam*) and the land of warfare (*dar al-harb*). In the land of warfare (European dominance), Islamic resistance was manifested in jihad, which could mean either a struggle of arms or a struggle of words and the soul. As we have discussed above, the jihad of words and the soul was a Muslim religious obligation that was spelled out in the text of the Quran:

> O ye who believe! Take not my enemies and yours as friends—offering them love, even though they have rejected the truth that has come out to strive

(jihad) in My Way and to seek Good Pleasure (Take them not as friends); holding secret converse of love with them. (LX, 1)[73]

In this context, W. D. Fard's racial teaching was a "jihad of words," and its efficacy among African Americans was due to its similarity to the language of nineteenth-century Christian Pan-Africanism which we discussed in Chapter 2. Edward Wilmot Blyden, Theophilus Gould Steward, James Theodore Holly, and Henry McNeal Turner, with their ideas of a black God, "black moral superiority," white American Christianity as a "clan religion," and "the mission of the darker races," had all laid the groundwork in black America for the acceptance of Fard's "jihad of words" against Europeans. In the 1950s and 1960s, the "jihad of words" as a potent religious and political strategy would continue and would reach a high point of influence with the work of Malcolm X.[74]

Chapter 6

MALCOLM X AND
HIS SUCCESSORS

CONTEMPORARY SIGNIFICATIONS
OF AFRICAN-AMERICAN ISLAM

If you don't know my name, you don't know your
own.   —James Baldwin

Against Europe I protest,
And the attraction of the West.
Woe for Europe and her charm,
Swift to capture and disarm!
Europe's hordes with flame and fire
Desolate the world entire,
Architect of sanctuaries
Earth awaits rebuilding arise!
Out of leaden sleep
Out of slumber deep Arise!   —Muhammad Iqbal

James Baldwin characterized the World War II period as a turning point in
African-American history: "The treatment accorded the Negro during the
Second World War marks for me a turning point in the Negro's relation to
America. To put it briefly, and somewhat too simply, a certain hope died,
a certain respect for white Americans faded." At the same time, Cornel
West has argued that "with the emergence of the United States as supreme
world power and the collapse of European colonialism in Asia and Africa"
at the end of World War II, some African Americans began to realize the
"possibilities for a post-European world." Thus the political and cultural
identities that African Americans constructed for themselves in this era
were related to global events involving the "cultural and political agency
of peoples of color" and "decolonization . . . in the Third World."[1]

World War II was also a watershed event in the Islamic world, for in its aftermath Syria, Jordan, Pakistan, Indonesia, and African Muslim countries achieved independence from colonialism as European power diminished. Around that time, Muslim societies began to reassert themselves and decide how to deal with the mixed legacy of Western culture. Independence was an ambiguous phenomenon, however, as British forces remained in Egypt until 1954—thirty-two years after its so-called independence—and in Iran until 1958—twenty-six years after its independence. Also, on the eve of decolonization of the Islamic world, the United States had already established military bases and businesses in various Muslim countries in order to exploit their natural resources (usually petroleum). Thus, in the aftermath of World War II, despite their improved political fortunes, many Muslim peoples still felt that the Islamic world's major task was to rid itself of Western political and economic dominance and thus some of them signified the United States as the "Great Satan" (better translated as "the Great Demon" or "the Great Devil").[2]

Indeed the emergence of Malcolm X as the major international spokesperson for black American Muslims in the 1960s was connected with this international resurgence of Islam in world affairs, the decolonization in Asia and Africa, and the demonization of America in the Muslim world. Malcolm X's eloquent articulation of black America's identity crisis and its search for "a more authentic identity," its disillusionment with the socioeconomic and political agenda of the white mainstream, and its "newfound sense of pride and power" reflected the agenda of contemporary Muslims all over the world.[3]

Moreover, Malcolm X was a star of the media. He was young, strong, handsome, and vibrant, and he changed his name each time he modified his religious and political identities. His "jihad of words" in defense of Islam was both forceful and seductive and echoed similar jihads of words against the West in the Muslim world. The theme of signification and identity is adumbrated through the words and ideas of Malcolm X, for this red-headed genius became the primary model for the signification of black Islamic identity in contemporary America. Indeed, in Malcolm's shifting relationships with the Nation of Islam, and with Islam in the Middle East and West Africa, and in his ambivalence between racial separation and multi-racialism in these contexts, we can discern the models for the various significations of Islamic identity in the ever-changing ideologies of Louis Farrakhan and Warith Deen Mohammed—the two foremost black Muslim leaders in America today. These issues will be a focal point of this chapter.

We will also analyze Elijah Muhammad's role in establishing Islam as a major factor in American religion and black American life in the 1950s, 1960s, and 1970s. For it must not be forgotten that the Honorable Elijah Muhammad and the organization that he built were the models for Malcolm X's racial-separatist significations of black Islamic identity. Moreover, Elijah Muhammad was The Messenger—the last surviving link between the original message of black American Islam that had come from the East early in the twentieth century and contemporary black America. As we shall see, his jihad of words, as it was expressed in his books, speeches, and newspaper articles, was also one of the most potent messages of Islam delivered to black America in the twentieth century, and the issue of names and identity and the relationship of black American Islam to global Islam were inseparable from this message. The Nation of Islam in the 1960s saw a transition from the concept of signification as a personal search for religious identity to an institutional quest for a collective public identity. This transition signaled that the Nation of Islam had truly become a major force in American religion and politics. Although it remained a religion, the inter-relation of religion and politics was central in its quest for a public religious identity.

However, to understand fully the meaning of the significations that Elijah Muhammad and Malcolm X formulated, we must begin with the latter's formative years, in the 1930s and 1940s, for this is when his changes in name and identity began. And it should be noted that the reconsideration of Malcolm X's religious and political identities that follows is based on a substantial body of new and old source materials that together have opened the door for revision of certain traditional ideas about him and the Nation of Islam.[4]

FROM MALCOLM LITTLE TO MALCOLM X: FAMILY CONTINUITY AND ISLAMIC IDENTITY

Malcolm Little was born in Omaha, Nebraska on May 19, 1925. He was one of the eight children of Earl Little and Louise Norton Little. Both parents were black nationalists—active members in Marcus Garvey's Universal Negro Improvement Association.

Until very recently, much of the scholarship on Malcolm X has focused on the pathology and deterioration of the Little family during the Great Depression and thus has de-emphasized the central role of family continuity in the initial formation of Malcolm X's Islamic identity. However, William Strickland has recently revised this traditional view of Malcolm X by focusing on "the history that made Malcolm." He notes that "the Malcolm X we know is unimaginable apart from the family into which he was born and the parents who gave him life. He is unimaginable apart from the Garveyism to which his parents were committed and the Garveyism out of which the Nation of Islam sprang." As we shall see, both Earl and Louise Little paid an extraordinary personal price for their political activism but, in spite of this, they passed on an extraordinary internationalist political/religious legacy to their children, who reconstructed their scattered family by converting to the Nation of Islam in the 1940s and brought their oldest brother, Malcolm, into the Nation while he was in prison.[5]

Louise Norton Little was born in the West Indies in the British colony of Grenada; her father was a white man of Scottish descent and her mother was a black woman, born in Grenada. Earl Little was born in 1890 in Georgia, where his early first marriage resulted in three children. In the early 1900s, both Earl and Louise immigrated to Canada, where they met and were married in 1919. Although there was a UNIA chapter in Montreal during this period, the available sources do not tell whether Earl and Louise were members of it. However, we do know that in Canada, Earl and Louise were exposed to a global cross-section of black peoples and cultures, for in the early 1900s "Montreal was a miniature version of Garvey's Pan-African world." In 1919, in the aftermath of the bloody "Red Summer," in which scores of black Americans were killed by whites in race riots around the country, the Littles returned to the United States. For a while, they lived in Philadelphia, where their first child, Wilfred, was born. Eventually, they settled in Omaha, where Earl Little became the president of the local chapter of the UNIA and Louise Little organized news releases for the UNIA's global newspaper, *The Negro World*.[6]

Malcolm X's oldest daughter, Attallah Shabazz, sheds new light on how her grandparents' political work and religious identities shaped her father's global religious and political identities:

> My father is what his parents were, and their parents. . . . [my grandparents] were internationalists. They were from the Garvey movement. They understood history from point go. And my grandmother, being from the Caribbean, was surrounded by Easterners, meaning North Africans and East Indians; all that had something to do with her nature. The circle of my father's life has a lot more to do with what went into it initially in the first decade of shaping his life. His commitment to people, social change, being self sufficient. My grandmother translated four languages—to transcribe into the newspaper, which my father and his siblings shopped around. All of that social involvement—the commitment, the responsibility started early. So that when my grandfather and my grandmother were taken away, and the children separated and dispersed through the system and then my father through the streets. Those were all distractions. If he did not have a strong track to begin with, he might not have found his way back. But he was nurtured from the beginning.
>
> Interestingly enough, my grandparents were from two different religions, even though in those days you became automatically what your husband was. Neither parent invaded the other one's spiritual rearing and spirituality. My grandfather, as a result of being the first generation born out of slavery, was exposed to Christianity. *My grandmother was exposed to Islam in a nonrigid way because of the culture around her.*[7]

By all accounts, Malcolm and his siblings had hard childhoods because of white racist opposition to their parents' political activities. In

1925, the Littles were expelled from Omaha by the powerful Ku Klux Klan. Not to be deterred from resistance, however, Earl Little moved his family to Milwaukee, Wisconsin, where he became president of the International Industrial Club, which petitioned President Calvin Coolidge to pardon Marcus Garvey in 1927. In 1929, the Little family moved again to Lansing, Michigan, where Earl purchased a home in a white neighborhood and planned to set up his own store. However, in the wake of a court battle to evict the Littles from their home, which was in a neighborhood supposedly protected from racial integration by a restrictive covenant, the racial harassment of the family escalated. Hostile white supremacists burned their new home to the ground. Although this incident was seared into Malcolm's early memory, it would be a mistake to characterize all of his "early childhood as a nightmare," as has traditionally been done, for in spite of the tragedy of this event, Earl Little temporarily recovered.[8]

He moved his family to East Lansing, built his own home, and grew the crops to feed them on his own land. Most important, he did not abandon his political work. Thus, Earl emerged from this crisis as a model of political resistance for Malcolm and his siblings, sowing the seeds for their political and religious consciousness and identity by taking them to UNIA meetings. As Malcolm's eldest brother Wilfred Little recalls:

> Back in those days in the city of Lansing there was no such thing as a UNIA hall. So my father would get together people who were interested and they would go in cars to Detroit, and in Detroit we'd have a chance to attend meetings where they would have speakers. Sometimes he would take me, or he would take Malcolm—the ones that were old enough to kinda understand.
>
> When you'd leave there you'd feel proud of yourself, you know—you'd be proud that you were Black. You knew that you had been somebody and you're gon' be somebody now if you got the chance, and you looked for every opportunity to accomplish that.[9]

And the Little children's lessons about black racial identity and consciousness continued outside of the UNIA hall, as their father and mother taught them to sing the UNIA national anthem proudly, even in the Lansing schools in which they were the only black children. Wilfred Little remembers that to his white teachers' chagrin, one day he stood up in class and sang the following words of the UNIA Universal Ethiopian Anthem after the Pledge of Allegiance to the American flag:

> Ethiopia, thou land of our fathers
> Thou land where the gods loved to be
> As the storm clouds a night suddenly gathers
> Our armies come rushing to thee.
> We must in the fight be victorious,
> When swords are thrust outward to glean;

For us will the vict'ry be glorious
When led by the red, black and green.
Advance, advance to victory!
Let Africa be free![10]

Furthermore, in his autobiography, Malcolm X recalled fondly that although he knew his father both as a preacher and political activist,

> the image of him that made me proudest was his crusading and militant campaigning with the words of Marcus Garvey. . . . One of the reasons I've always felt my father favored me was that to the best of my remembrance, it was only me that he sometimes took with him to the Garvey UNIA meetings which he held in different people's homes. . . . There were never more than a few people at any one time—twenty at most. But that was a lot, packed in someone's living room. I noticed how differently they all acted, although sometimes they were the same people who jumped and shouted in church. But in these meetings both they and my father were more intelligent and down to earth. It made me feel the same way.[11]

Although Malcolm X admitted that his childhood introduction to Garveyism did not immediately change the stereotyped image of Africa that he had learned from the dominant culture, the important point for us is that his mother and father planted in his consciousness the political and spiritual seeds of Pan-Africanism and Islam that later in his life blossomed into an extraordinary Pan-Africanist and Islamic identity under the influence of the Nation of Islam, the Arab Muslim world, and West African political and religious leaders. This was the gift that Earl and Louise Little gave to all of their children in the beginning. For as we shall see, in spite of the hardships that they faced, through three generations, the Littles remained an extraordinary family of African-American Muslims and internationalist political activists.[12]

It finally became clear to white supremacist groups in Lansing that they could not force Earl Little to abandon his militant political work on behalf of black people; and on September 28, 1931, he was killed mysteriously—crushed and almost torn in half by a streetcar in Lansing. His death was attributed to the Black Legion, a major white supremacist organization. This tragedy was the beginning of the end for the Little family. From 1931 to 1939, Louise Little struggled desperately to keep her family together during the Great Depression. However, the worsening economic times, loneliness, and unrelenting harassment by the public-relief authorities chipped away at her spirit year by year. Finally, Louise Little was pushed to her breaking point, as the state authorities took her children away from her one by one and sent them to foster homes. She suffered a nervous breakdown, and on January 3, 1939 she was legally declared insane and committed to the state mental hospital at Kalamazoo. She was forty-two years old at the time of her commitment and was not released from Kalamazoo until 1963.[13]

In the wake of their mother's commitment, the Little children—Malcolm, Wilfred, Hilda, Reginald, Yvonne, Philbert, Robert, and Wesley—were placed by the state authorities in separate foster homes in Lansing. This dispersal of the Little family had actually begun in 1937, when the state welfare authorities placed Malcolm in a temporary foster home. In August 1939, he was expelled from the Lansing school system for minor troublemaking and sent to a juvenile detention home in the town of Mason. This was his introduction to the corrections system, which would eventually be the catalyst and location for his first conversion to Islamic identity. In his autobiography, Malcolm declared:

> I think that an objective reader may see how in the society to which I was exposed as a black youth here in America, for me to wind up in a prison was really just about inevitable.[14]

In the detention home and in his junior high school in Mason, the young Malcolm came face to face with the brutal racial and economic inequities, as well as the racist significations of white Christian America. Although he excelled in academics and sports and was the president of his class in Mason Junior High School, his white teachers discouraged him from preparing for college and aspiring to be a lawyer because of his race. Malcolm's favorite teacher told him, "That's no realistic goal for a nigger." And his white classmates and the white people in the detention home often referred to him as "nigger," "darkie," "Rastus," and "coon."[15]

By the time Malcolm reached the eighth grade, American institutional racism had resulted in the brutal death of his father, the institutionalization of his mother, the separation of his siblings, and the beginning of deep self-hatred and self-destructive behavior. This is an important point, for just as it is impossible to fully understand Malcolm's later Islamic identity without discussing his father's internationalist political work and his mother's "nonrigid" exposure to Islam in her native Grenada, it is also important to analyze the influence of American racism on his religious and political life. William Strickland has correctly noted that Malcolm's Islamic identities are "unimaginable apart from the American racism that radicalized him as it radicalized so many who have wrestled with being both black and human in a persistently resistant America."[16] For the next decade of his life, Malcolm fulfilled the destiny of juvenile delinquency, self-hatred, and crime that American institutional racism had bequeathed to him. He became the mirror image of all the racist significations that white Christian America had constructed for young African-American men. James H. Cone has described this phase of his life as "the making of a bad nigger."[17]

In 1940, Malcolm Little began a new phase of his life when his elder half-sister, Ella Collins, invited him to Boston for a summer visit. Ella was destined to be an important family connection in the different stages of Malcolm's religious and political identity crises. In the years that followed, as Malcolm transformed his religious and political identities in the Nation of Islam, in Mecca, in the Muslim Mosque, Inc., and in the Organization of Afro-American Unity, Ella not only followed her brother's example but was also the family member who provided him with financial support, tough and honest advice, and advocacy in crucial situations. She was the matriarch of the Little family and stood by her brother through thick and thin. Initially, she impressed Malcolm because she was unconditionally proud of her blackness and was a homeowner and economic striver in Boston. In February 1941, she got legal custody of her brother from the state of Michigan and brought him to Boston to live with her, his half-sister Mary, and his half-brother Earl Jr. Malcolm was fifteen years old.[18]

In Boston, Malcolm quickly began to assume his legendary hustling identity, "Red," which was the precursor to his first Islamic name and identity. Red was the embodiment of all the negative significations of black men that American institutional racism had created and that conversion to the Nation of Islam would later destroy. He was a zoot-suit-wearing, rag-headed, conked-haired, lindy-hopping jitterbug; a high-school drop-out, shiftless, and chronically unemployed; sexually promiscuous, with a pro-clivity for white women; a thief, a hustler, a pimp, and a drug addict with a volatile and violent streak, but always wearing a smile for white people.[19]

Although Malcolm lived in middle-class surroundings with Ella in the Roxbury section of Boston, he preferred the fast life in the Dudley Station area of Roxbury and the South End, where many of the black nightclubs and bars were located. This is where he began his short career in criminal activities, which included selling narcotics, prostitution, con games, gambling, and eventually armed robbery. As Malcolm worked as a shoe shiner, a soda jerk, and a dishwasher in Boston and as a porter on the New Haven Railroad between Boston and New York, he soon realized that America's racist economic inequities were stacked against black men like him in the 1940s. He told his brother Wilfred:

> Hell, I will never make it trying to be right. The only people that are really making it are the ones that's trying to do wrong. . . . You'll never make it on these janitor jobs and selling sandwiches on these trains and shining shoes and and stuff like that.

As Malcolm began to understand the racial contradictions in the North, that Boston, the so-called "Cradle of Liberty" was really the most violently racist and segregated city in the Northeast, assuming the identity of Red and embarking on a new life of crime seemed like the only reasonable response.[20]

In March 1943, Malcolm moved to New York City to work briefly for the New Haven Railroad. However, Broadway and the bright lights of Manhattan attracted him to Harlem, the Mecca of black America during the World War II era. Employed as a waiter in Small's Paradise Bar in Harlem, he learned the ins and outs of hustling—from prostitution to con games to dope peddling to armed robbery. In his autobiography, Malcolm reminisced about his hustling days and revealed how he got the name "Detroit Red."

> New York was heaven to me. And Harlem was Seventh Heaven! I hung around in Small's and the Braddock bar so much that the bartenders began to pour a shot of bourbon, my favorite brand of it, when they saw me walk in the door. And the steady customers in both places, the hustlers in Small's and entertainers in Braddock, began to call me "Red," a natural enough nickname in view of my bright red conk.[21]

The conk—the chemical processing of coarse hair to make it straight— was the ultimate symbol of racial self-hatred for many African Americans. It represented the desire of some blacks to approximate European standards of beauty as closely as possible. In the 1940s, conking was a painful and unhealthy process—the lye that chemically straightened the hair could permanently burn and damage the scalp. The conk was one of the symbols of oppression that Malcolm's eventual conversion to the Nation of Islam would erase by emphasizing black pride and wholesome health practices. In his autobiography, the conk was a manifestation of internalized American racism. It symbolized black people's racial self-hatred and the denigration of their African physical characteristics. At the same time, it was a symbol of a black dialectical process which involved hatred of and fascination with the white dominant culture. For Malcolm, this dialectic was ultimately resolved by his initial conversion to a racial-separatist Islamic identity, which emphasized psychological and physical separation from white American culture and the hatred of white people.[22]

"Detroit Red," one of Malcolm's most flamboyant identities, did not last long. In January 1946, he was charged with larceny, breaking and entering, and carrying firearms. At twenty years of age, he began a six-year sentence in Charlestown Prison in Massachusetts on February 27, 1946—the same year that Elijah Muhammad finished his four-year sentence for draft resistance. This coincidence was pivotal in the history of Islam in America. While he was in prison in Michigan, Muhammad saw that black religious and political organizations had not developed programs to rehabilitate the lowest of the black lower class—the pimps, prostitutes, drug addicts, and young criminals like Detroit Red. After World War II, he changed the agenda of the Nation of Islam to concentrate on this group. He believed that knowledge of black peoples' true history and identity could transform this group into useful members of the black community. Thus signification, spiritual therapy and the discipline of

Islam were central in the programs that he developed to save these people. The results were astounding: fourteen years later, the movement's membership expanded to an estimated 100,000, and 75 percent of those people were between seventeen and thirty-five years old. By 1960, the Nation of Islam was the major outpost for Islam in the Western world, and much of its renewed vitality was due to the efforts of the dynamic Malcolm X, who converted to Islam in prison in 1947 and 1948.[23]

After a brief transfer to Concord Reformatory, Malcolm arrived at the Norfolk Prison Colony in March 1948. Norfolk was an enlightened prison colony which included an outstanding library and educational programs for its inmates. In this atmosphere, Malcolm was initially encouraged to develop his mind by Bimbi, the smartest black prisoner in Concord, who built his reputation among his fellow inmates with his words. In the meantime, some of Malcolm's siblings—Wilfred, Hilda, Philbert, and Reginald—had begun to reunite their family by converting to the Nation of Islam. Malcolm's oldest brothers, Wilfred Little and Abdul Aziz Omar (Philbert), have emphasized the central role of family continuity in their initial conversion to a racial-separatist Muslim identity. Wilfred initiated the process of conversion in his family:

> I came into the Muslim movement in 1947 and started bringing my brothers and sisters in. We already had been indoctrinated with Marcus Garvey's philosophy, so that was a good place for us. They didn't have to convince us we were Black and should be proud or anything like that.
>
> We all got together and decided we better let Malcolm know about this. Even though we had been scattered, we kept up with each other, and we tried to do things together as a family.[24]

However, it was Philbert who initially wrote to Malcolm to introduce him to Islam:

> So I wrote to Malcolm and told him if he would believe in Allah that he would get out of prison. And that's all I wrote because I knew he had very low tolerance for religion.[25]

William Strickland has noted that the Littles' "act of renewing family ties" through conversion to Islamic identity "was also a reconnection with those days when their mother read to them from *The Negro World* and then their father spoke to them of 'the great race work' to be done." Malcolm's own account of his conversion experience from Detroit Red to Satan (his first nickname in prison) to Malcolm X also emphasized the theme of family continuity and poignantly demonstrated the dramatic change in identity that his new Muslim name signified and why this experience became an inspiring model for other African-American Muslim converts in the corrections system. For initially, at the heart of Malcolm's conversion to Islamic identity was the global Islamic theme of the greater jihad, which involved an intense inner struggle "to turn his life around" and purify his soul for Islam:

> My sister Hilda . . . kept urging me to write to Mr. Muhammad. He understood what it was to be in the white man's prison, she said, because he himself had not long before gotten out of the federal prison at Milan, Michigan where he had served four years for evading the draft. . . . I did write to Elijah Muhammad. . . . At least twenty-five times I must have written that first one-page letter to him, over and over. I was trying to make it both legible and understandable. I practically couldn't read my handwriting myself; it shames me even to remember it. My spelling and my grammar were as bad, if not worse. Anyway, as well as I could express it, I said I had been told about him by my brothers and sisters, and I apologized for my poor letter.
>
> Mr. Muhammad sent me a typed reply. It had an all but electrical effect upon me to see the signature of the "Messenger of Allah." After he welcomed me into the "true knowledge," he gave me something to think about. The black prisoner, he said, symbolized white society's crime of keeping black men oppressed and deprived and ignorant, and unable to get decent jobs, turning them into criminals. He told me to have courage. He even enclosed some money for me, a five-dollar bill. . . .
>
> Regularly my family wrote to me, "Turn to Allah . . . pray to the East."
>
> The hardest test I ever faced in my life was praying. You understand. My comprehending, my believing the teachings of Mr. Muhammad had only required my mind's saying to me, "That's right!" or "I never thought of that." But bending my knees to pray—the act—well, that took me a week. . . .
>
> For evil to bend its knees, admitting its guilt, to implore the forgiveness of God, is the hardest thing in the world. It's easy for me to see and to say that now. But then, when I was the personification of evil, I was going through it. Again, and again, I would force myself back down into the praying-to-Allah posture. When finally I was able to make myself stay down—I didn't know what to say to Allah.
>
> For the next years, I was the nearest thing to a hermit in the Norfolk Prison Colony. I never have been more busy in my life. I still marvel at how swiftly my previous life's thinking pattern slid away from me, like snow off a roof. It is as though someone else I knew of had lived by hustling and crime. I would be startled to catch myself thinking in a remote way of my earlier self as another person.[26]

MALCOLM X AND THE JIHAD OF WORDS

Although the intense inner struggle of the greater jihad was initially at the heart of Malcolm's conversion to a Muslim identity, he distinguished himself in the Nation of Islam and in the world through the lesser jihad of words. Steven Barboza has characterized Malcolm's jihad of words as "talking back at white America—which translated as offering blacks a psychological alternative" to American institutional racism. Malcolm's jihad of words, however, was more significant than this. By virtue of the jihad of words he became the most important twentieth-century public advocate for Islam in America, and arguably in the world. At the same time, with his genius for the spoken word and his profound spirituality, Malcolm raised this global Islamic paradigm to a level of significance that surpassed the original vision of Ghulam Ahmad and the Ahmadiyya Movement in Islam. Malcolm's transformation of the jihad of words was closely related to the theme of signification and identity. For Malcolm, the jihad of words was not just defensive rhetoric on behalf of Islam, but also a potent intellectual tool for spiritual and political consciousness raising in African-American Islam.[27]

William Strickland has noted that "we fail to perceive Malcolm as a true intellectual because we regard as intellectuals those who communicate via the written word and to a certain audience." However, it is precisely in the context of Malcolm's astounding intellectual development in prison that we can begin to understand the power of his jihad of words and its relation to signification and identity in the Nation of Islam. Extensive and thoughtful reading, debating, and serious contemplation raised his religious and political consciousness about the situation of black people in America and the world and helped him to develop the discipline needed to become *Muslim*—literally, to submit completely to Allah. The specifics of Malcolm's intellectual work in prison became a model for Muslim ministers in the Nation of Islam who carried on the tradition of the jihad of words in the 1960s and beyond.[28]

One aspect of Malcolm's intellectual development was his study of what he called his "dictionary project"; he studied all the words in Webster's dictionary. Malcolm not only studied their meanings but also their etymology and the logic of their use. The logic of words led him to a love of debating, and soon he became a master of logically constructed arguments. He began to excel in the discussion groups and debates in his prison classes at Norfolk. Malcolm Jarvis, a fellow inmate, later recalled:

> They would be debating different things on race, religion, and Malcolm would back 'em to the wall with his questions and answers. And then while he was talking, I would be jotting down questions. I'd be jotting down a rebuttal and shove it under his hand, and he'd look down, and then he'd take over.[29]

Malcolm became sensitized to global political and religious issues by reading extensively in history, religion, philosophy, and the social sciences. In his eventual jihad of words, Malcolm used elements from his study of world history to advance the historical and religious doctrines of the Nation of Islam and to indict the white western world for its racism. These readings also helped Malcolm to understand his new Muslim identity in a global context. Together with his fellow inmate Malcolm Jar-vis, he sought the "knowledge and wisdom of the world" in his readings:

> Malcolm and I were playing the part of, like, Solomon in the Bible—we were seeking knowledge and wisdom of the world. That's what had us going into these books in Egyptology, hieroglyphics, psychiatry, psychology, theol-ogy. We studied Shintoism, we studied many things out of these books that we had at the library. We were just seeking basic knowledge of what makes the world tick. We were trying to acclimate our minds into thinking on a much higher level than that of the average person.[30]

Malcolm's readings in world history included books written by or about Will Durant, W. E. B. Du Bois, H. G. Wells, Arnold Toynbee, Frederick Olmstead, Harriet Beecher Stowe, Mahatma Gandhi, Herodotus, J. A. Rogers, and others. Through this study, he developed a deeper apprecia-tion for the Nation of Islam's most basic theme of racial-separatist signifi-cation and identity—that the black race was the original race of human-kind—by verifying empirically "the black race's historical greatness." At the same time, Malcolm's study of philosophy also verified this theme by tracing the intellectual roots of Western civilization back to the East. In his autobiography, he wrote:

> When I discovered philosophy, I tried to touch all the landmarks of philosophical development. Gradually, I read most of the old philosophers, Occidental and Oriental. The Oriental philosophers were the ones I came to prefer; finally, my impression was that most Occidental philosophy had largely been borrowed from the Oriental thinkers. Socrates, for instance, traveled in Egypt. Some sources even say that Socrates was initiated into some of the Egyptian mysteries. Obviously, Socrates got some of his wisdom among the East's wise men.[31]

As a result of his family's intervention, Elijah Muhammad's teachings, and rigorous intellectual and spiritual work, Malcolm had discovered "his new identity and his calling" in prison. As he began to tutor his fellow black prisoners and teach them about the Nation of Islam, he traveled the same path of activism and preaching that "his parents had trod" in Marcus Garvey's Universal Negro Improvement Association. Thus the theme of family continuity was echoed in the jihad of words that Malcolm began in prison.[32]

During the time of Malcolm's imprisonment, the social and economic power of black America was changing dramatically. These changes are important for understanding the appeal of both his jihad of words and the Nation of Islam's theme of identity and signification to the black masses during this period. As a result of a new racial consciousness and militancy during World War II and migration during the postwar years, a new and powerful black working class emerged at the end of the 1940s. The strengthened political consciousness of this new working class prepared the way for the dramatic growth of the Nation of Islam and the civil-rights revolution in the 1950s and 1960s, producing a mood of hope and certainty that racial barriers would be destroyed in America and organizing to ensure this goal. Richard M. Dalfiume has called the World War II era the "forgotten years" of the black revolution:

> The hypocrisy and paradox involved in fighting a world war for the four freedoms and against aggression by an enemy preaching a master race ideology, while at the same time upholding racial segregation and white supremacy, were too obvious. The war crisis provided American Negroes with an opportunity to point out, for all to see, the difference between the American creed and practice.[33]

During the war, A. Philip Randolph's march on Washington movement sowed the seeds for the mass militant political movements of the 1950s and 1960s. In 1941, Randolph scheduled a march of 100,000 blacks on Washington, D.C. to protest discrimination in the defense industries. Bowing to the pressure of this threat, one week before the scheduled march, President Roosevelt issued Executive Order 8802, abolishing discrimination in national defense and federal departments of the government. A. Philip Randolph, the head of the Brotherhood of Sleeping Car Porters, emerged from this controversy as the foremost black leader in America. He symbolized a kind of militance among lower-class blacks that had not appeared since the Garvey era and recognized the value of black consciousness and collective self-reliance in a movement that involved the black masses. Although Randolph was an advocate of coalition politics, he believed that "only power can effect the enforcement and adoption of a given policy" and that "power is the active principle of only the organized masses, the masses united for a definite purpose." The march on Washington movement was a positive sign that times were about to change for working-class blacks in the ghettos.[34]

The demographic fact behind the Nation of Islam's rise in the postwar years was the second Great Migration. Between the 1940s and the late 1960s, five million black Americans moved from the South to the "promised land" of the Northern cities. This mass movement enlarged Chicago's African-American population from almost 300,000 in 1940 to more than 800,000 in 1960 and produced similar changes in many American cities. These new migrants to the North sought the economic advancement and legal rights that Jim Crow had withheld from them in the South. In doing so, they transformed the race issue in America. According to Nicholas Lemann:

> this great migration changed the United States from a country where race was a regional issue and black culture existed mainly in rural isolation into one where race relations affected the texture of life in nearly every city and suburb;

it altered politics at every level and popular culture and the very idea of what American society is.[35]

Malcolm X was part of this "human tide" that moved northward in these years, and he became a pioneer in the effort to mobilize the black poor socially and politically by utilizing the jihad of words and the Nation of Islam's liberating message of signification and identity. He became the model for thousands of black men and women who were destined to write the following letter to W. D. Fard through Elijah Muhammad in order to convert to the Nation of Islam. Upon the Nation's acceptance of this letter, they received their "original" names and an X, which signified the African name that was lost in slavery:

> Dear Savior Allah, Our Deliverer:
>   I have been attending the teachings of Islam by one of your ministers, two or three times. I believe in It, and I bear witness that there is no God but Thee, and that Muhammad is Thy Servant and Apostle. I desire to reclaim my own. Please give me my original name. My slave name is as follows.[36]

Toward the end of his prison term, Malcolm's spiritual and political transformation intensified his ministry on behalf of the Nation of Islam at an astounding pace. As a result of his persuasive preaching, he converted Osborne and Leroy Thaxton, Malcolm Jarvis, and several others in the Norfolk Prison Colony in 1950. In March of that year, he led the Muslim prisoners in Norfolk in written and verbal protests against the prison's obligatory typhoid inoculations, which were prohibited by their religion, and the prison's refusal to accommodate the Muslims' special dietary requirements. Although prison authorities sent Malcolm back to Charlestown Prison to silence him, he continued his jihad of words by writing a letter to President Truman, protesting the United States' involvement in the Korean War. He wrote:

> Dear President Truman,
>   Tell Bradley to get in shape. It looks like another war. I have always been a Communist. I have tried to enlist in the Japanese Army, last war, now they will never draft or accept me in the U.S. Army. Everyone has always said "that nigger Malcolm is crazy" so it isn't hard to convince people that I am.
>   Malachi Shabazz[37]

By this time, Malcolm had decided on his own to adopt a Muslim name, "Malachi," which he believed was an appropriate Arabic replacement for his "slave name," Malcolm. "Malachi" was really a Hebrew name that meant "my messenger." Because Elijah Muhammad was already known as "The Messenger" of Allah and had planned to give Malcolm his X to signify his African name lost in slavery, he criticized his new disciple for his name change and for his independent letters to the press and the president. By January 1951, Malcolm X had acquiesced to Elijah Muhammad's chastisement. However, this episode foreshadowed the dramatic struggle over the racial separatist religious and political identity of the Nation of Islam that would occur between Elijah Muhammad and Malcolm X in the 1960s.[38]

MALCOLM X, ELIJAH MUHAMMAD, AND GLOBAL ISLAM: THE POLITICS OF RELIGIOUS IDENTITY

When Malcolm came out, he was full o' fire. . . . He got out at the right time and the right place, so he could expound. He came to Detroit, and he was surprised to find that there were so few people in this powerful teaching. He got on the podium, and he told them, "I'm ashamed, I'm surprised that you are sitting here, and so many empty seats." He said, "Every time you come here, this place should be full." And that excited the Honorable Elijah Muhammad, it excited the believers who had any energy. And we brought in people, just hundreds of them.
—Abdul Aziz Omar[39]

Malcolm X was twenty-seven years old when he was paroled from prison on August 7, 1952. That month, he received his X from Elijah Muhammad. Three of his brothers, Reginald, Wilfred, and Philbert, had already converted to the Nation of Islam. Upon his release, Malcolm lived with Wilfred in Detroit, where he worked for the Garwood Furniture Company and later for the Ford Motor Company during the day, recruiting new members for the Nation of Islam in the evening. Within less than a year, his efforts increased the membership of the Detroit Temple No. 1 to such an extent that Elijah Muhammad made him an assistant minister for the Nation of Islam and then, in the fall of 1953, the first minister for Boston Temple No. 11.[40]

Elijah Muhammad's son, Warith Deen Mohammad, recalled:

Malcolm was impressing [my] father as soon as he was released from prison. . . . He had been waiting for someone to deliver his message to a non-Muslim audience. . . . He wanted more visibility for the Nation of Islam. . . . He wanted to compete with Christian Black America.

As Elijah Muhammad evaluated how the federal government's deliberate campaign of persecution had decimated the young black male ranks of his movement in the 1940s, he saw in Malcolm X's youthful exuberance and gifted oratory two qualities that would help him to invigorate the Nation of Islam in the 1950s.[41]

Warith Deen Mohammed has noted that:

Before the Honorable Elijah Muhammad's release from prison, we were very much like any private spiritualist religious movement. Upon his release he changed our focus from the lessons of the Nation of Islam to doing something practical to changing our environment for the better.[42]

As Malcolm X quickly rose through the ranks of the Nation of Islam, he also became a primary facilitator of social change in the most depressed areas of the African-American environment. In March 1954, Elijah Muhammad rewarded Malcolm X's efforts by promoting him to minister of Philadelphia Temple No. 12, and then advancing him to New York Temple No. 7 three months later. He was sent to Detroit Temple No. 1 in September 1957. Soon Malcolm became the Nation of Islam's Chief Minister, traveling extensively through the cities of the United States to establish forty-nine new temples in the 1950s. Under his influence, the membership of the organization increased to 40,000 during this decade and primarily attracted black youth as new converts.[43]

The complete historical narrative of Malcolm X's ascendancy in the Nation of Islam has been the subject of several important social-science and biographical works. It will not be repeated here. However, little attention has been devoted to the religious significance of Malcolm X's work and its importance in establishing the Nation of Islam's signification and identity in the context of global Islam. Elucidation of these issues clears the way for understanding the Nation of Islam and related African-American Muslim groups primarily as religious movements with political implications rather than exclusively as political organizations or social movements as has been previously done. The major point here is that religion is the starting point for understanding the political significance of Malcolm X and the Nation of Islam.[44]

As the relationship between Elijah Muhammad and Malcolm X developed and the Nation of Islam became a national religious movement with international recognition in the Muslim world, the most fundamental questions about the politics of the organization's racial-separatist religious identity were raised. At stake was how the Nation of Islam defined its religious identity in relation to the politics of the Muslim world and the African-American freedom struggle in the 1960s. As we shall see, ultimately, this politics of religious identity developed into a "life and death" power struggle between Elijah Muhammad, Malcolm X, and different factions in the Nation of Islam over who would lead the African-American Muslim community in the United States. However, this struggle was dormant in the late 1950s and early 1960s, as Elijah Muhammad and Malcolm X worked together to define the religious identity of their movement in the Muslim world and in America. The relationship that developed between Malcolm X and his mentor Elijah Muhammad was a warm father-son friendship. The two men had much in common; both had grown up the hard way, were self-educated, and were the sons of strong racially aware black men. Together in 1959, they were poised to become the two most important Islamic leaders in North America.[45]

Although many Muslims and non-Muslims in America and abroad criticized the racial ideas of the Nation and refused to recognize it as Islamic, behind the scenes, national and international Muslim leaders monitored and maintained relations with either Malcolm or Elijah. For they grudgingly recognized that the Nation of Islam was the major outpost for their religion in the Western world. In 1959, Elijah Muhammad decided to settle, once and for all, the political question arising from the relation of the Nation of Islam's religious identity to global Islam. He sent Malcolm X, as an ambassador of the Nation of Islam, on a tour of the Middle East and West Africa. In July 1959, Malcolm met with Muslim religious and political officials in Cairo, who "received him with open arms" and prepared the official path for Elijah Muhammad to make the hajj to Mecca in 1960.[46]

Louis Lomax has noted that:

> The Hajj, the long . . . pilgrimage to Mecca that every [Muslim] looks forward to, is the final criterion of whether one is or is not a [Muslim]. Only certified followers of Islam are allowed to enter Mecca during the holy period of the pilgrimage. . . . Several days after he departed from New York, Elijah placed his credentials before the eagle-eyed hajj committee, the final judge of who may march to Mecca and pray. Elijah Muhammad was admitted without delay, and Black Muslims—the word was cabled back and came over the wire services—held meetings of praise and thanks all over the nation.[47]

Since the time of Mansa Musa, black Muslim leaders had used the hajj to respond to charges that their racial separateness and black political agenda were un-Islamic, for the hajj ensured "tacit recognition and implicit legitimization" of a leader and his people by the international Muslim community. This pilgrimage occurs during Dhu al-Hijja, the twelfth month of the Muslim calendar. The rites which take place at the Kaaba, the Zamzam Well, and the plain of Arafat commemorate the roots of monotheism in the lives of Abraham, his son Ishmael, and his servant, Hagar. Muslim solidarity is emphasized, as all pilgrims shed their worldly possessions to don a garment (the *ihram*) made of two white sheets, before they enter the sacred city of Mecca. No other ritual observance in Islam does more to create the impression of ethnic and racial equality in the religion. At the conclusion of the hajj, the pilgrims visit the tomb and mosque of Muhammad at Medina and can thereafter place Hajji or Hajja "at the beginning of their names."[48]

What was the political outcome of the 1960 hajj for the Nation of Islam's religious identity? Although Elijah Muhammad had been introduced to conservative orthodox Islam in Mecca and could have completely transformed the African-American identity of the Nation of Islam to that of conservative Islam, he deliberately chose to maintain a racial-separatist,

African-American, sectarian status for his religious movement. Thus, Muhammad maintained his primacy and power as the final authority on the religious identity of North America's dynamic African-American Muslim community. Yvonne Y. Haddad and Jane I. Smith have documented an Islamic tradition recognizing the legitimacy of sectarianism in global Islam:

> [Sectarianism] reflects the lengthy history of Islam's struggles to maintain correct belief. Sectarianism generally has been viewed as a challenge to central political authority as well as to theological canonicity, and efforts to define sects as existing outside of the mainline community have a rich history. According to Islamic tradition, frequently cited in treatises on heresiography, the Prophet Muhammad said that the Magians will be divided into seventy sects, the Jews into seventy-one, the Christians into seventy-two and the Muslims into seventy-three. In recent years various nationalist and sectarian leaders have used this tradition to plead for tolerance, claiming that sects are a part of the mosaic of Islam and that there is room within the faith for a variety of interpretations and ideas.[49]

At the time of Elijah Muhammad's pilgrimage to Mecca, an important Muslim official in Cairo echoed the above sentiments as he explained to Louis Lomax why the conservative Muslim world was tolerant of the Nation of Islam's racial-separatist and religiously radical version of Islamic identity:

> Of course your Black Muslims are improperly informed. But they are turning men to Allah, away from Christianity, toward Mecca. This is what we want. That is what we must have. We need new blood in western Islam. If Muhammad can give that new blood we welcome him. As for his teachings . . . we will see to it that the correct view is given to the black men in America. Now the thing is to get them facing Mecca.[50]

Louis Lomax has aptly characterized the Nation of Islam's separatist version of Islamic identity as "cultural island hopping" with a "continuously expanding line" between the two poles of identity. He wrote:

> They must maintain the "Islamic" tinge but at the same time keep their teaching within American terms of reference that Negroes can understand; they must take Negroes who have a struggle with English and teach them Arabic; they must convince the most Western of men that they are Arabs.[51]

Although he is often portrayed as an uninformed old man who knew little about the political and religious intricacies of global Islam, Elijah Muhammad had a profound understanding of the politics of religious identity in global Islam and black America. He knew that political and cultural self-determination was crucial to the success of any mass movement in the African-American community. Thus although Elijah was willing to acknowledge some mutual religious and political bonds of identity between the Nation of Islam and Muslims in the East, he was not willing to alter his basic program of black separatism and self-determination in America to conform completely to an Eastern conservative version of Islamic identity.[52]

According to Khallid Muhammad, Elijah believed that:

> Islam was a medicine to cure the ills of our people. . . . Medicine has to be prescribed in dosage according to the sickness [and] the condition of the people. Islam in China must meet the needs of the Chinese people . . . and throughout Africa and in Asia and the islands in the Pacific, in the Caribbean, in the Arabian peninsula, wherever, it has to meet the needs of the people. So a people who have been totally robbed of their name and their language, their religion, their culture, their god, their folkways, their mores. . . . Robbed of the very power in their being and still held in captivity in their land . . . and still under the yoke of extreme white supremacy and white racism, we have to be taught the same five pillars that all Muslims are taught. But the application of the teaching, the prescription of this medicine would have to be unique to the condition of the people in the last stage of its bondage.[53]

Although Elijah Muhammad's version of African-American Islamic identity was religiously radical in its racial separatism and in its political autonomy from the conservative Islam of the East, both Elijah Muhammad and Malcolm X considered themselves and the Nation of Islam as part of the international Islamic community. In his 1960 speech at the Harvard Law School Forum, Malcolm X said:

> There are over 725 million Muslims on the earth, predominantly in Africa, Asia, and the non-white world. . . . We here in America who are under the Divine Leadership of the Honorable Elijah Muhammad are an integral part of the world of Islam that stretches from the China Seas to the sunny shores of Africa.[54]

Malcolm's statement points to an important political fact about African-American Islam in the postwar era. The astounding and dramatic power that Malcolm X, Elijah Muhammad, and the Nation of Islam symbolized was inspired by and connected to the political reassertion of Islam in Asia and Africa after World War II. Between 1945 and the late 1960s, as European colonialism collapsed in the Islamic world, Indonesia, Pakistan, Syria, Jordan, Sudan, Egypt, Libya, Tunisia, Algeria, Morocco, Mauritania, Senegal, Guinea, Ivory Coast, Chad, Upper Volta, Niger, and Nigeria all won their independence from colonial rule.[55]

In the 1950s and 1960s, Gamal Abd al-Nasser, the Muslim president of Egypt and one of Malcolm's mentors, utilized the cultural and political agency of Islam more effectively than any other world leader to construct a post-colonial identity for his people. Nasser was a friend and supporter of the Nation of Islam. He pushed the British out of the Suez Canal zone in 1954 and nationalized it in 1956, proclaiming, "O Americans, may you choke to death in your fury!" When America refused to sell him arms in 1955, he began communications with the Communist block. Eventually, Nasser became a leader of the Pan-Arab movement and selectively utilized aspects of Islam to legitimate an Arab socialist revolution. During the 1960s, Arab socialist governments in Syria, Iraq, and Algeria also used aspects of Islam to legitimate their regimes and to construct new identities for their people. African Muslim states cultivated religious and political ties with Arab Muslim countries as the struggle for independence intensified in the Islamic world. Malcolm X and Elijah Muhammad were the Western heirs of this political ferment against white American and European power in the Muslim world.[56]

Another important symbol of this political ferment—one that connected the identities of African-American Muslims to the Third World community of Islam—was the Bandung Conference of Third World countries in 1955. According to Malcolm X:

> At Bandung all the nations came together, the dark nations from Africa and Asia . . . despite their economic and political differences they came together. All of them were black, brown, red or yellow. . . . They realized all over the world where the dark man was being oppressed, he was being oppressed by the white man; where the dark man was being exploited, he was being exploited by the white man. So they got together on this basis—they had a common enemy.[57]

Although the relations between Arab Muslim groups in America and the Nation of Islam were sometimes hostile in the 1960s because of these groups' differing ideas about race and prophecy, Elijah maintained close personal ties with the Lahore branch of the Ahmadiyya movement. Organizationally and doctrinally, the Lahoris were separate from the Qadian Ahmadis, whose story was told in Chapter 4. The Lahoris believed that Ghulam Ahmad, the founder of the Ahmadiyya movement, was a reformer but not a prophet. Thus they saw themselves as giving the same message of Islam as other Muslim groups. In 1949, Bashir Ahmad Minto, the first Lahore missionary in America, came to San Francisco from Pakistan. Until he returned in 1957, he operated a mosque and reading room on Castro Street under the auspices of the Muslim Society of the U.S.A. He was followed in 1959 by Muhammad Abdullah, a Pakistani who came to the United States from missionary work in the Fiji Islands. Abdullah was the link between the Ahmadis and the Nation of Islam in the 1950s, 1960s, and 1970s. He began a correspondence with Elijah Muhammad in 1955 while he was still in the Fiji Islands. By 1960, Abdullah was a teacher in the

International Muslim Brotherhood and came to Philadelphia to meet Elijah Muhammad's son Wallace, who was the minister of the Temple of Islam there. During the next few years, he taught Wallace Urdu and commentary on the Quran in order to influence him toward a multi-racial model of Islam. In 1961, Wallace arranged for Abdullah to meet his father at the Nation of Islam's national convention. When Abdullah had dinner with Elijah Muhammad at the conclusion of the convention, Muhammad asked him "What's the use of sending missionaries to England and preaching to white people?" Abdullah replied "The English sent missionaries to India to convert them to Christianity. To turn the tables gave the Indian a superiority complex." Abdullah recollected that Muhammad gave him one hundred dollars at the end of the dinner, and he refused to accept it. Muhammad said, "Brother, this is America, you need money." Behind the scenes, Muhammad Abdullah and his small organization remained allies and advisors to the Nation of Islam after Elijah Muhammad's death. The Lahoris believed that behind Elijah's rhetoric about white devils and racial separatism was a Muslim who followed the "real Islam" but who, because of Western prejudices about the religion, thought that he had to present something new. In 1961, Elijah told Abdullah, "Don't think I'm against prayer five times a day, making the hajj or fasting during Ramadan. Don't think I'm against following Islamic teachings. If I overload my followers, they will run away, so I'm teaching them bit by bit."[58] This relationship between Abdullah and the Muhammad family was important because it paved the way for the Nation of Islam's transition to multi-racial Islam that occurred in Wallace's leadership after his father's death in 1975.

However, despite the relationship with the Lahore Ahmadis, the hajj's spirit of solidarity did not penetrate relations between the Nation of Islam and some of the Pakistani members of the Qadian Ahmadis. The lack of cooperation between segments of the two groups was due to the black Muslims' perception of these more powerful Ahmadis as competition for the same following. Moreover, the Qadian Ahmadis offered only a religious program to their American converts and disapproved of the Nation of Islam's espousal of a black separatist identity in the 1960s. However, they understood the rationale behind the movement's identity:

> Since the white has treated the black as a distinct species and not as members of the human race, the "Black Moslem" leadership in retaliation freezes that division and applies the epithet of "Devil" to the slave-driving white, perhaps not too unjustly, even deservedly as the inhuman 100 year long lynchings of the Negro would certainly earn the perpetrators no better title.[59]

Ahmadiyya leaders fervently hoped that the Nation of Islam would someday follow all the beliefs and observances of global Islam and, in doing so, become the vanguard of the rise of the "sun of Islam" in the West. Although the Ahmadis maintained twenty-five missions in the

United States, in the 1960s they only had 3,000 American converts. They must have realized that the future of Islam in America did not rest solely with them.[60]

As a consequence of these connections with global Islam, the Nation of Islam offered "covert support for Arab and Pakistani causes" and fostered "greater foreign Muslim understanding of the African-American human condition." Also Elijah Muhammad insured a "high degree of global Islamic consciousness in his movement, in the future, by making the study of Arabic a focal point in the Nation of Islam's schools for its youth. In the 1960s, the University of Islam in Chicago was the largest Arabic school in the United States. And knowledge of Arabic was insured in the Nation of Islam's highest echelon of leadership when Elijah Muhammad sent his sons Akbar and Wallace to study at al-Azhar University in Egypt in the early 1960s.[61]

Elijah Muhammad's model of racial-separatist Islamic identity successfully carried the Nation of Islam through its golden age in the early 1960s. He had astutely played the politics of religious identity in the Muslim world with the help of his young roving ambassador, Malcolm X. But, as we shall see later, the tension between the African-American and the global Islamic poles of the Nation of Islam's religious identity was only temporarily resolved and would eventually break the Nation into warring factions. This tension was temporarily obscured in the early 1960s, however, as Elijah Muhammad and Malcolm X struggled to control the significations of the Nation of Islam in America.

THE POLITICS OF IDENTITY IN AMERICA

Although the Nation of Islam's religious identity was established in the Muslim world in 1960, in America, its leaders came face to face with another set of identity issues. At the root of these problems was America's ignorance and fear of Islam. In the 1960s, both black and white Americans had a monolithic understanding of Islam as a world religion. It was commonly believed that there was only one valid version of the religion, the "true" or "real" Islam—orthodox Islam. Thus, in the perception of most of the FBI and police officials, social scientists, religious leaders, and journalists who formulated significations of African-American Islam in the 1960s, the Nation of Islam was not Islam or even a religion; its radical racialist theology precluded that. Although most of these significations were rooted in ignorance about Islam, some of them originated in deliberate and cynical plans to undermine the Nation of Islam and to destroy its leaders.

At the same time, Elijah Muhammad and Malcolm X attempted to counter these negative significations through a dynamic jihad of words which included public lectures by the Nation's ministers, articles published in its own newspaper, and research conducted by selected non-Muslim scholars and political activists. In the final evaluation, however, significations of the Nation of Islam during this period were complicated by the movement's own internal political contradictions. For its global religious identity was based on relations with Third World nations that were politically radical in spite of the fact that in America, under the leadership of Elijah Muhammad, the Nation of Islam was a politically conservative organization.[62]

In 1959, the American media began to make Malcolm X and Elijah Muhammad into national figures. *Life, Look, Newsweek, Time,* and *Reader's Digest* covered the Nation of Islam. Soon Malcolm X became a frequent guest speaker on college campuses and radio and television programs. Most important, from July 13–17, 1959, in the five-part television documentary "The Hate That Hate Produced," Mike Wallace and Louis E. Lomax branded the Nation as a major anti-American hate group. Wallace and Lomax sent shock waves throughout the country as they told "a story of the rise of black racism, of a call for black supremacy among a growing segment of American Negroes," who, they said, "used a good deal of the paraphernalia of the traditional religion of Islam, but . . . are fervently disavowed by orthodox Muslims." In this signification, the global Islamic roots of the Nation of Islam's religious identity were obscured by Wallace's contention that the Nation was a "hate group" rather than a real religion.[63]

In one sense, Wallace's attempt to marginalize the Nation failed—its membership doubled because of the publicity that it received from "The Hate That Hate Produced." In another sense, however, Wallace may have succeeded, accomplishing one of the indirectly stated objectives of his negative signification of the Nation of Islam. He had mentioned in the program that white Southerners "would set off a federal investigation" if they preached "a gospel of hate" similar to the Nation of Islam's.[64] Accordingly, around the time of the Wallace and Lomax documentary, the FBI began to monitor Malcolm X, Elijah Muhammad, and the Nation of Islam's activities more closely. Through a multi-faceted program of wiretapping, infiltration, and media manipulation, the intelligence community created their own significations of the Nation of Islam. These significations were related to the FBI's Cointelpro/Racial Matters program in the 1960s. According to the Church Committee Report:

> COINTELPRO is the FBI acronym for a series of covert programs against domestic groups. . . . The unexpressed major premise of the programs was that a law enforcement agency has the duty to do whatever is necessary to combat perceived threats to the existing social and political order.[65]

As the Nation of Islam grew and increased its appeal to middle-class blacks in the late 1950s, J. Edgar Hoover wrote to the Justice Department requesting more wiretapping of the movement. According to his memo:

> Members fanatically follow the teachings of Allah as interpreted by Muhammad; they disavow allegiance to the United States; and they are taught they need not obey the laws of the United States. . . . It is believed that a technical surveillance . . . will furnish . . . data concerning [the] fanatical and violent nature of the current plans of the NOI to expand its activities throughout the United States.[66]

In the wake of Malcolm X's tour of the Middle East and West Africa and the growing eminence of the Nation of Islam in the Muslim world, the FBI formulated a signification of the Nation that was intended to discourage authorization for Elijah Muhammad's hajj by orthodox Muslim religious authorities in the Saudi Arabia. On August 20, 1959, the FBI circulated the following anonymous document to African Muslim leaders:

> As the great silver plane circled over the blazing sand of Saudi Arabia, it was viewed by a lowly camel driver and his son, Karim. "Tell me, Papa Abdul, what is that great bird hovering there in the sky?" "Son, that is no bird; it's an airplane bringing Elijah Poole—oop, I mean Elijah Muhammad—to Mecca!" "Papa Abdul, how do you know such worldly things about our visitors?" "Why, son, it's no secret in Saudi Arabia who Poole is and how he's distorted the Moslem faith. He and his uninformed followers are the subject of every bull session at every camel stop on this desert." "Tell me, Pop, who is this man Poole?"
>
> "Well, Karim, all I know about him is what I read in the latest issue of 'Camel Tracks'—you know, the magazine like the one we get from the oil company with all the pictures—that he is a Negro American who was born in Sandersville, Georgia, some 60 years ago. He hasn't done a day's work since about 1930 when he started spoofing the Negroes in Detroit, Michigan, with his own butchered version of our beloved Moslem faith. We true Moslems have all been alerted to stay away from him and his kind. He teaches . . . hate and deceit for the purpose of extracting millions from his gullible followers for his own personal glorification, whereas the true Moslem believes in love and respect for all mankind."[67]

Although Elijah Muhammad understood the seriousness of the significations that the media and the intelligence community had formed to control the Nation of Islam in America and to marginalize its relations with the Muslim world and potentially with revolutionary governments in the Third World, he was determined to counter these negative images with his own significations. Cautiously, he launched a jihad of words on several fronts in America. The first step in this jihad of words was to establish a newspaper for the Nation of Islam. In 1960, Malcolm X founded

Muhammad Speaks and a magazine called *The Messenger* in New York City. Although *The Messenger* quickly folded, *Muhammad Speaks* eventually became one of the most popular newspapers in black America, with a reported circulation of 500,000 at its peak. From its inception, *Muhammad Speaks* was a high-quality publishing venture, and its editorial staff was composed primarily of non-Muslim African-American intellectuals. Initially James Baldwin was approached to edit the newspaper. When he declined this offer, C. Eric Lincoln and Louis Lomax helped to produce the first issues. In its first year, the production of the newspaper was moved from New York to the Nation of Islam's headquarters in Chicago. In its heyday in the 1960s, *Muhammad Speaks* was staffed primarily by reporters and editors affiliated with the black Left, and its emphasis was internationalist with incisive, politically oriented news from the Third World. Meanwhile, Christine Johnson was recruited by Malcolm X to write the textbooks for the Nation of Islam's schools. Johnson was reportedly a member of the Communist Party and traveled frequently to the Soviet Union. These internationalist and radical political figures, working behind the scenes of the Nation of Islam's publications, emphasized the relationship of the Nation to global political and religious movements in Africa and Asia. This emphasis countered the media's signification of the religion as a parochial hate group.[68]

In the early 1960s, Elijah Muhammad allowed two black social scientists—C. Eric Lincoln and E. U. Essien-Udom—and a black journalist, Louis Lomax, to conduct case studies of the Nation of Islam. C. Eric Lincoln's work on the Nation of Islam began as his doctoral thesis at Boston University's School of Theology. In 1961, his thesis, *The Black Muslims in America*, was expanded and published by Beacon Press. Lincoln was a trusted ally of the Nation of Islam and a close personal friend of Elijah Muhammad and Malcolm X. His book is still the classic study of the Nation of Islam and a classic in sociological literature. Both Elijah Muhammad and Malcolm X hoped that Lincoln's research would work in their favor and help to dispel the negative signification of their religion that had been formulated by the media and the intelligence community. But Lincoln, who was a sociologist of religion, formulated his own social-scientific signification of the Nation of Islam that echoed some of the images of the movement that had already been created by the white establishment. Lincoln's signification focused on the establishment of the Nation of Islam as a logical consequence of what he perceived as the pathology of urban, lower-class, black nationalism. Lincoln coined the term "Black Muslims" to differentiate followers of the Nation of Islam from orthodox Muslims, whom he called "moslems." He advanced the theory that black Islam was primarily a social protest movement rooted in the anxiety and discontent of black lower-class migrants in the northern industrial cities. Finally, scholarship yielded to polemics in the foreword to *The Black Muslims in America*, where Gordon Allport stated that the Nation of Islam's "implications for the future are in a sense frightening . . . [and] the tie to Islam is, of course, an historical monstrosity."[69]

In his *Autobiography*, Malcolm X commented on Lincoln's signification of the Nation of Islam's identity:

> Dr. C. Eric Lincoln's book was published amid widening controversy about us Muslims, at just about the time we were starting to put on our first big mass rallies.
>
> Just as the television "Hate That Hate Produced" title had projected the "hate teaching" image of us, now Dr. Lincoln's book was titled *The Black Muslims in America*. The press snatched at that name. "Black Muslims" was in all the book reviews, which quoted from the book only what was critical of us, and generally praised Dr. Lincoln's writing.
>
> The public mind fixed on "Black Muslims." From Mr. Muhammad on down, the name, "Black Muslims," distressed everyone in the Nation of Islam. I tried at least two years to kill off that "Black Muslims." Every newspaper and magazine writer and microphone I got close to: "No! We are black people here in America. Our religion is Islam: We are properly called 'Muslims'!" But that "Black Muslims" never got dislodged.[70]

Clearly, in Lincoln's signification, the Nation of Islam was not a religion but rather a social protest movement because of its focus on race issues. His work, especially *The Black Muslims in America*, completed the construction of "the myth of a race-blind Islam" which began with the work of Edward W. Blyden in the nineteenth century. "The myth of a race-blind Islam" refers to a discourse and an intellectual tradition that have created and perpetuated ahistorical and sensationalist representations of Islam and black nationalism.

E. U. Essien-Udom was a Nigerian political scientist at Harvard University. Although his book, *Black Nationalism: A Search for Identity in America*, did not receive as much critical attention as Lincoln's work, it also contributed to "the myth of a race-blind Islam" in its characterization of the Nation of Islam as "a special type of political behavior" rather than a religion because of its focus on race. Essien-Udom's work also focused on the theme of the pathology of the black "subculture" and advanced the thesis that the Nation of Islam's theology reflected "the social history of the Negro in America, especially the psychological trauma and personality disturbances to which that history has given rise."[71] This myth has functioned as a major intellectual impediment to the analysis of the global implications of the Nation of Islam and related religious movements. It also ignores the fact that religion is the starting point for understanding the social and political significance of the Nation of Islam.

Although Louis Lomax was involved in the production of "The Hate That Hate Produced," his book *When the Word Is Given* was one of the few studies of its time to emphasize that the Nation of Islam was a religion connected to global Islam. Gossipy and dynamic, Lomax's significations of the Nation focused on its cultural creativity. Lomax was intimately in touch with the pulse of the religious movement as he imaginatively transported his reader to the Nation's inner sanctum—its restaurants, where his vivid significations suggested the sweet taste of the Muslim bean pies and the perfume of its Eastern incense.[72]

Malcolm X attempted to counter the negative significations of the Nation of Islam through a dynamic jihad of words. The power of Malcolm X's jihad of words in America first came to public attention on April 14, 1957 at a Harlem police station, when he and more than one hundred of his followers successfully demanded the hospitalization of Hinton Johnson, a Nation of Islam member who had been brutally beaten by the police. By the early 1960s, Malcolm X had become the national spokesperson for the Nation of Islam and an international figure who carried out his jihad of words on behalf of Elijah Muhammad in the temples of the Nation of Islam, on the streets of Harlem, in lecture halls, and on college campuses all over America. Indeed, Malcolm X's rise as a public figure was supported by Elijah Muhammad, who recognized that his protegé's jihad of words fostered respectability for the Nation and corrected the negative significations of Islam that were formulated by the white American establishment.[73]

When Ghulam Ahmad, the founder of the Ahmadiyya Movement of Islam, said, "We have killed the infidels with a sword of arguments and the one who wants to kill us has no hope of success,"[74] he was pointing to the power of the jihad of words as a potentially revolutionary tool in the modern era of colonialism. Malcolm's spiritual and intellectual development and his family legacy helped him transform his jihad of words while still in prison. In the 1960s, with the support of Betty Shabazz (his new wife), years of oratorical training in the Nation of Islam, and unlimited access to television and the media, Malcolm revolutionized the concept. It was obvious to most observers that Malcolm X's jihad of words had prophetic potential in America. Through his oratory, he had the power to radically change the consciousness of his followers. Amina Rahman, a convert to the Nation of Islam in the 1960s, remembered Malcolm X's oratorical power:

> I've seen Malcolm make men cry, and strong women. Seen him bring a crowd to the point of wanting to riot and pull them back from the edge very quickly. He could almost play them, move them back and forth, dancing close to the edge, but with just incredible control.[75]

Benjamin Karim, an assistant minister in Temple No. 7 in Harlem, remembered the same kind of consciousness-raising power in Malcolm X's oratory:

> I was holding an umbrella over his head. It started drizzling. Now, I'm looking at this crowd while the Minister's talking. People stopped blinking

their eyelids, as though they were in a trance. Then you would see some-
body—probably the fluid evaporated in the eyeball, and they realized something was amiss—as though they had come out of a trance. Then they'd go
right back into it without blinking. It was strange. It started raining but all of
those people stayed, thousands, blocking off the street for two blocks in both
directions.[76]

And Malcolm X's power for consciousness raising through the jihad of
words was not limited to the African-American community. He had a
significant following among college students and developed a college
ministry. C. Eric Lincoln recalled the beginning of this ministry and its
impact on students and professors:

> In the old days when Malcolm first became a sort of spokesperson for the
> movement, he was forbidden to speak before or to any white people. At that
> time, I was a graduate student at Boston University. . . . I will never forget the
> day Malcolm came in with an honor guard of fifteen Muslims including his
> protege, Louis Farrakhan. To everybody's great surprise, he was permitted to
> come and address this very learned seminar at Boston University. In an hour
> and a half lecture he had so impressed these very well educated people that
> they gave him a standing ovation. The next week, I had a call from a professor
> at Harvard that said "Hey can you get Malcolm to come to Harvard to speak
> to us. . . . The next call I got was from Malcolm X. . . . "Look here, Professor
> Lincoln, I don't mind speaking to these devils but can't you get me a chance to
> speak to some black college students somewhere?" So I sent him to Clark
> College in Atlanta.[77]

As the Nation of Islam reached its peak of influence in the early 1960s,
it opened new temples and businesses around the country. Seeing the
popularity of *Muhammad Speaks* in the black community, seeing the ascendancy of the Fruit of Islam in New York, Chicago, Los Angeles, and in other
major cities, and most of all, rejoicing in Malcolm X's defeat of its opposition on television, Elijah Muhammad believed that he had successfully
negotiated the politics of the Nation of Islam's racial-separatist religious
identity in America. The Nation of Islam was exactly what he wanted it to
be—a politically conservative religious movement outside the mainstream
of black civil-rights activism in the sixties. Instead of demonstrating for
civil rights in the future, Elijah Muhammad demanded that his people use
the discipline of Islam to separate from the white race in America and to
develop an economic and cultural base in their own communities in
anticipation of the day when the Nation of Islam would receive its own
separate territory in the United States. However, in his satisfaction with
the Nation's conservative status quo in America, Elijah Muhammad underestimated the prophetic and radical political potential of Malcolm X's
jihad of words, which would soon transform his political and religious

identity beyond the radical religious and conservative political boundaries of the Nation of Islam in America.[78]

THE SPLIT: THE POLITICS OF RELIGIOUS
IDENTITY EXPLODE

Abul Khatib has written that "Seeking justice and removing oppression are universal human pursuits and the morality of the just struggle is
firmly enshrined in the human conscience. Jihad is the Muslim paradigm
of the liberation struggle."[79]

The liberation of black people in America was the ultimate aim of the
Nation of Islam. By the 1960s, Elijah Muhammad had formulated a po-
tent racial-separatist Muslim identity and economic program for African
Americans that he believed would ultimately lead them to liberation; and
"he wanted to compete with Christian black America for the black follow-
ing." According to his son, Warith Deen Mohammed, at the center of this
Islamic identity were the idea of divinity in the person of W. D. Fard and
Elijah Muhammad's association with that divinity as the Messenger of
God:

> God incarnate. . . . God in the flesh, God as a man. . . . We believed that God
> was like the Egyptian pharaohs, descended from an invisible reality, that
> divinity was passed on from father to son. Nothing said about where God
> came from except on earth. We were told that God does not exist in any form
> except man. . . . No Hell . . . No Heaven . . . except on earth.[80]

Although Elijah Muhammad dealt cautiously with politics in the Muslim world and America in order to control the public image and significations of the Nation of Islam, in his view, religion was the road to black
liberation in America. Thus, he argued for a separate black territory and
the release of all Muslims from the federal prisons in order to create a black
Muslim theocracy in America. He awaited the Battle of Armageddon,
when he believed that Allah "would end the era of white supremacy" in
the West and the black race would reign supreme. Elijah's road to black
liberation was politically conservative, with its emphasis on black capitalism and late-nineteenth-century racial-separatist civilizationist ideas (in
which African-Americans' links to their West and Central African cultural
roots were denigrated). At the same time, this was a spiritually radical and
authoritarian road to liberation, as Elijah believed that Allah in the person
of W. D. Fard had given divine authority to him and his blood descendants.[81]

Although Malcolm X believed in this version of a religious identity in
the Nation of Islam and was a loyal follower of Elijah Muhammad until
1964, there was great potential for radical political power in his jihad of
words. His ability to "make it plain" to the black masses began to attract

the attention of radical Third World political and religious leaders as early as the late 1950s. His association and/or friendships with Ahmad Sukarno of Indonesia, Kwame Nkrumah of Ghana, Fidel Castro of Cuba, Gamel Abd al-Nasser and Mahmoud Yousse Shawarbi of Egypt, Patrice Lumumba of the Belgian Congo, and Ben Bella and Mahmoud Boutiba of Algeria gradually exposed him to radical Third World political ideas in the 1960s.[82] All of these leaders were patrons of the Nation of Islam in the early sixties. In light of these influences, it was inevitable that Malcolm X's jihad of words would eventually test the conservative political boundaries of the Nation of Islam's religious identity by evolving into a radical critique of capitalism and Western global imperialism. In addition, the direction of Malcolm X's rhetoric in the 1960s implicitly begged for a dynamic political connection between the Nation of Islam, the black Left, and civil-rights organizations. In the final evaluation, this kind of connection was also discouraged by the conservative racial separatism of Elijah Muhammad. Thus, in the Nation of Islam, there was significant ideological tension between conservative black nationalist and radical black nationalist ideologies.[83]

This ideological tension between elements of religion and politics exacerbated the subtle differences between Elijah Muhammad and Malcolm X regarding the public identity of their religious movement. When these differences finally came to a head in 1963, they could have been contained and resolved in the Nation of Islam had they not been exploited by inside and outside forces that wanted to divide and conquer the movement. As we shall see, "the scramble for power in the Nation" and the sensationalistic significations of the media and the intelligence community caused the politics of religious identity to explode in the Nation of Islam in 1964. The complete background of events and issues that led to the split between Elijah Muhammad and Malcolm X is long and complex and will not be fully explored here. However, the following account highlights the most important aspects of this story for our purposes.[84]

In the early 1960s, no event signaled the ideological differences that would later explode between Elijah Muhammad and Malcolm X more portentously than the murder of Ronald Stokes by the Los Angeles Police Department. On April 27, 1962, Stokes (who was the twenty-year-old secretary of the Nation of Islam's Los Angeles Mosque No. 27) "was shot at point blank range" and then beaten in the street by one of the police officers. When the police later invaded the mosque to search its male members, who were suspected of theft, all the Muslim men were forced to face the wall as police officers "rip[ped] their suit jackets up to the neckline . . . and then rip[ped] each man's trousers from the bottom of the inner seam to the belt loop before snatching them off." Five other Muslim men were shot—some in the back—one was permanently paralyzed and others were beaten by the police. Several police officers were also shot in the crossfire of police bullets. Although it was officially determined that all of the Muslims involved were unarmed, the coroner's jury ruled that Ronald Stokes's murder "was justifiable under the lawful performance of duty and self defense." And the Muslims who were arrested at the mosque were convicted of assault.[85]

Benjamin Karim, Malcolm X's assistant in the Harlem Mosque No. 7, recalled that "Malcolm mourned deeply for Ronald Stokes," who was an old friend from Roxbury; and Malcolm had a deep attachment to the Los Angeles mosque because he had established it himself in 1957. His initial reaction to the Stokes murder was to launch an armed retaliatory rebellion against the Los Angeles Police Department. Reportedly, he said, "I am going to Los Angeles to die."[86]

Malcolm X preached at Ronald Stokes's funeral in Los Angeles on May 5, 1962, with more than two thousand people present, including representatives of various civil rights groups that had formed a coalition to protest the murder. News of the murder reached the Muslim world, as Gamal Abd al-Nasser and Kwame Nkrumah publicly condemned the atrocity.[87]

In a press conference at the Los Angeles Statler-Hilton Hotel on May 4, Malcolm X initiated a jihad of words to politically mobilize the black community in Los Angeles. His language was angry and strong:

> Seven innocent unarmed black men were shot down in cold blood by Police Chief William J. Parker's Los Angeles City Police . . . [in] one of the most ferocious inhuman atrocities ever inflicted in a so-called democratic and civilized society. . . . [This was a] brutal and cold blooded murder by Parker's well-armed storm troopers.[88]

At a protest rally organized by the County Civic League in Los Angeles on May 24, 1962, Malcolm X again set the stage for organized political action and, according to the FBI report of the event, he alluded to the kind of radical internationalist political coalition that he would eventually embrace in 1964. He preached

> Not a Muslim but a black man was shot down. . . . For you're brutalized because you're black and when they lay a club on the side of your head, they do not ask your religion. You're black that's enough. [FBI agents at this event reported that he also said that] black people all over the world are uniting. Socialists, communists and liberalists all are coming together to get rid of the common enemy with white skin.[89]

Clearly, Malcolm X had laid the groundwork in Los Angeles to expand the political horizons of the Nation of Islam's racial-separatist religious identity. In Malcolm X's jihad of words in the wake of Ronald Stokes's murder, there was potential for either organized violent rebellion, coalition politics with the NAACP, and/or an alliance with the black Left. However, as William Strickland has noted,

In private, Malcolm and many other Muslims awaited instructions from Chicago to avenge their dead. They waited on word from the Messenger to begin the Battle of Armageddon that Elijah Muhammad promised would end the era of white supremacy. Instead . . . [Elijah Muhammad's] message from Chicago . . . instructed them to stick with nonviolence: "Hold fast to Islam. . . . Allah has promised that no devil will ever get away with the death of a Muslim. We are going out into the streets to begin war with the devil. Not the kind of war he expects . . . no, we are going to let the world know he is the devil; we are going to sell newspapers."[90]

Ultimately, Malcolm X submitted to Elijah Muhammad's religious solution to this event, which he believed called for radical political action to confront police brutality in Los Angeles. Although Elijah's politically conservative view of the Nation of Islam's religious identity had prevailed in public, back in New York, Malcolm confided his dissatisfaction privately to Brother Louis 2X and Minister Benjamin Karim:

You know, we talk about people being bitten by dogs and mowed down by fire hoses, we talk about our people being brutalized in the civil rights movement and we haven't done anything to help them. . . . And now we've had one of our own brothers killed . . . and still we haven't done anything. . . . We spout our militant revolutionary rhetoric and we preach Armageddon. . . . But when our own brothers are brutalized or killed, we do nothing.[91]

To sum up, Elijah Muhammad's and Malcolm X's different reactions to the murder of Ronald Stokes demonstrated clearly the ideological rift that was growing between these two men. And the ideological position that each of these leaders held represented the potential for formulating two different versions of religious identity for the Nation of Islam. Muhammad's conservative black nationalism, couched in a static version of religious separatism, encouraged political isolation and discouraged political alliances. It emphasized "private economic market mechanisms for group advancement" as a substitute for political action in the black community. As Muslims sold weekly quotas of *Muhammad Speaks,* as they donated large portions of their personal income to the Nation, and as Malcolm X gave all of the money that he earned in the college lecture circuit to the organization, the Nation of Islam built an economic empire of Muslim schools, businesses, and mosques that dotted the urban landscape of America. By the early 1960s, Elijah Muhammad had purchased more than "one-half million dollars worth of real estate in Chicago alone" on behalf of the Nation. Although Muhammad was realizing his goal of economic and moral respectability for the Nation of Islam in black America, his version of a racial-separatist religious identity held little potential for political evolution. He was a cautious administrator who had been a political prisoner in the 1940s, partly because of his internationalist politi-

MALCOLM X, *1963, shown with the dome of the Connecticut Capitol behind him as he arrived in Hartford for a two-day visit.* Used by permission of the Bettmann Archives. UPI/CORBIS-Bettmann.

cal associations. He fully understood the danger of a radical political emphasis in his movement.[92]

On the other hand, Malcolm X's growing radical black nationalism offered the possibility of political growth and evolution in the context of a black religious identity. Malcolm X's travels as an ambassador in the United States and throughout the Muslim world and the United States to advance the insulated religious and political interests of the Nation of Islam taught him that there was a need for political alliances with other organizations that represented the interests of blacks and other disenfranchised non-European peoples. Black political unity would allow black people to deal more militantly with racial oppression and global imperialism. Although Elijah Muhammad's teachings led Malcolm X to cultivate the religious and cultural links between African Americans and the Third World, it was the latter's radical black nationalism that began to emphasize the political and economic links between the systems of racial oppression in Africa and America.[93]

By 1963, although Malcolm X's political ideas were still encompassed in the Nation of Islam's religious identity, there was a new political emphasis in his jihad of words. In some of his speeches, he moved away from the strictly religious concerns of the Nation of Islam and talked almost exclusively about the politics of racial oppression from an internationalist perspective. His "Message to the Grassroots" was typical of this trend. It was a classic radical black nationalist speech and an important signal to insiders and outsiders that Malcolm X had outgrown the political conservativism of the Nation of Islam. The Northern Grass Roots Leadership Conference was a nationalist event sponsored in Detroit on November 9–10, 1963 by Albert B. Cleage, Jr.—the founder of the Shrine of the Black Madonna, the Freedom Now Party, and the Group on Advanced Leadership. At this conference, in the midst of a five-hour meeting of more than two thousand people at King Solomon Baptist Church, Malcolm X called for black political coalition and unity regardless of the religious differences among blacks:

> What you and I need to do is learn to forget our differences. When we come together, we don't come together as Baptists or Methodists. You don't catch hell because you're a Baptist, and you don't catch hell because you're a Methodist . . . you don't catch hell because you're a Democrat or a Republican, you don't catch hell because you're a Mason or an Elk, and you sure don't catch hell because you're an American, because if you were an American you wouldn't catch hell. You catch hell because you're a black man. . . .
>
> We have this in common: we have a common oppressor, a common exploiter, and a common discriminator. But once we all realize that we have a common enemy, then we unite—on the basis of what we have in common. And what we have foremost in common is that enemy—the white man.[94]

As Malcolm X continued, he pointed out the difference between the Third World revolutions and the "Negro Revolution," and used the former as a model for raising African-American political consciousness:

> Of all our studies, history is best qualified to reward our research. And when you see that you've got problems, all you have to do is examine the historic method used all over the world by others who have problems similar to yours. Once you see how they got theirs straight, then you know how you can get yours straight. There's been a revolution, a black revolution, going on in Africa. In Kenya, the Mau Mau were revolutionary; they were the ones who brought the word "Uhuru" to the fore. The Mau Mau, they were revolutionary, they believed in scorched earth, they knocked everything aside that got in their way, and their revolution also was based on land, a desire for land. In Algeria, the northern part of Africa, a revolution took place. The Algerians were revolutionists, they wanted land. France offered to let them be integrated into France. They told France, to hell with France, they wanted some land, not some France. And they engaged in a bloody battle.
>
> So I cite these various revolutions, brothers and sisters, to show you that you don't have a peaceful revolution. You don't have a turn-the-other-cheek revolution. The only kind of revolution that is nonviolent is the Negro revolution. The only revolution in which the goal is loving your enemy is the Negro

revolution. It's the only revolution in which the goal is a desegregated lunch counter, a desegregated theater, a desegregated park, and a desegregated public toilet; you can sit down next to white folks—on the toilet. That's no revolution. Revolution is based on land. Land is the basis of all independence. Land is the basis of freedom, justice, and equality.

The white man knows what a revolution is. He knows that the black revolution is world-wide in scope and in nature. The black revolution is sweeping Asia, is sweeping Africa, is rearing its head in Latin America. The Cuban Revolution—that's a revolution. They overturned the system. Revolution is in Asia, revolution is in Africa, and the white man is screaming because he sees revolution in Latin America. How do you think he'll react to you when you learn what a real revolution is? You don't know what a revolution is. If you did, you wouldn't use that word.[95]

In "The Message to the Grassroots," the evolving independent political dimension of Malcolm X's religious identity was introduced to the American public with a dramatic and influential flair. Here, his jihad of words shifted from the Nation of Islam's politically conservative paradigm of the black liberation struggle to a Third World model of that struggle. It is noteworthy that Malcolm X delivered this speech several weeks before his suspension from the Nation by Elijah Muhammad. This suspension occurred because Malcolm X spoke out radically on a political issue that could potentially damage the religious image of the Nation of Islam. However, before we discuss this suspension, the "scramble for power in the Nation" and the significations of the intelligence community must be examined as an important prelude to this event.

At the beginning of his career in the Nation of Islam, Elijah Muhammad had advised Malcolm X about the price of fame:

> Brother Malcolm, I want you to become well known. Because if you are well known, it will make me better known . . . but Brother Malcolm, there is something you need to know. You will grow to be hated when you become well known. Because usually people get jealous of public figures.[96]

And this warning came true. By 1961, Elijah Muhammad moved from Chicago, the national headquarters of his religious movement, to Phoenix in order to nurse his chronic bronchial asthma. As a result of his move, there were now "three different leadership centers" for the Nation of Islam: the national headquarters in Chicago, the Messenger's home in Phoenix, and Malcolm X's headquarters in Harlem. As William Strickland has noted, these multiple leadership centers were "a prescription for trouble, chaos, and intrigue, augmented by the fact that Elijah Muhammad's bad health inevitably raised the question of who would take over the Nation upon his death."[97]

The question of succession was vital to the religious identity of the

Nation of Islam. According to the significations that Elijah Muhammad had formulated for his movement, leadership and divinity would be passed on to his blood descendants—members of the "royal family." At the time of his birth in 1933, Elijah's son Wallace D. Muhammad had been named for succession to power because he was named after Wallace D. Fard, the founder of the Nation, who came to be regarded as God after his disappearance in the 1930s. However, in the early 1960s, Wallace, his brothers Akbar and Ayman, and his nephew Hasan Sharif stood in the shadow of Malcolm X as they dabbled in orthodox Islam and questioned Elijah Muhammad's religious authority. Thus, many of the key ministers in the Nation of Islam viewed Malcolm X as the logical successor to the Messenger, and this created problems.[98]

In 1961, Elijah Muhammad gave Malcolm X "free rein" as national spokesperson for the Nation. And some of the ministers began to resent his power in the media and the placement of his powerful allies in the Nation's ministry: Louis X, Malcolm X's protegé, was the chief minister in Boston; Benjamin Karim was the assistant minister in New York; and Malcolm X's brothers, Philbert and Wilfred, were chief ministers in Lansing and Detroit. Malcolm was also a close friend and ally of Wallace D. Muhammad, and his half-sister Ella and his wife, Betty, were influential in the organizations for Muslim women. By 1962, Elijah Muhammad's son Herbert, who was the publisher of *Muhammad Speaks*, ordered the staff of the newspaper to publish as little as possible about Malcolm X. Raymond Sharrief, who was the national head of the Fruit of Islam and Elijah Muhammad's son-in-law, was another jealous and powerful critic of Malcolm X in the Chicago headquarters. John Ali and Captain Joseph, the heads of operations in Phoenix and New York respectively, were also formidable rivals of Malcolm's. Together, Malcolm X's critics in Chicago, Phoenix, and New York attempted to convince Elijah that his highly visible representative had too much power in the Nation and in the media.[99]

In spite of these internal tensions, Malcolm X's political popularity continued to grow in America in 1963, as he became an outspoken critic of Martin Luther King, Jr.'s nonviolent movement and debated the integrationist strategies of the NAACP and CORE—Congress for Racial Equality. Malcolm's popularity among the black masses in Harlem was unquestionable, and he was a frequent speaker in massive street rallies and at Adam Clayton Powell, Jr.'s Abyssinian Baptist Church. However, to the dismay of his rivals in the Nation of Islam, by 1963 his critique of the civil-rights movement was no longer based primarily on the religious differences between black Muslims and black Christians, but instead on the social class contradictions in the black community. This trend was clear in the field Negro–house Negro segment of the "Message to the Grassroots" speech in late 1963:

> There were in black history two kinds of negroes. There was the old house negro and the field negro. The house negro always looked out for his master.

When the field negroes got too much out of line, he held them back in check. . . . If the master got hurt, he'd say, "What's the matter boss? We sick?" However, there were the field negroes who lived in the huts, who had nothing to lose. They wore the worst kind of clothes. They ate the worst food. They caught hell. They felt the sting of the lash. And they hated this land. . . .

I am a field negro. If I can't live in the house as a human being, I'm praying for that house to blow down, I'm praying for a strong wind to come along. . . . If the master don't treat me right and he's sick, I'll tell the doctor to go the other way. But if we are all going to live as human beings, then I am for a society in which human beings can practice brother and sisterhood.[100]

As Malcolm X's jihad of words continued to shift in this political direction, some of the Nation's officials began to question the seriousness of his religious commitment and identity. What was his primary goal: to gain converts for the Nation of Islam or to advance his radical black nationalist political agenda? Alex Haley's work with Malcolm X was the last straw in the minds of the Nation's Chicago bureaucrats, who were jealous of Malcolm X's public notoriety and questioned his religious identity and political ambitions. Haley, a freelance journalist, was commissioned to write Malcolm X's autobiography in 1963. At this point in time, no one was working on Elijah Muhammad's autobiography, and he was the Messenger of the movement. Haley's work could not help but exacerbate the internal tensions in the Nation of Islam.[101]

Also, the significations that he formulated for the Nation of Islam in his work were problematic. Haley's work perpetuated "the myth of a race-blind Islam" that was predominant in the work of C. Eric Lincoln and E. U. Essien-Udom, as Haley did not sympathize with the views of the Nation. Manning Marable has noted that Haley was . . . not a student of black nationalism; politically he was profoundly integrationist, and inclined toward supporting Republicans." Although Malcolm X's *Autobiography* was not published until 1965, an earlier interview with Malcolm X was published in *Playboy* magazine in May 1963. In this "candid conversation with the militant major-domo of the black Muslims," Haley not only used the "Black Muslim" label formulated by C. Eric Lincoln, but more importantly he focused on the "hate group" image developed by Mike Wallace in 1959. In the introduction to the *Playboy* interview, Haley portrayed the Nation of Islam not as a religion but instead as a "black supremacy version of Hitler's Aryan racial theories . . . amalgamating elements of Christianity and Mohammedanism (both of which officially and unequivocally disown it)." He continued: "Our view is that this interview is both an eloquent statement and damning self-indictment of one noxious facet of rampant racism." As Haley repeatedly referred to Islam as "Mohammedism" and "Muslimism" in this interview, he echoed the significations of European orientalists and demonstrated his ignorance about Islam as a world religion.[102]

The activities of the intelligence community were also an important prelude to Malcolm X's split with the Nation of Islam. Their monitoring and manipulation of the significations of the movement were unrelenting, as Marable had demonstrated:

> The FBI had been planting agents in the Nation of Islam since the 1940s and as Malcolm evolved as a leader and the Nation of Islam grew, the FBI intensified its infiltration and surveillance of the organization. The Nation of Islam's temples were illegally wire-tapped, members were watched, and tax records were scrutinized. As of 1955, Malcolm's letters were illegally opened, transcribed, and re-mailed by the Feds. By 1960, the surveillance on Malcolm escalated to the point whereby a group of agents were specifically assigned to trail and document his activities and strategies.[103]

The FBI's intent was to undermine the Nation of Islam by creating or exploiting dissension among its membership. By early 1963, the FBI was closely monitoring tensions between Malcolm X and the Muhammad family:

> On several dates during February, March, and April 1963, there was developing a feeling of resentment and animosity against the subject by Elijah Muhammad's family. This resentment apparently stems from Malcolm's taking charge and running the NOI convention in Chicago, Illinois, in February 26, 1963, when illness precluded Elijah Muhammad's attendance. . . .
> This resentment was further aggravated by subject's remaining in Chicago for several weeks after the convention where he made numerous appearances and speeches in the Chicago area. On the request of members of the family, Elijah Muhammad, who was still in Phoenix, Arizona, ordered subject to return to New York City which he did . . . canceling his future scheduled appearances around Chicago.[104]

In 1963, the press released a statement that Elijah Muhammad was the father of the children of three of his former secretaries. Malcolm X investigated this rumor and determined that it was true. He confronted Elijah Muhammad about the rumor, and the latter confirmed it. Since Muhammad was a moral and spiritual symbol for the Nation of Islam, Malcolm X, with the help of Wallace D. Muhammad, found Biblical and Quranic passages to explain these sexual relationships to the public. This incident was probably one of the turning points in Malcolm X's relationship with Elijah Muhammad. Malcolm could no longer idolize his former mentor or believe in his divinity. Malcolm X's confirmation of the grounds for this scandal bolstered the Nation of Islam's contentions that he was becoming more powerful than Elijah Muhammad.[105]

When President Kennedy was assassinated on November 22, 1963, Elijah Muhammad instructed all his ministers to avoid discussing the event. In an interview in Manhattan, on December 1, Malcolm X violated this injunction by saying:

I saw it as a case of chickens coming home to roost. I said it was the same thing as had happened with Medgar Evers, with Patrice Lumumba, with Madam Nhu's husband.[106]

As punishment for these comments, on December 4, Elijah Muhammad suspended Malcolm X for three months. Most of the "instant experts" on Islam at that time misinterpreted the significance of both Malcolm's statement and Elijah's response to it. They did not understand that this was a classic conflict between Elijah Muhammad's conservative goal of respectability for his movement and Malcolm X's radical political ideas. The public identity of the Nation of Islam was at stake. C. Eric Lincoln, who was in constant touch with both men during this period, has articulated the most sensible interpretation of this conflict:

> Elijah was beginning to gain respectability in the world community. He was saying more positive things than he was saying before. At the Savior's Day Meeting, the businessmen and politicians were coming from Chicago. . . . At just this moment that Elijah was beginning to reach this respectability, Malcolm made this unfortunate statement that could shatter any move to respectability that Elijah wanted . . . so he had to set Malcolm down. That was what that was all about. Those other tales [were] by instant experts on Islam.[107]

Initially, Malcolm X wanted to and could have returned to the Nation of Islam, for there was deep love and respect between these two men that was not initially altered by this conflict. Elijah Muhammad told Lincoln during the early part of Malcolm's suspension: "It's nothing but a sham, it's a put up. The boy knows that all he has to do is come home and take his punishment."[108] Warith Deen Mohammed was also very familiar with the emotional depth of the relationship between these two men. He said: "I couldn't see how that relationship could have changed to one of hate for each other. . . . It was instigated fear and distrust."[109]

However, as the media, the FBI, and divisive forces in the Nation of Islam inflated the conflict between Elijah and Malcolm, the latter's suspension turned into a nasty affair that made reconciliation between the two men only a remote possibility. Malcolm X launched a vicious jihad of words on television, the radio, and in the newspapers denouncing the Nation of Islam's theology and Elijah Muhammad's morality. In the wake of this rhetoric, Malcolm X began to hear rumors in February 1964 that he was going to be killed by an assassin from the Nation. Then he received word from Elijah Muhammad that his suspension would continue "for an indefinite period."[110]

Malcolm X broke all ties with the Nation of Islam on March 8, 1964 and formally announced his separation at a press conference at the Park Sheraton Hotel in New York on March 11. The sweeping religious and political changes that he undertook from that time until his assassination on February 21, 1965 were destined to become potent models for signification and identity in contemporary African-American Islam.[111]

MALCOLM X: THE MASTER OF SIGNIFICATION, THE MODEL FOR IDENTITY

Although Malcolm X's split with the Nation of Islam was precipitated partly by the inter-relation of religion and politics in his religious identity, it would be a mistake to say that "religion was not the dominant concern of Malcolm's thought or activity . . . after his Black Muslim days," as George Breitman has done. It is important that during the last year of his life, Malcolm X's political evolution originated in the dramatic changes occurring in his religious identity.[112]

Despite his flawed reading of the role of religion in Malcolm X's career, Breitman has formulated the most cogent analysis of the final year of Malcolm's life. For analytical purposes, he has divided this final year into two phases: the first, a "transition period," from March to May 1964; and the second, a final phase, from June 1964 to February 1965. The transition period is the most important phase for understanding Malcolm X's changes in religious identity.[113]

During this period, Malcolm underwent two dramatic changes in his religious identity that became significant models for contemporary African-American Islam. First, Malcolm X established multi-racial orthodox Islam as an option for African-American Muslims. Then, he explored the religious and cultural links between African-American Islam and its West African roots. As we shall see, each of these changes in Malcolm's religious identity was accompanied by the adoption of a new name. Thus, he can aptly be called the master of signification in African-American Islam.[114]

At the very beginning of his separation from the Nation of Islam, Malcolm founded the Muslim Mosque, Inc., which was based on orthodox Muslim principles. On March 11, 1964, he discussed the religious and political significance of this new organization.

> This will give us a religious base, and the spiritual force necessary to rid our people of the vices that destroy the moral fiber of our community.
> Muslim Mosque, Inc. will have its temporary headquarters in the Hotel Theresa in Harlem. It will be the working base for an action program designed to eliminate the political oppression, the economic exploitation, and the social degradation suffered daily by twenty-two million African-Americans.[115]

Then, in April 1964, Malcolm went to Mecca to make the obligatory pilgrimage called the hajj. This experience transformed his ideas on Islam and race relations in the Muslim world. When Malcolm X saw people of different colors and races worshipping together, apparently as brothers and sisters in Islam, he came to the conclusion that the Nation of Islam's racial separation had no place in the multi-racial orthodox Islam which he accepted in Mecca. Malcolm changed his name to El Hajj Malik El-Shabazz. As his wife would say later, "He went to Mecca as a Black Muslim and there he became only a Muslim."[116]

Malcolm's pilgrimage to Mecca also changed his theological understanding of racism. He could no longer lend credence to the Yacub myth of the Nation of Islam, and he now understood racism primarily as an economic and political consequence of capitalism. The white race was not inherently demonic; the American social and political system that perpetuated racism was. In a passage that indicates how dramatically making the hajj transformed Malcolm X's racial attitudes, he declared:

> The color-blindness of the Muslim world's religious society and the color blindness of the Muslim world's human society; these two influences had each day been making a greater impact, and an increasing persuasion against my previous way of thinking . . . there were tens of thousands of pilgrims, from all over the world. They were all colors, from blue-eyed blondes to black-skinned Africans. But we were all participating in the same ritual, displaying a spirit of unity and brotherhood that my experiences in America had led me to believe never could exist between the white and non-white.[117]

On a superficial level, it appeared that Malcolm X, like other naive observers of Islamic countries, believed that this area of the world was free from the evils of racism. However, more substantively, we must ask how such an astute observer of human affairs could have missed the patterns of racial separatism that had such deep roots in the Islamic world.

In Malcolm's time, approximately twenty percent of the inhabitants of Africa were non-European whites. The majority of them lived in northern Africa, which was the border zone between the native black and the white populations of the continent. Although northern Africa was color-conscious, the racial discrimination that had always been present there manifested itself in terms of class—the North Africans were used to seeing black people at the lower end of the socio-economic scale. Until the 1950s, some of northern Africa's leaders did not even identify with Africa, but instead with Europe. In 1870, for example, Khediwe Ismail stated that Egypt "does not lie in Africa but in Europe."[118]

The ideological identification of Arab northern Africa with the African continent did not begin until the 1950s. Before that time, Morocco, Libya, and Tunisia did not even have formal diplomatic ties with the countries of middle Africa, which were predominantly black. In 1952, Gamal Abd al-Nasser of Egypt said, "We are in Africa," but on a paternalistic note, he continued, "We will never in any circumstances relinquish our responsibility to support, with all our might, the spread of enlightenment and civilization to the remotest depths of the jungle." This remark indicated that his relatively new identification of Arab Africa with Africa was not as pristine as some suggested.[119]

In spite of these difficulties, an ideology of cooperation between northern and middle Africa was firmly entrenched in the minds of many Africans by the 1960s. The roots of this change in worldview can be traced to the African intellectuals. For more than one hundred fifty years, the leaders of Islamic northern Africa had been struggling with the impact of westernization on their societies. Ideologically this issue was seen as a conflict between the "alien new" and the traditional old. By the 1950s this conflict was for the most part resolved and westernization was internalized and accepted. In the context of the various nationalist struggles that were occurring on the African continent at that time, African intellectuals—both black and white—began to look within their own environments for an alternative identification. The "Third World" concept emerged from this ideological void. Thus Arab intellectuals in northern Africa began to identify with the black people of middle Africa. This worldview was emotionally attractive and successful because it led to a kind of color-blind cooperation in political and cultural affairs that benefited the entire African continent and the Islamic world. Indeed this was the ideology that so impressed Malcolm X during his pilgrimage to Mecca in 1964, and it was an integral part of the multi-racial rhetoric of orthodox Sunni Islam, which he embraced in place of the Nation of Islam. Deep down, Malcolm must have known that there were no racial utopias in Islam and that both the Nation of Islam and Sunni Islam had racial problems. Perhaps the euphoria of conversion to the former interpretation of the religion and the solidarity created by the hajj had temporarily blinded him to the racial and ethnic realities of the lands where orthodox Islam was predominant.[120]

Several months after his pilgrimage, Malcolm demonstrated an awareness of the racial tensions in the orthodox Islamic world. On a radio program in New York in December 1964, a caller asked him: "Why do the Arabs discriminate against the black man? And especially I read about the Sudan where they attacked and killed Negroes just because they were black." Malcolm replied:

> When I went to West Africa, I noticed that there was a strong feeling among the Africans against the Arabs . . . when you study the divisive forces at work on the African continent today, you'll find that these divisive forces are not indigenous to the African or the African continent, but are coming from the outside.[121]

However, when another caller pressed him to explain, "the Arab role . . . as slave traders and the hatred that would stem from that," Malcolm was forced to confront his own contradictions about the roots of racism in orthodox Islam. He replied:

> I don't condone slavery, no matter who it's carried on by. And I think that every power that has participated in slavery of any form on this earth in history has paid for it, except the United States. All of your European powers

that colonized . . . the part that the Arabs played in the enslavement of Africans, all of them who played a part have lost their empires, lost their power, lost their position except the United States.[122]

Although the hajj was a significant factor in Malcolm X's new religious identify, its importance has been over-emphasized by many commentators who have used it to de-emphasize Malcolm's continued hostility toward white Americans. Although "Malik Shabazz after Mecca" no longer considered whites as intrinsically evil, his change of consciousness about whites occurred primarily to facilitate religious and political coalitions with white Muslims in Asia and Africa, and not with white Americans. And as Lawrence Mamiya has demonstrated:

> He did not allow whites to join his newly formed organization, the Muslim Mosque, Inc. and the Organization for Afro-American Unity. He saw the possibilities of working with whites on selected issues but not membership. Malcolm's overwhelming concern was for the black masses, and he saw white membership as leading to an erosion of black independence.[123]

When Malcolm X departed from Mecca and North Africa, he traveled to Nigeria, which began the West African phase of his transition period. This West African tour was the most dynamic influence in his new religious and political identity for several reasons. First, West Africa was a homecoming for Malcolm in two respects—it connected him to his ancestors' land of origin and to African-American Islam's original source—the homelands of America's first African Muslim slaves. Malcolm's formulation of the spiritual and political connections between African America and West Africa was perhaps more profound than that of Edward Wilmot Blyden, the father of Pan-Africanism in the late nineteenth century. For the civilizationist tendencies of African-American Islam were dissolved in the absence of criticism of African traditional religions in his significations. And in his connecting the African struggles for independence with the African-American liberation struggle, Malcolm's version of Pan-Africanism changed the basic goals of that struggle, from a national agenda of civil rights to an international agenda of human rights.[124]

The high point of Malcolm's trip to Nigeria occurred on May 8, 1964 at the University of Ibadan, when the Nigerian Muslim Student's Society gave him the name Omowale, which means "the son who has come home." Ruby M. and E. U. Essien-Udom were present at the event and recalled Malcolm's political impact on Nigeria:

> From the time Malcolm came to Nigeria until he left he generated an unbelievable excitement. For those of us who had known Malcolm in the United States, it was a joy to experience once again that rare combination of oratorial brilliance and fearlessness compiled with naked honesty and a

genuine humility that made Malcolm so compelling and disarming. In his speech at Trenchard Hall at the University of Ibadan, Malcolm stressed the necessity for the African nations to lend their help in bringing the Afro-American's case before the United Nations. He argued that the Afro-American community should cooperate with the world's Pan-Africanists; and that even if they remained in America physically, they should return to Africa philosophically and culturally and develop a working unit between the framework of Pan-Africanism. Following his speech at Trenchard Hall, the Nigerian Muslim Student's Society had a reception for Malcolm in the Student's Union Hall and made him an honorary member of their society. They endowed him with the new name Omowale, meaning "the son who has come home." This gesture symbolized the wholehearted acceptance of Malcolm as a person and leader which we clearly observed among the radical youths and intellectuals in Nigeria. In his television and radio appearances in Nigeria, Malcolm stressed the need for African support to bring the charge of violation of Afro-American human rights by the United States before the United Nations.[125]

From Nigeria, Malcolm traveled to Ghana, which was known then as the "political Mecca" of Pan-Africanism. In Ghana, Malcolm spoke at the events sponsored by the community of African-American expatriates, the University of Ghana, the Kwame Nkrumah Ideological Institute, and the Ghanaian Parliament. He discussed Pan-Africanism with President Kwame Nkrumah, Shirley Graham Du Bois, and the Chinese, Cuban, and Algerian ambassadors. On his final day in Ghana, Malcolm received an honor from the Nigerian Muslim official, Al Hajj Iba Wali, that signaled the Pan-Africanist connection between West Africa and African-American Muslims. He gave Malcolm the regal African turban and robe of the Nigerian Muslims and a copy of the Quran. And Malcolm donned his new African clothing as a symbol of global black unity.[126]

Malcolm returned to the United States on May 21, 1964, after making short trips to Liberia, Senegal, and Morocco. By the time of his return, his experiences with radical political leaders in the Middle East and West Africa had convinced him of the need for an African-American political organization that would be separate from the Muslim Mosque, Inc. Thus, on June 29, 1964, he established a secular political body, the Organization of Afro-American Unity, which was designed to unite African Americans concerned with the global issue of human rights. Although much has been made of Malcolm's attempts to reconcile his political ideas with those of the mainstream leaders of the civil-rights movement during the final period of his split with the Nation of Islam, this tendency is not supported by the aims and objectives of the OAAU. These aims and objectives focused on

the letter and spirit of the Organization of African Unity established [in] Ethiopia, May 1963. . . . Pan-Africanism, self-determination, culture, national unity, anti-imperialism, education, economic security, self defense, and world-wide concerns.

In fact, the black power movement that arose after Malcolm's death adopted the major principles behind the OAAU.[127]

The inter-relation of religion and politics remained problematic in the religious identity that Malcolm formulated both for the Muslim Mosque, Inc. and for himself. This organization never seriously challenged the hegemony of the Nation of Islam among African-American Muslims. And there is evidence that many members of the former organization were dissatisfied with Malcolm's overwhelming political emphasis in his last days and longed for a more exclusively religious solidarity. At the same time, many African Americans who were not Muslims, but who were politically inspired by Malcolm, felt abandoned in 1965 during the long hot summer of black urban uprisings in America. At the time of these rebellions, Malcolm was away in Africa and the Muslim world seeking support for his campaign to bring the United States government before the United Nations for its human-rights violations against black Americans. Toward the end of his life, Malcolm's jihad of words had shifted from a focus on religion to a scathing critique of capitalism as an intrinsically evil economic system with connections to global racial oppression and imperi-alism. He saw socialism as a possible corrective.[128]

Malcolm's political plans were never fully realized, however, because death came too soon. Stalked by the shadows of his enemies in the Nation of Islam, the FBI, the CIA, and the New York City Police Department, Malcolm knew in his final days that he was marked for death, and he was desperate. He was assassinated during a speaking engagement at the Audubon Ballroom in Manhattan on February 21, 1965, and Talmadge Hayes, Thomas 15X Johnson, and Norman 3X Butler, all former Nation of Islam members, were sentenced to life in prison. In 1977, however, Hayes confessed that he had falsely accused Johnson and Butler and that the real assassins (besides himself) were residing in New Jersey. Defense Attorney William Kunstler was unsuccessful in obtaining a new trial. He suggested that the FBI and the New York City Police Department were involved in Malcolm X's murder. Indeed, the FBI had Malcolm under close observa-tion for years and had also infiltrated the Nation of Islam. Although the full truth about Malcolm X's assassination may never be known, recently, there has been a renewed interest among scholars about his assassination. And it is noteworthy that two of the most important assassination theories are linked to different ideas about the signification of Malcolm X and the Nation of Islam.[129]

Michael Friedly and Karl Evanzz have recently formulated assassina-tion theories that respond to Louis Lomax's ideas about the intelligence community's role in Malcolm's death. In 1968, in *To Kill a Black Man*, Lomax wrote:

This racist American society assassinated both Malcolm X and Martin Luther King, Jr. The men arrested may have pulled the trigger, but they by no means acted alone; American society was not only in concert with the assassins but there is every evidence that they were the hired killers.

Lomax died mysteriously in Los Angeles in a car accident during the production of a film on the assassination.[130]

Friedly, whose work on Malcolm X's assassination has resurrected the hate group image of the Nation of Islam, disavows any governmental involvement in the assassination and blames it solely on internal dissent in the Nation of Islam. He writes:

> Internal dissent and factional battles are natural attributes of all human societies, and the struggle between Malcolm X and Elijah Muhammad was a natural manifestation of that conflict. Lomax's statement may have some validity in that resorting to violence rather than negotiation may have been an imposed factor in the controversy. But his larger implications are overstated and distribute blame unnecessarily to communities that had no effect on the assassination of Malcolm X.[131]

Evanzz, however, believes that Lomax "solved the riddle of [Malcolm's] assassination twenty-five years ago." The former's book, *The Judas Factor: The Plot to Kill Malcolm X*, is based on Lomax's theory that Malcolm X was set up for murder by a former associate (referred to as Judas), who allegedly was connected to the intelligence community. Based on government documents that were declassified in the mid-1970s, *The Judas Factor* posits the theory that both the FBI and CIA were involved in Malcolm's death and used his split with Elijah Muhammad as the smokescreen for this involvement. According to Evanzz's evidence, signification was at the center of the intelligence community's campaign against Malcolm X and other black radicals in the sixties, and that the FBI and the CIA

> conducted a media manipulation program wherein some print, radio, and television reporters were fed distorted, inaccurate, and sometimes wholly fabricated "information" for the sole purpose of destroying targeted individuals and groups . . . [and] the majority of organizations targeted by the intelligence community, both left- and right-wing, had been infiltrated by the FBI or CIA, or both.[132]

In Evanzz's theory, both the FBI and the CIA had strong motives for the assassination. The FBI was afraid of an eventual "alliance" between black radicals under the leadership of Malcolm X and black "moderates" led by Martin Luther King, Jr. The CIA was threatened by Malcolm X's internationalist political activities and had directed a sector of the agency—the division that was implicated in the assassination and overthrow of several

Third World leaders—to monitor "Malcolm X's activities up to the hour of his assassination."[133]

My analysis of Malcolm X's activities in the last year of his life support Karl Evanzz's theory of the intelligence community's perception of Malcolm X as a significant political threat both in America and in the international context. His jihad of words in the final period of his life articulated a cogent plan for black liberation that included a separation of religion and politics, open expressions of disgust with the American system, and a United Nations initiative to expand the civil-rights movement into an international black alliance for human rights. All of these ideas were highlighted in "The Ballot or the Bullet," a speech he gave on April 3, 1964 at Cory Methodist Church in Cleveland. On that occasion, he preached:

> Although I'm still a Muslim, I'm not here tonight to discuss my religion. I'm not here to try and change your religion. I'm not here to argue or discuss anything that we differ about, because it's time for us to submerge our differences and realize that it's best for us to first see we have the same problem. . . .
>
> If we don't do something real soon, I think you'll have to agree that we're going to be forced either to use the ballot or the bullet. . . .
>
> No, I'm not an American, I'm one of 22 million black people who are victims of Americanism. One of the 22 million black people who are victims. The United Nations has what's known as the charter of human rights, it has a committee that deals in human rights. . . .
>
> Expand the civil rights struggle to the level of human rights, take it to the United Nations, where our African brothers can throw their weight on our side, where our Asian brothers can throw their weight on our side, where our Latin-American brothers can throw their weight on our side. . . .
>
> Let the world know how bloody his hands are. Let the world know the hypocrisy that's practiced over here. Let it be the ballot or the bullet.[134]

The ideas of national and global black political unity were adumbrated even more forcefully at the first public rally of the Organization of Afro-American Unity in New York on June 28, 1964:

> We have formed an organization known as the Organization of Afro-American Unity which has the . . . aim and objective—to fight whoever gets in our way, to bring about the complete independence of people of African descent here in the Western Hemisphere, and first here in the United States, and bring about the freedom of these people by any means necessary.
>
> That's our motto. . . . And then, once we are united among ourselves in the Western Hemisphere, we will unite with our brothers in the motherland, on the continent of Africa. . . .
>
> Since self-preservation is the first law of nature, we assert the Afro-American's right to self defense. . . . Instead of the various black groups

declaring war on each other, showing how militant they can be cracking each other's heads, let them go down South and crack some of those cracker's heads. . . .

We propose to support and organize political clubs to run independent candidates for office and to support any Afro-American already in office who answers to and is responsible to the Afro-American community. . . .

The Afro-American community must accept the responsibility for regaining our people who have lost their place in society. We must declare an all-out war on organized crime in our community. A vice that is controlled by policemen who accept bribes and graft must be exposed. We must establish a clinic, whereby one can get aid and care for drug addiction.

Our cultural revolution must be the means of bringing us closer to our African brothers and sisters. It must begin in the community and be based on community participation. Afro-Americans will be free to create only when they can depend on the Afro-American community for support, and Afro-American artists must realize that they depend on the Afro-American community for inspiration. . . .

This cultural revolution will be the journey to our rediscovery of ourselves. History is a people's memory and without a memory man is demoted to the level of the lower animals. . . .

Armed with the knowledge of our past, we can with confidence charter a course for our future. Culture is an indispensable weapon in the freedom struggle. We must take hold of it and forge the future with the past.[135]

On July 17, 1965, Malcolm delivered an appeal for support to the delegates of the Organization of African Unity in Cairo, Egypt. He urged this "African summit," composed of the rulers of independent African nations, to help him bring the case of the human-rights violations of the United States before the United Nations. This was a bold initiative that was undoubtedly scrutinized by the intelligence community because of its potential to disrupt American foreign policy and to create an alliance between the African-American political group and African governments. Malcolm X's appeal to the Organization of African Unity was based on the racial and political links between African Americans and Africans:

Your Excellencies:

The Organization of Afro-American Unity has sent me to attend this historic African summit conference as an observer to represent the interests of 22 million African Americans whose human rights are being violated daily by the racism of American imperialists.

The Organization of Afro-American Unity has been formed by a cross-section of America's African-American community, and is patterned after the letter and spirit of the Organization of African Unity. . . .

Since the 22 million of us were originally Africans who are now in America not by choice but only by a cruel accident in our history, we strongly believe that African problems are our problems and our problems are African problems. . . .

We also believe that as heads of the independent African states you are the shepherd of all African peoples everywhere, whether they are still at home on the mother continent or have been scattered abroad. . . .

The Organization of Afro-American Unity, in cooperation with a coalition of other leaders and organizations, has decided to elevate our freedom struggle above the domestic level of civil rights. We intend to internationalize it by placing it at the level of human rights. Our freedom struggle for human dignity is no longer confined to the domestic jurisdiction of the United States government.

We beseech the independent African states to help us bring our problem before the United Nations, on the grounds that the United States government is morally incapable of protecting the lives and the property of 22 million African-Americans. And on the grounds that our deteriorating plight is definitely becoming a threat to world peace.[136]

During the final weeks of Malcolm's life, he began to talk about the African-American freedom struggle as an aspect of "a worldwide revolution" against racism, corporate racism, classism, and sexism. Utilizing the concept of jihad, and the political lessons that he had learned from his Muslim contacts in the Middle East and Africa, he constructed a model of black liberation that appealed to Muslims and non-Muslims alike. And aspects of his radical black nationalism appealed to African Americans throughout the black political spectrum—from the NAACP to the black Left. Because of his potential (if he had lived) to unite many black Muslims and black Christians in America and abroad in a liberation struggle that could have significantly challenged the corporate capitalist power base of the white American establishment, there is no question that the American intelligence community had the incentive to be involved in Malcolm X's murder. Indeed, since Malcolm X's death, no Muslim leader has constructed an African-American religious and political identity that has had the potential to lead black people to liberation in America. For the ultimate lesson of the African-American Muslim paradigm of Malcolm X's life is that the price for such an identity is death.[137]

WARITH DEEN MOHAMMED AND LOUIS FARRAKHAN: MUSLIM IDENTITIES IN THE SHADOWS OF MALCOLM X

In many respects, Malcolm X represented the culmination of the various religious identities that could be formulated in African-American Islam. "His stamp on the American Islamic landscape [was] enduring, his influence undeniable," as he explored the racial-separatist model of the religion in the Nation of Islam, an Arab-centric multi-racial orthodox Muslim identity in Mecca, and the West African roots of African-American

Islam in Ghana. At the same time, Malcolm X's political identity at the end of his life represented the culmination of the radical black nationalist tradition expressed through jihad, the Islamic paradigm of the liberation struggle. Louis Farrakhan and Warith Deen Mohammed, the two most important black Muslim leaders in America today, are in a sense the spiritual heirs of Malcolm X, for the Muslim identities that they have formulated for their movements are based on the racial-separatist model of Malcolm X during his association with the Nation of Islam and his multi-racial emphasis after his pilgrimage to Mecca. Lawrence Mamiya has referred to this model for identity as the "Old Malcolm" based on racial particularism. An identity modeled on the "New Malcolm," in contrast, would be based on universalism or multi-racialism. However, it is noteworthy that neither Farrakhan nor Mohammad has realized the radical strategies for political liberation inherent in the concept of jihad as Malcolm did, for both men advocate conservative black nationalist strategies for bringing African Americans into the mainstream of American capitalist structures. Before discussing the programs of these contemporary leaders, we must explore the historical significance of Elijah Muhammad's death, which will shed light on their identities.[138]

Elijah Muhammad, the spiritual leader of the Nation of Islam, died on February 25, 1975. He was regarded by his followers as the "last Messenger of Allah" because of his close association with Wallace D. Fard, the Nation of Islam's deified prophet and founder who disappeared in 1934. His particular combination of political savvy, religious wisdom, money, and love for his people, made him the most prominent Muslim leader on the North American continent for the forty years that he headed the Nation of Islam. Under his leadership, the black Muslim movement acquired one million followers and seventy-six mosques in the United States and abroad. Its holdings, which included the Guaranty Bank and Trust Company, thousands of acres of farmland, the *Muhammad Speaks* newspaper (with the largest circulation of any African-American newspaper), housing complexes, aircraft, and retail and wholesale businesses, were estimated at $85,000,000 by the 1970s.[139]

More important, Elijah Muhammad made the American public aware of the religion of Islam, which was no small feat in a country that started as a bastion of Protestant Christianity and that later evolved a "civil religion" based on Judeo-Christian values. However, he did not accept orthodoxy for his movement until 1974, a few months before his death, and this development was the result of over fourteen years of ideological conflict with his son Wallace. Both Wallace and his brother Akbar had converted to orthodox Islam in the 1960s, having studied Islam at the prestigious al-Azhar University in Egypt.[140]

Wallace D. Muhammad was born in 1933. He was named after Wallace D. Fard, who predicted that Elijah Muhammad's seventh child would be a male who would eventually succeed his father. Wallace, who had made several pilgrimages to Mecca, did not accept the divinity of W. D. Fard, a view for which Elijah Muhammad excommunicated his son from the Nation of Islam several times. Wallace also remained a supporter and confidant of Malcolm X even after Malcolm fell out of favor with Elijah Muhammad.[141]

Wallace D. Muhammad became the Supreme Minister of the Nation of Islam immediately after his father's death on February 26, 1975. During the first years of his leadership, he mandated sweeping changes in the racial-separatist black Muslim movement in order to bring it into line with a multi-racial orthodox Muslim identity. These changes included a reinterpretation of the theology of the organization. The new leader abolished the doctrine of black racial supremacy and for the first time allowed whites to subscribe to the religion. He refuted W. D. Fard's divinity, preferring to emphasize Fard's contributions as the founder of the movement, as a community worker, and as a reform psychologist. Wallace Muhammad held that Fard's doctrine about "white devils" was not meant to be understood literally, interpreting it as a psychological smoke screen for his community work among the black lower class. Wallace did not consider Elijah Muhammad the "Messenger of Allah," but rather as the man who reinterpreted Fard's doctrines. He praised his father for achieving the "First Resurrection" of black Americans by introducing them to Islam. However, he claimed that the "Second Resurrection" was to occur not as an "apocalyptic event" as his father had suggested, but instead as a change in the mission of the Nation of Islam. Now its mission was directed not only at black America, but also at the entire American environment. Wallace recognized Malcolm X's contributions to the movement and renamed the Harlem mosque Malcolm Shabazz Mosque.[142]

Muhammad changed the terminology of the organization in order to achieve orthodox identity. He renamed the Nation of Islam the "World Community of Al-Islam in the West" in 1976, the "American Muslim Mission" in 1980, and the "Muslim American Community" in the 1990s. To avoid association with Wallace D. Fard's doctrines, Wallace Muhammad changed his own name to Warith Deen Mohammed (formerly Warith Deen Muhammad). Warith Deen means "inheritor of the faith" in Arabic. At first, he called black people Bilalians in honor of Bilal Ibn Rabah, the Ethiopian who was a close friend of the Prophet Muhammad, redesignating the newspaper *Muhammad Speaks* as *The Bilalian News*. Warith's followers now call themselves the Muslim American Community, and their newspaper is called *The Muslim Journal* (formerly *The American Muslim Journal*). Ministers of Islam were renamed "imams," and temples were renamed "mosques" and "masjids" (an Arabic word for "mosque").[143]

The rituals and beliefs of the Muslim American Community are now closer to orthodox Muslim customs. The members of the group practice the pillars of Islam and believe in one God and in Muhammad as his last prophet. The fast of Ramadan, which occurred in December when Elijah Muhammad was alive, is now celebrated according to the lunar calendar used by orthodox Muslims. In the masjid, worshipers face the east and sit on the floor to pray, both traditional Islamic practices.[144]

Furthermore, the Muslim American Community has abandoned the anti-American stance of its predecessor, the Nation of Islam. It no longer demands a separate state from the United States government, and its members now salute the American flag and vote. Warith Deen Mohammed has paid the organization's long-term debts and back taxes. The movement has sold most of its businesses, and in 1979, it signed a 22-million-dollar contract to manufacture rations for the U.S. Department of Defense. The older American Muslim Mission supported the Equal Rights Amendment and hoped that one of its members would eventually become an influential politician or corporate executive. Essentially, Imam Mohammed has done away with the racial-separatist identity of his organization in order to fully Americanize it.[145]

There have also been some important signs from the East. Warith was the only American official who was asked to attend the Tenth Annual Islamic Conference of Ministers of Foreign Affairs in Fez, Morocco. He is considered to be the primary facilitator for Islamic missionary activities in the United States. In 1978, several oil-rich Arab Muslim countries designated him the "sole consultant and trustee" of the monies of all Islamic organizations involved in missionary activities in America. Also, the international Muslim community is financing the construction of a 14- to 16-million-dollar mosque on the South Side of Chicago, and already over 2 million dollars have been raised for this project. On the other hand, some Islamic groups in the United States are displeased with the Muslim American Community's status in the Muslim world and continue to equate Warith Deen with Elijah Muhammad's teachings which they despised.[146]

In 1978, Warith Deen Mohammed decentralized his organization's leadership structure by resigning as spiritual leader and becoming an ambassador-at-large, representing the organization in domestic and international affairs. The community is now governed by a council of six imams, each of whom has complete authority in his area of the country and equal power on the national level. This is a radical change from Elijah Muhammad's organization, in which he was the autocrat and all decisions for the Nation of Islam were made in Chicago.[147]

Lately, Warith Deen Mohammed has moved away from the complete capitulation of his movement to a version of orthodox Islam (heavily influenced by Saudi Arabia) that occurred in the 1970s and 1980s. In a recent interview at Duke University, he suggested plans for an unique American "school of thought" that would be independent of Arabian religious authorities:

I have great affection for the school of thought of Saudi Arabia. I don't belong to any particular school of thought and I don't advise any of my colleagues to begin to promote any school of thought in America. We will eventually have a school of thought in America, that's my hope, that's my belief. . . . As long as our thought represents the essentials in the Quran and life of the Prophet. Islam has had different schools of thought. What's wrong with different schools of thought? We are encouraged to have our own opinion. Islam is not a static religion. I don't think we stopped growing.[148]

In 1976, Warith Deen Mohammed estimated that there were 70,000 members in his organization. However, since that time the movement has lost thousands of members who disagree with the changes that he has made and who wish to return to the racial-separatist identity prescribed by the Nation of Islam. On March 7, 1978, Louis Haleem Abdul Farrakhan announced his departure from The World Community of Islam in the West, in an interview in *The New York Times*. In 1979, he began publishing *The Final Call*, a newspaper that was named after Elijah Muhammad's publication in Chicago in 1934. *The Final Call* urges black people to return to the belief in Allah in the person of W. D. Fard and his messenger, Elijah Muhammad. Farrakhan believes that this is an eschatological issue—it represents the last chance for black people to attain power and freedom in the United States.[149]

Louis Farrakhan's movement shares the objectives held by the Nation of Islam under Elijah Muhammad. His program discourages integration with white people and advocates black control of black community resources. It demands equal opportunities in education and employment, along with economic and social justice for all blacks in the United States. Farrakhan's organization also demands the release of black prisoners who make up the majority of the prison population in the United States. The most extraordinary aspect of the new Nation of Islam's program is its "demand for a separate land" for blacks. This point was also part of Elijah Muhammad's program. And Farrakhan has also re-established the paramilitary group, the Fruit of Islam, which Warith Deen Mohammed had dismantled because of his opposition to its violent tactics.[150] In the wake of Farrakhan's departure from the path established by Warith, "at least a dozen competing fragments" of the former Nation of Islam appeared. The three most influential are led by John Muhammad (Elijah's brother) in Detroit, Silis Muhammad in Atlanta, and Emmanuel Abdullah Muhammad in Baltimore.

Minister Farrakhan believes that Warith Deen Mohammed has misinterpreted his father's teachings. In his view, when Elijah Muhammad stated that white people were devils, he meant it in a literal sense. Furthermore, Farrakhan agrees with Elijah Muhammad's unique interpretation of the Bible and the Quran as the most appropriate scriptural messages for the liberation of the black masses. He considers orthodox Islam inappropriate for African Americans because it does not take into account their condition in the United States or discrimination against them in the Islamic world. This latter issue is very important because it points to Farrakhan's and Mohammed's different views about the international community. Where Warith Deen Mohammed sees the possibility for true equality between Arab and black Muslims and is considered an Arabized intellectual in some circles, Louis Farrakhan sees the problems of race and color differences in the Islamic world and rejects a multi-racial Arab-centric Muslim identity. In a speech in Harlem in 1980 he declared:

> I am here as a servant of Allah [not Mecca]. I see Muslims taking advantage of blacks in Arabia and Africa. I will not jump over one black Christian to find brotherhood with a Muslim. . . . If you [orthodox Muslims] are so interested in the black man in America, why don't you clean up the ghettos in Mecca. . . . The ghettoes in the Holy City where the Sudanese and other black African Muslims live are some of the worst I've seen anywhere. . . . I see racism in the Muslim world, clean it up![151]

Louis Farrakhan began his life as Louis Eugene Walcott on May 11, 1933 in New York City. He was raised in Roxbury, Massachusetts as an Episcopalian in St. Cyprian's Church and earned his high-school diploma at Boston Latin School. He then studied for two years at Winston-Salem's Teachers College in North Carolina. Farrakhan is a former calypso singer and professional violinist who converted to the Nation of Islam in 1955 and studied with Malcolm X. He is considered a Muslim by the international community because he has made the pilgrimage to Mecca and speaks fluent Arabic. However, Mecca did not change Farrakhan's ideas about prophecy in the Nation of Islam. On Savior's Day on February 24, 1991, Farrakhan preached

> We believe that Allah came to us in the name of W. Farrad Muhammad, the messiah of the Christians and the Mahdi of the Muslims. . . . Many of my Muslim brothers say this is un-Islamic. . . . I visited Mecca and I sat with the scholars and this is the main point we wrangled over. . . . And when I finished they shut their mouths.[152]

Lawrence H. Mamiya argues that changes in the socioeconomic conditions of the Nation of Islam explain the present ideological changes in the organization's identity. He draws on Max Weber's *Protestant Ethic and the Spirit of Capitalism* to illustrate "a dialectical relationship between religious ideas and socioeconomic conditions." Just as Weber maintained that Calvinistic Protestantism created the attitudes which made its believers into successful capitalists, so Mamiya argues that the Nation of Islam, which started as a lower-class religious organization, over the years emphasized thrift and economic independence to such an extent that it eventually evolved into a middle-class organization. This change in socioeconomic conditions resulted in fertile ground for the ideological changes that Warith D. Mohammed has made in the mostly middle-class Muslim American community. On the other hand, Louis Farrakhan's resurrected Nation of Islam continues to appeal to the black lower class.[153]

Weber's concept of "elective affinity" also plays an important part in Mamiya's analysis. This concept is concerned with a believer's selection of religious ideology, which is often based on the relationship between socio-economic conditions and the underlying message of a religion is again primary. Poor blacks will probably tend to select the resurrected Nation of Islam over the Muslim American Community since the former movement continues to emphasize the black nationalist message which Elijah Muhammad originally designed to attract the black lower class. The Muslim American Community, with its new identification with a multi-racial Islamic tradition and the Arabic language and its emphasis on full participation in American society and relaxation of discipline, will probably be most attractive to a well-educated middle-class membership. Mamiya emphasizes that this is not a deterministic analysis, for there are activities for poor blacks in the Muslim American Community, and there are middle-class members in the resurrected Nation of Islam. But there are general trends in each organization. The social class of the followers often influences which group they will select and which aspect of the identity they will utilize in their lives.[154]

The future bodes well for Warith Deen Mohammed's Muslim American Community since it has identified with the multi-racial orthodox Islamic world and has the late Elijah Muhammad's vast resources at its disposal. International Islamic leaders see Warith's organization as an opportunity to establish a permanent Islamic outpost in the United States. They have even named him Mujaddin—reviver of religion—and have given him the authority to certify all pilgrimages to Mecca from North America. Furthermore, Wallace's multi-racialism has made his movement more attractive to potential white converts in the United States. The Muslim American Community's schools are noteworthy—they offer courses in Arabic from the elementary grades through high school. It is likely that future American scholars in Islamic studies will emerge from this group.[155]

The resurrected Nation of Islam relies on Louis Farrakhan's personal charisma and the appeal of black nationalism for its continued growth. The conservative backlash which has resulted in racial discrimination, along with the economic problems, high unemployment rates, and the crack cocaine crisis that have affected black Americans in the 1980s and 1990s under the Reagan, Bush, and Clinton administrations ensure that the racial-separatist identity offered by Farrakhan's movement will appeal to the masses. However, some of his activities have alienated mainstream black leaders and the white political establishment in the United States.[156]

In April 1984, Farrakhan incurred the wrath of black journalists around the country when he allegedly threatened Milton Coleman, a reporter for

The Washington Post, and said that black reporters who are critical of black leaders are traitors to the black race. Farrakhan made these statements after Coleman reported that the black presidential candidate, Rev. Jesse Jackson, had called Jews "Hymies" and New York City "Hymietown." In late June of that year, a reporter for the *Chicago Sun-Times* quoted a radio sermon in which Louis Farrakhan referred to the establishment of Israel as "an outlaw act" and its religion as "gutter religion." According to George E. Curry, the NAACP and the white political establishment responded quickly and decisively to Louis Farrakhan's words as "Farrakhan was promptly denounced by President Reagan, Vice President Bush, NAACP Executive Director Benjamin L. Hooks, and Democratic presidential candidates Walter Mondale and Gary Hart. The United States Senate voted 95–0 to censure Farrakahn for his 'hateful bigoted expressions of anti-Jewish and racist sentiments.'"[157]

In May 1985, Louis Farrakhan made one of the most radical moves in the history of the Nation of Islam when his organization received a 5 million dollar loan from Colonel Muammar el-Qaddafi, the Libyan leader. Farrakhan referred to Qaddafi as a "fellow struggler in the cause of liberation of our people." This interest-free loan was intended to develop black economic independence in the United States through a planned national corporation called POWER or People Organized and Working for Economic Rebirth. Perhaps Qaddafi was initially attracted to the Nation of Islam because of Farrakhan's antisemitic representation in the media. However, Qaddafi's animosity toward the United States, and Farrakhan's association with him will ensure close governmental scrutiny of the new Nation of Islam in the future.[158]

In spite of the differences between Farrakhan's and W. D. Mohammed's religious and political identities, their views on some issues converge. First, the leadership of both movements is connected to the bloodline of Elijah Muhammad. Of course, Warith is Elijah's son, but even most informed observers do not know that Louis Farrakhan married into the Muhammad family, and that Tynetta Muhammad, Elijah Muhammad's second wife, and her sons are officials in Farrakhan's Nation of Islam. Farrakhan's son-in-law is also his chief of staff. All of this suggests that the Nation of Islam and the Muslim American Community will continue to be ruled by family dynasties in the foreseeable future. And, at the Nation of Islam's Mosque Maryam in Chicago, orthodox prayer rituals are followed.

Second, Farrakhan's movement no longer advocates separation from the American political mainstream. In his own words, "We are coming out of the mosque now to try to serve the broader community." Recently, three Muslims from the Nation of Islam ran for electoral office in the Washington, D.C. area. Warith Deen Mohammed's Muslim American Community is also actively involved in American political life. In the 1980s, his group formed the Muslim Political Action Committee in Greater Washington, D.C. and vigorously campaigned for ex-Mayor Marion Barry.[159]

Finally, both the Muslim American Community and the Nation of Islam have mobilized against the marketing and distribution of crack cocaine, which has created unprecedented waves of violence and fear in black urban communities in the 1980s and 1990s. In the late 1980s, the black residents of Mayfair Mansion, a housing project in Washington, D.C., that had been taken over by drug dealers, called in the Nation of Islam to patrol their neighborhood. With the cooperation of the police department, the Muslims eliminated the drug traffic and crime in the development in a short period of time and have maintained Mayfair Mansion as a crime-free area for two years. This story exemplifies the Nation of Islam's success in fighting crime in poor black communities throughout the United States.[160]

Louis Farrakhan and Warith Deen Mohammed underline the fact that there is more than one kind of Muslim identity in African-American Islam today, each with a different relationship to the international community and a different stance on racial-separatist and multi-racial community experience.[161]

VARIETIES OF MUSLIM IDENTITIES

Since the 1970s both the Lahore and Qadian branches of the Ahmadiyya movement in America have been affected by the persecution of their co-religionists in Pakistan. In 1974, the Pakistani Parliament passed a resolution declaring the Ahmadis a non-Muslim group and the National Assembly of Pakistan began to consider an amendment to the penal code which would make the profession of certain Ahmadi beliefs a crime punishable by imprisonment. This communal strife has continued in the 1980s as Islamic fundamentalists in Pakistan increased their persecution of the Ahmadiyya community in 1982. In May 1985, the orthodox community blamed the Ahmadis for the destruction of a mosque in Sukkur, Pakistan. Two people were killed in this incident.[162]

Many Pakistanis distrust the Ahmadis because they are well educated, whereas the majority of the Muslims in Pakistan are not. This is basically a struggle between a progressive middle-class minority and the fundamentalist masses who are in the majority. The Pakistani controversy has influenced Arab, Indian, and Pakistani Muslims' attitudes toward the Ahmadiyya movement in the United States. These Muslims scorn the Ahmadis in America and do not participate in their missionary work. However, the latter still consider themselves a part of worldwide multi-racial Islam.[163]

Mubarak Ahmad has been the chief missionary of the Qadian branch of the Ahmadiyya movement in the United States since 1983. Under his leadership, the movement has acquired ten new American missions. Ahmad salutes the various black Muslim groups in the United States and is particularly pleased by Warith Deen Mohammed's Muslim American

Community, which is presently moving closer to orthodoxy. He emphasizes that the Ahmadiyya movement is "a peace loving community that does not believe in terrorism or hijacking." The movement's motto is "love for all, hatred for none." The total U.S. membership is about 10,000 of which 45 percent are black Americans, and 55 percent are Pakistanis and Indians. The Ahmadis have branches in more than forty American cities, and their "numbers are growing."[164]

The original mission in Chicago is still functioning on South Wabash Avenue. This group has 300 members (50 are black Americans, and the remaining members are Indians and Pakistanis, with a few white Americans). On October 23, 1994, the Ahmadiyya movement dedicated a new $350,000 mosque named Masjid Al-Sadiq, on the site of their first mission house in America. College students are a special target group for the Ahmadis, who have lectured at the University of Chicago. Also, the movement donates its literature to university and public libraries.[165]

The Lahore branch of the Ahmadiyya movement is active in the San Francisco Bay area in California. Although their numbers are small, with fewer than 100 members in the United States, they publish a monthly magazine entitled *The Islamic Review*. Their mission is to translate the Quran into as many different languages as possible, including Spanish, French, Japanese, Chinese, and Russian. Muhammad Abdullah, the imam for Oakland, is one of the oldest Muslim leaders in America. In the 1960s he was a mentor for Warith Deen Mohammed and continues to maintain a close personal and organizational relationship with him.[166]

Other Muslim groups in black America in recent years include the Hanafi Muslims, who came to public attention in January 1973 when some of their members were massacred in Washington, D.C., and in March 1977 when they protested the film "Muhammad." Although no comprehensive scholarly study of this movement has yet been published, we do know that they draw their beliefs and practices from the Hanafite Sunni texts and testaments. Abu Hanifa founded one of the four schools of Islamic religious law (*sharia*) in the eighth century. This religiously conservative group, which was initially led by Hamaas Abdul Khaalis, interprets the Quran literally and focuses its militant protests on religious rather than sociopolitical issues.[167]

The Islamic Party of North America: The Community Mosque was established in 1971 in a black ghetto community in Washington, D.C. by Yusuf Muzaffaruddin Hamid. Hamid, who studied with various Muslim teachers in Pakistan in the 1960s, wished "to facilitate the sharing and understanding of the Islamic way of life, and teaching Muslims their prayers while sharing with them programs which Islamized their lifestyles." In its heyday, the Party was an African-American neighborhood-based movement with branches in New Jersey, Georgia, Maryland, Virginia, Pittsburgh, and Chicago. After the formal organization of the Party ended, Hamid founded another small group in Georgia. Until his death in the early 1990s, he continued to emphasize the need to interpret the Quran, hadith, and other scriptural components of Islam in the particularistic context of black American culture.[168]

Darul Islam, also called the Abode of Islam, was founded in Brooklyn in 1962 by Yahya Abdul-Kareem, Ishaq Abduga Shaheed, and Rajab Mahmu. Racial separatism has influenced this movement since its early days: its first converts were former members of the Black Power Movement, and "it has never been very open to immigrant communities." Darul Islam is one of the "most influential" Islamic philosophies among African Americans, with branches in many major urban areas of the United States. Knowledge of the Quran, hadith, and the Arabic language are heavily emphasized in the religious life of this community. The Indian Shaykh Jalani influenced two of the Darul Islam's founders and some of its members to establish a new group called the Fuqra at the end of the 1970s.[169]

Darul Islam, led by Imam Jamil Al-Amin, has established approximately thirty branches in America and the Caribbean. Based on the Quran and formal Islamic prayer, Imam Jamil's philosophy focuses on the African-American struggle for social justice. Although he considers racial identity a very important aspect of what Islam can offer black people, Jamil's philosophy goes beyond race: "You have to go beyond the whole concept of nationalism when you are talking about successful struggle. . . . Peoplehood is based upon belief more than anything else."[170]

Some African-American Muslims are members of Sufi groups in the United States. According to Aminah Beverly McCloud,

> Sufis have found the way to God in allegorical symbolic interpretations of the Quran and the life of the prophet Muhammed. . . . [Their] (way to God) elaborates a method for individual spirituality under the guidance of a shaykh and specifically a type of Sufi order.

At the present time, African Americans are followers of two important tariqas (Sufi "paths")—Tijaniyyah and Naqshabandiyyah. The Tijanis' roots are in an order founded in Algeria in the eighteenth century by Abul-Abbas ben Muhammad ben al-Mukhter al-Tijani. In America, Shaykh Hassan Cisse is the leader of a tariqa of about two thousand followers, in which some black Americans have been "initiated and authorized" as teachers on the east coast and in the midwest. Naqshabandiyyah was founded in central Asia in the fourteenth century by Kwajah Baha al-Din Muhammad Naqshaband. This tariqa established itself in the Americas in 1986 and has communities in many key cities in the United States. African Americans who are Naqshabandi signal their affiliation by wearing red turbans. Their shaykh, Maulan Shaykh Nazim Adil Qubrusi, was born in Turkey.[171]

Among the remaining Muslim groups, the Ansaaru Allah Community of Brooklyn has existed since about 1970. This eclectic and messianic body was formerly called the Nubian Islamic Hebrew Mission. The founder of the Ansaars, Al Hajj Al Imam Isa Abd Allah Muhammad Al Mahdi, is said to be the great-grandson of Al Imam Muhammad Al Mahdi, who was a leader in the holy war against the British in the Sudan in the late nineteenth century. The Ansaars believe that their founder will have 144,000 followers in the year 2000, when the millennium will occur.[172]

The Ansaaru Allah Community uses the Bible and the Quran to support their beliefs and identity. They offer approximately eighty publications for sale to the general public. The identity and beliefs of their movement draw from the teachings of Judaism, Christianity, and Islam. Like the Nation of Islam, they preach the inferiority of the white race and the supremacy of their own group. The Ansaars, who consider themselves to be the chosen people of God and their original homeland to be the Sudan, call themselves Nubians and believe that Arabic is their original language.[173]

In Los Angeles, Masjid Rasoul is the spiritual home of an African-American Shiite Muslim community that was established ten years ago. P. Q. Halifu is one of the leaders of this group, which believes that the Prophet Muhammad chose Ali and his descendants as the rightful leaders of the Muslim community. Shiites make up approximately 10 percent of the Muslims in the United States. Also based in Los Angeles is the Islamic Moorish Empire of the West, Inc., a splinter group of the Moorish Science Temple of America, which honors Noble Drew Ali as its founder but does not consider him a prophet. In 1993, they published the first edition of their newspaper, *The Moorish Chronicles*.[174]

Over the last thirty years, there has been dramatic growth in the number of Muslims in the United States. Today, experts estimate that America's Muslim population is somewhere between 4 to 6 million, which could make Islam the second largest religion in the United States. According to Yvonne Haddad, America's Muslims operate "more than 600 mosques/Islamic centers, two Islamic colleges, scores of parochial day schools, several hundred weekend schools, women's organizations, youth groups, and professional and civic organizations." Thus, today, Islam is not just in the international news but is an integral part of the landscape of America.[175]

THE FUTURE

The shape of this new community is important for understanding the future direction of Islam in contemporary black America. Black Americans comprise about 42 percent of the Muslims in the United States. South Asian Muslims constitute almost 25 percent, Arabs approximately 12 percent, and the remaining 21 percent are from Iran, West Africa, Southeast Asia, Eastern Europe, and white America. California (1 million Muslims), New York (800,000 Muslims), and Illinois (400,000 Muslims) are the states with the largest Muslim populations. Much of this dramatic growth is due to the arrival of recent Muslim immigrants who came to the United

Nation of Islam leader **LOUIS FARRAKHAN** *addresses the Million Man March, Monday, October 16, 1995, on Capitol Hill. Farrakhan proclaimed divine guidance in bringing to Washington the largest assemblage of black Americans in history. Farrakhan's son Mustafa is at left.* AP Photo/Doug Mills. Used by permission.

States after the American immigration laws were reformed in the 1960s. These Muslim immigrants are generally middle-class professionals who maintain cultural and linguistic ties to their countries of origin.

What do these developments have to do with Islam in black America?[176] Although there are no conclusive statistics yet, some observers believe that the immigrant community as well as the leadership of Warith Deen Mohammed have influenced many black American Muslims to embrace somewhat orthodox interpretations of Islam. Dawud Assad, president of the U.S. Council of Masjid, says that "eighty-five to ninety percent of our converts are black. . . . They become better Muslims than the Muslim immigrants. The blacks are very God-fearing." Moreover it appears that African Americans who are converting to orthodox Islam throughout the United States are learning Arabic, the universal language of the religion, and are deconstructing the racial separatism of the traditional black Muslim movements. Al-Amin Abdul-Latif, the imam of a storefront mosque in Brooklyn, is typical of this trend, as racial equality is the focus of many of his sermons: "Adam and Moses and Jesus were all Muslims," he preached at a Friday service, "not because they were black, not because they were white, but because they submitted their wills to Allah."[177]

Appearances, however, can be deceiving. Although orthodox Islam is undoubtedly progressing significantly among black Americans and racialist rhetoric is not as prevalent as it was in the 1960s, true integration between black and nonblack Muslims has not yet occurred. There are few truly racially integrated Islamic communities. Even nonblack Muslim groups are for the most part ethnically segregated. Although Muslims of different races and nationalities sometimes pray together in some mosques, foreign Muslims, second- and third-generation immigrant Muslims, and black Muslims are constructing an Islamic agenda in America in different national organizations and settings. The needs of the first two groups are served primarily by the Muslim Student Association, the Federation of Islamic Associations, the Islamic Society of North America, the Muslim World League, and the American Muslim Council. Although the Arab Americans who are predominant in these groups are affected by the negative media images of Islam and United States foreign policy in the Middle East, they are for the most part fulfilling the American dream and reconciling their religious identity "as successfully as [their] American Christian and Jewish counterparts." On the other hand, because of their racial status in America, black Muslims, whether they are orthodox or not, are dealing with a different circle of identification. Their mosques and centers are still located primarily in the black urban communities, and no matter how effectively they Arabize their movements, they know that they must deal with the political and social agenda of black America in the 1990s in order to do effective missionary work in this setting.[178]

Finally, the recent sensationalist attention that Louis Farrakhan and his former spokesperson Khallid Muhammad have received in the American media underlines the tension between separatism and universalism and between religion and politics in the identities of African-American Muslims. The religious significance of Farrakhan, who is one of the most popular African-American leaders today, has been overshadowed by some of his controversial political and social statements. At the same time, although he is arguably the most powerful Muslim leader in America, this fact has also been overshadowed by the media's emphasis on issues that have little to do with the essence of the religion of Islam in America. This media emphasis on sensationalism in its images of African-American Muslims is not new. Malcolm X was also a victim of this tendency.[179]

However, in spite of his many detractors, Louis Farrakhan's movement is "striking a responsive chord in Black America." Recently, 20,000 people purchased tickets (at prices ranging from $25 to $250) to hear Farrakhan speak at Javits Center in New York City; at least "5000 people were turned away because there were no more seats left in the auditorium." His "Stop the Violence Rallies for Black Men," which are held in various cities throughout the United States, are always presented to a full house. In these troubled political times, no other African-American leader can regularly draw tremendous crowds. But what accounts for "the Farrakhan phenomenon"? The Epilogue will shed light on this issue by examining how and why African Americans who are not Muslims have commodified Islam in their quest for identity.[180]

COMMODIFICATION OF IDENTITY

"Neither social scientists nor ruling elites . . . are likely to fully appreciate the incitement a successful act of defiance may represent for a subordinate group, precisely because they are unlikely to be much aware of the hidden transcript from which it derives much of its energy. . . .

When the first declaration of the hidden transcript succeeds, its mobilizing capacity as a symbolic act is potentially awesome. At the level of tactics and strategy, it is a powerful straw in the wind. It portends a possible turning of the tables. . . . At the level of political beliefs, anger, and dreams it is a social explosion. That first declaration speaks for countless others, it shouts what has historically had to be whispered, controlled, choked back stifled, and suppressed. If the results seem like moments of madness, if the politics they engender is tumultuous, frenetic, delirious, and occasionally violent, that is perhaps because the powerless are so rarely on the public stage and have so much to say and do when they finally arrive."[1]   —James C. Scott

In the wake of several decades of "surveillance by the established religious authorities" and the federal government and of "existence at the margins of public life" as the hidden transcript of the oppressed, African-American Islam has finally arrived on the center stage of American religion and politics. At the end of the twentieth century, it has developed "to new levels as an outspoken and tumultuous competitor of doctrine and practices" in both religion and politics. But what does all of this portend for African-American identity formation?[2]

As the hegemonic discourses of the majority community appear to be destined to continue in America during the twenty-first century, the potent counter-conceptions and cultural and political strategies of African-American Islam will undoubtedly maintain their influence among black Americans. And as global Islam continues its militant ascendancy, new generations of African Americans will undoubtedly utilize the compelling significations of Islam in their lives, commodifying selective aspects of African-American Islamic identities.[3]

Today, most African Americans are aware that Islam has deep roots in their culture. Since the 1960s, the Nation of Islam's leaders, businesses, newspapers, radio programs, food, and distinctive clothing have become visible and routinized aspects of black communities in America's inner cities. Although most black Americans are Christians, they tend not to share with America's open hostility toward Islam. As Akbar Muhammad has pointed out, since African Americans have "no real political stake in America, political opposition to the Muslim world is unworthy of serious consideration." On the contrary, the political ideas of black Muslim leaders—from Elijah Muhammad to Malcolm X, and from Warith Deen Mohammed to Louis Farrakhan—are the subject of constant debate in contemporary black America.[4]

In this context, aspects of black Muslim identity have become commodities in black America, taking the form of stylized, media-oriented "cultural products" with little of their original religious content or substance.[5] Bean pies, incense, the television series *Roots*, Muslim clothing, Arabic names and expressions, and the speeches of Louis Farrakhan have all become products for mass consumption in contemporary black America.

Even Malcolm X must be considered in the context of this process. After his death, he became an icon in African-American culture; black artists, intellectuals, and celebrities tended to commodify his image and political ideas in a way that makes it easy to forget that Islam was at the center of his spiritual-political journey, beginning as Malcolm Little and progressing through Malcolm X to al-Hajj Malik Shabazz. Sonia Sanchez and Gwendolyn Brooks have written poems about his life and death. Amiri Baraka (formerly Le Roi Jones) was spiritually and artistically influenced by Malcolm X and the Nation of Islam in the 1960s. The novelists Alex Haley in *Roots* and Ishmael Reed in *Mumbo Jumbo*, inspired by Malcolm's life, have used Islam as central themes in their work. Malcolm's influence is also evident in two provocative black autobiographies—Nathan McCall's *Makes Me Wanna Holler* and Sanyika Shakur's *Monster*. Jazz musicians such as Yusef Lateef, Ahmad Jamal, Idris Sulayman, and Sahib Shahab and professional athletes like Muhammud Ali, Kareem Abdul Jabar, Ahmad Rashad, and Jamal Wilkes have converted to Islam and adopted Arabic names. Mike Tyson reportedly converted to Islam while in prison. Grand Puba and the Islamic rap musicians Lakim Shabazz, Poor Righteous Teachers, Eric B. and Rakim, King Sun, Movement X, Prince Akeem, Ice Cube, KMD, and a Tribe Called Quest all mention Malcolm X and the Nation of Islam in their lyrics. No artist, however, has commodified Malcolm X's identity more effectively than Spike Lee in his 1989 film *Do the Right Thing*, and then in *Malcolm X* in 1992. Spike Lee's superb cinematic portrayal of Malcolm X's life in the latter movie has recently inspired renewed interest and debate about Islam and black nationalism in black America.[6]

The film *Malcolm X* has also spurred new African-American interest in Louis Farrakhan's message. Farrakhan is "the most revered leader among the Black masses," as Ron Daniels has noted, and "his appeal is widespread. In addition to the dispossessed and disadvantaged, Farrakhan's rallies include large numbers of Black professionals, business people, and members of the Black middle class." Of course, Farrakhan's appeal is partially explained by his "militant voice" of black separatism, which resonates throughout black America at a time when many African Americans believe that black elected officials are powerless to improve their lot.[7]

Commodification of identity, however, is also a provocative way to understand "the Farrakhan phenomenon." Farrakhan's message presents multi-faceted significations of African-American Islamic identity that include specialized aspects for black men, women, and children; strategies for black economic and political empowerment; Afrocentric interpretations of history; an African-American Islamic worldview and cultural ethos; as well as potent psychological strategies to enhance black pride and self-respect. In the context of this rich tapestry of cultural, political, economic, and spiritual offerings, African Americans have commodified selective aspects of Farrakhan's message. Ron Daniels agrees with this evaluation of the Nation of Islam leader's appeal to black America. He writes, "In my view, many who go to hear Farrakhan or give him a favorable approval rating do not necessarily agree with all of his pronouncements or concur with every aspect of his program."[8]

Of course, the focal point of Farrakhan's attraction and fame is his jihad of words. As he "talks back" at America, reminding its rulers of this country's slavery and Jim Crow past, he presents black people with a "psychological alternative," a "nonpacifist" way of resisting oppression. And as the mainstream media and the political establishment focus on the antisemitic aspects of Louis Farrakhan's and Khallid Muhammad's jihad of words, commodifying the Nation of Islam as a hate group and its leaders as "ministers of rage," they are missing the message and the impact that many black Americans are drawing from African-American Islam today.[9]

Across black America—in black churches and mosques, in black enclaves in cities and suburbs, in black colleges and universities, in Black Studies departments and in black student associations in predominantly white colleges and universities, and in black political organizations—people are quietly acknowledging that in the future, Islam may provide some important answers to African-American economic, political, and cultural questions that have not been resolved by black Christian leaders.

Already, in black urban areas across the country, black Christian leaders are organizing special seminars to educate their people about Islam and to stem the tide of what they perceive as an alarming rate of African-American conversions to Islam. Mike Wilson, the founder and director of Project Joseph, which conducts "Muslim awareness seminars" for members of black churches throughout the United States to educate them about the threat posed by Islam, believes that "if the conversion rate continues unchanged, Islam could become the dominant religion in Black urban areas by the year 2020."[10]

Although there is little hard evidence available to confirm or refute this assertion, Islam has recently become an increasingly significant aspect of the African-American experience. As the commodification process popularizes elements of Islamic culture among non-Muslims, Islam could indeed prevail in black America in the twenty-first century.

NOTES

INTRODUCTION. WHAT SHALL WE CALL HIM?

1. Flora Lewis, "Jackson as African American," *New York Times,* January 11, 1989.

2. Isabel Wilkerson, "Many Who Are Black Favor a New Term for Who They Are," *New York Times,* January 31, 1989.

3. Bayard Rustin, "Blacks? African-Americans?" *New York Times,* February 1, 1989. Actually, the origin of "the names controversy" in African-American culture can be traced back to the early nineteenth century. See Sterling Stuckey, *Slave Culture* (New York: Oxford University Press, 1987), pp. 193–244.

4. Noble Drew Ali, "What Shall We Call Him?" *Moorish Literature,* n.d., p. 5.

5. Charles H. Long, *Significations* (Philadelphia: Fortress Press, 1986), p. 3.

6. Charles H. Long, interview, by author, May 12, 1992, Santa Barbara, Calif.

7. James C. Scott, *Domination and the Arts of Resistance: Hidden Transcripts* (New Haven: Yale University Press, 1990). Ranajit Guha, *Elementary Aspects of Peasant Insurgency* (Delhi: Oxford University Press, 1983). Antonio Gramsci, *Selections from the Prism Notebooks* (London: Wishart, 1971). Barrington Moore, Jr., *Injustice: The Social Bases of Obedience and Revolt* (White Plains, N.Y.: M. E. Sharpe, 1987).

8. John L. Esposito, *Islam the Straight Path* (New York: Oxford University Press, 1991), p. 93. Vincent J. Cornell, "Jihad: Islam's Struggle for the Truth," *Gnosis Magazine* (Fall 1991): 18.

9. This theme of racial-separatist/multi-racial Islam builds on the theme of McCloud's work which postulates "a tension between two philosophies" in African-American Islam: asabiya, the tendency toward nation-building and separation from other communities and "ummah, the tendency toward integration with a unified global Islam." See Aminah Beverly McCloud, *African American Islam* (New York: Routledge, 1995), back cover.

10. Carol L. Stone, "Estimate of Muslims Living in America," in Yvonne Y. Haddad, ed., *The Muslims of America* (New York: Oxford University Press, 1991), p. 29. An "official count" of Muslims in the United States is difficult to ascertain since most mosques do not have "membership rolls." However, most specialists in Islam in America estimate the count at four million to six million people. See Mary H. Cooper, "Muslims in America," *The CQ Researcher* (April 30, 1993): 363–83. A survey conducted by Isham Bagby and Wade Clark Roof indicates 500,000 "mosque-goers" in America. However this survey did not include the Nation of Islam. John Dart, "A Closer Look at Islam in the West,"*Los Angeles Times,* December 10, 1994.

11. James A. Michener, "Roots, Unique in Its Time," *New York Times Book Review,* February 26, 1977, p. 41.

12. See C. Eric Lincoln, *The Black Muslims in America* (Boston: Beacon, 1961); Allan D. Austin, *African Muslims in Antebellum America* (New York: Garland, 1984); Clifton Marsh, *From Black Muslims to Muslims* (Metuchen, N.J.: Scarecrow, 1984); Yvonne Haddad and Adair Lummis, *Islamic Values in the United States* (New York: Oxford University Press, 1987); Yvonne Haddad, ed., *The Muslims of America,* (New York: Oxford University Press, 1991); Yvonne Haddad and Jane Smith,

Mission to America (Gainesville: University Press of Florida, 1993); and Steven Barboza, *American Jihad: Islam after Malcolm X* (New York: Doubleday, 1994). Generic studies of the African-American Muslim community are few and incomplete. However, chief among them is Aminah Beverly McCloud's *African American Islam,* the first comprehensive textbook, and C. Eric Lincoln's *The Black Muslims in America,* which is still the most distinguished social scientific study of the Nation of Islam.

CHAPTER 1. MUSLIMS IN A STRANGE LAND

1. Daniel Panger, *Black Ulysses* (Athens: Ohio University Press, 1982), p. 3.

2. Nuñez Cabeza de Vaca, *Relation of Nuñez Cabeza de Vaca,* trans. Buckingham Smith (Ann Arbor: University of Michigan Microfilm, 1966), published in Spanish in 1542; R. R. Wright, "Negro Companions of the Spanish Explorers," *American Anthropologist* 4 (1902): 223; Clyde-Ahmad Winters, "Afro-American Muslims from Slavery to Freedom," *Islamic Studies* 17, No. 4 (1978): 187–205.

3. From a letter to Amos Beman, in Dorothy Sterling, ed., *Speak Out in Thunder Tones: Letters and Other Writings by Black Northerners, 1787–1865* (Garden City, N.Y.: Doubleday, 1973), p. 29; also in Allan D. Austin, *African Muslims in Antebellum America: A Sourcebook* (New York: Garland, 1984), p. 3.

4. Allan Austin, "Kunta Kinte's Fellows: African Roots in Antebellum America," typed manuscript of paper presented at the American Academy of Religion National Meeting, Chicago, Illinois, November 1988; Albert J. Raboteau, *Slave Religion* (New York: Oxford University Press, 1978), p. 4.

5. Bernard Lewis, *Race and Slavery in the Middle East* (New York: Oxford University Press, 1990), p. 18; Janet L. Abu-Lughod, *Before European Hegemony: The World System A.D. 1250–1350* (New York: Oxford University Press, 1989).

6. St. Clair Drake, *Black Folk Here and There,* vol. 2 (Los Angeles: Center for Afro-American Studies, UCLA), pp. 80, 85–86. The Quran was one of the first documents that recognized the humanity of slaves and gave them legal rights in this part of the world. Surahs of the Quran that discuss slavery include 2:177–78; 4:36; 4:92; 9:60; 16:71; 23:6; 24:31–33; 24:58; 30:28; 33:50–52; 58:3; and 70:29–31.

7. Drake, *Black Folk Here and There,* vol. 2, p. 91.

8. Phillip K. Hitti, *History of the Arabs,* 10th ed. (New York: Macmillan, 1970), pp. 235, 332, in Orlando Patterson, *Slavery and Social Death: A Comparative Study* (Cambridge: Harvard University Press, 1982), pp. 93, 176, 178; Lewis, *Race and Slavery in the Middle East;* John R. Willis, ed., *Slaves and Slavery in Muslim Africa* (London: Frank Cass, 1985); Drake, *Black Folk Here and There,* vol. 2, pp. 127–29; Ayi Kwei Armah, *Two Thousand Seasons* (Nairobi: East African Publishing House, 1973). For more information on Yaqub al-Mansur, see Ali Ibn Abd Allah, *Rondh el Kartus,* trans. A. de Beaumier (Paris, 1860), pp. 303–26, and Ibn Khaldun, *Histoire des Berbères,* trans. M. de Slane (Paris, 1927), pp. 205–16.

9. Vincent F. Cornell, "Jihad: Islam's Struggle for Truth," *Gnosis Magazine* (Fall 1992): 18, 22; passages in the Quran that deal with jihad include: 2:217–18, 4:74 (*qatil*), and 4:95.

10. Drake, *Black Folk Here and There,* vol. 2, pp. 87–88, 90–91.

11. Ibid., pp. 101–103; John Esposito, *Islam: The Straight Path* (New York: Oxford University Press, 1988), p. 60.

12. Michael G. Morony, *Iraq after the Muslim Conquest* (Princeton: Princeton University Press, 1984), pp. 6–7.

13. Kenneth W. Harrow, *Faces of Islam in African Literature* (Portsmouth, New Hampshire: Heinemann, 1991), pp. 3, 7. See David Robinson, "An Approach to Islam in West African History," in Harrow, *Faces of Islam in African Literature.*

14. Mervyn Hiskett, *The Development of Islam in West Africa* (New York: Longman, 1984), p. 1.

15. Ibid., pp. 2, 12–14; Abd al-Aziz al-Bakri, *Kitab al-masalik wa-'l-mamalik bilad Ifriqiya wa-'l-Maghrib,* ed. Baron MacGuckin de Slane—French title, *Déscription de l'Afrique* Septentrionale (Algiers, 1911); also in Levtzion, *Corpus of Early Arabic Sources for West African History,* pp. 79–80.

16. Ancient historical accounts of the saga of Ghana and the Almoravids include al-Bakri, *Kitab al-masalik wa-'l-mamalik;* Ibn Khaldun, *Kitab tarikh al-duwal al-Islamiya bi'l-Maghrib min Kitab al-'Ibar,* ed. M. G. de Slone, 2 vols. (Paris, 1847); al-Zuhri, *Kitab al-Ja'rafiyya,* ed. Hadj-Sadok, *Bulletin d'Etudes Historiques et Scientifiques de l'Afrique Occidentale Française* 21 (1968); al-Idrisi, *Kitab nuzhat al-mushtaq fi ikhtiraq al-afaq,* ed. R. Dozy and M. J. de Goeje (Leyde, 1866); Hiskett, *The Development of Islam in West Africa,* pp. 6–8; Peter B. Clarke, *West Africa and Islam* (London: Edward Arnold, 1982), pp. 17–24; and Levtzion, *Ancient Ghana and Mali* (London: Metuchen, 1973), pp. 29–52.

17. Hiskett, *The Development of Islam in West Africa,* pp. 44–58.

18. Levtzion, "Merchants vs. Scholars and Clerics in West Africa: Differential and Complementary Roles," in Levtzion and Fisher, eds. *Rural and Urban Islam in West Africa* (London: Lynne Rienner, 1987), pp. 21–37.

19. Levtzion, "Rural and Urban Islam in West Africa: An Introductory Essay," in *Rural and Urban Islam in West Africa,* pp. 1–20.

20. It is important to note that West Africans utilized names to define their new Muslim identities and to make Islam their own as the indigenous cultures of the Sudan and of West Africa brought to Islam a potent model for signification and identity in their traditional naming practices. Here West Africans adapted to the influence of orthodox Islam by indigenizing Arabic names and mixing Arabic and African indigenous names. And of course, these naming practices were destined to become a model for the signification of Arabic names in twentieth century African-American culture.

Although West African naming practices were complex and differed from ethnic group to ethnic group, Robert Paustian has demonstrated that there were "certain general naming themes" that indicated a West African concern with names and provided the cultural tools for the indigenization of Arabic names. Generally, birth names were the most important West African names because a baby was not considered fully human until formally named in a naming ritual. However, more important for our purposes is Paustian's theme that there was considerable leeway for people to "take many names besides birth names in later life." Thus, as West African naming practices evolved over time, a second name could be added to denote a family connection, a place, a personal trait, or Islamic influence. A final general West African naming theme that is relevant here concerns the use of anthroponyms, or what Paustian designates as "phrase names." Many West African names contained "phrases or aphorisms" that served "the dual purpose of both personal identification and the expression of attitudes, sentiments, and historical facts." This is important because the historical circumstances surrounding individual or group conversion to Islam could be chronicled in the "phrase name." In connection with this final theme it should be noted that both West African birth names and names taken later in life often reflected important contemporary events and that undoubtedly in some cases Islamic influence was also a major factor in this kind of naming practice. See P. Robert Paustian, "The Evolution of Personal Naming Practices among American Blacks," *Names* 26, No. 2 (1978), pp. 177–82; Takawira Mafikdze, "The Origin and Significance of African Personal Names," *Black World* 9 (1970), pp. 4–6; Kwaku Adzei, "The Meaning of Names in Ghana," *Negro Digest* 12 (1962), pp. 95–99; Heinz A.

Wieschhoff, "The Social Significance of Names among the Ibo of Nigeria," *American Anthropologist* 43 (1941), pp. 212–22; Melville J. Herskovits, *Dahomey* (New York: Augustin, 1938), pp. 263–64; Dawud Hakim, *Arabic Names and Other African Names with Their Meanings* (Philadelphia: Hakim, 1970); Mataebere Iwundu, "Igbo Anthroponyms: Linguistic Evidence for Reviewing the Igbo Culture," *Names* 21, No. 1 (March 1973), pp. 46–49; Ihechukwu Madubuike, *Handbook of African Names* (Washington, D.C.: Three Continents, 1976); N. Puckett, "Names of American Negro Slaves," in *Studies in the Science of Society*, ed. George P. Murdock (New Haven: Yale University Press, 1937), pp. 471–94; "American Negro Names," *Journal of Negro History* 23 (1938), pp. 35–48, and *Black Names in America* (Boston: G. K. Hall, 1975); Lorenzo D. Turner, *Africanisms in the Gullah Dialect* (Chicago: University of Chicago Press, 1949); J. L. Dillard, *Black English* (New York: Random House, 1972).

21. Ibn Fadl al-Umari, *Masalik al-Absar fi mamalik al-amsar,* in Levtzion, *Corpus of Early Arabic Sources for West African History,* pp. 268–69.

22. Morroe Berger, "The Black Muslims," *Horizon* (Winter 1964): 51.

23. Ibn Khaldun, *Kitab tarikh,* vol. 1, pp. 264–68; Levtzion, *Ancient Ghana and Mali,* pp. 63–72.

24. St. Clair Drake, *Black Folk Here and There,* vol. 2, p. 144.

25. Said Hamdun and Noel King, eds. and trans., *Ibn Battuta in Black Africa* (London: Rex Collings, 1975), pp. 33, 47, 48.

26. Leo Africanus, *Description de l'Afrique,* trans. A. Epaulard (Paris, 1956); Berger, "The Black Muslims," p. 51.

27. Drake, *Black Folk Here and There,* vol. 2, p. 144; al-Sadi, *Tarikh al-Sudan,* Arabic text and French trans. O. Hondas (Paris, 1911), pp. 5, 6, 23.

28. Hiskett, *The Development of Islam in West Africa,* pp. 38–40; al-Sadi, *Tarikh al-Sudan,* pp. 124–27; Thomas A. Hale, *Scribe, Griot, and Novelist: Narrative Interpreters of the Songhay Empire* (Gainesville: University Press of Florida, 1990), and "Can a Single Foot Follow Two Paths? Islamic and Songhay Belief Systems in the Timbuktu Chronicles and the Epic of Askia Muhammad," in Harrow, *Faces of Islam in African Literature,* pp. 131–40. For Askia Muhammad's rationalization of the enslavement of thousands of black Africans, see Leo Africanus, *The History and Description of Africa and of the Notable Things Therein Contained* (New York: B. Franklin, 1963), pp. iii, 825. For the reasons that early black Islamic rulers participated in the domestic enslavement and export of other blacks, see Claude Meillassoux, *The Anthropology of Slavery* (Chicago: University of Chicago Press, 1991), p. 43ff.

29. Al-Sadi, *Tarikh al-Sudan,* pp. 154–55, 159–60; Levtzion, *Ancient Ghana and Mali,* pp. 88–89.

30. Lovejoy, *Transformations in Slavery,* pp. 66–78; al-Sadi, *Tarikh al-Sudan,* pp. 106, 259–64, 276.

31. Lovejoy, *Transformations in Slavery,* p. 30; Ahmad Baba, *Mi'raj al-Su'ud ila Nayl Hukm majlub al-Sud* (1614). It should be noted that the Songhay empire was reportedly based on slave labor. This situation was not unprecedented; see Allan G. Fisher, *Slavery and Muslim Society in Africa* (London: C. Hurst, 1970), p. 28ff.

32. Drake, *Black Folk Here and There,* vol. 2, p. 180.

33. Lovejoy, *Transformations in Slavery,* pp. 18–22. There is a scholarly debate about who was primarily responsible for the transformation of African slavery in the modern era. John Thornton in *Africa and Africans in the Making of the Atlantic World, 1400–1680* (Cambridge: Cambridge University Press, 1992) argues "that Africa was a voluntary and active participant in the Atlantic world. Africa's economic and military strength gave its political and economic elites the capacity to determine how trade with Europe developed." This view inflates the military

and economic strength of Africa on the eve of modernity and shifts the blame from Europe for the Atlantic slave trade. Paul Lovejoy in *Transformations in Slavery* corrects the assumption that African slavery, among Africans and Arabs, was benign and demonstrates how African slavery was part of the production process in the Muslim world. However, this interpretation also takes the heat off European responsibility by focusing on African and Arab exploitation. Bernard Lewis in *Race and Slavery in the Middle East* also focuses on Arab responsibility for the African slave trade. The most convincing arguments regarding the transformation of African slavery come from scholars who focus on external stimuli: Eric Williams in *Capitalism and Slavery* (Chapel Hill: University of North Carolina Press, 1944), demonstrates how African slavery was connected to the birth of capitalism in the West; while Patrick Manning in *Slavery and African Life* (Cambridge: Cambridge University Press, 1990) notes that "what distinguishes Africa and Africans with regard to slavery . . . is *modernity*. The enslavement of Africans increased in the modern period, a time when the enslavement of most other peoples was dying out."

34. Herbert S. Klein, *African Slavery in Latin America and the Caribbean* (New York: Oxford University Press, 1986), pp. 12–18; Long, *Significations*, pp. 2–6.

35. João José Reis, *Slave Rebellion in Brazil*, trans. Arthur Brakel (Baltimore: The Johns Hopkins University Press, 1993), based on transcripts of the trials of the rebels at Conceicão da Praia, Brazil. At the Amistad Trial in New Haven, Connecticut, Richard R. Madden identified one of the African mutineers as a Muslim by saying an Islamic prayer to him. The African Muslim responded to the prayer in Arabic: "Allah akbar"—God is great. Howard Jones, *The Mutiny on the Amistad* (New York: Oxford University Press, 1987), p. 108; Madden deposition, November 20, 1839, 133 U.S. District Court Records for Connecticut, Federal Archives and Record Center, Waltham, Massachusetts.

36. John Washington, "Some Account of Mohammedu Sisei, a Mandingo, of Nyani-Mara in the Gambia," *Journal of the Royal Geographical Society* 8 (1838): 449–54; Richard R. Madden, *A Twelve Months' Residence in the West Indies, During the Transition from Slavery to Apprenticeship, with Incidental Notices of the State of Society, Prospects and Natural Resources of Jamaica and Other Islands*, 2 vols. (Philadelphia: Carey, Lea, and Blanchard, 1835); Folarium Shyllon, *Black People in Britain, 1555–1833* (New York: Oxford University Press, 1977), p. 60.

37. For a brilliant analysis of intellectual resistance to slavery, see William D. Piersen, *Black Legacy* (Amherst: University of Massachusetts Press, 1993). Janet D. Cornelius has analyzed slave literacy as resistance, in *When I Can Read My Title Clear* (Columbia: University of South Carolina Press, 1991). This chapter is a challenge to Orlando Patterson's major thesis, in *Slavery and Social Death* (Cambridge: Harvard University Press, 1982), that slave systems erase social identity. Patterson fails to distinguish between what slave systems attempt to do and what they succeed in doing; he forfeits agency to the ruling/master classes and their appurtenances, thus concealing entirely the possibilities that the enslaved have any choices in the matter.

38. Charles Ball, *A Narrative of the Life and Adventures of Charles Ball, a Black Man*, 3rd ed. (Pittsburgh: John T. Skyrock, 1854), p. 143.

39. Reis, *Slave Rebellion in Brazil*, p. 154; Sidney W. Mintz and Richard Price present a pathbreaking study of how African slaves were acculturated in America, in *The Birth of African-American Culture* (Boston: Beacon, 1992), first published by Institute for the Study of Human Issues, 1976.

40. Cornell, "Jihad: Islam's Struggle for Truth," p. 18; Adbul Khatib, "The Need for Jihad," *Gnosis Magazine* (Fall 1991): 24.

41. Thomas Bluett, *Some Memoirs of the Life of Job, the Son of Boonda in Africa; Who*

Was a Slave about two Years in Maryland; and afterwards being brought to England was set free, and sent to his native land in the year 1734 (London: Richard Ford, 1734), in Austin, *African Muslims in Antebellum America.*

42. Ibid., p. 79.

43. Ibid., p. 80.

44. Ibid., pp. 81–93. Francis Moore, a Royal African Company associate furnished the most extensive information about Job's years after his return to Africa; see Francis Moore, *Travels into the Inland Parts of Africa . . . with a Particular Account of Job Ben Solomon* (London, 1738). See also Philip D. Curtin, ed., *Africa Remembered* (Madison: University of Wisconsin Press, 1967), pp. 17–59. Job's Arabic manuscripts can be found in the British Library, and the portrait which was published in *Gentleman's Magazine* (in June 1750) is at Amherst College.

45. Yarrow Mamout's age is estimated as 134 years in *The Image of the Black in Western Art,* vol. 4 (Cambridge: Harvard University Press, 1989), p. 112. Peale's portrait of Yarrow Mamout was painted on January 30 and 31, 1819 and is presently at the Historical Society of Pennsylvania. Peale's diary is at the American Philosophical Society Library in Philadelphia, and part of the text of the diary was published in Austin, *African Muslims in Antebellum America,* pp. 69–70.

46. Ibid.

47. Abd al-Rahman Ibrahima, personal letter, New Haven, Connecticut, 1828 in the John Trumbull Papers, Yale University. The following are biographies or sketches of Abd al-Rahman Ibrahima's life: Frederick Freeman, *Yaradee: A Plea for Africa* (Philadelphia: J. Whetham, 1836); Edward Everett, "Abdul Rahaman," speech, "The Colonization of Africa" (1853) in Everett, *Orations and Speeches on Various Occasions* (Boston: Little, Brown, 1859); Charles Snyder, "The Biography of a Slave," in *The African Repository* (American Colonization Society); P. J. Staudenraus, *The African Colonizationist Movement, 1861–1865* (New York: Columbia University Press, 1961); Louis Harlan, "The Prince: The Biography of a Slave," and B. Marie Perinbam, "Abd-al-Rahman: A Critical Note" in *Job Ben Solomon and Abd al-Rahman: The Stories of Two Men in Slavery* (Washington, D.C.: American Historical Association, 1970); Terry Alford, *Prince among Slaves* (New York: Oxford University Press, 1977); John Blassingame, *Slave Testimony* (Baton Rouge: Louisiana State University Press, 1977); and Austin, *African Muslims in Antebellum America.*

48. Cyrus Griffin, Natchez *Southern Galaxy,* May 29, June 5 and 12, and July 5, 1828; "Abduhl Rahahman: The Unfortunate Muslim Prince," *African Repository* 4 (May 1828): 77–81; Terry Alford, *Prince among Slaves,* pp. 3–22.

49. Ibid.

50. Ibid.

51. Ibid.; for information about John Ormond from one of his partners, see Adam Afzelius, Diary, February 26, 1796 in Alexander Peter Kup, ed., *Sierra Leone Journal, 1795–1796* (Uppsala, Sweden, 1967), p. 76, 98n.

52. "Abduhl Rahahman," *African Repository* 4 (May 1828): 80; Alford, *Prince among Slaves,* pp. 22–23.

53. Alford, *Prince among Slaves,* pp. 24–36.

54. *Massachusetts Journal* (September 4, 1828); Abduhl Rahahman, *African Repository* 4 (May 1828): 80; Alford, *Prince among Slaves,* pp. 69–72.

55. Marschalk to Thomas Reed, Natchez, October 3, 1826, in Thomas Mullowny to Henry Clay, Tangier, March 27, 1827, "Dispatches from the United States Consuls in Tangier," vol. 4 (1819–1830), *State Department Records,* National Archives and Records Service, Washington, D.C.; Alford, *Prince among Slaves,* p. 98.

56. Ibid., pp. 99–100, Mullowny to Clay, Tangier, March 27, 1827.

57. John Quincy Adams, Adams diary, July 10, 1827, Adams Papers, Massachusetts Historical Society; Clay to Marschalk, Washington, D.C., January 12, 1828,

Domestic Letters, M40, *State Department Records,* National Archives and Records Service; Austin, *African Muslims in Antebellum America,* pp. 129–30; *Freedom's Journal* (New York, October 24, 1828): 244–45; John Russwurm, "Traveling Scraps," *Freedom's Journal* (August 29, 1828): 79; some of Ibrahima's Arabic writing is in the American Philosophical Society Library in Philadelphia.

58. Edward M. Gallaudet, *Life of Thomas Hopkins Gallaudet* (New York: Holt, 1888), pp. 231–34; *Freedom's Journal* (June 20, 1828): 109; "Abdul Rahaman," New York *Journal of Commerce* (October 16, 1828); Alford, *Prince among Slaves,* pp. 159–61.

59. Vincent P. Franklin, *Black Self-Determination,* pp. 87–90.

60. Alford, pp. 163–64.

61. *Freedom's Journal* (May 28, 1829): 406; (December 20, 1828): 299; *African Repository* (July 1828): 158; (November 1829): 281; (April 1830): 60; (August 1830): 182; (November 1830): 283.

62. Austin, *African Muslims in Antebellum America,* p. 386.

63. Georgia Bryan Conrad, *Reminiscences of a Southern Woman* (Hampton, Virginia: Hampton Institute, n.d.), p. 13.

64. Charles Spalding Wylly, *The Seed That Was Sown in Georgia* (New York: Neale, 1910); Wylly, the grandson of Thomas Spalding, recalled that his grandfather owned slaves of "Moorish or Arabian descent, devout Mussulmans, who prayed to Allah . . . morning, noon, and evening."

65. William B. Hodgson, *Notes on Northern Africa, the Sahara and Sudan* (New York: Wiley and Putnam, 1844), p. 73; Joseph H. Greenberg, "The Decipherment of the 'Ben Ali Diary,' a Preliminary Statement," *Journal of Negro History* (July 1940); Ella May Thornton, "Bilali—His Book," *Law Library Journal* 48 (1955): 228–29; Bilali's diary is in the library of Georgia State University, in Atlanta. Recently, Ronald A. T. Judy has translated Bilali's (Ben Ali's) diary and analyzed the various accounts of his life in *(Dis)Forming the American Canon: African-Arabic Slave Narratives and the Vernacular* (Minneapolis: University of Minnesota Press, 1993). See also William S. McFeely, *Sapelo's People: A Long Walk into Freedom* (New York: W. W. Norton, 1994).

66. Zephaniah Kingsley, *Treatise on the Patriarchal or Co-operative System of Society,* 2nd ed. (1829); rpt., Freeport, N.Y.: Books for Libraries, 1970, pp. 13–14; Wylly, *The Seed That Was Sown in Georgia,* p. 52; E. Merton Coulter, *Thomas Spulding of Sapelo* (Baton Rouge: Louisiana State University, 1940), pp. 190–93; Caroline Couper Lovell, *The Golden Isles of Georgia* (Boston: Little, Brown, 1933), pp. 103–104.

67. Savannah Unit of the Georgia Writer's Project of the Works Projects Administration, *Drums and Shadows* (Athens: University of Georgia, 1940); rpt. Garden City, N.Y.: Doubleday-Anchor, 1972; Charles T. Davis and Henry Louis Gates, Jr., eds., *The Slave's Narrative* (New York: Oxford University Press, 1985).

68. Savannah Unit of the Georgia Writer's Project, *Drums and Shadows,* pp. 158–70.

69. Ibid.

70. "Letter of James Hamilton Couper, Esq.," in Austin, *African Muslim Slaves in Antebellum America,* pp. 321–25; originally published by William Brown Hodgson in *Notes on Northern Africa, the Sahara, and the Sudan* (New York, 1844), pp. 68–75; also see Curtin, *Africa Remembered,* pp. 145–51. See Judy, *(Dis)Forming the American Canon,* pp. 187–207, for detailed analysis of James Hamilton Couper's writings about Salih Bilali.

71. Ibid.

72. Ibid.

73. Savannah Unit of Georgia Writer's Project, *Drums and Shadows;* Lydia Parrish, *Slave Songs of the Georgia Sea Islands* (Athens: University of Georgia Press,

1992) first published in 1942; she also met and got stories of Salih Bilali and Bilali's descendants. No one has systematically analyzed the impact of these Muslims and their traditions on Gullah culture.

74. Ibid., pp. 154, 168–69, 170–73.

75. Ibid., pp. 166–67.

76. Ibid., p. 148.

77. Theodore Dwight, Jr., "Condition and Character of Negroes in Africa," *Methodist Quarterly Review* (January 1864): pp. 77–90. Also in Austin, *African Muslims in Antebellum America*, p. 424.

78. "Colonization Meeting," *African Repository* 9 (January 1835); "Colonization Meeting in New York," *African Repository* (July 1835); Austin, *African Muslims in Antebellum America*, pp. 409–11; Tom W. Shick, *Emigrants to Liberia, 1820 to 1843* (Newark: Department of Anthropology, University of Delaware, 1971), p. 60. See Judy, *(Dis)Forming the American Canon*, pp. 167–87.

79. *Who Was Who in America: Historical Volume 1607–1896*, p. 231; Dwight, "Remarks on the Sereculehs, an African Nation, Accompanied by a Vocabulary of Their Language," *American Annals of Education and Instruction* 5 (1835): pp. 451–56; Austin, *African Muslims in Antebellum America*, pp. 411–12.

80. Dwight, "Remarks on the Sereculehs, an African Nation," pp. 451–56; and "An Account of the Serreculies, or Serrawallies, with hints respecting several other tribes or families of people composing the Foula nation," American Ethnological Society *Transactions* 1 (New York, 1845); Lamin O. Sanneh, *The Jakhanke* (London: International African Institute, 1979).

81. Said's letter was published in Dwight's "Condition and Character of Negroes in Africa" and in Austin, *African Muslims in Antebellum America*, pp. 431–32.

82. Ibid.

83. Omar Ibn Said's original autobiographical manuscript in Arabic has been lost. "Autobiography of Omar Ibn Said, Slave in North Carolina, 1831," *American Historical Review* 30 (July 1925): 787–95, was introduced and annotated by J. Franklin Jameson. Earlier translators of the manuscript included Alexander I. Cotheal (1848), who was an associate of Richard F. Burton, who translated *A Thousand and One Nights,* and Issac Bird (1793–1876). Bird's translation was the basis of the *AHR* article and was revised by F. M. Mousa, an officer of the Egyptian Legation in Washington, D.C. Said's manuscripts and portrait are found at the Davidson College Library, Davidson, North Carolina; Andover Newton Theological Seminary, Newton Centre, Massachusetts; Wilson Library, University of North Carolina, Chapel Hill; and North Carolina Archives, Raleigh.

84. See Gregory Bedell, "Prince Moro," *Christian Advocate* (July 1825), pp. 306–307; Ralph R. Gurley, *African Repository* 13 (July 1837): 201–203; Wilmington *Chronicle* (January 22, 1847); M. B. Grier, "Uncle Moreau," *North Carolina University Magazine* 3 (September 1854): 307–309; William S. Plumer, "Meroh, a Native African," New York *Observer* (January 8, 1863); George E. Post, "Arabic-Speaking Negro Mohammedans in Africa," *African Repository* (May 1869), pp. 129–33; *Asheville Citizen* (August 3, 1887); John C. Foard, *North America and Africa* (Statesville, N.C., 1904), p. 66; J. Franklin Jameson, "Autobiography of Omar ibn Said, Slave in North Carolina, 1831," *North American Historical Review* 30 (July 1925); Louis T. Moore, "Prince of Arabia," *Greensboro Daily News* (February 13, 1927); George H. Calcott, "Pious N.C. Slave Wrote Life Story in Arabic," in a Greensboro newspaper, ca. 1953; George H. Calcott, "Omar ibn Said: A Slave Who Wrote an Autobiography in Arabic," *Journal of Negro History* 39 (1954): 58–63; Walter S. McDonald, "General Owen Gave Home in Bladden to African Prince Taken as a Slave," *The Bladden Journal* (September 8, 1960); Margaret McMaham, "Bladden Slave Was Also a Prince," Fayetteville *News and Observer* (March 17, 1968); Thomas C. Parramore, *Carolina Quest* (Englewood Cliffs, N.J.: Prentice-Hall, 1978), p. 191;

Clyde-Ahmad Winters, "Afro-American Muslims—From Slavery to Freedom," *Islamic Studies* 17 (1978): 187–205; Clyde-Ahmad Winters, "Roots and Islam in Slave America," *Al-Ittihad* (October and November, 1978).

85. Jameson, "Autobiography of Omar Ibn Said, Slave in North Carolina, 1831," pp. 787–95.

86. John W. Blassingame, "Using the Testimony of Ex-Slaves: Approaches and Problems," in Charles T. Davis and Henry Louis Gates, Jr., eds., *The Slave's Narrative* (New York: Oxford University Press, 1985), pp. 8–93. Edward W. Said, *Orientalism* (New York: Vintage, 1978).

87. The Taylor letter is in the Franklin Trask Library, Andover Newton Theological Seminary, Newton Centre, Mass., reprinted in Austin, *African Muslims in Antebellum America*, p. 455; Moore, "Prince of Arabia" (1927); Austin, *African Muslims in Antebellum America*, p. 471; there are shades of jihad in Said's last "Lord's Prayer." It translates: "When victory comes from God, soon, along with good news to the believers, and thou seest men entering the religion in companies, for God, celebrate ye, then, thy Lord and ask His forgiveness. Surely He is ever merciful. Finished. My name is Umar—or Ya'amar." Austin, *African Muslims in Antebellum America*, pp. 479, 519–20.

88. For examples, see reprints of three Said manuscripts in Austin, *African Muslims in Antebellum America*, pp. 456, 471–72; Reis, *Slave Rebellion in Brazil*, pp. 96–103. For more information on Muslim slaves' use of Arabic as a secret language for conspiracies, see Cedric J. Robinson, *Black Marxism* (London: Zed Press, 1983), pp. 207–10.

89. The story of the Yang letter is in Mathew B. Grier, "Uncle Moreau," *North Carolina Presbyterian* (July 23, 1859); the letter from Karfae can be found in George E. Post, "Arabic-Speaking Negro Mohammedans in Africa," *African Repository* (May 1869), pp. 129–33.

90. See Hollis R. Lyneh, ed., *Black Spokesman: Selected Published Writings of Edward Wilmot Blyden* (New York: Humanities Press, 1971) and *Edward Wilmot Blyden: Pan-Negro Patriot* (New York: Oxford University Press, 1967).

91. Samuel Moore, *Biography of Mahommah G. Baquaqua* (Detroit, 1854). Original with photo available at Burton Historical Collection, Detroit Public Library; reprinted in Austin, *African Muslims in Antebellum America*, pp. 594–644.

92. Moore, *Biography of Mahommah G. Baquaqua* in Austin, *African Muslims in Antebellum America*, pp. 610–25.

93. Ibid., pp. 626–38; Andrew T. Foss and E. Mathews, *Facts for Baptist Churches* (Utica: American Baptist Free Mission Society, 1850), original in Miller Library, Colby College; reprinted in Austin, *African Muslims in Antebellum America*, pp. 591–94.

94. Austin, *African Muslims in Antebellum America*, p. 588.

95. Moore, *Biography of Mahommah G. Baquaqua* in Austin, *African Muslims in Antebellum America*, pp. 640–44.

96. Ibid.

97. Austin, "Kunta Kinte's Fellow: African Roots in Antebellum America," p. 1, typed manuscript, presented at the American Academy of Religion National Meeting, Chicago, Illinois, November 1988.

98. Norwood P. Hallowell, "A Native of Bornu," *Atlantic Monthly* (October 1867): pp. 485–95, also in Austin, *African Muslims in Antebellum America*, pp. 661–79.

99. Ibid., pp. 661–76.

100. Ibid., pp. 671–72.

101. Ibid., pp. 676–78.

102. Ibid., p. 679.

103. Ibid.

104. Sterling Stuckey, *Slave Culture* (New York: Oxford University Press, 1987), p. 198; Suzanne Miers and Igor Kopytoff, eds., *Slavery in Africa* (Madison: University of Wisconsin Press, 1977), pp. 14–18.

105. Austin, "Kunta Kinte's Fellows," p. 6.

106. Bernard Lewis, *Islam and the West* (New York: Oxford University Press, 1993), pp. 15–19.

107. Ibid. Judy argues that the "African-Arabic" Muslim slave narratives "challenge the claim of traditional Enlightenment discourse that literacy and reason are the privileged properties of Western culture." See *(Dis)Forming the American Canon.*

108. Long, *Significations*, p. 4. James C. Scott's work on hegemony and resistance explicitly links the theme of slave identities in the New World to issues of "political discourse among subordinate groups." Here, a hidden transcript which can be produced by subordinate groups outside the realm of the power of their dominators may become a potent and "sharply dissonant political culture" which opposes and "reacts back on" the public transcripts of elite groups. Furthermore, Scott's analysis elucidates the linguistic and metaphysical resistance strategies of African Muslim slaves in America by positioning religion at center of the most potent hidden transcripts credited to North American slaves. He writes: "Inasmuch as the major historical forms of domination have presented themselves in the form of a metaphysics, a religion, a worldview, they have provoked the development of more or less equally elaborate replies in the hidden transcript. . . . Perhaps resistance to ideological domination requires a counter ideology—a negation—that will effectively provide a general normative form to the host of resistant practices invented in self defense by any subordinate group. . . . Slave owners in both the West Indies and North America took great pains to prevent the creation of sites where a hidden transcript could be created and shared. . . . However hobbling the surveillance it did not prevent the rapid development of linguistic codes impenetrable to outsiders [and] . . . an autonomous religious vision emphasizing deliverance." Scott, pp. 18, 29, 115, 118, 126, 127.

109. Stuckey, *Slave Culture*, pp. 198–200.

110. Austin, "Kunta Kinte's Fellows," p. 6. Michael Mullin, in *Africa in America* (Urbana: University of Illinois Press, 1992), has demonstrated that slaves who preserved their African ethnicity "retained a more collective identity and were more likely to be treated as a people and to resist by organizing with others," p. 15.

111. Vincent P. Franklin, *Black Self-Determination*, 2nd ed. (New York: Lawrence Hill, 1992); first published 1984. For a distinctive study of literacy as a widespread and important tool of resistance to slavery, see Janet Duitsman Cornelius, *When I Can Read My Title Clear* (Columbia: University of South Carolina Press, 1991). Stuckey, *Slave Culture*, p. ix; Sterling Stuckey believes that "African religions and ethnic differences were considered a handicap and steadily lost ground before the need for unity against overwhelming odds" in the nineteenth century (p. 119). The evidence that I have gathered demonstrates the opposite trend: that preservation of specific African identities in America, in some cases, served as paradigms for Pan-Africanist resistance and unity in the nineteenth century.

CHAPTER 2. PAN-AFRICANISM AND THE NEW AMERICAN ISLAM

1. Wilson J. Moses, *The Golden Age of Black Nationalism, 1850–1925* (New York: Oxford University Press, 1988), first published 1978, p. 65; John Hope Franklin and Alfred A. Moss, Jr., *From Slavery to Freedom* (New York: McGraw-Hill, 1988), 6th ed. In this context, the South refers to the Southern plantocracy.

Important selected source materials on the life of Edward Wilmot Blyden include **1. Secondary sources:** Hollis R. Lynch, *Edward Wilmot Blyden: Pan-Negro*

Patriot, 1832–1912 (New York: Oxford University Press, 1967) is the seminal work in this category. A very different assessment of Blyden is found in V. Y. Mudimbe, *The Invention of Africa* (Bloomington: Indiana University Press, 1988). Wilson J. Moses provocatively analyzes the life of Blyden in the context of nineteenth-century black nationalism in *The Golden Age of Black Nationism, 1850–1925* (New York: Oxford University Press, 1988). Dennis Hickey and Kenneth C. Wylie present an interesting assessment of Islam in Blyden's work in *An Enchanting Darkness: The American Vision of Africa in the Twentieth Century* (East Lansing: Michigan State University Press, 1993). **2. Manuscripts:** The Papers of the American Colonization Society, Library of Congress, Washington, D.C., and the Presbyterian Board of Foreign Missions, 375 Riverside Drive, New York City, are the two most important collections of Blyden's papers and correspondence in the United States. Other Blyden materials are in John E. Bruce Papers, Schomburg Collection, Harlem Branch of the New York Public Library; Hemphill Papers, Duke University, Durham, North Carolina; John Miller Papers, Princeton University; and Papers of the Trustees of Donations for Education in Liberia, Massachusetts Historical Society, Boston. **3. Published books of Edward W. Blyden:** *Christianity, Islam, and the Negro Race* (1888; rpt. Edinburgh: University of Edinburgh Press, 1967), *Vindication of the Negro Race* (Monrovia, 1857), and *Liberia's Offering* (New York, 1862) are three of Blyden's most important works.

2. Hollis R. Lynch, *Edward Wilmot Blyden, Pan-Negro Patriot,* pp. 4–6; Blyden to Coppinger (September 13, 1884), *Papers of the American Colonization Society,* vol. 21, Library of Congress, Washington, D.C.; *New York Colonization Journal* (December 1, 1850); Blyden to Lowne, February 1852, papers of the Presbyterian Board of Foreign Missions (375 Riverside Drive, New York).

3. Moses, *The Golden Age of Black Nationalism, 1850–1925,* p. 18. *Constitution of the African Civilization Society* (New Haven, 1861). Seminal studies of Pan-Africanism include C. L. R. James, *A History of Pan-African Revolt* (Washington, D.C., 1969) and *Communism* (New York, 1970); Immanuel Geiss, *The Pan-African Movement* (New York, 1974); J. Ayodele Langley, *Pan-Africanism and Nationalism in West Africa, 1900–1945* (Oxford, 1975); and George Shepperson, "Pan-Africanism and 'Pan Africanism': Some Historical Notes," *Phylon* (Winter 1962), pp. 346–58. It should be noted that, although some black nationalists were involved in the colonization movement, many African Americans opposed it because of its racism.

4. Moses, *The Golden Age of Black Nationalism, 1850–1925,* pp. 17, 27. Moses has noted that Howard Brotz, Theodore Draper, and Harold Cruse are scholars that have analyzed black nationalism primarily in the context of geographical separatist movements, while August Meier, Elliot Rudwick, and John Bracey say that black nationalism is not always equated with "territorial separatism."

5. Clifton E. Marsh, *From Black Muslims to Muslims* (Metuchen, N.J.: Scarecrow, 1984), pp. 16–17.

6. Moses, *The Golden Age of Black Nationalism, 1850–1925,* p. 27.

7. Lynch, *Edward Wilmot Blyden, Pan-Negro Patriot,* pp. 54–59. Blyden: "The Negro in Ancient History," *Methodist Quarterly Review,* 52 (January 1869), pp. 62–78; "Mohammedanism in the Negro Race," *Fraser's Magazine,* New Series 12 (November 1975), pp. 598–615; "Christianity and the Negro Race," *Fraser's Magazine,* New Series 13 (May 1876): pp. 554–68.

8. Said, *Orientalism,* p. 3.

9. Austin, *African Muslims in Antebellum America,* pp. 485–86; George E. Post, "Arabic-Speaking Negro Mohammedans in Africa," *African Repository* (May 1869), pp. 129–31; Henry M. Schieffelin, ed., *The People of Africa: A Series of Papers on Their Character, Condition, and Future Prospects* (New York: Anson D. F. Randolph, 1871), pp. 69–73.

10. Ibid.

11. Blyden, *Christianity, Islam, and the Negro Race* (Edinburgh: University of Edinburgh Press, 1967), pp. xiii-xiv; first published 1887. Lynch, *Edward Wilmot Blyden, Pan-Negro Patriot*, pp. 67–70.

12. Ibid.

13. V. Y. Mudimbe, *The Invention of Africa*, p. 116. Blyden, *Christianity, Islam, and the Negro Race*, p. 233.

14. Blyden, *Christianity, Islam, and the Negro Race*, p. 113. Mudimbe, *The Invention of Africa*, p. 117. Moses, *The Golden Age of Black Nationalism*, p. 10.

15. Lynch, *Edward Wilmot Blyden, Pan-Negro Patriot*, pp. 193–94. Blyden, "Africa and the Africans," *Fraser's Magazine* (August 1878), p. 194. *West African Reporter* 9 (November 25, 1882).

16. Moses, *The Golden Age of Black Nationalism, 1850–1925*, pp. 20–21, 48–49; Mudimbe, *The Invention of Africa*, pp. 100–105; Blyden, *Christianity, Islam, and the Negro Race*, pp. 94–95, 126, 348, 349, 368. *Liberia's Offering* (New York, 1862), p. 156. Charles A. and Mary R. Beard, *The American Spirit: A Study of the Idea of Civilization in the United States* (New York, 1942).

17. Blyden, *Christianity, Islam, and the Negro Race*, pp. 122, 124, 227. "Mixed Races in Liberia," *Smithsonian Institute Annual Report* (Washington, D.C., 1870), pp. 386–89. Mudimbe, *The Invention of Africa*, pp. 107–109, 118–19. Arthur De Gobineau, *Essai sur l'inégalité des races humaines* (1853). Moses, *The Golden Age of Black Nationalism, 1850–1925*, pp. 21, 48–49.

18. Hiskett, *The Development of Islam in West Africa*, pp. 227–43.

19. Mudimbe, *The Invention of Africa*, p. 115.

20. Dennis Hickey and Kenneth C. Wylie have done the best job of analyzing the reasons for the lack of critical attention given to the issue of Islam and racism among Africans and African Americans. See *An Enchanting Darkness: The American Vision of Africa in the Twentieth Century*.

21. Mudimbe, *The Invention of Africa*, pp. 127–28. Lynch, *Edward Wilmot Blyden: Pan-Negro Patriot*, p. 246; *Selected Letters of Edward Wilmot Blyden* (Millwood, N.Y.: KTO Press, 1978).

22. Lynch, *Selected Letters of Edward Wilmot Blyden*, p. 82, "Blyden to the Rev. Henry Van," October 11, 1871, pp. 94–95; Blyden to the Rev. Henry Van, September 6, 1871, pp. 88–89.

23. Ibid.

24. "Blyden to the Rev. John C. Lowrie," May 9, 1876, in Lynch, *Selected Letters of Edward Wilmot Blyden*, pp. 202–207.

25. Ibid., p. 331; "Blyden to William Coppinger," October 2, 1885, in Lynch, *Selected Letters of Edward Wilmot Blyden*, pp. 346–49.

26. "Blyden to the Rev. John Miller," December 6, 1888, ibid., pp. 399–401. Moses N. Moore, "Edward Blyden and the Presbyterian Mission in Liberia," *Union Seminary Quarterly Review* (Spring 1995).

27. Ibid., pp. 99, 459; "Blyden to Mary Kingsley," May 7, 1900, ibid., pp. 460–65.

28. Edwin Redkey, ed., *Respect Black: The Writings and Speeches of Henry McNeal Turner* (New York: Arno Press and the New York Times, 1971), p. viii.

29. Adelaide Cromwell Hill and Martin Kilson, eds., *Apropos of Africa* (Garden City, N.Y.: Anchor, 1971), pp. 48–54; Turner, "Freetown, Sierra Leone, Africa," November 16, 1891, ibid., pp. 266–68; "York Island, Sherbro River, Africa," December 9, 1891; ibid., pp. 277–80. For the history of other African-American missionaries in Africa, see Sylvia M. Jacobs, *Black Americans and the Missionary Movement in Africa* (Westport, Conn.: Greenwood Press, 1982).

30. Ibid., p. 55; J. H. Smyth, "The African in Africa and the African in America"; ibid., pp. 56–67.

31. Peter Gilbert, ed., *Selected Writings of John Edward Bruce: Militant Black Journalist* (New York: Arno Press and the New York Times, 1971), p. 49.

32. Albert J. Raboteau, "Ethiopia Shall Soon Stretch Forth Her Hands: Black

Destiny in Nineteenth-Century America," university lecture in religion at Arizona State University, Tempe (January 27, 1983), pp. 12–13; Theophilus Gould Steward, *The End of the World; or Clearing the Way for the Fullness of the Gentiles* (Philadelphia, 1888).

33. Akbar Muhammad, "Interaction between 'Indigenous' and 'Immigrant' Muslims," *Hijrah Magazine* (March/April 1985), p. 14.

34. Catherine Albanese, *America: Religions and Religion* (Belmont, Calif.: Wadsworth, 1981), p. 189.

35. Esposito, *Islam,* p. 128.

36. Ibid., p. 129.

37. Mohammed Alexander Russell Webb, *Islam in America* (New York: Oriental Publishing Co., 1893), p. 69.

38. Richard H. Seeger, "World's Parliament of Religions, Chicago, Illinois, 1893," Ph.D. dissertation, Harvard University, 1986; published as *The World's Parliament of Religions: The East/West Encounter, Chicago, 1893* (Bloomington: Indiana University Press, 1995). See also Webb, *The Armenian Troubles and Where the Responsibility Lies* (privately printed); *The Five Pillars of Practice* (privately printed); *An Outline of the Mohammedan Faith* (privately printed); *Polygamy and Purdah* (privately printed); *A Guide to the Names: A Detailed Exposition of the Moslem Order of Ablutions and Prayer* (New York: by the author, 1893), p. 27; *Islam: A Lecture Delivered at the Framji Cowasji Institute, Bombay, India, Thursday Evening 10th November 1892* (Bombay: Bombay Gazette Stream Printing Works, 1892), p. 8; *Lectures on Islam* (Lahore: Mohammedan Tract and Book Depot, 1893), p. 48; *The Three Lectures* (Madras: Lawrence Asylum Press, 1892), p. 53; "Muhammad: The Most Misunderstood Messenger of God," *The Minaret* 10, No. 2 (Spring 1989): 9–12; and Emory H. Tunison, "Muhammad Webb, First American Muslim," *The Arab World* 1, 3 (45): 13–18.

39. Webb, *Islam in America,* pp. 67–69. *New York Times* (February 24 and October 8, 1893; July 14, 1894; December 1, 1895; October 1, 1901; and October 3, 1916). *New York Tribune* (February 24 and 28, 1893). Webb's staff for his publishing ventures included Nefeesa M. T. Keep, R. Othman White, John H. Lant, Leon Landsburg, Erwin Nabakoff, and Harry Jerome Lewis. Webb purchased a farm in Ulster Park, New York and was accused of "financial chicanery" by his staff. See Mark Ferris, "To 'Achieve the Pleasure of Allah': Immigrant Muslims in New York City, 1893–1991" in Haddad and Smith, eds., *Muslim Communities in North America* (Albany: State University of New York Press, 1994), pp. 210–11.

40. Mohammed Alexander Russell Webb, *Islam in America,* pp. 58–70; Akbar Muhammad, "Interaction between 'Indigenous' and 'Immigrant' Muslims in the United States: Some Positive Trends," *Hijrah Magazine* (March/April 1985), p. 14.

41. Webb, "The Influence of Social Condition," in J. W. Hanson, ed., *World's Congress of Religions at the World's Columbian Exposition* (Boston: J. S. Round, 1894), pp. 528–29. Conversation with Akbar Muhammad at the American Society of Church History Annual Meeting, Chicago, Illinois, January 6, 1995.

42. Raboteau, "Ethiopia Shall Soon Stretch Forth Her Hands," p. 1.

43. Benjamin William Arnett, "Christianity and Negro," in J. W. Hanson, ed., *The World's Congress of Religions at the World's Columbian Exposition* (Boston: J. S. Round, 1894), p. 750; Frederick Douglass and Ida B. Wells, *The Reason Why the Colored American Is Not in the World's Columbian Exposition* (n.p., 1893), pp. 3–4. For an analysis of racism in the representations of non-European cultures in the exhibits of the World's Columbian Exposition, see Charles H. Long, "New Space, New Time: Disjunctions and Context for a New World Religion," prepared for a Conference on "Race Discourse and the Origin of the Americas: A New World View of 1492" at the Smithsonian Institution, October 31–November 1, 1991.

CHAPTER 3. THE NAME MEANS EVERYTHING

1. Booker T. Washington, *Up from Slavery*, in John Hope Franklin, ed., *Three Black Classics* (New York: Avon, 1901), p. 41; Charles H. Lippy and Peter W. Williams, eds., *Encyclopedia of the American Religious Experience*, vol. 3 (New York: Scribner's, 1988), s.v. "Black Militant and Separatist Movements," by Lawrence H. Mamiya and C. Eric Lincoln; Louis R. Harlan, *Booker T. Washington: The Making of a Black Leader, 1856–1901* (New York: Oxford University Press, 1972) and *Booker T. Washington: The Wizard of Tuskegee, 1901–1915* (New York: Oxford University Press, 1983).

2. C. Eric Lincoln, "The American Muslim Mission in the Context of American Social History," Earle H. Waugh, Baha Abu-Laban, and Regala B. Qureshi, eds., *The Muslim Community in North America* (Edmonton: University of Alberta Press, 1983), p. 219. Some specialists in African-American Islam, such as Ernest Allen, have questioned whether the Moorish Science Temple of America was really Islamic because its founder composed his own "Holy Koran" by drawing on obscure Christian works. However, I have chosen not to decide whether this organization was officially Islamic because I believe that such a decision is in the purview of Muslim religious authorities and not historians of African-American Islam. Thus, in this book, when an organization declares itself as Islamic, that declaration makes it a valid subject for study as a part of Islam in America.

3. Akbar Muhammad, "Interaction between 'Indigenous' and 'Immigrant' Muslims in the United States: Some Positive Trends," *Hijrah Magazine* (March/April 1985): 14. Although the Moorish Science Temple began in 1913, little is known about its activities until 1925. The Moorish Science Temple has been criticized as a non-Islamic movement by some scholars and Muslims. However, McCloud has demonstrated that "Noble Drew Ali was clear on what constitutes Islam" and on "Quranic principles concerning the nature of reality as spiritual and the nature of human existence as co-eternal with the existence of time." See McCloud, *African American Islam*, pp. 9–13.

4. Martin Marty, *Modern American Religion: The Noise of Conflict, 1919–1941* (Chicago: University of Chicago Press, 1989), pp. 1–14.

5. Florette Henri, *Black Migration* (Garden City, N.Y.: Anchor, 1975), p. 68; Seth M. Scheiner, "The Negro Church and the Northern City, 1890–1930," in W. G. Shade and R. C. Herrenkohl, eds., *Seven on Black* (Philadelphia: J. B. Lippincott, 1969), p. 95.

6. Ibid., p. 96; Kenneth L. Kusmer, *A Ghetto Takes Shape* (Urbana: University of Illinois Press, 1976), p. 158. The Great Migration will be discussed in the context of contemporary migration theory and African-American religious historiography in Chapter 5.

7. Kenneth Kusmer, "The Black Urban Experience in American History," in Darlene Clark Hine, ed., *The State of Afro-American History* (Baton Rouge: Louisiana State University Press, 1986), pp. 91–122. The early sociological studies of black urban life were primarily historical and focused on the so-called pathological adjustment of black southern migrants to the North. Typical of the trend were W. E. B. DuBois, *The Philadelphia Negro* (Philadelphia, 1899); R. R. Wright, *The Negro in Pennsylvania* (Philadelphia, 1909); Mary White Ovington, *Half a Man* (New York, 1911); Clyde V. Kiser, *Sea Island to City* (New York, 1931); Emmett J. Scott, *Negro Migration during the War* (New York, 1920); Robert Weaver, *The Negro Ghetto* (New York, 1948); and Thomas J. Woofter, *Negro Problems in Cities* (New York, 1928). Three early exceptions to this trend were St. Clair Drake and Horace Clayton, *Black Metropolis* (New York, 1945) (which rooted the study of Chicago's South Side ghetto in historical context); James Weldon Johnson, *Black Manhattan* (New York, 1925); and Alain Locke, ed., *The New Negro* (New York, 1925). Both Johnson's book and Locke's emphasized the dynamism and cultural creativity of urban blacks.

8. Kusmer, *A Ghetto Takes Shape*, p. 36; Sheiner, "The Negro Church and the Northern City," p. 95.

9. Ibid.; Kusmer, "The Black Urban Experience," pp. 106–107.

10. Howard Rabinowitz, *Race Relations in the Urban South, 1865–1890* (New York, 1987), pp. 192–93.

11. For information on the development of black communities in Harlem, Chicago, and Detroit, see Gilbert Osofsky, *Harlem: The Making of a Ghetto* (New York: Harper and Row, 1963) and Scheiner, *Negro Mecca* (New York, 1965); St. Clair Drake and Horace Clayton, *Black Metropolis* (New York: Harcourt, 1945); Allan H. Spear, *Black Chicago* (Chicago: University of Chicago Press, 1967); Thomas Philpott, *The Slum and the Ghetto* (New York, 1978); David Alan Levine, *Internal Combustion* (Westport, Conn.: Greenwood Press, 1976); August Meier and Elliot Rudwick, *Black Detroit and the Rise of the U.A.W.* (New York, 1979); and Richard W. Thomas, "The Black Urban Experience in Detroit, 1916–1967," in Thomas and Homer Hawkins, eds., *Blacks and Chicanos in Urban Michigan* (New York, 1979). Also see Gerber, *Black Ohio and the Color Line, 1865–1915* (Urbana, 1976); Herbert Gutman, *The Black Family in Slavery and Freedom* (New York, 1926); Thomas C. Cox, *Blacks in Topeka, Kansas, 1865–1915* (Baton Rouge, 1982); Oliver Zuny, *The Changing Face of Inequality* (Chicago, 1982); and William Trotter, *Black Milwaukee* (Urbana, 1985).

12. Kusmer, *A Ghetto Takes Shape*, p. 36; ibid., p. 157; August Meier and Elliot Rudwick, *From Plantation to Ghetto* (New York: Hill and Wang, 1966), p. 236. The Ku Klux Klan had approximately 4 million members during the 1920s.

13. Clifton E. Marsh, *From Black Muslims to Muslims* (Metuchen, N.J.: Scarecrow, 1984), pp. 30–31.

14. John Higham, *Strangers in the Land* (New York: Atheneum, 1963), p. 5.

15. August Meier and Elliot Rudwick, *From Plantation to Ghetto* (New York: Hill and Wang, 1966), p. 242.

16. Ibid., p. 243.

17. Daniel Walden, ed., *W. E. B. DuBois: The Crisis Writings* (Greenwich, Conn.: Fawcett, 1972), p. 21; Elliot M. Rudwick, *W. E. B. DuBois: Propagandist of the Negro Protest* (New York: Atheneum, 1968); Arnold Rampersad, *The Art and Imagination of W. E. B. DuBois* (New York: Schocken, 1976); and David Lewis, *W. E. B. DuBois, 1868–1919* (New York: Henry Holt, 1993).

18. Meier and Rudwick, *From Plantation to Ghetto*, p. 226; Theodore G. Vincent, *Black Power and the Garvey Movement* (San Francisco: Ramparts Press, 1971), p. 56.

19. Franklin, *Black Self-Determination*, pp. 13–25.

20. Darlene Clark Hine, "Lifting the Veil, Shattering the Silence: Black Women's History in Slavery and Freedom," in Hine, ed., *The State of Afro-American History*, pp. 223–49; Theodore G. Vincent, *Black Power and the Garvey Movement*; Stephen R. Fox, *The Guardian of Boston* (New York, 1971); Elinor Des Verney Sinette, *Arthur Alfonso Schomburg* (Detroit: New York Public Library and Wayne State University Press, 1989); Moses, *Golden Age of Black Nationalism*, pp. 220–71.

21. Theodore G. Vincent, *Black Power and the Garvey Movement*, p. 33.

22. Ibid., p. 39. Besides the journals that I have already mentioned in the chapter, several others began publication during the World War I period. A. Philip Randolph and Chandler Owen began the publication of *The Messenger*, a socialist journal, in 1917. In 1918, Garvey's weekly newspaper *Negro World* first appeared. Cyril Briggs first published *The Crusader* in 1918. It advocated black nationalism and revolution. William Briggs's *Challenge* and Hubert Harrison's *Negro Voice*—both militant journals—first appeared in 1918.

23. Moses, *The Golden Age of Black Nationalism*, pp. 267–71.

24. Alain Locke, ed., *The New Negro* (New York: Atheneum, 1992), first published 1925, p. 7. For cogent analysis of the political side of the New Negro movement, see Ernest Allen, Jr., "The New Negro: Explorations in Identity and Social Conscious-

ness, 1910–1922," in Agnes Heller and Lois Rudwick, eds., *1915: The Cultural Moment* (New Brunswick, N.J.: Rutgers University Press, 1991), pp. 48–68.

25. Ibid., pp. 4–6; Moses, *The Golden Age of Black Nationalism,* pp. 258–61; Faith Berry, *Langston Hughes: Before and Beyond Harlem* (New York: Carol, 1992), first published in 1983; Arnold Rampersad, *The Life of Langston Hughes,* 2 vols. (New York: Oxford University Press, 1988).

26. Genna Rae McNeil, review of *Race First* by Tony Martin, in *Journal of Negro History* (October 1977), p. 405. The Colored Farmers Alliance in the 1880s was an important forerunner to Garvey's mass movement; however, we don't know the former's real numbers and probably never will.

27. Vincent, *Black Power and the Garvey Movement,* pp. 13, 91; Marty, *The Noise of Conflict,* p. 117.

28. Robert A. Hill, ed., *Marcus Garvey and the Universal Negro Improvement Association Papers,* vol. 3, p. 302.

29. Ibid., vol. 1, p. lxxxvii.

30. Randall K. Burkett, *Garveyism as a Religious Movement* (Metuchen, N.J.: Scarecrow, 1978), pp. 7, 8; Robert N. Bellah, "Civil Religion in America," in Donald R. Cutler, ed., *The Religious Situation* (Boston: Beacon, 1968), pp. 331–56; Conrad Cherry, *God's New Israel* (Englewood Cliffs, N.J.: Prentice Hall, 1971).

31. Hill, ed., *Marcus Garvey and the Universal Negro Improvement Association Papers,* vol. 3 (Berkeley: University of California Press, 1984), p. 302.

32. E. Franklin Frazier, "Garvey: A Mass Leader," in John Henrick Clarke, ed., *Marcus Garvey and the Vision of Africa* (New York: Vintage, 1974), pp. 236–41.

33. Burkett, *Garveyism as a Religious Movement,* p. 112.

34. Duse Mohammed Ali, *In the Land of Pharaohs* (London: Frank Cass, 1968), pp. x-xi.

35. Robert A. Hill, "The First England Years and After, 1912–1916," in Clarke, ed., *Marcus Garvey and the Vision of Africa,* pp. 41–43. Michael D. Biddiss, "The Universal Races Congress of 1911," *Race* 13, No. 1 (1971): 37–46. G. Spiller, ed., *Papers on Inter-Racial Problems Communicated to the First Universal Races Congress* (London: P. S. King, 1911).

36. Ibid., p. xv; "A Mosque in London," *African Times and Orient Review* (July 1912); "British Government and Muhammadans" (November 1912); "Cross versus Crescent" (December/January 1913); "The Downfall of Islam" (April 1913); "Ahmad Bey El-Bakry and His Son, Ehsan Effendi El-Bakry" (October 1913); "The Political Union of Muslims and Hindus in India" (January 1917); "The Shereef of Mecca Recognized as King of Hejaz" (February 1917). In the August 1917 issue there were two references to the Ahmadis. The first was a picture with the following caption—"Where East Meets West on Terms of Equality. The Eid-ul-Fitr Ahmadiya Mosque, Woking, England. English, Scotch, Irish, African, Indian, Egyptian at Woking, England." Also there was an advertisement for *The Islamic Review and Muslim India,* an Ahmadi publication, edited by Haji Khwadja Kamal-ud-Din and Maulvie Sadr-ud-Din; *African Times and Orient Review* (July 1912), p. 1.

37. Marcus Garvey, "The British West Indies in the Mirror of Civilization," *African Times and Orient Review* 1 (October 1913); Vincent, *Black Power and the Garvey Movement,* p. 94; Mohammed Ali, *In the Land of the Pharaohs,* pp. xvii–xviii.

38. Robert A. Hill, "The First England Years and After, 1912–1916," p. 50.

39. Ibid., pp. 68–70; Garvey, "A Talk with Afro-West Indians: The Negro Race and Its Problems" (n.d.), extant copy in West India Reference Library, Jamaica.

40. Robert A. Hill, "The First England Years and After, 1912–1916," pp. 43, 49–54. J. E. Casely Hayford, *Ethiopia Unbound, Studies in Race Emancipation* (London: Frank Cass, 1969), first published 1911, p. xxiii.

41. Robert A. Hill, "The First England Years and After, 1912–1916," pp. 49–54. Hayford, *Ethiopia Unbound,* pp. 165–66.

42. Ibid., pp. 165–72.

43. Ibid., p. 69.

44. Ibid., p. 197. Hill, "The First England Years, 1912–1914," p. 54.

45. Duse Mohammed Ali, *In the Land of the Pharaohs,* pp. xviii-xxv. Robert Hill has noted that the relationship between Garvey and Mohammed Ali was contentious at times, although the source of this contention is not evident. Hill, "The First England, 1912–1914," pp. 43–44.

46. Vincent, *Black Power and the Garvey Movement,* pp. 109–21. *New York Times,* August 4, 1920; Marty, *The Noise of Conflict,* p. 119.

47. Tony Martin, *Race First* (Westport, Conn.: Greenwood Press, 1976), p. 74.

48. Ibid., pp. 67, 75; *Negro World* 4 (February 1922).

49. Arnold J. Ford, "The Universal Ethiopian Hymnal," 1922, Marcus Garvey and Universal Negro Improvement Association Papers, University of California, Los Angeles; Barkett, *Garveyism as a Religious Movement,* pp. 178–81.

50. *Negro World,* March 25, 1921.

51. *Negro World,* March 4, 1922.

52. *Negro World,* September 15, 1923.

53. Burkett, ed., *Black Redemption* (Philadelphia: Temple University Press, 1970), p. 15.

54. Noble Drew Ali, *The Holy Koran of the Moorish Science Temple of America* (Chicago, 1927), p. 59.

55. Muhammad Abdullah Ahari El, *Sharif Abdul Ali (Noble Drew Ali—His Life and Teachings)* (Chicago: Magribine Press, 1989), pp. 3–4. It should be underlined that all of the above tales are legends. Peter Lamborn Wilson, "Shoot-Out at the Circle 7 Koran: Noble Drew Ali and the Moorish Science Temple," *Gnosis Magazine* 12 (Summer 1989), pp. 44–45. Also see Wilson, *Sacred Drift: Essays on the Margins of Islam* (San Francisco: City Lights, 1993), pp. 15–18, for the most thorough account of the legends concerning Noble Drew Ali's early life. On page 28 of *Sacred Drift,* Wilson offers evidence in the form of a 1927 flyer from the Moorish Science Temple that its leader might have been "a professional circus magician." A possible source of Muslim ideas in the circus was "The Barnum and Bailey New Big Indo-Arabic Spectacle the Wizard Prince of Arabia," which toured America at the turn of the century. See Joseph Newman, ed., *200 Years: A Bicentennial Illustrated History of the United States* (Washington, D.C.: U.S. News and World Report, 1973), vol. 2, pp. 102–103.

56. Ibid., pp. 5–7. McCloud, *African American Islam,* pp. 10–11.

57. Ali, *The Holy Koran,* pp. 56–58; Ahari-El, *Sharif Abdul Ali,* pp. 12–14. With regard to the influence of the Quran on the Moorish community, McCloud writes that "there were several English translations and commentaries of the Quran in existence at the time." These included "the first Muslim Translation of Muhammad Abdul Hakim Khan of Patiala in 1905. Whether these translations were available to African American Muslims at the time of the century is still a question." See McCloud, *African American Islam,* p. 200.

58. Ali, *The Holy Koran,* pp. 56–58. Wilson considers "The Holy Koran" as "a modern apocryphon . . . in which the images of established religious and canonical texts acquire a kind of mutuality, a tendency to drift to reflect the subjectivities of visionaries who sift through fragments in order to produce more fragments." See *Sacred Drift,* pp. 19–25.

59. Catherine Albanese, *America: Religions and Religion,* 2nd ed. (Belmont, Calif.: Wadsworth, 1992), pp. 266–68. Peter Lamborn Wilson notes that Noble Drew Ali's *Holy Koran* was also inspired by Nicholas Notovich's *La Vie Inconnue de Jesus Christ* (1894), Miozra Ghulam Ahmad's *Jesus in India* (1899), and Budgett Meakin's *The Moorish Empire* (1899); Peter Lamborn Wilson, "Shoot-Out at the Circle 7 Koran: Noble Drew Ali and the Moorish Science Temple," *Gnosis Magazine* 12 (Summer

1989), p. 45; Jay Kinney, "Sufism Comes to America," *Gnosis Magazine* 30 (Winter 1974), p. 18. McCloud has noted that Noble Drew Ali's texts have much in common with "the literature of the Druze of Syria," who had a community "in the immediate area" of the Moorish Science Temple. She has also noted possible Shiite influences in Noble Drew Ali's teachings and Ismaili Muslim influence in the Moorish community's three daily prayers. McCloud, *African American Islam*, p. 201. Caesar E. Farah, *Islam: Beliefs and Observances*, 4th ed. (New York: Barron's, 1987), pp. 179–80.

60. Idries Shah, *The Sufis* (New York: Doubleday, 1964), p. xix.

61. Peter Lamborn Wilson, "Shoot-Out at the Circle 7 Koran: Noble Drew Ali and the Moorish Science Temple," p. 46.

62. Ibid.

63. *Negro World*, April 1922; Mark C. Carnes, *Secret Ritual and Manhood in Victorian America* (New Haven: Yale University Press, 1989), pp. 3, 5, 6, 158.

64. Judith N. Shklar, "Subversive Genealogies," *Daedalus* (Winter 1972), pp. 129–30.

65. Cedric Robinson, "White Signs in Black Times: The Politics of Representation in Dominant Texts" (Santa Barbara: International Conference on Black Theoretical Practice, May 1989).

66. Stanley Lieberson, *A Piece of the Pie* (Berkeley: University of California Press, 1980), pp. 31–35.

67. Ibid.

68. Yvonne Y. Haddad and Jane I. Smith, *Mission to America* (Gainesville: University Press of Florida, 1993), pp. 1–22.

69. Kenneth W. Harrow, *Faces of Islam in African Literature* (Portsmouth, N.H.: Heinemann, 1991), pp. 7–8.

70. Ibid., p. 9.

71. Ibid.

72. Federal Bureau of Investigation, Chicago File 14–41.

73. C. Eric Lincoln, *The Black Muslims in America* (Boston: Beacon, 1961), pp. 54–55; "Negro in Illinois: Churches and Religious Cults" (1940), Illinois Writers Project, Vivian G. Harsh Collection, Carter G. Woodson Regional Library Center, Chicago, Illinois, p. 8.

74. *Associated Negro Press*, March 20, 1929. Author's telephone interview with Ernest Allen, Jr., April 1994.

75. Ibid. McCloud believes that "Noble Drew Ali was murdered in 1930 and buried in Burr Oak Cemetery in Chicago." McCloud, *African American Islam*, p. 18. According to McCloud, the prophet's first wife, Pearl Ali, is still alive and resides in Chicago. McCloud, *African American Islam*, pp. 17–18.

76. "Negro in Illinois," pp. 6–7. Hill, *Marcus Garvey and U.N.I.A. Papers*, vol. 7 (Berkeley: University of California Press, 1990), p. 82; Federal Bureau of Investigation reports on the Moorish Science Temple of America, File 62–25889; Peter Lamborn Wilson, "Shoot-Out at the Circle 7 Koran: Noble Drew Ali and the Moorish Science Temple," p. 48; Wendell Berge, Assistant Attorney General, "Memorandum to the Director FBI," January 23, 1943. In the 1930s, a group of Moorish Americans led by Walter Smith Bey were influenced by the teachings of Dr. Yusef Khan, an Ahmadi Muslim from India. For details about this development, see Jameela A. Hakim, "History of the First Muslim Mosque of Pittsburgh, Pennsylvania," in J. Gordon Melton and Michael A. Koszenzi, eds., *Islam in North America: A Sourcebook* (New York: Garland, 1992), pp. 153–63. Wilson offers the best account of the final shoot-out and the succession of leaders after Drew Ali's death. See *Sacred Drift*, pp. 38–47.

77. FBI Report, Chicago File 61–293, p. 19; FBI Report, Detroit File 100–6603, pp. 40881–82.

78. FBI Report, "The Moorish Science Temple . . . Internal Security—Sedition," New York City File 100–33742, p. 295; Hill, *U.N.I.A. Papers,* vol. 7, p. 717. See Ernest Allen, "Waiting for Tojo: The Pro-Japan Vigil of Black Missourians, 1932–1943," *Gateway Heritage* (Fall 1994), pp. 16–32.

79. FBI Report, "Confidential, Moorish Science Temple of America," February 26, 1943, pp. 46–48.

80. Ibid.

81. FBI Report, "Moorish Science Temple of America: Robert Washington organizer," Jackson, Mississippi, August 7, 1942, File 100–793, p. 127.

82. FBI Report, "Moorish Science Temple of America File 100–4692; "C. Kirkman Bey," Kansas City, Missouri File 100–4692; Ernest Allen, Jr., "When Japan Was Champion of the Darker Races: Satokata Takahashi and the Development of Our Own, 1933–1942," *The Black Scholar* 24 (Winter 1993/1994).

83. FBI Report, "Colonel C. Kirkman Bey: with aliases, et al., Moorish Science Temple of America," Detroit, Michigan, April 21, 1943, File 100–6603, p. 336.

84. Ibid. FBI Report, "Moorish Science Temple of America, Inc., Baltimore, Maryland, May 13, 1953, File 25–18253, pp. 1–6.

85. FBI Report, A. H. Crowl, Special Agent to Director FBI, Re: "The Moorish Science Temple of America, Robert Washington, Organizer, Internal Security," Springfield, Illinois, April 8, 1942, File 62–25889–7, p. 99; [title deleted], Chicago, Illinois, September 21, 1943, File 14–39; "At Pulaski, Illinois" [date and file number unknown]; Detroit File 100–6603; "Colonel C. Kirkman Bey, with Aliases, et al. Moorish Science Temple of America," Knoxville, Tennessee, January 1, 1943, File 100–1368; Herbert K. Moss, Special Agent to Director FBI, Re: "Moorish Science Temple of America, Internal Security—Sedition; Overthrow or Destruction of Government," Louisville, Kentucky, February 15, 1943, File 62–25889–62, pp. 400–401; Letter to Director FBI, Re: "Moorish Science Temple of America, Inc., et al. Internal Security—Selective Service, Sedition, Birmingham, Alabama, May 18, 1943, File 100–15442; "Moorish Science Temple of America, Inc., et al.," New Haven, Connecticut, September 14, 1942, File 100–5963; Confidential Memo from War Department, Security and Intelligence, Re: "Moorish Science Temple," Great Barrington, Massachusetts, September 4, 1945, File 100–10995–53; J. R. Ruggles to Special Agent in Charge, New York, Re: "William Briggs—Bey Internal Security," Savannah, Georgia, February 11, 1943, File 100–33742–38; and E. I. Bobbit, Special Agent, "Memorandum for the File," Re: Prince George County, Virginia Internal Security, Richmond, Virginia, September 25, 1942, File 100–4361.

86. "Moorish Science Temple, New Haven Division letter to President Franklin D. Roosevelt," February 24, 1943.

87. Hine, ed., *The State of Afro-American History,* pp. 223–49.

88. FBI Summary Report, File 100–35742, pp. 265–30068; FBI Report, Moorish Science Temple of America, May 28, 1943, pp. 241–54; *Moorish Voice,* November 1942; January, February, March, April, May, June 1943—available at the FBI headquarters in Washington, D.C.

89. John L. Esposito, *The Islamic Threat, Myth or Reality* (New York: Oxford University Press, 1943), p. 58.

90. FBI Files 100–5698 and 100–5943. "Prince Is among Moors at Convention," *Berkshire Evening Eagle,* September 18, 1944. "Moors Get Government Backing to Help Relieve Food Problem," *People's Voice,* April 17, 1943.

91. Memorandum to U.S. Government from Informant [name deleted], October 12, 1978, File 157–5338–18, p. 108; Special Agent in Charge, Philadelphia to Director FBI, Re: Moorish Science Temple of America, December 5, 1973, File 157–7522–7, pp. 140–41.

92. *Moorish Guide* 1, No. 7 (July 1982), p. 3. McCloud, *African American Islam,* p. 56.

93. "Mine Eyes Have Seen the Glory of Noble Drew Ali," *The Sun*, October 31, 1978; Haddad and Smith, *Mission to America*, p. 86. Wilson reports that the Moorish Science Temple has been expanding since the "centenary of Noble Drew Ali's birth" in 1986. New groups include The Moorish Great Seal, The Moorish Natural and Divine Movement, The Moorish Circle of Fulfillment, The United Moorish Republic, and The Moorish Orthodox Church (which was actually established in the 1950s by Europeans). See *Sacred Drift*, pp. 48–50.

94. Hill, *Marcus Garvey and U.N.I.A. Papers*, vol. 7, p. 82.

95. Lincoln, "American Muslim Mission in the Context of American Social History," p. 219.

CHAPTER 4. THE AHMADIYYA MISSION TO AMERICA

1. Roi Ottley, *New World A-Coming* (Boston: Houghton Mifflin, 1943), pp. 56–57. This chapter is based on the author's previous research: "Islam in the United States in the 1920s: The Quest for a New Vision in Afro-American Religion," Ph.D. dissertation, Princeton University, 1986; "The Ahmadiyya Mission to Blacks in America in the 1920s," *Journal of Religious Thought* 44, No. 2 (Winter/Spring 1988), pp. 50–66; and "The Ahmadiyya Movement in America," *Religion Today* (U.K.) 5, No. 3 (1990). The background material on the Ahmadiyya Movement in Islam is voluminous. Some important selected sources include **1. The published writings of Ghulan Ahmad:** *The Philosophy of the Teachings of Islam* (London: Ahmadiyya Centenary Publications, 1979), one of his most important works. *The Essence of Islam: Extracts from the Writings of the Promised Messiah*, vol. 1, trans. Muhammad Zafrullah Khan (London: Ahmadiyya Centenary Publications, 1978). *Tadkirah*, trans. Khan (London: Saffron Books, 1976). *Tawzih-i-Maram*, trans. Iqbul Ahmad (Lahore: Anjuman Ahmadiyya, 1966). *Message of Peace* (Lahore: Anjuman Ahmadiyya, 1986). **2. Publications of the Ahmadiyya Movement:** Malawi Sher Ali, ed. and trans., *The Holy Quran* (Rabwah, Pakistan: Oriental and Religious Publishing Co., n.d.). *The Muslim Sunrise, The American Ahmadi Journal*, published continuously, with a few breaks, since the early 1920s, is the most important source of information on Ahmadiyya history in the United States. The earliest volumes of the journal can be found in the New York Public Library and its annexes. Recently a microfilm version of a full run of the earliest volumes was produced through the efforts of Ernest Allen, Jr., and can be purchased through the New York Public Library. Early volumes of *The Review of Religions*, an older Ahmadi journal, also provide primary source material for the movement's early days in Armenia. The journal can be found in the annexes of the New York Public Library. A. R. Dard, *Life of Ahmad* (Lahore: Sultan Brothers, 1949). Muhammad Ali, *The Ahmadiyya Movement* (Lahore: The Ahmadiyyah Anjuman Isha'at Islam, 1975). **3. Secondary sources:** Yohannan Friedmann's pioneering book *Prophecy Continuous: Aspects of Ahmadi Religious Thought and Its Medieval Background* (Berkeley: University of California Press, 1989), builds on two earlier important works on the Ahmadiyya Movement, Humphrey J. Fisher, *Ahmadiyya* (London: Oxford University Press, 1963) and Spencer Lavan, *The Ahmadiyya Movement* (Delhi: Manohar Book Service, 1974). Important secondary literature on the Ahmadiyya Movement's history in America includes Yvonne Y. Haddad and Jane I. Smith, *Mission to America: Five Islamic Sectarian Communities in North America* (Gainesville: University Press of Florida, 1993) and the author's work cited above.

2. John Esposito, *Islam: The Straight Path* (New York: Oxford University Press, 1988), p. 137.

3. Yohanan Friedmann, *Prophecy Continuous*, pp. 2–3.

4. Ibid., pp. 4–10.

5. Caesar F. Farah, *Islam* (New York: Barrons, 1987), pp. 247–49.

6. Ibid., pp. 104–50.

7. Friedmann, *Prophecy Continuous*, pp. 49–82.

8. Murray R. Titus, *Islam in India and Pakistan* (Calcutta: YMCA Publishing House, 1959), p. 257; Kenneth Cragg, *Counsels in Contemporary Islam* (Edinburgh: University of Edinburgh Press, 1965), p. 156.

9. Spencer Lavan, *The Ahmadiyya Movement* (Delhi: Monohar Book Service, 1974), p. 1; Humphrey J. Fisher, *Ahmadiyyah* (London: Oxford University Press, 1963), pp. 80–82.

10. Lavan, *The Ahmadiyya Movement*, p. 45; Ghulam Ahmad, *Tawhih-Maram*, trans. Iqbal Ahmad (Lahore: Ahmadiyyah Anzuman Ishbat-i-Islam, 1966), first Urdu ed., 1891, p. 5; Ahmad, *Masih Hindustan Men* (Qadian, 1912; written in 1899), p. 27.

11. A. R. Dard, *Life of Ahmad* (Lahore: Sultan Brothers, 1949), p. 272.

12. Lavan, *The Ahmadiyya Movement*, p. 93.

13. Ibid., pp. 95, 110–14; "God Bless the British Government," *The Review of Religions* 15 (January 1918), pp. 1–11.

14. "Peer Becomes Muslims," *The Review of Religions* 12 (December 1913), p. 513; "Religion of Islam—Spread of the Faith in This Country," *The Sheffield Evening Telegraph* (November 29, 1913).

15. Sher Ali, "America's Intolerance," *The Review of Religions* 19 (April/May 1920), p. 158.

16. "Ahmadiyya Mission News," *The Review of Religions* 19 (July 1920), p. 24.

17. Mufti Muhammad Sadiq, *The Moslem Sunrise* 1 (April 1922), p. 1.

18. Mufti Muhammad Sadiq, "One Year's Missionary Work in America," *The Moslem Sunrise* 1 (July 1921), p. 12.

19. "Ahmadiyya Mission News," *The Review of Religions* 19 (July 1922), p. 24.

20. Mufti Muhammad Sadiq, "No Polygamy," *The Moslem Sunrise* 1 (July 1921), p. 9.

21. Sher Ali, "America's Intolerance," *The Review of Religions* 19 (April/May 1920), pp. 158–60.

22. "Ahmadiyya Mission News," *The Review of Religions* 19 (July 1922), p. 24.

23. Yvonne Y. Haddad, "The Muslim Experience in America," *The Link* 2 (September/October 1979), p. 2.

24. As cited by J. Gordon Melton, "The Attitude of Americans toward Hinduism from 1883–1983 with Special Reference to the International Society for Krishna Consciousness," Evanston, Illinois, May 1985.

25. *Harvard Encyclopedia of American Ethnic Groups*, s.v. "Immigration: History of U.S. Policy," by William S. Bernard, pp. 4590–91.

26. Gary R. Hess, "The Forgotten Asian Americans: The East Indian Community in the United States," in *The Asian American*, ed. Norris Hundley, Jr. (Santa Barbara: Clio Books, 1976), pp. 169–71.

27. "Ahmadiyya Mission News," *The Review of Religions* 19 (July 1920), p. 242.

28. *Press*, Philadelphia, February 19, 1920.

29. Fred Metcalf, comp., *The Penguin Dictionary of Modern Humorous Quotations* (London: Penguin, 1987), p. 174.

30. Roi Ottley, *New World A-Coming* (Boston: Houghton Mifflin, 1943), p. 20; "Ahmadiyya Mission News," *The Review of Religions* 19 (July 1920), p. 24.

31. "Ahmadiyya Mission News," *The Review of Religions* 19 (July 1920), p. 24.

32. Ibid.

33. "Brief Report of the Work in America," *The Moslem Sunrise* 2 (June 1923), p. 166.

34. Spencer Lavan, *The Ahmadiyya Movement* (New Delhi: Manohar Book Services, 1974), p. 107.

35. "Ahmadiyya Mission News," *The Review of Religions* 19 (July 1920), pp. 30–40.

36. Mufti Muhammad Sadiq, "One Year's Moslem Missionary Work in America," *The Moslem Sunrise* (July 1921), p. 13.

37. Mufti Muhammad Sadiq, "Brief Report of the Work in America," *The Moslem Sunrise* 1 (October 1921), p. 13.

38. "Our American Mission," *The Review of Religions* 19 (October 1920), p. 352.

39. Yvonne Y. Haddad and Adair T. Lummis, *Islamic Values in the United States* (New York: Oxford University Press, 1987), pp. 13–14.

40. *Harvard Encyclopedia of American Ethnic Groups*, s.v. "Arabs," by Alixa Naff, p. 131.

41. Atif A. Wasfi, *An Islamic-Lebanese Community in U.S.A.* (Beirut: Beirut Arab University, 1971), p. 86.

42. Ibid., pp. 6–7.

43. Yvonne Y. Haddad, "The Muslim Experience in the United States," p. 1.

44. Yhaya Aossey, Jr., *Fifty Years of Islam in Iowa, 1925–1975* (Cedar Rapids, Iowa: Unity, n.d.).

45. Abdo A. Elkholy, *The Arab Moslems in the United States* (New Haven, Conn.: College and University Press, 1966), p. 2.

46. Haddad and Lummis, *Islamic Values in the United States*, p. 11.

47. *Harvard Encyclopedia of American Ethnic Groups*, s.v. "Bosnian Muslims," by William G. Lockwood, p. 185.

48. *Harvard Encyclopedia of American Ethnic Groups*, s.v. "Turks," by Talat Sait Halman, pp. 993–95.

49. *Harvard Encyclopedia of American Ethnic Groups*, s.v. "Albanians," p. 26. Shaykh Daoud published *Islam: The True Faith, the True Religion of Humanity*, 2nd ed. (1965), and his group published a magazine for women, called *Sahabiyat*. He died in 1980. See McCloud, *African American Islam*, pp. 21–24.

50. Interview with Abid Haneef, Burlington, Massachusetts, December 1986. One of Sadiq's earliest followers recalled, "He began visiting various denominations of churches and the Syrian restaurants. . . . Since he knew colloquial Arabic language, he made a great hit with the Arabs of Syria, Lebanon and Palestine." See Haddad and Smith, *Mission to America*, p. 61, and M. Yusaf Khan, "Some of Our Missionaries," *Muslim Sunrise* 42 (December 1975), p. 14.

51. Mufti Muhammad Sadiq, "My Advice to the Muhammadans in America," *The Moslem Sunrise* 2 (October 1921), p. 29.

52. "Islamic Society in America," *The Review of Religions* 19 (October 1920), p. 353.

53. *The Moslem Sunrise* 1 (July 1921), p. 31.

54. "Suggested Islamic Organ in America," *The Review of Religions* 19 (October 1920), p. 353.

55. *The Moslem Sunrise* 1 (July 1921), p. 1.

56. "Brief Report of the Work in America," *The Moslem Sunrise* 2 (October 1921), pp. 36–37.

57. Mufti Muhammad Sadiq, "Islam Defended: A Denial That It Teaches Its Adherents to Hate and to Kill," *The Moslem Sunrise* 1 (July 1921), p. 14.

58. "In Defense of Islam and Moslem," *The Moslem Sunrise* 1 (January 1922), p. 72.

59. *Syracuse Sunday Herald*, June 25, 1922.

60. "Jewish Massacres," *The Moslem Sunrise* 2 (October 1921), p. 40.

61. "The Only Solution of Color Prejudice," *The Moslem Sunrise* 2 (October 1921), p. 41.

62. Mufti Muhammad Sadiq, "Warm Controversy on Mohammedanism," *The Moslem Sunrise* 1 (July 1921), p. 16.

63. *The Moslem Sunrise* 1 (July 1922), p. 117.

64. Manning Marable, "Religion and Black Protest Thought," in *African American Religious Studies: An Interdisciplinary Anthology*, ed. Gayrand S. Wilmore (Durham: Duke University Press, 1989), p. 329.

65. C. Eric Lincoln, "The Muslim Mission in the Context of American Social History," in *African American Religious Studies: An Interdisciplinary Anthology*, ed. Gayrand S. Wilmore (Durham: Duke University Press, 1989), pp. 341–42.

66. Roger Didier, "Those Who're Missionaries to Christians," *The Moslem Sunrise* 1 (October 1922), pp. 139–40.

67. *The Moslem Sunrise* 1 (October 1921), p. 26.

68. Ibid. (October 1922), p. 138. According to Haddad and Smith, Sadiq "was forced to go to Chicago . . . after it became clear that [he] was not preaching orthodox Islam." See *Mission to America*, p. 61 and Mary Caroline Holmes, "Islam in America," *Moslem World* 16 (1926), p. 262–66.

69. Ibid. (October 1921), p. 36.

70. Ibid., 2 (January 1923), p. 166.

71. Ibid., 1 (July 1922), p. 119.

72. Ibid. (April and July 1923), p. 270.

73. Ibid.

74. Ibid., 2 (January 1923), p. 175.

75. Ibid., p. 191.

76. See Albert J. Raboteau, *Slave Religion* (New York: Oxford University Press, 1978), p. 152; Donald G. Matthews, *Religion in the Old South* (Chicago: University of Chicago Press, 1977), pp. xvi-xvii; Clifton H. Johnson, ed., *God Struck Me Dead* (Boston: Pilgrim Press, 1969).

77. Thomas D. Hamm, *The Transformation of American Quakerism* (Bloomington: Indiana University Press, 1988), p. xv.

78. *The Moslem Sunrise* 2 (January 1923), p. 175.

79. Ibid.

80. Ibid., p. 161.

81. Ibid., 3 (January 1924), p. 45; ibid., 2 (January 1923), p. 167.

82. David E. Apter, "Political Religions in the New Nation," in Clifford E. Geertz, ed., *Old Societies and New States* (New York: Free Press of Glencoe, 1963), p. 77.

83. Robert H. Hill, ed., *Marcus Garvey and the Universal Negro Improvement Association Papers*, vol. 1 (Berkeley: University of California Press, 1983), p. 521.

84. "Ganesh Rao to the Editor," *Negro World*, in Hill, ed., *Marcus Garvey Papers*, vol. 4, pp. 495–96. Sudarshan Kapur has demonstrated that African Americans were also aware of Indian nationalism through the "consciousness of Gandhi and his movement," which had been pervasive in the black press since the early twentieth century; see *Raising up a Prophet* (Boston: Beacon, 1992), p. 158.

85. *The Moslem Sunrise* 2 (April 1923), p. 263.

86. Ibid. (January 1923), p. 184.

87. "Ben E. Rogers, William E. DuBois, Marcus Garvey and Pan Africa," *Journal of Negro History* 40 (April 1955), p. 159.

88. Theodore Vincent, *Black Power and the Garvey Movement* (Palo Alto: Ramparts Press, 1972), p. 195.

89. *The Moslem Sunrise* 1 (October 1922), p. 140.

90. Laurence Moore, *Religious Outsiders and the Making of Americans* (New York: Oxford University Press, 1986), p. 19; Will Herberg, *Protestant, Catholic, Jew: An Essay in American Religious Sociology* (Garden City, N.Y., 1945); Martin E. Marty, "Ethnicity: The Skeleton of Religion in America," *Church History* 41 (March 1972).

91. *Chicago Herald Examiner* (November 3, 1929); *The Moslem Sunrise* 3 (July 1930), p. 11.

92. Ibid.

93. *The Moslem Sunrise* 3 (July 1930), p. 12.

94. *The Moslem Sunrise* 3 (December 1930), pp. 21–23.

95. *The Moslem Sunrise* 4 (October/January 1931–1932), p. 18; *The Moslem Sunrise* 8 (October 1935), pp. 29–30. Bengalee's wife came to America in 1936 to work with the Ahmadi women. He was also assisted by Khalid Nasir, Ghulam Yasin, and Mirza Monawar Ahmad in the 1930s. See Haddad and Smith, *Mission to America*, p. 63, and "Some Nostalgic Memories of the Early Years of the American Mission," *The Muslim Sunrise* 42 (December 1975): 13–15.

96. Ibid.

97. *The Moslem Sunrise* 6 (April-July 1933), p. 43. Other important African-American converts in the 1930s were Hamida Chamber (Chicago), Hamida Aziza (Dayton), Alia Shahid (Pittsburgh), and Bashir Afzal. Interview with Muzaffar Ahmad Zafar, National Vice President of the Ahmadiyya Movement in Islam, October 3, 1992, Chino, California.

98. Noorul Islam, "Activities of the Ahmadiyya Moslem Mosque in Chicago," *The Moslem Sunrise* (first quarter 1940), pp. 18–21. McCloud, *African American Islam*, pp. 21, 24–27.

99. "Blot on the Good Name of America," *The Moslem Sunrise* 15 (third quarter 1943), p. 26.

100. "Segregation in the Christian Churches," *The Moslem Sunrise* 20 (first quarter 1948), p. 26; "Mixed Congregation," *The Muslim Sunrise* 27 (first quarter 1955); H. H. Lippincot, *The Christian Century* (February 9, 1955); "Northern Churches and Racism," *The Muslim Sunrise* 28 (third quarter 1956), pp. 9–10; Frank Loescher, *The Christian Century* (February 8, 1956); "Segregation in the Churches," *The Moslem Sunrise* 27 (second quarter 1955), pp. 6–7; *Newsweek* (September 27, 1954).

101. "Solution of Color Prejudice, Islam or Christianity," from Alan Burns, *Colour Prejudice* (London, 1948); *The Moslem Sunrise* 21 (fourth quarter, 1949), p. 29.

102. Ibid.; P. L. Prattis, "The Moslem Missionary Proposes to Show Us the True Way of Allah and the Prophet," *The Moslem Sunrise* 11 (July 1939), pp. 28–29; Omar Cleveland, "The Democracy in Islam," *The Moslem Sunrise* 4 (April-July 1931), p. 17; "The Great Quest" 11 (October 1939), pp. 18–19; "Happiness" 12 (first quarter 1940), p. 25; "Ideals of Islam" 13 (November 1941), p. 31; "Muhammad" 14 (first quarter 1942), pp. 29–30; "Islamic Culture" 15 (second quarter 1943), pp. 29–30.

103. S. E. Brush, "Ahmadiyyat in Pakistan," *The Muslim World* (April 1955), pp. 145–47.

104. Abdul Kadir Khan, "The Agony of Kashmir," *The Moslem Sunrise* 20 (second quarter 1948), pp. 1–22; Edgar Snow, "An American Journalist Looks at Pakistan," *The Moslem Sunrise* 20 (third quarter 1948), pp. 16–17; also *Saturday Evening Post* (July 17, 1948).

105. S. E. Brush, "Ahmadiyyat in Pakistan," *The Muslim World* (April 1955), p. 170.

106. Sufi Bengalee, "Jewish Rights and Claims to Palestine," *The Moslem Sunrise* 11 (January 1939), pp. 21–22.

107. "The Palestine Problem," *The Moslem Sunrise* 26 (fourth quarter 1954), pp. 21–25; "Anti-Semitism in Israel," *The Muslim Sunrise* 26 (third quarter 1954), pp. 4–5.

108. John T. Wood, "Democracy's First Line of Defense: Islam," *The Muslim Sunrise* 24 (third quarter 1952), pp. 18–22; Stephen B. L. Penrose, "American Stake in the Middle East," *The Muslim Sunrise* 25 (fourth quarter 1953), pp. 26–27.

109. McCloud, *African American Islam*, pp. 20–21.

110. Author's telephone interview with Muzaffar Ahmad Zafr, Dayton, Ohio, December 7, 1994.

111. C. O. Simpkins, *Coltrane: A Biography* (Baltimore: Black Classic Press, 1989), first published 1975, pp. 39–40, 115.
112. Interview with Muzaffar Ahmad Zafr, December 7, 1994. McCloud, *African-American Islam,* p. 21.
113. Interview with Muzaffar Ahmad Zafr, December 7, 1994. Author's telephone interview with Rashid Ahmed, Milwaukee, Wisconsin, December 11, 1994.
114. Interview with Mazaffar Ahmad Zafr, December 7, 1994.
115. McCloud, *African American Islam,* p. 21.
116. Interview with Rashid Ahmed.
117. Interview with Rashid Ahmed.
118. McCloud, *African American Islam,* pp. 53–54.
119. Author's telephone interview with Maneer Hamid, Philadelphia, Pennsylvania, December 12, 1994.
120. Author's telephone interview with Dhul Waqar Yaqub, Chicago, Illinois, December 11, 1994.
121. McCloud, *African American Islam,* p. 58.

CHAPTER 5. MISSIONIZING AND SIGNIFYING

1. "A Picturesque Colony," *New York Tribune,* October 2, 1892, p. 2.
2. Alixa Naff, *Becoming American: The Early Arab Immigrant Experience* (Carbondale: Southern Illinois University Press, 1985).
3. Elijah Muhammad, *Message to the Blackman in America* (Chicago: Muhammad Mosque of Islam, 1965), p. 17.
4. Erdmann D. Beynon, "The Voodoo Cult among Negro Migrants in Detroit," *American Journal of Sociology* 43 (July 1937-May 1938), p. 896. From an interview with Sister Carrie Mohammed.
5. Ibid. From Beynon's interview with Sister Denke Majied.
6. Ibid., p. 895.
7. Mayor's Inter-racial Committee, *The Negro in Detroit,* vol. 3 (Detroit: Detroit Bureau of Government Research, 1926), pp. 2, 18.
8. "Nation of Islam Deserted," *African Mirror* (August/September 1979), p. 37.
9. C. Eric Lincoln, *The Black Muslims in America* (Boston: Beacon, 1973), p. 13.
10. "Nation of Islam Deserted," p. 37; Elijah Muhammad, *Message to the Blackman in America,* pp. 32, 210.
11. Benyon, "Voodoo Cult among Negro Migrants in Detroit," p. 896. From Benyon's interview with Brother Challar Sharrieff.
12. Clifton E. Marsh, *From Black Muslims to Muslims* (Metuchen, N.J.: Scarecrow, 1984), p. 52. From an interview with Warith D. Muhammad.
13. "Nation of Islam Deserted," *African Mirror* (August/September 1979), p. 37.
14. Benyon, "Voodoo Cult among Negro Migrants in Detroit," pp. 897, 901; W. D. Fard, *Teaching for the Lost Found Nation of Islam in a Mathematical Way, Problem Number 30.*
15. Marsh, *From Black Muslims to Muslims,* p. 53. From *Muhammad Speaks,* Special Issue, April 1972.
16. Benyon, "Voodoo Cult among Negro Migrants in Detroit," p. 907.
17. C. Eric Lincoln, "The American Muslim Mission in the Context of American Social History," in Earle H. Waugh, Baha Abu-Laban, and Regula B. Qureshi, eds., *The Muslim Community in North America* (Edmonton: University of Alberta Press, 1983), p. 221; Malu Halsa, *Elijah Muhammad* (New York: Chelsea House, 1990), p. 105.
18. Carole Marks, *Farewell—We're Good and Gone* (Bloomington: Indiana University Press, 1989), pp. 1, 110, 111, 165, 170.
19. Ibid., pp. 165, 175.

20. "Nation of Islam Deserted," *African Mirror* (August/September 1979), p. 38.

21. Elijah Muhammad, *Message to the Blackman in America*, p. xiv.

22. Gayraud Wilmore, *Black Religion and Black Radicalism*, 2nd ed. (Maryknoll, N.Y.: Orbis, 1983); see also Randall Burkett and David Wills, "Afro-American Religious History, 1919–1939: A Resource Guide and Bibliographical Essay" (Cambridge, Mass., 1989), for a reassessment of Wilmore's deradicalization thesis; C. Eric Lincoln and Lawrence H. Mamiya, *The Black Church in the African American Experience* (Durham: Duke University Press, 1990), p. 121.

23. Marsh, *From Black Muslims to Muslims*, p. 53.

24. David Allan Levine, *Internal Combustion: The Races in Detroit, 1915–1926* (Westport, Conn.: Greenwood Press, 1976), pp. 3, 12, 39, 44.

25. Louis Lomax, *When the Word Is Given* (Cleveland: World, 1963), p. 50.

26. Levine, *Internal Combustion*, p. 137.

27. August Meier and Elliott Rudwick, *From Plantation to Ghetto*, 3rd ed. (New York: Hill and Wang, 1976), p. 260; Louis Lomax, *When the Word Is Given* (Cleveland: World, 1963), p. 50.

28. Marsh, *From Black Muslims to Muslims*, pp. 55–56.

29. Charles Long, *Significations* (Philadelphia: Fortress Press, 1986), p. 2.

30. C. Eric Lincoln, "American Muslim Mission," p. 222.

31. Elijah Muhammad, *Message to the Blackman in America*, p. iii.

32. Sulayman Nyang, "Convergence and Divergence in an Emergent Community: A Study of Challenges Facing U.S. Muslims," in Yvonne Haddad, ed., *The Muslims of America* (New York: Oxford University Press, 1991), p. 239.

33. Elijah Muhammad, *Our Savior Has Arrived* (Chicago: Muhammad's Temple of Islam No. 2, 1974), p. 10.

34. Z. I. Ansari, "Aspects of Black Muslim Theology," *Studia Islamica* (1981), p. 165; Elijah Muhammad, *Message to the Blackman in America*, p. 274.

35. Abubaker Y. Al-Shingiety, "The Muslim as the 'Other': Representation and Self-Image of Muslims in North America," in Yvonne Haddad, ed., *The Muslims of America*, p. 55.

36. John Higham, *Strangers in the Land* (New York: Atheneum, 1963), p. 156.

37. Martin Marty, *The Noise of Conflict, 1919–1941* (Chicago: University of Chicago Press, 1991), pp. 259, 261.

38. Akbar Muhammad, "Interaction between 'Indigenous' and 'Immigrant' Muslims in the United States: Some Positive Trends," *Hijrah Magazine* (March/April 1985), p. 74.

39. Author's interview with Muhammad Abdullah, Hayward, California, September 1989.

40. C. Eric Lincoln, "American Muslim Mission," pp. 222–23.

41. Author's interview with Khallid Muhammad, Santa Barbara, California, December 7, 1993.

42. Judith Stein, *The World of Marcus Garvey* (Baton Rouge: Louisiana State University Press, 1986), pp. 5, 256, 266, 281.

43. Long, *Significations*, p. 1.

44. Elijah Muhammad, *Message to the Blackman in America*, p. 17; Lincoln, *The Black Muslims in America*, p. 14; Nia Damali, *Golden Names for an African People* (Atlanta: Blackwood Press, 1986).

45. Benyon, "Voodoo Cult among Negro Migrants in Detroit," p. 897; Lincoln, *The Black Muslims in America*, p. 14.

46. Elijah Muhammad, *Message to the Blackman in America*, pp. 10, 17; interview with Khallid Muhammad, Santa Barbara, California, December 7, 1993.

47. Akbar Muhammad, "Interaction between 'Indigenous' and 'Immigrant' Muslims in the United States: Some Positive Trends," p. 74; Abubaker Y. Al-

Shingiety, "The Muslim as the 'Other': Representation and Self-Image of Muslims in North America," pp. 53, 58; Lincoln, "The American Muslim Mission in the Context of American Social History."

48. Elijah Muhammad, *The Fall of America* (Chicago: Muhammad's Temple of Islam No. 2, 1973), p. 150.

49. Dennis Hickey and Kenneth C. Wylie, *An Enchanting Darkness: The American Vision of Africa in the Twentieth Century* (East Lansing: Michigan State University Press, 1993), pp. 270–71.

50. See Benyon, "Voodoo Cult among Negro Migrants in Detroit," p. 900.

51. FBI Files: Office Memorandum from Special Agent in charge of Detroit to Director of FBI, Re: W. D. Fard, January 7, 1958, File 100–26356, pp. 214–15, and November 29, 1957, File 100–26356, p. 150; Lincoln, *The Black Muslims in America*; E. U. Essien-Udom, *Black Nationalism*.

52. Z. I. Ansari, "Aspects of Black Muslim Theology," *Studia Islamica* 53 (1981); Z. I. Ansari, "The Religious Doctrines of the Black Muslims of America, 1930–1980," *Journal of Islamic Social Sciences* (1987), p. 200.

53. Muhammad Abdullah, interviews in Hayward, California, June 6, 1987 and October 8, 1989; Akbar Muhammad, "Interaction between 'Indigenous' and 'Immigrant' Muslims in the United States: Some Positive Trends"; for a tantalizing summary of the different stories of Fard's identity, see Prince-A-Cuba, "Black Gods of the Inner City," *Gnosis Magazine* (Fall 1992), pp. 56–63.

At the annual meeting of the American Society of Church History in Chicago in January 1995, Muhammad said that he had seen Fard's handwriting in Arabic and it led him to think of Fard as an "Ottoman Turk." Also, according to Muhammad, "There was something truly Muslim" in the esoteric nature of the teachings of the early Nation of Islam. Thus he believed that Fard was a Sevener affiliated with the Shiites because of their association with "eso-tericism." Also the early Nation of Islam's "mode of prayer—the position of the feet and supplication of the hands" suggested Shiite influence to Akbar Muhammad.

54. FBI Report, Correlation summary in Wallace Don Ford, January 15, 1958, Files 105–63642, pp. 160–66.

55. Ibid., pp. 166–68. FBI Reports: Memorandum, J. Walter Yeagley, Assistant Attorney General, Internal Security Division to Director FBI, Re: Nation of Islam, September 9, 1963 and September 13, 1963, File 105–63642–44. Wallace Don Ford, File 100–44922, pp. 1, 2 and File 100–43165–1S (1), p. 16.

56. Karl Evanzz, *The Judas Factor: The Plot to Kill Malcolm X* (New York: Thunder's Mouth Press, 1992), pp. 132–46; FBI Reports: Memorandum by Special Agent in Charge, Chicago to Director of FBI, Re: Wallace Dodd Fard, July 30 and July 31, 1963, File 105–63642–36, pp. 282, 288; Memo to W. C. Sullivan, Re: Nation of Islam, July 30, 1963, pp. 317–18, File 105–63642; George Bonds, Jr. to J. Edgar Hoover, Re: Ed Montgomery article on Nation of Islam in the *Los Angeles Sunday Examiner,* July 28, 1963, File 105–63642–4B, pp. 328–29; Conversation between Simmons of *The California Eagle* and Elijah Muhammad, File 100–33683, pp. 283–87. Ed Montgomery, "Muslim Founder White Masquerader" *Los Angeles Sunday Examiner,* July 28, 1963; Mohd Yakub Khan, "White Man God for Cult of Islam," *New Crusader* (Chicago) August 15, 1959; Elijah Muhammad, "Beware of Phony Claims," File 105–63642, pp. 340–41. Airtel Airmail, Special Agent in charge, Miami, to Director of FBI, Re: Wallace Don Fard, January 21, 1958, File 105–63642–19, pp. 219–20. Special Agent in charge, Chicago, to Director of FBI, Re: Nation of Islam, March 13, 1963, File 105–38683, p. 260.

57. Beynon, "Voodoo Cult among Negro Migrants in Detroit," p. 902; Malu Halsa, *Elijah Muhammad,* p. 54.

58. Ibid., p. 903; *Detroit News,* November 22, 23, and 27, 1932; *Detroit Free Press,* December 2 and 7, 1932.

59. Elijah Muhammad, *Message to the Blackman in America,* p. 24; Louis Lomax, *When the Word Is Given* (Cleveland: World, 1963), p. 53.

60. Lomax, *When the Word Is Given,* p. 54; Evanzz, *The Judas Factor,* p. 30.

61. Interview with Khallid Muhammad, Santa Barbara, California, December 7, 1993.

62. Elijah Muhammad, *Message to the Blackman in America,* pp. 263–64.

63. Allen, "When Japan Was 'Champion of the Darker Races,'" FBI Report: "Foreign Inspired Agitation among American Negroes," 1942–1943, File 671, pp. 179–94.

64. Ibid.; Marsh, *From Black Muslims to Muslims,* pp. 60–61; Malu Halsan, *Elijah Muhammad* (New York: Chelsea House, 1990), pp. 59–65.

65. Interview with Khallid Muhammad, Santa Barbara, California, December 7, 1993; "Cultists Riot in Courtroom," *Chicago Tribune,* March 6, 1935; Mazaffar Ahmad Zafr, National Vice President of the Ahmadiyya Movement in Islam, has noted that African-American jazz musicians who were converts to Islam kept the spirit of their religion alive in black America in the 1940s and 1950s. They include Ahmad Jamal, Muhammad Sadiq (who played with Charlie Parker and Jay McShan), Dizzy Gillespie, Mustafa Daleel, and Talif Daoud. Interview with author, Chino, California, October 3, 1992.

66. Marsh, *From Black Muslims to Muslims,* pp. 60–61.

67. Manning Marable, *Race, Rebellion and Reform* (Jackson: University Press of Mississippi, 1991), p. 15; Nicholas Lemann, *The Promised Land* (New York: Alfred A. Knopf, 1990).

68. Sydney Ahlstrom, *A History of the American People* (New Haven: Yale University Press, 1972), p. 875; Burkett and Wills, "Afro-American Religious History, 1919–1939," pp. 1–2; Marty, *The Noise of Conflict, 1919–1941,* pp. 258–59.

69. Burkett and Wills, "Afro-American Religious History, 1919–1939," p. 2.

70. John L. Esposito, *Islam: The Straight Path* (New York: Oxford University Press, 1988), pp. 128–29, 146; Larry A. Posten, "Da'wa in the West," in Yvonne Haddad, ed., *The Muslims of America,* p. 125.

71. Akbar Muhammad, "Interaction between 'Indigenous' and 'Immigrant' Muslims in the United States: Some Positive Trends," p. 14; Larry A. Posten, "Da'wa in the West," pp. 125–26.

72. Akbar Muhammad, "Interaction between 'Indigenous' and 'Immigrant' Muslims in the United States: Some Positive Trends," p. 14.

73. Frances Robinson, *Atlas of the Islamic World since 1500* (New York: Facts on File, 1982), pp. 17, 140; Esposito, *Islam: The Straight Path,* p. 1239; Vincent J. Cornell, "Jihad Islam's Struggle for Truth," *Gnosis Magazine* (Fall 1991), p. 19.

74. Albert J. Raboteau, "Ethiopia Shall Stretch Forth Her Hands: Black Destiny in Nineteenth-Century America," *The University Lecture in Religion,* Arizona State University, Tempe, Arizona, January 27, 1983, pp. 11, 14.

CHAPTER 6. MALCOLM X AND HIS SUCCESSORS

1. Quoted in Richard M. Dalfiume, "The 'Forgotten Years' of the Negro Revolution," *Journal of American History* 55 (June 1968), p. 90; Frances Robinson, *Atlas of the Islamic World since 1500* (New York: Facts on File, 1982), p. 158; Cornel West, "Postmodernism and Black America," *Zeta Magazine* (1988), p. 10.

2. Robinson, *Atlas of the Islamic World since 1500,* pp. 158–59.

3. John Esposito, *Islam: The Straight Path* (New York: Oxford University Press, 1988), p. 164.

4. These source materials include **1. Biographical treatments:** Peter Goldman, *The Death and Life of Malcolm X,* 2nd ed. (Urbana: University of Illinois Press, 1979), first published 1973, one of the best and most complete biographies to date; Hakim

Jamal, *From the Dead Level: Malcolm X and Me* (New York: Random House, 1972), written by Malcolm X's cousin-in-law; Benjamin Karim with Peter Skutches and David Gallen, *Remembering Malcolm* (New York: Carroll and Graf, 1992), an intimate insider's perspective on Malcolm X and the Nation of Islam, as told by his former assistant minister in the Harlem mosque; Louis Lomax, *To Kill a Black Man* (Los Angeles: Holloway House, 1968); Malcolm X with Alex Haley, *The Autobiography of Malcolm X* (New York: Ballantine, 1986), first published 1964, the most important source for research and a classic in African-American literature; Bruce Perry, *Malcolm: The Life of a Man Who Changed Black America* (Barrytown, N.Y.: Station Hill, 1991), a flawed psychological portrait of Malcolm X that is notable for its emphasis on sensationalism; William Strickland and Cheryll Y. Greene, *Malcolm X: Make It Plain* (New York: Viking, 1994), complete with a brilliant and revised biography, oral history selections and striking photographs (a companion to the PBS documentary film with the same title), the best single source of information on Malcolm X's life; and Eugene Victor Wolfenstein, *The Victims of Democracy: Malcolm X and the Black Revolution* (Berkeley: University of California Press, 1981), a complicated and intriguing study that utilizes Marxist and Freudian theory to examine Malcolm's life. **2. Speeches:** George Breitman, ed., *Malcolm X Speaks* (New York: Grove, 1965) and *By Any Means Necessary* (New York: Pathfinder, 1970), speeches, interviews, and documents that date from Malcolm X's split with the Nation of Islam to his death; George Breitman, ed., *Malcolm X on Afro-American History* (New York: Pathfinder, 1970); Steve Clarke, ed., *February 1965: The Final Speeches of Malcolm X* (New York: Pathfinder, 1992), speeches and interviews from the last three weeks of Malcolm X's life; Archie Epps, ed., *Malcolm X: Speeches at Harvard* (New York: Pragon House, 1991), first published in 1968 as *The Speeches of Malcolm X at Harvard*, includes an interpretive essay (written by the editor of the volume) and speeches from 1961 to 1964; Benjamin Karim, ed., *The End of White World Supremacy* (New York: Seaver, 1971), speeches from Malcolm X's final year in the Nation of Islam; and Bruce Perry, ed., *Malcolm X: The Last Speeches* (New York: Pathfinder, 1989). **3. Assassination studies:** Karl Evanzz, *The Judas Factor: The Plot to Kill Malcolm X* (New York: Thunder's Mouth, 1992), the best of this genre; and Michael Friedly, *Malcolm X: The Assassination* (New York: Carroll and Graf/Richard Gallen, 1992). **4. Political studies:** George Breitman, *The Last Year of Malcolm X: The Evolution of a Revolutionary* (New York: Merit, 1967); James H. Cone, *Martin and Malcolm and America: A Dream or a Nightmare* (Maryknoll, N.Y.: Orbis, 1991), brilliant, the best of this genre, but flawed in its dialectical treatment of Malcolm and King; Y. N. Kly, ed., *The Black Book: The True Political Philosophy of Malcolm X* (Atlanta: Clarity Press, 1986); and Shawna Maglangbayan, *Garvey, Lumumba, Malcolm: Nationalist-Separatists* (Chicago: Third World Press, 1972). **5. Essays and interviews:** Steven Barboza, *American Jihad: Islam after Malcolm X* (New York: Doubleday, 1994)—the interviews in this book reveal much new information about Malcolm X and Islam in America; John Henrik Clark, ed., *Malcolm X: The Man and His Times* (New York: Collier, 1969), still the best collection of essays on Malcolm X; Alex Haley, ed., *The Playboy Interviews* (New York: Ballantine, 1962); Gerald Horne, "'Myth' and the Making of Malcolm X," *American Historical Review* 98 (April 1993): 440–50; "Malcolm X: A Tribute," *Steppingstones* (Winter 1983); Manning Marable, "On Malcolm X: His Message and Meaning," *Open Magazine Pamphlet Scenes* (November 1992); Joe Wood, ed., *Malcolm X: In Our Own Image* (New York: St. Martin's, 1992). **6. Nation of Islam studies:** E. U. Essien-Udom, *Black Nationalism* (Chicago: University of Chicago, 1962); C. Eric Lincoln, *The Black Muslims in America* (Boston: Beacon, 1961), the classic study of the Nation of Islam; Louis Lomax, *When the Word Is Given* (Westport, Conn.: Greenwood Press, 1975), first published 1963, a fascinating study by the late journalist who was a personal friend of Malcolm X; and Clifton E. Marsh, *From Black Muslims to Muslims*

(Metuchen, N.J.: Scarecrow, 1984). **7. FBI materials:** Clayborne Carson, Spike Lee, and David Gallen, *Malcolm X: The FBI File* (New York: Carroll and Graf, 1991).

5. Strickland and Greene, *Malcolm X: Make It Plain,* pp. 4–5.

6. Ibid, pp. 8–9. Haley, *The Autobiography of Malcolm X,* Chapter 1. (Hereafter cited as Malcolm X, *The Autobiography.*)

7. Steven Barboza interview with Attallah Shabazz, *American Jihad,* pp. 211–12. Also see Jan Carew, *Ghosts in Our Blood: With Malcolm X in Africa, England, and the Caribbean* (Chicago: Lawrence Hill, 1994) for an analysis of Malcolm X's West Indian heritage in his identity transformation in the last year of his life.

8. Strickland and Greene, *Malcolm X: Make It Plain,* pp. 10–11; also see the oral histories of Wilfred and Philbert Little, on p. 21. Malcolm X, *The Autobiography,* Chapter 1. Cone, *Martin and Malcolm and America,* Chapter 4.

9. Wilfred Little's oral history in Strickland and Greene, *Malcolm X: Make It Plain,* p. 23.

10. Ibid., p. 20.

11. Malcolm X, *The Autobiography,* p. 6.

12. Malcolm X, *The Autobiography,* p. 7; Abdul Aziz Omar (Philbert Little), oral history in Strickland and Greene, *Malcolm X: Make It Plain,* p. 15.

13. Malcolm X, *The Autobiography,* Chapter 1; Cone, *Martin and Malcolm and America,* pp. 42–45. Goldman, *The Death and Life of Malcolm X,* pp. 28–29. See the oral histories of Wilfred Little, Abdul Aziz Omar, Yvonne Woodward, Jenny Washington, and Florentine Baril in Strickland and Greene, *Malcolm X: Make It Plain,* pp. 24–29, 33; see also the physician's certificate verifying Louise Little's insanity, p. 32.

14. Malcolm X, *The Autobiography,* Chapter 2. Quotation cited in Cone, *Martin and Malcolm and America,* p. 38.

15. Malcolm X, *The Autobiography,* Chapter 2. Oral histories of Wilfred Little, Jim Cotton, and Cyril McGuire in Strickland and Greene. *Malcolm X: Make It Plain,* p. 34. Cone, *Martin and Malcolm and America,* pp. 45–47. Quotation cited in Carson et al., *Malcolm X: The FBI File,* p. 58. Wolfenstein, *The Victims of Democracy,* Chapter 4.

16. Strickland and Greene, *Malcolm X: Make It Plain,* p. 6. Wolfenstein, *The Victims of Democracy,* Chapter 1.

17. Cone, *Martin and Malcolm and America,* Chapter 2.

18. Malcolm X, *The Autobiography,* Chapter 3. Strickland and Greene, *Malcolm X: Make It Plain,* p. 36, photographs, pp. 35, 48; oral history of Ella Collins, p. 35. Goldman, *The Death and Life of Malcolm X,* p. 30. Cone, *Martin and Malcolm and America,* p. 47. Wolfenstein, *The Victims of Democracy,* p. 153.

19. Malcolm X, *The Autobiography,* Chapters 3–9.

20. Ella's house was at 72 Dale Street, which was in lower Roxbury and not on "the hill" in upper Roxbury as other biographical accounts have reported. Also there were not enough black people in Roxbury to make a real ghetto in the 1940s. The South End was the black ghetto section of Boston during this period. Ibid., Chapters 3–4. Cone, *Martin and Malcolm and America,* pp. 47–48. Strickland and Greene, *Malcolm X: Make It Plain,* p. 38; oral histories of Malcolm Jarvis, Wilfred Little, Ella Collins, and Yvonne Woodward, pp. 46–51, 52–55; photographs, pp. 46–51; and map of Malcolm X's Boston years, p. 57.

21. Malcolm X, *The Autobiography,* Chapters 5–6. Oral histories of Malcolm Jarvis and Abdul Aziz Omar in Strickland and Greene, *Malcolm X: Make It Plain,* p. 56.

22. Malcolm X, *The Autobiography,* pp. 52–55. Horne, "'Myth' and the Making of Malcolm X," p. 447.

23. Malcolm X, *The Autobiography,* Chapters 9–10. Malcolm was involved in an interracial burglary ring and believed that he was given a stiffer sentence because of his relationships with white women. See the oral histories of Malcolm Jarvis and Ella Collins in Strickland and Greene, *Malcolm X: Make It Plain,* pp. 57–59;

Malcolm's court records, p. 58; a photograph of a Charlestown prison, p. 59; and Malcolm's mug shots, p. 37.

24. Malcolm X, *The Autobiography*, Chapter 10. See the oral histories of Wilfred Little, Abdul Aziz Omar, and Cyril McGuire in Strickland and Greene, *Malcolm X: Make It Plain*, pp. 59–60; photograph of the Little brothers in 1949, p. 60.

25. Ibid.

26. Strickland and Greene, *Malcolm X: Make It Plain*, pp. 39–40. Malcolm X, *The Autobiography*, pp. 161–70.

27. Barboza, *American Jihad*, p. 18.

28. Strickland and Greene, *Malcolm X: Make It Plain*, pp. 41–42. Karim, *Remembering Malcolm*, pp. 95–106.

29. Malcolm X, *The Autobiography*, Chapter 11. Strickland and Green, *Malcolm X: Make It Plain*, p. 41; oral histories of Malcolm Jarvis and Stanley Jones, pp. 62–64.

30. Ibid.

31. Malcolm X, *The Autobiography*, pp. 174–79.

32. Strickland and Greene, *Malcolm X: Make It Plain*, p. 42.

33. Marable, *Race, Reform, and Rebellion*, p. 117; Richard M. Dalfiume, "The 'Forgotten Years' of the Negro Revolution," *Journal of American History* 55 (June 1968): 106.

34. Herbert Garfinkel, *When Negroes March* (New York: Atheneum, 1969), pp. 2–3; Dalfiume, "The 'Forgotten Years' of the Negro Revolution," p. 98.

35. Nicholas Lemann, *The Promised Land: The Great Migration and How It Changed America* (New York: Alfred A. Knopf, 1990), dustcover; Gary Nash, "The Voices of Real People," *Los Angeles Times Book Review*, November 3, 1991, p. 9. Gerald Horne has theorized that the demise of the black Left after 1948 was in part responsible for white America's partial tolerance of the Nation of Islam, which—in spite of its controversial race rhetoric—supported capitalism. See Horne, "Myth and the Making of Malcolm X," pp. 442–43.

36. Evanzz, *The Judas Factor*, pp. 3–4.

37. Ibid., pp. 10–12. Malcolm X, *The Autobiography*, p. 222. FBI File 100–399321, "Malcolm K. Little," May 4, 1953; see Carson et al., *Malcolm X: The FBI File*, pp. 97–115.

38. See Malcolm's letters to Elijah Muhammad, in Evanzz, *The Judas Factor*, pp. 12–14. FBI File 100–399321. Malcolm K. Little, May 4, 1953; see Carson et al., *Malcolm X: The FBI File*, pp. 97–115.

39. Abdul Aziz oral history in Strickland and Greene, *Malcolm X: Make It Plain*, p. 65.

40. Marsh, from *Black Muslims to Muslims*, p. 71. Malcolm stayed with his sister Ella in Boston for one day immediately after he was released from prison. See Malcolm X, *The Autobiography*, p. 214.

41. Videotape of "A Conversation with Imam W. Deen Mohammed: Muslim American Spokesman." Duke University Living History Program, April 16, 1992, Part 1.

42. Imam Warith Deen Mohammed oral history in Strickland and Greene, *Malcolm X: Make It Plain*, p. 61.

43. Ibid., pp. 70–72. Malcolm X, *The Autobiography*, Chapter 13.

44. See Lincoln, *The Black Muslims in America*; Essien-Udom, *Black Nationalism*; Evanzz, *The Judas Factor*; Strickland and Greene, *Malcolm X: Make It Plain*; Malcolm X, *The Autobiography*; Lomax, *When the Word Is Given*; and Karim, *Remembering Malcolm*.

45. Strickland and Greene, *Malcolm X: Make It Plain*, pp. 43–44.

46. Lomax, *When the Word Is Given*, pp. 71–72. Evanzz, *The Judas Factor*, pp. 77–78. Malcolm X left New York on July 5, 1959 and traveled to Egypt, Saudi Arabia, Iran, Syria, and Ghana on behalf of the Nation of Islam. On his passport issued for

this tour, on May 27, 1959, he was first designated as Malik El-Shabazz. See FBI File 105–8999, November 17, 1959, New York office, "Malcolm K. Little" in Carson et al., *Malcolm X: The FBI File,* pp. 173–80. Malcolm's work as an international ambassador for the Nation of Islam had begun in June 1956, when he was invited by Adam Clayton Powell, Jr. to speak on the occasion of a visit by Achmad Sukarno, the Muslim president of Indonesia, to the Abyssinian Baptist Church in New York. On July 26, 1958, Malcolm X was part of a group of New York City black leaders who met with President Nkrumah of Ghana. Malcolm X talked with Nkrumah again on August 17, 1958. See Evanzz *The Judas Factor,* pp. 67–74.

47. Lomax, *When the Word Is Given,* p. 69.

48. Frances Robinson, *Atlas of the Islamic World since 1500* (New York: Facts on File, 1982), pp. 93–95.

49. Haddad and Smith, *Mission to America,* p. 1.

50. Lomax, *When the Word Is Given,* p. 73.

51. Ibid., p. 66.

52. Franklin, *Black Self-Determination,* p. 6.

53. Author's interview with Khallid Abdul Muhammad, former national assistant to the Honorable Minister Louis Farrakhan, in Santa Barbara, California on December 7, 1993.

54. Lomax, *When the Word Is Given,* pp. 131–32.

55. Esposito, *Islam: The Straight Path,* pp. 167–68.

56. *The Islamic Threat* (New York: Oxford University Press, 1992), p. 72.

57. Malcolm X, "Message to the Grass Roots," November 9, 1963, Detroit, Michigan, in Breitman, ed., *Malcolm X Speaks,* pp. 5–6.

58. Author's interview with Muhammad Abdullah, June 30, 1987 and October 16, 1989, in Hayward, California.

59. Author's interview with Abid Haneef, Burlington, Massachusetts, December 29, 1986; A. G. Soofi, "Islam and 'Black Moslems,'" *The Review of Religions* 58 (July 1964), p. 245. A. R. Khan Bengalee, "The Ahmadiyya Movement in Islam vs. the So-called Black Muslim Movement of America," *The Review of Religions* 60 (January 1966), p. 7.

60. See "Ahmadiyya Muslim Missionary in the Western Hemisphere," *The Review of Religions* 56 (October 1962), p. 38; "A New Mosque in America," *The Review of Religions* 60 (January 1966), pp. 31–32. Mirza Mubarak Ahmad, *Our Foreign Missions* (Rabwah, West Pakistan: Ahmadiyya Muslim Foreign Missions, 1965), pp. 62–63; *The Review of Religions* (May 1959), p. 1. Bengalee, "The Solution of the Racial Problem," *The Review of Religions* 57 (September 1963), pp. 531–33. Soofi, "Letter from America," *The Review of Religions* (November 1967), pp. 344–47; "Letter from America," *The Review of Religions* 64 (March 1969), pp. 102–103; "Letter from America," *The Review of Religions* 64 (March 1969), p. 106.

61. Akbar Muhammad, "Interaction between 'Indigenous' and 'Immigrant' Muslims in the United States," p. 14. Lomax, *When the Word Is Given,* photograph opposite p. 97.

62. Strickland and Greene, *Malcolm X: Make It Plain,* p. 94.

63. FBI File 100–399321, "Malcolm X Little," July 16, 1959, in Carson et al., *Malcolm X: The FBI File,* pp. 159–72. "The Hate That Hate Produced" was shown on the "Newsbeat" show on WNTA-TV, Channel 13, New York.

64. Strickland and Greene, *Malcolm X: Make It Plain,* p. 85.

65. Evanzz, *The Judas Factor,* p. 65.

66. Ibid., pp. 66–67.

67. Ibid., pp. 78–79.

68. Strickland and Greene, *Malcolm X: Make It Plain,* p. 84. John Woodford, "Testing America's Promise of Free Speech: *Muhammad Speaks* in the 1960s: A Memoir," *Voices of the African Diaspora* (CAAS, University of Michigan) 7, No. 3

(Fall 1991), pp. 3–16. "A Conversation with Imam W. Deen Mohammed," Duke University. The Nation of Islam had columns in the New York *Amsterdam News* and the Los Angeles *Herald Dispatch* in the 1950s.

69. Lincoln, *The Black Muslims in America*, p. xvii. Essien-Udom, *Black Nationalism*. Lomax, *When the Word Is Given*.

70. Malcolm X, *The Autobiography*, p. 247.

71. Essien-Udom, *Black Nationalism*, pp. 57, 122, 325, 326.

72. Lomax, *When the Word Is Given*, p. 19.

73. Strickland and Greene, *Malcolm X: Make It Plain*, p. 77. Malcolm X, *The Autobiography*, pp. 236–39.

74. Yohanan Friedmann, *Prophecy Continuous* (Berkeley: University of California Press, 1989), p. 177.

75. Oral history of Amina Rahman in Strickland and Greene, *Malcolm X: Make It Plain*, p. 113.

76. Benjamin Karim oral history in ibid., p. 115.

77. "A Conversation with Imam Warith Deen Mohammed."

78. Imam Warith Deen Mohammed oral history in Strickland and Greene, *Malcolm X: Make It Plain*, p. 126.

79. Abul Khatib, "The Need for Jihad," *Gnosis Magazine* (Fall 1991): p. 24.

80. "A Conversation with Imam Warith Deen Mohammed," Duke University.

81. See Elijah Muhammad, *Message to the Blackman in America* (Chicago: Muhammad Mosque of Islam No. 2, 1965), for an explication of this program.

82. Evanzz, *The Judas Factor*, Chapters 7 and 8; Rosemari Mealy, *Fidel and Malcolm X* (New York: Ocean Press, 1993).

83. Marable, "On Malcolm X," p. 6.

84. Strickland and Greene, *Malcolm X: Make It Plain*, p. 83.

85. Evanzz, *The Judas Factor*, p. 85; Goldman, *The Death and Life of Malcolm X*, pp. 97–99. FBI file No. 100–399321, "Malcolm X. Little," November 16, 1962 in Carson et al., *Malcolm X: The FBI File*, pp. 217–19.

86. Karim, *Remembering Malcolm*, pp. 134–35; Strickland and Greene, *Malcolm X: Make It Plain*, p. 81.

87. Evanzz, *The Judas Factor*, pp. 119–22.

88. *Los Angeles Herald Dispatch*, May 10, 1962.

89. Ibid., May 24, 1962.

90. Strickland and Greene, *Malcolm X: Make It Plain*, p. 82.

91. Karim, *Remembering Malcolm*, p. 138.

92. Marable, "On Malcolm X," p. 6.

93. Ibid., p. 7.

94. Breitman, ed., *Malcolm X Speaks*, pp. 3–4.

95. Ibid., pp. 8–9.

96. Strickland and Greene, *Malcolm X: Make It Plain*, p. 83.

97. Ibid., p. 83.

98. Barboza, *American Jihad*, pp. 99–114, 268–71.

99. Strickland and Greene, *Malcolm X: Make It Plain*, pp. 90–91.

100. Breitman, *Malcolm X Speaks*, pp. 10–11.

101. Alex Haley, *The Playboy Interviews* (New York: Ballantine), pp. ix-x.

102. Ibid., pp. 20–22.

103. Marable, "On Malcolm X," pp. 10–11.

104. FBI File No. 100–399321, "Malcolm X. Little," November 15, 1963 in Carson et al., *Malcolm X: The FBI File*, pp. 242–44.

105. Malcolm X, *The Autobiography*, pp. 294–99.

106. Ibid., pp. 300–302.

107. "A Conversation with Imam Warith Deen Mohammed," Duke University.

108. Ibid.

109. Ibid.

110. Ibid., pp. 308–309.

111. Carson et al., *Malcolm X: The FBI File*, pp. 72–73.

112. Breitman, *The Last Year of Malcolm X*, p. 7.

113. Ibid., p. 22.

114. Malcolm X, *The Autobiography*, Chapters 17 and 18.

115. Breitman, *Malcolm X Speaks*, pp. 20–21.

116. Malcolm X, *The Autobiography*, pp. 81, 82.

117. Ibid., pp. 338–39.

118. Shawna Maglangbayan, *Garvey, Lumumba, Malcolm: Nationalist-Separatists* (Chicago: Third World Press, 1972), Part 3.

119. Ibid.

120. Ibid.

121. Bruce Perry, ed., *Malcolm X: The Last Speeches* (New York: Pathfinder, 1989), pp. 104–106.

122. Ibid.

123. Mamiya, "From Black Muslim to Bilalian," in Koszegi and Melton, *Islam in North America: A Sourcebook* (New York: Garland, 1992).

124. Ruby M. and E. U. Essien-Udom, "Malcolm X: An International Man," in Clarke, ed., *Malcolm X: The Man and His Times*, pp. 255–67.

125. Ibid., pp. 246–47.

126. Alice Windom and John Henrik Clarke oral histories in Strickland and Greene, *Malcolm X: Make It Plain*, pp. 180–81.

127. Breitman, ed., *By Any Means Necessary*, pp. 33–67.

128. Robert Little, John Henrik Clarke, and Percy Sutton oral histories in Strickland and Greene, *Malcolm X: Make It Plain*, pp. 174, 176, 189.

129. Marsh, *From Black Muslims to Muslims*, pp. 83–87.

130. Friedly, *Malcolm X: The Assassination*, p. 210. Evanzz, *The Judas Factor*, p. xxiv.

131. Friedly, *Malcolm X: The Assassination*, pp. 210–11.

132. Evanzz, *The Judas Factor*, pp. xix–xxiv.

133. Ibid.

134. Breitman, ed., *Malcolm X Speaks*, pp. 21–44.

135. Breitman, ed., *Malcolm X: By Any Means Necessary*, pp. 33–67.

136. Breitman, ed., *Malcolm X Speaks*, pp. 72–87.

137. Clark, *February 1965: The Final Speeches*, pp. 106–70. Marable, "On Malcolm X," pp. 14–15.

138. Mamiya, "From Black Muslim to Bilalian," in Koszegi and Melton, eds. *Islam in North America*, pp. 166–69. "Interview with Imam Warith Deen Mohammed," Duke University. Louis Farrakhan, *A Torchlight for America* (Chicago: FCN, 1993). Martha F. Lee, *The Nation of Islam: An American Millenarian Movement* (New York: Edwin Mellen, 1988), pp. 77–78.

139. Marsh, *From Black Muslims to Muslims*, pp. 90–91.

140. Ibid., pp. 90–92. Lincoln, "American Muslim Mission in the Context of American Social History," pp. 216, 224.

141. Marsh, *From Black Muslims to Muslims*, pp. 92–93.

142. Ibid., p. 95. Lee offers the best detailed analysis of the changes in Chapter 4 of *The Nation of Islam: An American Millenarian Movement*. Mohammed's theological and ritual innovations can be traced in his books: *The Teachings of W. D. Muhammad* (Chicago: The Honorable Elijah Muhammad Mosque No. 2, 1976); *Book of Muslim Names* (Chicago: Honorable Elijah Muhammad Mosque No. 2, 1976); *The Man and the Woman in Islam* (Chicago: The Honorable Elijah Muhammad Mosque No. 2, 1976); *As the Light Shineth from the East* (Chicago: WDM Publishing, 1980); *Prayer and al-Islam* (Chicago: Muhammad Islamic Foundation, 1982); *Imam*

W. Deen Muhammad Speaks from Harlem, N.Y. (Chicago: W. D. Muhammad Publications, 1984); and *An African-American Genesis* (Chicago: Progressions, 1986). See also Mattias Gardell, "The Sun of Islam Will Rise in the West: Minister Farrakhan and the Nation of Islam in the Latter Days," in Yvonne Y. Haddad and Jane I. Smith, eds., *Muslim Communities in North America* (Albany: State University of New York Press, 1994).

143. Lincoln, "American Muslim Mission in the Context of American Social History," p. 228. Elaine Rivera, "The Very Positive Face of Islam: Little Known Muslim Leader Has a Huge Following in U.S.," *Houston Chronicle,* May 21, 1994.

144. Ibid.

145. Ibid., pp. 228–29.

146. Ibid., pp. 222–31.

147. Marsh, *From Black Muslims to Muslims,* pp. 99–100.

148. "A Conversation with Imam W. Deen Mohammed."

149. Lawrence H. Mamiya, "Minister Louis Farrakhan and the Final Call: Schism in the Muslim Movement," in *The Muslim Community in North America,* p. 237. Lee, *The Nation of Islam: An American Millenarian Movement,* p. 94.

150. Ibid., pp. 242–43. See Lee, *The Nation of Islam: An American Millenarian Movement,* Chapter 5 for details. C. Eric Lincoln, *The Black Muslims in America,* 3rd ed. (Trenton, N.J.: Africa World Press, 1994), p. 267; McCloud, *African American Islam,* pp. 83–88.

151. Ibid., pp. 238–42.

152. Louis Farrakhan, "Who Is God," Christ Universal Temple, Chicago, Illinois, February 24, 1991, videotape. Lincoln, *The Black Muslims in America,* p. 268.

153. Ibid., pp. 245–46. Warith Deen Mohammed discusses this Muslim "work ethic" in *An African-American Genesis,* pp. 37–38.

154. Ibid.

155. Ibid., pp. 250–51.

156. Ibid., pp. 252–53.

157. Ibid. George E. Curry, "Farrakhan, Jesse, and Jews," *Emerge,* July/August 1994, pp. 28–40. See also Gardell "The Sun of Islam Will Rise in the West," pp. 36–40.

158. *New York Times Index,* May 1–15, 1985 (New York: New York Times Publishing, 1985): p. 49.

159. Farrakhan, "Who Is God," videotape.

160. Farrakhan interview. "Cliff Kelley Show," WGCI Radio Station, Chicago, Illinois, 1990; Sulayman S. Nyang, "Convergence and Divergence in an Emergent Community: A Study of Challenges Facing U.S. Muslims," in *The Muslims of America,* p. 245.

161. Farrakhan interview, "Cliff Kelley Show."

162. *A Response to the Article Entitled "The Qadiyanies: A Non-Muslim Minority in Pakistan"* (Athens, Ohio: Faye-i-Umar Press, n.d.), pp. 1, 29; *New York Times Index 1982* (New York: New York Times Publishing, 1983), p. 490; *New York Times Index* (May 16–31, 1985), p. 63.

163. Telephone interview with Muhammad Afzal Mirza, Ahmadi missionary in charge of the midwest region, Chicago, Illinois, January 22, 1986.

164. Interview, Mubarak Ahmad, Ahmadi missionary in charge of the United States, Washington, D.C., November 22, 1986. McCloud, *African American Islam,* p. 57. Author's interview with Maneer Hamid. Booklet, "Hazrat Mirza Tahir Ahmad" (n.d.), p. 4.

165. Ibid.

166. Interview, Muhammad Abdullah, Hayward, Calif., June 30, 1987.

167. Barboza, *American Jihad,* pp. 213–22.

168. McCloud, *African American Islam,* pp. 64–69.

169. Ibid., pp. 69–72.

170. Ibid., pp. 85–88.

171. Ibid., pp. 88–94.

172. Wilson J. Moses, *Black Messiahs and Uncle Toms* (University Park: Pennsylvania State University Press, 1982), p. 191.

173. Haddad and Smith, *Mission to America,* Chapter 5. Isa Muhammad's publications are voluminous. The selective bibliography below comes from *Mission to America,* pp. 215–16. Unless otherwise indicated, these works were all published in Brooklyn by Ansaru Allah Community. Muhammad, Isa, "Al Imam Isa Visits Egypt 1981" (n.d.), "Al Imam Isa Visits the City of Brotherly Love" (1979), *Al-Quran al-Muqaddasa: Al-Wasiyya al-Akhirah* (1977), *The Ansar Cult* (1988), "Are the Ansars (in the West) a Self-Made Sect?" (n.d.), *The Book of Laam* (Brooklyn: Nubian Islam Hebrews, n.d.), "Childhood and Reproduction" (n.d.), "Christ Is the Answer" (n.d.), "Disco Music: The Universal Language of Good or Evil?" (n.d.), "The Dog" (n.d.), "Four Horsemen of the Apocalypse: Can the Holy Qu'ran Solve It?" (n.d.), "Hadrat Faatimah" (n.d.), *The Holy Quran: The Last Testament* (n.p.: published by the author, 1977), "Islamic Beauty Aids and Customs" (n.d.), "Islamic Cookery" (n.d.), "Islamic Marriage Ceremony and Polygamy" (1977), "Men Who Dress in Women's Clothes" (n.d.), "Menstruation" (n.d.), "The Muslim Woman" (n.d.), "The Night of the 100 Raka'at" (n.d.), "The Paleman" (n.d.), "Racism in Islam" (n.d.), "The Sex Life of a Muslim" (n.d.), "Sons of Canaan" (n.d.), "Sons of the Green Light" (n.d.), "Thoughts of Muslim Women in Poetry" (n.d.), "What and Where Is Hell?" (n.d.), "Why Allah Should Not Be Called God" (n.d.), "Why the Beard?" (n.d.), "Why the Nosering?" (n.d.), "Why the Veil?" (n.d.), "Your Body" (n.d.).

174. Author's telephone interview with P. Q. Halifu, December 1993. Cooper, "Muslims in America," p. 370. Nyang, "Islam in the United States of America: A Review of the Sources" in Koszengi and Milton, eds., *Islam in North America,* pp. 15–17. Author's interview with Abdul-Qawi-Bey, Santa Barbara, Calif., September 1993; *The Moorish Chronicles* 1, No. 1 (May 1993).

175. Haddad, *The Muslims of America,* p. 3.

176. Mary H. Cooper, "Muslims in America," *CQ Researcher* (April 30, 1993), p. 364.

177. Ari L. Goldman, "Mainstream Islam Rapidly Embraced by Black American," *The New York Times,* February 21, 1989, pp. A1, B34.

178. Nyang, "Convergence and Divergence in an Emergent Community," in *The Muslims of America,* pp. 240–42. See Christine Kollars, "Masjid ul-Mutkabir: The Portrait of an African American Orthodox Muslim Community," in Haddad and Smith, eds., *Muslim Communities in North America,* pp. 475–500.

179. In a recent "Time/CNN poll of 504 African-Americans," 67 percent of the respondents rated Farrakhan "an effective leader." According to this poll, African Americans are familiar with Farrakhan "more than any other black political figure except Jesse Jackson and Supreme Court Justice Clarence Thomas." See William A. Henry III, "Pride and Prejudice," *Time,* February 28, 1994, p. 32. Also a recent poll in the *Chicago Sun-Times* indicated "a very favorable approval rating for Louis Farrakhan" among African Americans. See Ron Daniels, "The Farrakhan Phenomenon," *Z Magazine,* June 1994, p. 17.

180. Daniels, "The Farrakhan Phenomenon, pp. 15, 17.

EPILOGUE. COMMODIFICATION OF IDENTITY

1. James C. Scott, *Domination and the Arts of Resistance: Hidden Transcripts* (New Haven: Yale University Press, 1990), pp. 224, 227.

2. Ibid., p. 226.

3. Provocative works that analyze the persistence of racism in America at the end of the century include Derrick Bell, *Faces at the Bottom of the Well: The Permanence of Racism* (New York: Basic Books, 1992) and *And We Are Not Saved: The Elusive Quest for Racial Justice* (New York: Basic Books, 1987); Andrew Hacker, *Two Nations: Black and White, Separate, Hostile, Unequal* (New York: Scribner's, 1992); and Manning Marable, *Race, Reform, and Rebellion: The Second Reconstruction in Black America, 1945–1990,* 2nd ed. (Jackson: University Press of Mississippi, 1992).

4. Akbar Muhammad, "Interaction between 'Indigenous' and 'Immigrant' Muslims in the United States: Some Positive Trends," *Hijrah Magazine* (March/April 1985), 74.

5. Cornel West, "Postmodernism and Black America," *Zeta Magazine* (1988), 12.

6. Joe Wood, ed., *Malcolm X: In Our Own Image* (New York: St. Martin's, 1992). Gerald Horne, "Myth and the Making of 'Malcolm X,'" *American Historical Review* 98 (April 1993): 440–50. Marvin X and Faruk, "Islam and Black Art: An Interview with Le Roi Jones," *Negro Digest* (January 1969): 4–10, 77–80. Ira Berkow, "After Three Years in Prison, Tyson Gains His Freedom," *New York Times,* March 26, 1995. Alex Haley, *Roots: The Saga of an American Family* (Garden City, N.Y.: Doubleday, 1976). Ishmael Reed, *Mumbo Jumbo* (New York: Macmillan, 1972). Nathan McCall, *Makes Me Wanna Holler: A Young Black Man in America* (New York: Random House, 1994). Sanyika Shakur, A.K.A. Monster Kody Scott, *Monster: The Autobiography of an L.A. Gang Member* (New York: Atlantic Monthly Press, 1993). Howie Evans, "Mike Tyson: 'I'll Take My Thoughts to My Grave,'" *Amsterdam News* 85, No. 25, Saturday, June 18, 1994. Thomas Hauser, *Muhammad Ali: His Life and Times* (New York: Simon and Schuster, 1991). According to Ernest Allen, Jr., many of the Islamic rappers are members of the Five Percent Nation of Islam, a splinter group of the Nation of Islam that was founded in Harlem by Clarence 13X in 1964. The Five Percenters focus on the secret literature of W. D. Fard and believe that all black men are gods. They see themselves in the five percent of African Americans who are the "poor righteous teachers" of their race. In their significations, Harlem is Mecca, Brooklyn is Medina, and women are "'Moons' who [bask] in the luminous wisdom of male 'Suns'." Allen, "Making the Strong Survive: The Contours and Contradictions of Message Rap" in William Eric Perkins, ed., *Droppin' Science: Critical Essays on Rap Music and Hiphop Culture* (Philadelphia: Temple University Press, 1996). Joseph D. Eure and James G. Spudy, eds., *Nation Conscious Rap* (New York: P. C. International Press). Lawrence A. Stanley, ed., *Rap: The Lyrics* (New York: Penguin, 1992). Julie Dash, *Daughters of the Dust: The Making of an African American Woman's Film* (New York: New Press, 1992). Spike Lee with Lisa Jones, *Do the Right Thing* (New York: Fireside, 1989). Spike Lee with Ralph Wiley, *By Any Means Necessary: The Trials and Tribulations of the Making of* Malcolm X (New York: Hyperion, 1992).

7. Daniels, "The Farrakhan Phenomenon," p. 17. Eugene Cose, *The Rage of a Privileged Class* (New York: HarperCollins, 1993). Faith Berry, "The 'King' of the Hour at the March on Washington," *The Miami Times,* Thursday, September 8, 1983. Faith Berry to Minister Louis Farrakhan, October 31, 1983; Minister Louis Farrakhan to Faith Berry, November 3, 1983.

8. Minister Louis Farrakhan, *A Torchlight for America* (Chicago: FCN, 1993). Richard Muhammad, "Farrakhan Draws 9,000 Men to Washington, D.C. Meeting: Black Men on the Move," *The Final Call,* April 13, 1994. "Muhammad University of Islam, Educating Our Own," *The Final Call,* March 16, 1994. Minister Ava Muhammad, *Your Creative Force* (1993), *Principles of Femininity* (1991), and *A Light-Giving Sun* (1991), videocassettes. Daniels, "The Farrakhan Phenomenon," p. 18.

9. Steven Barboza, *American Jihad: Islam after Malcolm X* (New York: Doubleday, 1994), p. 18. "Ministry of Rage: Louis Farrakhan Spews Racist Venom at Jews and All White America. Why Do So Many Blacks Say He Speaks for Them?" *Time,*

February 28, 1994, the cover. The Historical Research Department, The Nation of Islam, *The Secret Relationship between Blacks and Jews* (Chicago: The Nation of Islam, 1991). For a concise summary of Khallid Muhammad's controversial speech at Kean College in New Jersey on November 19, 1993, see William A. Henry III, "Pride and Prejudice," *Time,* February 28, 1994, pp. 11, 20–34. After the speech, Farrakhan dismissed Muhammad from his official duties on behalf of the Nation of Islam. However, Khallid Muhammad still presents the message of Minister Louis Farrakhan and the Nation of Islam in numerous speaking engagements across the country. He appears to have a close working association with Unity Nation, a student group started at Howard University in 1988 to promote black nationalism. Carla Hall, "Ex-Farrakhan Aide Brings His War of Words to L.A.," *Los Angeles Times,* May 27, 1994. Tom Gorman and Psyche Pascual, "Ex-Aide to Farrakhan Shot in Legs," *Los Angeles Times,* May 30, 1994. Tom Gorman and Carla Hall, "Muhammad Attack Suspect Heavily Armed," *Los Angeles Times,* May 31, 1994. Andrea Ford and Mark Arax, "Muhammad Case Suspect Has a Record of Violence," *Los Angeles Times,* June 1, 1994. The above articles from the *Los Angeles Times* refer to the attempted assassination of Khallid Muhammad at the University of California, Riverside on May 27, 1994 by James E. Bess, a former Nation of Islam minister. See also the letter from the Office of the Chancellor, Riverside, California to Friends of the University of California, Riverside, May 30, 1994. The Nation of Islam's latest media controversy is Qubilah Shabazz's alleged "murder plot" against Louis Farrakhan. See Don Terry, "Shabazz Reaches a Settlement in Far-rakhan Murder Plot Case," *New York Times,* May 2, 1995.

10. Andrés Tapia, "Churches Wary of Inner City Islamic Inroads: More Blacks See the Muslim Message as an Appealing Alternative to Christianity," *Christianity Today* (January 10, 1994), p. 36.

SELECT BIBLIOGRAPHY

Ahari-El, Muhammad Abdullah. *Sharif Abdul Ali (Noble Drew Ali—His Life and Teachings),* Chicago: Magribine Press, 1989.

Ahmad, Aziz. *Islamic Modernism in India and Pakistan, 1857–1964.* London: Oxford University Press, 1967.

Ahmad, Hazrat Mirza Bashir-ud-Din Mahmud. *Ahmadiyyat or The True Islam.* Qadian, India: Tahrik-l-Jadid, 1937.

———. *Invitation to Ahmadiyyat.* London: Routledge & Kegan Paul, 1980.

Ahmad, Hazrat Mirza Ghulam. *The Essence of Islam: Extracts from the Writings of the Promised Messiah,* Vol. 1. Translated by Muhammad Zafrullah Khan. London: Ahmadiyya Centenary Publications, 1978.

———. *Masih Hindustan Men.* Qadian, 1912.

———. *Message of Peace.* Lahore, India: Anjuman Ahmadiyya, 1986.

———. *The Philosophy of the Teachings of Islam.* London: Ahmadiyya Centenary Publications, 1979.

———. *Tadhkirah.* Trans. Muhammad Zafrullah Khan. London: Saffron Books, 1976.

———. *Tawzih-i-Maram.* Trans. by Iqbul Ahmud. Lahore: Anjuman Ahmadiyya, 1966.

Ahmad, Hazrat Mizra Nasir. *Message of Love and Brotherhood in Africa.* Rabwah, Pakistan: Nusrat Art Press, 1970.

Akbar, Muhammad. "Interaction between 'Indigenous' and 'Immigrant' Muslims." *Hijrah Magazine* (March/April 1985): 13–15.

Alford, Terry. *Prince among Slaves.* New York: Harcourt Brace Jovanovich, 1977.

Ali, Abdullah Yusuf. *The Holy Qur'an: Text, Translation and Commentary.* Brentwood: Amana Corporation, 1989.

Ali, Malawi Sher, ed. and trans. *The Holy Quran.* Rabawah, Pakistan: Oriental and Religious Publishing Col., n.d.

Ali, Muhammad. *The Ahmadiyya Movement.* Lahore: Ahmadiyyah Anjuman Isha'at Islam, 1975.

Ali, Noble Drew. *The Holy Koran of the Moorish Science Temple of America.* Chicago, 1927.

———. "Koran Questions for Moorish Americans," n.d.

———. "A Warning from The Prophet in 1928," n.d.

———. "What Shall We Call Him?" *Moorish Literature,* n.d.

Ali, Sher. "America's Intolerance," *The Review of Religions* 19 (April/May 1920): 158.

Allen, Ernest Jr. "When Japan Was Champion of the Darker Races: Satokata Takahashi and the Development of Our Own, 1933–1942," *The Black Scholar* 24 (Winter 1994).

Allison, Robert J. *The Crescent Obscured: The United States and the Muslim World, 1776–1815.* New York: Oxford University Press, 1995.

Ansari, Zafar Ishaq. "Aspects of Black Muslim Theology." *Studia Islamica* 53 (1982).

————. "W. D. Mohammed: The Making of a 'Black Muslim' Leader (1933–1961)." *The American Journal of Islamic Social Sciences* 2 (1985): 245–62.

Armah, Ayi Kwei. *Two Thousand Seasons.* Nairobi: East African Publishing House, 1973.

Austin, Allan D. *African Muslims in Antebellum America: A Sourcebook.* New York: Garland, 1984.

Ball, Charles. *A Narrative of the Life and Adventures of Charles Ball, a Black Man,* 3rd ed. Pittsburgh: John T. Skyrock, 1854.

Barboza, Steven. *American Jihad: Islam after Malcolm X.* New York: Doubleday, 1994.

Battle, V. D. W. "The Influence of Al-Islam in America on the Black Community." In *The Black Scholar,* 33–412. California: Black Scholar Press, 1988.

Ben Said, Muhammad Ali. "A Native of Bornoo," *Atlantic Monthly* (October 1876): 483–95.

Benyon, Erdmann D. "The Near East in Flint, Michigan: Assyrians and Druze and Their Antecedents." *Geographical Review* 24, No. 2 (1944): 239–74.

————. "The Voodoo Cult among Negro Migrants in Detroit." *American Journal of Sociology* 43 (July 1937–May 1938): 894–907.

Berger, Morroe. "The Black Muslims," *Horizon* 6 (Winter 1964): 49–64.

Berry, Faith. *Langston Hughes: Before and Beyond Harlem.* New York: Carol Publishing, 1992; first pub. 1983.

Betts, Robert Brenton. *The Druze.* New Haven: Yale University Press, 1988.

Blassingame, John. *Slave Testimony: Two Centuries of Letters, Speeches, Interviews, and Autobiographies.* Baton Rouge: Louisiana State University Press, 1977.

Bluett, Thomas. *Some Memoirs of the Life of Job, the Son of Boonda in Africa.* London: Richard Ford, 1734.

Blyden, Edward Wilmot. "Christianity and the Negro Race," *Fraser's Magazine,* New Series 13 (May 1876): 554–68.

————. *Christianity, Islam and the Negro Race,* 1888; rpt. Edinburgh: University of Edinburgh Press, 1967.

————. *Liberia's Offering,* New York, 1862.

————. "Mohammedanism in the Negro Race," *Fraser's Magazine,* New Series 12 (November 1875): 598–615.

————. "The Negro in Ancient History," *Methodist Quarterly Review* 52 (January 1869): 62–78.

Bousquet, G. H. "Moslem Religion's Influences in the United States," *Modern World* (25 January 1935): 40–44.

Braden, Charles S. "Moslem Missionaries in America," *Religion in Life* 28, No. 3 (Summer 1959): 331–48.

Breitman, George. *The Last Year of Malcolm X: The Evolution of a Revolutionary.* New York: Merit, 1967.

————, ed. *By Any Means Necessary: Speeches, Interviews, and a Letter by Malcolm X.* New York: Pathfinder Press, 1970.

————, ed. *Malcolm X Speaks: Selected Speeches and Statements.* New York: Grove Press, 1965.

Brotz, Howard. *The Black Jews of Harlem: Negro Nationalism and the Dilemmas of Negro Leadership.* New York: Free Press of Glencoe, 1964.

Brown, Leon Carl. "Color in North Africa," *Daedalus* (Spring 1967): 464–82.

Burkett, Randall K. *Garveyism as a Religious Movement: The Institutionalization of a Black Civil Religion.* Metuchen, N.J.: Scarecrow Press, 1978.

Caldwell, Wallace E. "A Survey of Attitudes Toward Black Muslims in Prison." *Journal of Human Relations* 16 (1968): 220–38.

Calverly, E. E. "Negro Muslims in Hartford." *Muslim World* 55, No. 1 (January 1965): 340–45.

Carew, Jan. *Ghosts in Our Blood: With Malcolm X in Africa, England, and the Carribbean.* Chicago: Lawrence Hill Books, 1995.

Carnes, Mark C. *Secret Ritual and Manhood in Victorian America.* New Haven: Yale University Press, 1989.

Carson, Clayborne, Spike Lee, and David Gallen. *Malcolm X: The FBI File.* New York: Carroll and Graf, 1991.

Clark, Kenneth B. *King, Malcolm, Baldwin: Three Interviews.* Middletown, Conn.: Wesleyan University Press, 1985.

Clarke, John Henrik. *Malcolm X: The Man and His Times.* New York: Macmillan, 1969.

———, ed. *Marcus Garvey and the Vision of Africa.* New York: Random House, 1974.

Clarke, Peter B. *West Africa and Islam: A Study of Religious Development from the 8th to the 20th Century.* London: Edward Arnold, 1982.

Clarke, Steve, ed. *February 1965: The Final Speeches of Malcolm X.* New York: Pathfinder Press, 1992.

Clegg, Claude Andrew, III. *An Original Man: The Life and Times of Elijah Muhammad.* New York: St. Martin's Press, 1997.

Cleveland, Omar. "The Democracy in Islam," *The Moslem Sunrise* 4 (April-July 1931).

Cone, James H. *Martin and Malcolm and America: A Dream or a Nightmare.* Maryknoll, N.Y.: Orbis Press, 1991.

Cooper, Mary H. "Muslims in America," *The CQ Researcher* (April 30, 1993): 363–83.

Cornelius, Janet Duitsman. *"When I Can Read My Title Clear": Literacy, Slavery, and Religion in the Antebellum South.* Columbia: University of South Carolina Press, 1991.

Cornell, Vincent J. "Jihad: Islam's Struggle for the Truth," *Gnosis Magazine* (Fall 1991).

Cronon, Edmund David. *Black Moses: The Story of Marcus Garvey and the Universal Negro Improvement Association.* Madison: University of Wisconsin Press, 1966.

Cruse, Harold. *The Crisis of the Negro Intellectual.* New York: Morrow, 1967.

Cushmere, Bernard. *This is the One: Messenger Muhammad: We Need Not Look for Another.* Phoenix, Ariz.: Truth Publications, 1971.

Damali, Nia. *Golden Names for an African People.* Atlanta: Blackwood Press, 1986.

Daniels, Ron. "The Farrakhan Phenomenon," *Z Magazine* (June 1994).

Dard, A. R. *Life of Ahmad.* Lahire: Sultan Brothers, 1949.

Dash, Julie. *Daughters of the Dust: The Making of an African American Woman's Film.* New York: New Press, 1992.

Davis, Charles T., and Henry Louis Gates, Jr., eds. *The Slave's Narrative.* New York: Oxford University Press, 1985.

Drake, St. Clair. *The Redemption of Africa and Black Religion.* Chicago: Third World Press, 1970.

———. *Black Folk Here and There: An Essay in History and Anthropology,* vol. 2. Los Angeles: Center for Afro-American Studies, UCLA, 1990.

Drake, St. Clair, and Horace R Cayton. *Black Metropolis: A Study of Negro Life in a Northern City.* New York: Harcourt Brace, 1945.

Draper, Theodore. *The Rediscovery of Black Nationalism.* New York: Viking, 1970.

DuBois, W. E. B. *The Philadelphia Negro.* New York: Schocken, 1967.

———. *The Souls of Black Folk.* Chicago: A. C. McClurg, 1903.

Duse, Mohammed Ali. *In the Land of the Pharaohs.* London: Frank Cass and Co., 1968.

El-Amin Mustafa. *The Religion of Islam and the Nation of Islam: What Is the Difference?* Newark: El-Amin Productions, 1991.

Elkholy, A. *The Arab Moslems in the United States.* New Haven: College and University Press, 1983.

Epps, Archie, ed. *The Speeches of Malcolm X at Harvard.* New York: Morrow, 1968.

Esposito, John L. *Islam: The Straight Path.* New York: Oxford University Press, 1988.

———. *The Islamic Threat: Myth or Reality?* New York: Oxford University Press, 1992.

Essien-Udom, Essien Udosen. *Black Nationalism: A Search for Identity in America.* Chicago: University of Chicago Press, 1962.

Eure, Joseph D., and Richard M. Jerome, eds. *Back Where We Belong: Selected Speeches by Minister Louis Farrakhan.* Philadelphia: P. C. International, 1989.

Evanzz, Karl. *The Judas Factor: The Plot to Kill Malcolm X.* New York: Thunder's Mouth Press, 1992.

Farrakhan, Louis. *A Torchlight for America.* Chicago: FCN Publishing, 1993.

Fauset, Arthur H. *Black Gods of the Metropolis: Negro Religious Cults of the Urban North.* Philadelphia: University of Pennsylvania Press, 1971.

———. "Moorish Science Temple of America." In *Religion, Society, and the Individual,* edited by J. Milton Yinger, 458–507. New York: Macmillan, 1968.

Fisher, Allan G., and Humphrey J. Fisher. *Slavery and Muslim Society in Africa: The Institution in Saharan and Sudanic Africa and the Trans-Saharan Trade.* London: C. Hurst, 1970.

Fisher, Humphrey J. *Ahmadiyya.* London: Oxford University Press, 1963.

Franklin, Vincent P. *Black Self-Determination: A Cultural History of the Faith of the Fathers.* New York: Lawrence Hill, 1984.

Frazier, E. Franklin. *The Negro Church in America.* / C. Eric Lincoln. *The Black Church since Frazier.* New York: Schocken, 1976.

Friedly, Michael. *Malcolm X: The Assassination.* New York: Carroll and Graf/ Richard Gallen, 1992.

Friedmann, Yohanan. *Prophecy Continuous.* Berkeley: University of California Press, 1989.

Garvey, Marcus. "The British West Indies in the Mirror of Civilization," *African Times and Orient Review* 1 (October 1913).

Gilbert, Peter, ed. *Selected Writings of John Edward Bruce: Militant Black Journalist.* New York: Arno Press and The New York Times, 1971.

Goldman, Peter. *The Death and Life of Malcolm X.* New York: Harper and Row, 1973.

Haddad, Yvonne Yazbeck. "A Century of Islam in America," *The Muslim World*

Today, Occasional Paper, No. 4. Washington Islamic Affairs Programs, Middle East Institute, 1986.

———, ed. *The Muslims of America*. New York: Oxford University Press, 1991.

———, and Adair T. Lummis. *Islamic Values in the United States: A Comparative Study*. New York: Oxford University Press, 1987.

———, and Jane I. Smith. *Mission to America: Five Islamic Sectarian Communities in North America*. Gainesville: University Press of Florida, 1993.

———, and Jane I. Smith, eds. *Muslim Communities in North America*. Albany: State University of New York Press, 1994.

Halasa, Malu. *Elijah Muhammad: Religious Leader*. New York: Chelsea House, 1990.

Hale, Thomas A. *Scribe, Griot, and Novelist: Narrative Interpreters of the Songhay Empire*. Gainesville: University Press of Florida, 1990.

Haley, Alex. *The Autobiography of Malcolm X*. New York: Ballantine Books, 1965.

———. *Roots: The Saga of an American Family*. Garden City, N.Y.: Doubleday, 1976.

———, ed. *The Playboy Interviews*. New York: Ballantine Books, 1962.

Hallowell, Norwood P. "A Native of Borno," *Atlantic Monthly* (October 1876): 485–95.

Hamdun, Said, and Noel King, eds. and trans. *Ibn Battuta in Black Africa*. London: Rex Collings, 1975.

Hanson, J. W., ed. *World's Parliament of Religions at the World's Columbian Exposition*. Boston: J. S. Round, 1894.

Harlan, Louis R. *Booker T. Washington: The Making of a Black Leader, 1856–1901*. New York: Oxford University Press, 1972.

———. *Booker T. Washington: The Wizard of Tuskegee, 1901–1915*. New York: Oxford University Press, 1983.

Harrow, Kenneth W. *Faces of Islam in African Literature*. Portsmouth, N.H.: Heinemann, 1991.

Hauser, Thomas. *Muhammad Ali: His Life and Times*. New York: Simon and Schuster, 1991.

Hayford, J. E. Casely. *Ethiopia Unbound, Studies in Race Emancipation*. London: Frank Cass, 1969; first pub. 1911.

Henri, Florette. *Black Migration: Movement North, 1900–1920*. Garden City, N.Y.: Anchor, 1975.

Hickey, Dennis, and Kenneth C. Wylie. *An Enchanting Darkness: The American Vision of Africa in the Twentieth Century*. East Lansing: Michigan State University Press, 1993.

Higham, John. *Strangers in the Land: Patterns of American Nativism, 1860–1925*. New York: Atheneum, 1963.

Hill, Adelaide Cromwell, and Martin Kilson, eds. *Apropos of Africa: Afro-American Leaders and the Romance of Africa*. Garden City, N.Y.: Anchor, 1971.

Hine, Darlene Clark, ed. *The State of Afro-American History*. Baton Rouge: Louisiana State University Press, 1986.

Hiskett, Mervyn. *The Development of Islam in West Africa*. New York: Longman, 1984.

Hitti, Phillip K. *History of the Arabs*, 10th ed. New York: Macmillan, 1970.

Horne, Gerald. "Myth and the Making of Malcolm X," *American Historical Review* 98 (April 1993): 440–50.

Jacobs, Sylvia M. *Black Americans and the Missionary Movement in Africa.* Westport, Conn.: Greenwood Press, 1982.

Jamal, Hakim A. *From the Dead Level: Malcolm X and Me.* New York: Random House, 1972.

Jameson, J. Franklin. "Autobiography of Omar Ibn Said: Slave in North Carolina, 1831," *American Historical Review,* 30 (July 1925): 787–95.

Jones, Howard. *The Mutiny on the Amistad: The Saga of a Slave Revolt and Its Impact on American Abolition, Law, and Diplomacy.* New York: Oxford University Press, 1987.

Jones, Oliver Jr. "The Black Muslim Movement and the American Constitutional System," *Journal of Black Studies* 13, No. 4 (June 1983): 417–37.

Judy, Ronald A. T. *(Dis) Forming the American Canon: African-Arabic Slave Narratives and the Vernacular.* Minneapolis: University of Minnesota Press, 1993.

Kaplan, H. M. "The Black Muslims and the Negro American's Quest for Communion: A Cast Study in the Genesis of Negro Protest Movements," *British Journal of Sociology* 20 (1969): 164–76.

Kapur, Sudarshan. *Raising Up a Prophet: The African-American Encounter with Gandhi.* Boston: Beacon, 1992.

Karim, Benjamin. *Remembering Malcolm.* New York: Carroll and Graf, 1992.

———, ed. *The End of White World Supremacy, by Malcolm X.* New York: Aracade Publishing, 1971.

Khatib, Abul. "The Need for Jihad," *Gnosis Magazine* (Fall 1991).

Kinney, Jay. "Sufism Comes to America," *Gnosis Magazine* 30 (Winter 1974).

Klein, Herbert S. *African Slavery in Latin America and the Caribbean.* New York: Oxford University Press, 1986.

Kly, Y. N., ed. *The Black Book: The True Political Philosophy of Malcolm X.* Atlanta: Clarity Press, 1986.

Knight, Barbara B. "Religion in Prison: Balancing Free Exercise, No Establishment and Equal Protection Clauses," *Journal of Church and State* 26 (Autumn 1984): 437–54.

Koszegi, Michael A., and J. Gordon Melton. *Islam in North America: A Sourcebook.* New York: Garland, 1992.

Kusmer, Kenneth L. *A Ghetto Takes Shape: Black Cleveland, 1870–1930.* Urbana: University of Illinois Press, 1976.

Landes, Ruth. "Negro Jews in Harlem," *Jewish Journal of Sociology* 9 (1967): 175–89.

Lane, James H. "A Contemporary Revitalization Movement in American Relations: The Black Muslims." In *The Black Church in America,* edited by Hart M. Nelsen. New York: Basic Books, 1971.

Lavan, Spencer. *The Ahmadiyya Movement: A History and Perspective.* Delhi: Manohar Book Service, 1974.

Lee, Martha F. *The Nation of Islam: An American Millenarian Movement.* Lewiston, N.Y.: Mellen, 1988.

Lee, Spike, and Ralph Wiley. *By Any Means Necessary: The Trials and Tribulations of the Making of Malcolm X.* New York: Hyperion, 1992.

Leigh, David J. "Malcolm X and the Black Muslims' Search for Ultimate Reality," *Ultimate Reality and Meaning: Interdisciplinary Studies in the Philosophy of Understanding* 13 (March 1990): 33–49.

Lemann, Nicholas. *The Promised Land: The Great Black Migration and How It Changed America.* New York: Alfred A. Knopf, 1990.

Levine, David Allan. *Internal Combustion: The Races in Detroit, 1915–1926*. Westport, Conn.: Greenwood Press, 1976.

Lewis, Bernard. *Race and Color in Islam*. New York: Harper & Row, 1971.

———. *Race and Slavery in the Middle East: An Historical Enquiry*. New York: Oxford University Press, 1990.

Lewis, David Levering. *W. E. B. DuBois: Biography of a Race, 1868–1919*. New York: Henry Holt, 1993.

Lincoln, C. Eric. "The American Muslim Mission in the Context of American Social History." In *The Muslim Community in North America*, edited by Earl H. Waugh, Baha Abu-Laban, Regula B. Qureshi. Edmonton: University of Alberta Press, 1983.

———. *The Black Church since Frazier. See* Frazier, E. Franklin.

———. "The Black Muslims and Black Acceptance." In *The Black Experience in Religion*, edited by C. Eric Lincoln. Garden City, N.Y.: Doubleday, 1974.

———. "The Black Muslims as a Protest Movement." In *The Black Church in America*, edited by Hart M. Nelson, Raytha L. Yokely, and Anne K. Nelsen. New York: Basic Books, 1971.

———. *The Black Muslims in America*, 3rd ed. Trenton, N.J.: Africa World Press, 1994.

Locke, Alain, ed. *The New Negro*. New York: Atheneum, 1992; first pub. 1925.

Lomax, Louis E. *To Kill a Black Man*. Los Angeles: Holloway House, 1968.

———. *When the Word Is Given: A Report on Elijah Muhammad, Malcolm X, and the Black Muslim World*. Cleveland: World Publishing, 1963.

Long, Charles H. "New Space, New Time: Disjunctions and Context for a New World Religion," paper presented at conference "Race Discourse and the Origin of the Americas: A New World View of 1492," at the Smithsonian Institute, October 31–November 1, 1991.

———. *Significations: Signs, Symbols, and Images in the Interpretation of Religion*. Philadelphia: Fortress Press, 1986.

Lovejoy, Paul E. *Transformations in Slavery: A History of Slavery in Africa*. Cambridge: Cambridge University Press, 1983.

Lynch, Hollis R. *Edward Wilmot Blyden: Pan-Negro Patriot, 1832–1912*. New York: Oxford University Press, 1967.

———, ed. *Black Spokesman: Selected Published Writings of Edward Wilmot Blyden*. New York: Humanities Press, 1971.

———, ed. *Selected Letters of Edward Wilmot Blyden*. Millwood, N.Y.: KTO Press, 1978.

Madhubuti, Haki R. "Black Books Bulletin Interviews—Minister Louis Farrakhan," *Black Books Bulletin*. Chicago: Institute of Positive Education, 1978.

Maesen, William A. "Watchtower Influences on Black Muslim Eschatology: An Exploratory Study," *Journal for the Scientific Study of Religion* 21, No. 2 (June 1982): 321–25.

Maglangbayan, Shawna. *Garvey, Lumumba, Malcolm: Nationalist-Separatists*. Chicago: Third World Press, 1972.

Malcolm X. *Malcolm X on Afro-American History*, 3rd ed. New York: Pathfinder, 1990.

———. *See also* Haley, Alex.

Mamiya, Lawrence H. "From Black Muslim to Bilalian: The Evolution of a Movement," *Journal for the Scientific Study of Religion* 23 (June 1982): 138–52.

————. "Minister Louis Farrakhan and the Final Call: Schism in the Muslim Movement." In *The Muslim Community in North America*, edited by Earl H. Waugh, Baha Abu-Laban, and Regula B. Qureshi, 234–51. Edmonton: University of Alberta Press, 1983.

————, and C. Eric Lincoln. "Black Militant and Separatist Movements." In *Encyclopedia of the American Religious Experience: Studies of Traditions and Movements*, vol. 2, edited by Charles H. Lippy and Peter W. Williams, 755–71. New York: Scribner's, 1988.

Manning, Patrick. *Slavery and African Life: Occidental, Oriental, and African Slave Trades.* Cambridge: Cambridge University Press, 1990.

Marable, Manning. "On Malcolm X: His Message and Meaning," *Open Magazine Pamphlet Series.* November 1992.

Marsh, Clifton E. *From Black Muslims to Muslims: The Transition from Separatism to Islam, 1930–1980.* Metuchen, N.J.: Scarecrow Press, 1984.

Marshall, W. A. "Education in the Nation of Islam during the Leadership of Elijah Muhammad, 1935–1975." New York: Schomburg Library Collections (Sc MicroF 10660), n.d.

Martin, Tony. *Race First: The Ideological and Organizational Struggles of Marcus Garvey and the Universal Negro Improvement Association.* Westport, Conn.: Greenwood Press, 1976.

Marty, Martin. *Modern American Religion: The Noise of Conflict, 1919–1941.* Chicago: University of Chicago Press, 1989.

McCall, Nathan. *Makes Me Wanna Holler: A Young Black Man in America.* New York: Random House, 1994.

McCloud, Aminah Beverly. *African American Islam.* New York: Routledge, 1995.

McNeil, Gemna Rae. Review of *Race First* by Tony Martin, *Journal of Negro History* (October 1977): 405.

Meillassoux, Claude. *The Anthropology of Slavery: The Womb of Iron and Gold.* Chicago: University of Chicago Press, 1991.

Michener, James E. "Roots, Unique in Its Time," *New York Times Book Review* 26 (February 1977).

Mintz, Sidney W., and Richard Price. *The Birth of African-American Culture: An Anthropological Perspective.* Boston: Beacon, 1992.

Mohammed, Warith Deen. *An African-American Genesis.* Chicago: Progressions, 1986.

————. *Focus on Al-Islam.* Chicago: Zakat, 1988.

————. *Al-Islam Unity and Leadership.* Chicago Sense Maker, 1991.

Moore, Francis. *Travels into the Inland Parts of Africa with a Particular Account of Job Ben Solomon.* London, 1738.

Moore, R. Laurence. *Religious Outsiders and the Making of Americans.* New York: Oxford University Press, 1986.

Moore, Samuel. *Biography of Mahommah G. Baquaqua: A Native Zoogoo, in the Interior of Africa.* Detroit: Printed for the author, Mahommah Gardo Baquaqua, by Pomery, Tribune Office, 1854.

Morony, Michael G. *Iraq after the Muslim Conquest.* Princeton: Princeton University Press, 1984.

Moses, Wilson Jeremiah. *Black Messiahs and Uncle Toms: Social and Literary Manipulations of a Religious Myth.* University Park: Pennsylvania State University Press, 1982.

———. "Marcus Garvey: A Reappraisal," *Black Scholar* 4 (November–December 1972): 38–49.

Mudimbe, V. Y. *The Invention of Africa.* Bloomington: Indiana University Press, 1988.

Muhammad, Elijah. *The Fall of America.* Chicago: Muhammad's Temple of Islam, No. 2, 1973.

———. *Message to the Blackman in America.* Chicago: Muhammad Mosque of Islam, No. 2, 1963.

———. *Our Saviour Has Arrived.* Chicago: Muhammad's Temple of Islam, No. 2, 1974.

———. *The Supreme Wisdom: Solution to the So-Called Negroes' Problems.* Chicago: Muhammad Mosque of Islam, No. 2, 1957.

———. *The Theology of Time.* Hampton, Va.: United Brothers Graphics Printing, 1992.

Muhammad, Isa. *The Ansar Cult.* Brooklyn: Ansaru Allah Community, 1988.

———. *The Book of Laam.* Brooklyn: Nubian Islamic Hebrews, n.d.

———. *Al-Quran al-Muqaddasu: Al-Wasiyya al-Akhirah.* Brooklyn: Ansaru Allah Community, 1977.

Muhammad, Jabril. *Is It Possible That the Honorable Elijah Muhammad Is Still Alive?* New York: Resurrecting Light Communications, 1983.

Muhammad, Wallace D. *As the Light Shineth from the East.* Chicago: WDM Publishing, 1980.

———. *Book of Muslim Names.* Chicago: The Honorable Elijah Muhammad Mosque, No. 2, 1976.

———. *Imam W. Deen Muhammad Speaks from Harlem, N.Y.* Chicago: W. D. Muhammad Publications, 1984.

———. *The Man and the Woman in Islam.* Chicago: The Honorable Elijah Muhammad Mosque, No. 2, 1970.

———. *Prayer and al-Islam.* Chicago: Muhammad Islamic Foundation, 1982.

———. *The Teachings of W. D. Muhammad.* Chicago: The Honorable Elijah Muhammad Mosque, No. 2, 1976.

Naff, Alixa. *Becoming American: The Early Arab Immigrant Experience.* Carbondale: Southern Illinois University Press, 1985.

Nation of Islam Historical Research Department. *The Secret Relationship between the Blacks and Jews.* Chicago: The Nation of Islam, 1991.

Norman, Barbara Ann. "The Black Muslims: A Rhetorical Analysis," Ph.D. dissertation, University of Oklahoma, 1985.

Nuñez Cabeza de Vaca, Alvar. *Relation of Nuñez Cabeza de Vaca,* trans. Buckingham Smith. Ann Arbor: University Microfilms, 1966; published in Spanish in 1542.

Osofsky, Gilbert. *Harlem, the Making of a Ghetto: Negro New York, 1890–1930.* New York: Harper & Row, 1965.

Ottley, Roi. *"New World A-Coming": Inside Black America.* Boston: Houghton Mifflin, 1943.

Panger, Daniel. *Black Ulysses.* Athens: Ohio University Press, 1982.

Parenti, Michael. "The Black Muslims: From Revolution to Institution," *Social Research* 31 (1964): 975–94.

Parrish, Lydia. *Slave Songs of the Georgia Sea Islands.* Athens: University of Georgia Press, 1992.

Patterson, Orlando. *Slavery and Social Death: A Comparative Study.* Cambridge: Harvard University Press, 1982.

Paustian, P. Robert. "The Evolution of Personal Naming Practices among American Blacks," *Names* 26, No. 2 (1978): 177–82.

Perkins, William Eric, ed. *Droppin' Science: Critical Essays in Rap Music and Hiphop Culture.* Philadelphia: Temple University Press, 1996.

Perry, Bruce. *Malcolm: The Life of a Man Who Changed Black America.* Barrytown, N.Y.: Station Hill Press, 1991.

———, ed. *Malcolm X: The Last Speeches.* New York: Pathfinder, 1989.

Piersen, William D. *Black Legacy: America's Hidden Heritage.* Amherst: University of Massachusetts Press, 1977.

Raboteau, Albert. "Ethiopia Shall Soon Stretch Forth Her Hands: Black Destiny in Nineteenth Century America." University lecture in religion at Arizona State University, Tempe, January 27, 1983.

———. *Slave Religion: The "Invisible Institution" in the Antebellum South.* New York: Oxford University Press, 1978.

Rampersad, Arnold. *The Art and Imagination of W. E. B. DuBois.* New York: Schocken Books, 1990; first pub. 1976.

Redkey, Edwin S. *Black Exodus: Black Nationalist and Back-to-Africa Movements, 1890–1910.* New Haven: Yale University Press, 1969.

———, ed. *Respect Black: The Writings and Speeches of Henry McNeal Turner.* New York: Arno Press, 1971.

Reis, João José. *Slave Rebellion in Brazil: The Muslim Uprising of 1835 in Bahia,* trans. Arthur Brakel. Baltimore: The Johns Hopkins University Press, 1993.

Richardson, E. Allen. *Islamic Cultures in North America.* New York: Pilgrim Press, 1981.

Robinson, Francis. *Atlas of the Islamic World since 1500.* New York: Facts on File, 1982.

Rogers, Ben F. "William E. B. DuBois, Marcus Garvey, and Pan Africa," *Journal of Negro History* 40 (April 1955): 154–65.

Rose, Willie Lee. "An American Family," *New York Review of Books* 11 (November 1976): 3–4.

Ross, Vivian Hudson. "Black Muslim Schools: Institutionalization of Black Nationalism: Implications for the Altering of Self-Concept in Ghetto Schools," Ph.D. dissertation, University of Michigan, 1976.

Rudwick, Elliott M. "DuBois versus Garvey: Race Propagandists at War," *Journal of Negro Education* 27 (Fall 1959): 421–29.

———. *W. E. B. DuBois: Propagandist of the Negro Protest.* New York: Atheneum, 1968.

Sadiq, Mufti Muhammad. "My Advice to the Muhammadans in America," *The Moslem Sunrise* 2 (October 1921): 29.

———. "No Polygamy," *The Moslem Sunrise* 1 (July 1921): 9.

———. "One Year's Missionary Work in America," *The Moslem Sunrise* (July 1921): 12.

———. "Warm Controversy on Mohammedanism," *The Moslem Sunrise* 1 (July 1921): 16.

Said, Edward W. *Orientalism.* New York: Pantheon, 1978.

Savannah Unit of the Georgia Writer's Project of the Works Projects Administration. *Drums and Shadows: Survival Studies among the Georgia Coastal Negroes.* Athens: University of Georgia Press, 1940.

Scott, William R. "Arnold Ford's Back-to-Ethiopia Movement," *Pan African Journal* 8 (Summer 1975): 191–202.

Seager, Richard H. "World's Parliament of Religions, Chicago, Illinois, 1893," Ph.D. dissertation, Harvard University, 1986. (Later published as *The World's Parliament of Religions: The East/West Encounter, Chicago, 1893* [Bloomington: Indiana University Press, 1995].)

Shabazz, Hakim B. *Essays on the Life and Teaching of Master W. Fard Muhammad.* Hampton, Va.: United Brothers & United Sisters Communications Systems, 1990.

Shakur, Sanyika. *Monster: The Autobiography of an L.A. Gang Member.* New York: Atlantic Monthly Press, 1993.

Shalaby, Ibrahim M., and John H. Chilcott. *The Education of a Black Muslim.* Tucson: Sahuaro, 1972.

Shepperson, George. "Notes on Negro American Influences on the Emergence of African Nationalism," *Journal of African History* 1, No. 2 (1960): 299–312.

Shklar, Judith N. "Subversive Genealogies," *Daedalus* (Winter 1972): 129–54.

Spear, Allan H. *Black Chicago: The Making of a Negro Ghetto, 1890–1920.* Chicago: University of Chicago Press, 1967.

Steward, Theophilus Gould. *The End of the World, or, Clearing the Way for the Fullness of the Gentiles.* Philadelphia: A.M.E. Church Book Rooms, 1888.

Strickland, William, and Cheryll Y. Greene. *Malcolm X: Make It Plain.* New York: Viking, 1994.

Stuckey, Sterling. *Slave Culture: National Theory and the Foundations of Black America.* New York: Oxford University Press, 1987.

Tapia, Andrés. "Churches Wary of Inner City Islamic Inroads: More Blacks See the Muslim Message as an Appealing Alternative to Christianity," *Christianity Today* (January 10, 1994).

Thornton, John. *Africa and Africans in the Making of the Atlantic World, 1400–1680.* Cambridge: Cambridge University Press, 1992.

Thurman, Howard. *With Head and Heart: The Autobiography of Howard Thurman.* New York: Harcourt, Brace, Jovanovich, 1979.

Turner, Richard Brent. "The Ahmadiyya Mission to Blacks in America in the 1920s," *The Journal of Religious Thought* 44, No. 2 (Winter/Spring 1988): 50–66.

———. "The Ahmadiyya Movement in America," *Religion Today* 5, No. 3 (1990).

———. "Islam in the United States in the 1920s: The Quest for a New Vision in Afro-American Religion." Ph.D. dissertation, Princeton University, 1986.

———. "What Shall We Call Him? Islam and African American Identity," *The Journal of Religious Thought* 51, No. 1 (Fall 1995): 1–28.

Tyler, Lawrence L. "The Protestant Ethic among the Black Muslims," *Phylon* 27 (1966): 5–14.

Vincent, Theodore G. *Black Power and the Garvey Movement.* Berkeley: Ramparts Press, 1971.

Walden, Daniel, ed. *W. E. B. DuBois: The Crisis Writings.* Greenwich, Conn.: Fawcett Publications, 1972.

Wallace, Mike, and Louis E. Lomax, producers. "The Hate That Hate Produced," "Newsbeat" broadcast in New York City's WNTA-TV, July 10–17, 1959.

Waugh, Earl, Baha Abu-Laban, and Regula B. Qureshi, eds. *The Muslim Community in North America*. Edmonton: University of Alberta Press, 1983.

Webb, Mohammed Alexander Russell. *Islam in America: A Brief Statement of Mohammedanism and an Outline of the American Islamic Propaganda*. New York: Oriental Publishing Co., 1893.

West, Cornel. "Postmodernism and Black America," *Zeta Magazine*, 1988.

Williams, Eric. *Capitalism and Slavery*. Chapel Hill: University of North Carolina Press, 1944.

Williams, George Washington. *History of the Negro Race in America from 1619 to 1880*. New York: G. P. Putnam, 1882.

Williams, Raymond Brady. *Religions of Immigrants from India and Pakistan: New Threads in the American Tapestry*. Cambridge: Cambridge University Press, 1988.

Wilmore, Gayraud. *Black Religion and Black Radicalism: An Interpretation of the Religious History of Afro-American People*, 2nd ed. Maryknoll, N.Y.: Orbis Books, 1983.

Wilson, Peter Lamborn. *Sacred Drift: Essays on the Margins of Islam*. San Francisco: City Lights Books, 1993.

———. "Shoot-out at the Circle 7 Koran: Noble Drew Ali and the Moorish Science Temple." *Gnosis Magazine* 12 (Summer 1989).

Winters, Clyde Ahmed. "Afro-American Muslims from Slavery to Freedom," *Islamic Studies* 17, No. 4 (1978): 187–205.

———. "Roots and Islam in Slave America," *Al-Ittihad* 3 (October-November 1976): 18–20.

Wolfenstein, Eugene Victor. *The Victims of Democracy: Malcolm X and the Black Revolution*. Berkeley: University of California Press, 1981.

Wood, Joe, ed. *Malcolm X: In Our Own Image*. New York: St. Martin's Press, 1992.

Wright, R. R. "Negro Companions of the Spanish Explorers," *American Anthropologist* 4 (1902).

X, Malcolm. *See* Malcolm X.

INDEX

Bengalee, Sufi Mutiur Rahman, 132–33, 137, 266n.95
Berlin conference (1885), 53
Bey, C. Kirkman, 100, 103
Bey, H. Peter, 104
Bey, Mary Clift, 105
Bey, Walter Smith, 260n.76
Beynon, Erdmann D., 163
Bilali, 32–34, 35–36, 249n.65. *See also* Salih Bilali
Bird, Issac, 250n.83
Black nationalism: slavery and history of Islam, 5; Pan-Africanism and, 49–50; Du-Bois and, 77; during World War I era, 78; Garvey and, 80–90; and political dimensions of Malcolm X's religious identity, 207–209, 223; and territorial separatism, 253n.4
Blakey, Art, 139
Bliss, Daniel, 40
Bluett, Thomas, 25–26
Blyden, Edward Wilmot, 40, 47, 48–59, 81, 85–86, 90, 252–53n.1
Boston: and formative years of Malcolm X, 181, 272n.20
Boutiba, Mahmoud, 204
Braden, Charles, 132
Brazil: slave revolt of 1835, 23, 40
Breitman, George, 214
Briggs, Cyril, 78, 257n.22
Briggs, William, 257n.22
Brooks, Gwendolyn, 239
Brown, Katie, 34
Bruce, John Edward, 61, 84, 90
Buchanan, Agnes Foster, 117
Buddhism: U.S. missions in early 1900s, 62
Burkett, Randall, 82
Butler, Norman 3X, 219

Canada: black community in early 1900s, 177
Capitalism: Europe and slave trade in West Africa, 23; Malcolm X's critique of, 204, 215, 219
Captain Joseph, 210
Carew, Jan, 272n.7
Carnes, Mark C., 95
Castro, Fidel, 204
Central Intelligence Agency (CIA), 220–21
Challenge (journal), 257n.22
Christianity: African Muslim slaves and resistance to conversion, 24–25; Blyden on Islam and, 52; Turner on racism in, 59–62; Ahmadiyya movement and, 113, 123–24, 135
Cisse, Hassan, 233
Civil rights movement: and Elijah Muhammad, 202; and Malcolm X, 210–11
Class: and racial discrimination in north Af-

rica, 215; and religious identity of W. D. Mohammed and Louis Farrakhan, 228–29
Clay, Henry, 31
Cleage, Albert B., Jr., 208
Cleveland, Omar, 136
Clothing: Ahmadiyya movement and Muslim, 126
Coleman, Milton, 229–30
Collins, Ella, 181, 272n.20
Colonialism: and Islamic modernism, 62–63; and British rule in India, 110; and Nation of Islam, 172; and global Islam after World War II, 193–94
Colored Catholic Congresses, 66
Colored Farmers Alliance, 258n.26
Coltrane, John, 139
Columbus, Christopher, 22–23
Communism: and Ahmadiyya movement, 137
Cone, James H., 180, 271n.4
Conrad, Georgia, 32
Conwell, James. *See* Abdullah, Brother
CORE (Congress for Racial Equality), 210
Cornelius, Janet D., 247n.37, 252n.111
Cornell, Vincent J., 4–5
Cornish, Samuel, 31
Cotheal, Alexander J., 250n.83
Couper, James Hamilton, 34
Cox, John Coates, 28, 30
The Crisis (NAACP), 76
Culture. *See* Popular culture, African-American
Curry, George E., 230

Daleel, Fard, 139
Dalfiume, Richard M., 187
Daniels, Ron, 240
Daoud, Talib, 139
Darul Islam, 233
Dayton (Ohio), Ahmadiyya community, 140
De Guzman, Mimo, 102
De Jaspas, Melchour, 26
Department of Justice. *See* Federal Bureau of Investigation
Detroit: W. D. Fard and establishment of Nation of Islam, 148–51; Great Migration and Great Depression, 155–56
Development of Our Own, 167, 168
Dharmapala, Angarika, 62
Din, Ahmad, 126, 127
Din, Maulvi Muhammad, 130
Dingle-El, Richardson, 106
Do the Right Thing (film, 1989), 240
Douglass, Frederick, 66
Dowling, Levi H., 94
Dred Scott decision (1857), 49
DuBois, W. E. B., 76–78, 79
Dwight, Theodore, Jr., 36–37
Dwight, Timothy, Jr., 40

Lincoln, C. Eric, 6, 72, 124, 158, 162, 164, 199, 202, 213
Little, Earl, and Louise Norton Little, 176–80
Little, Malcolm. *See* Malcolm X
Little, Philbert. *See* Omar, Abdul Aziz
Little, Wilfred, 178, 183
Locke, Alain, 79–80, 256n.7
Lomax, Louis, 159, 191, 192–93, 197, 199, 200–201, 219–20, 271n.4
Long, Charles H., 2–3, 4, 45, 160, 255n.43
Los Angeles: Malcolm X on police brutality in, 204–206
Louis X, 210
Lovejoy, Paul E., 22, 247n.33
Lowrie, John C., 57
Lumumba, Patrice, 204
Lynch, Hollis R., 56

al-Mahdi, Ibrahim, 14
Malcolm X: and resurgence of global Islam after World War II, 175; formative years of, 176–84; Nation of Islam and jihad of words, 184–89; Nation of Islam and politics of religious identity, 189–214; after split with Nation of Islam, 214–23, 273–74n.46; and commodification of identity, 239; source materials on, 270–72n.4
Malcolm X (film, 1992), 240
Mali: history of Islam in, 18–20
Mamiya, Lawrence H., 217, 224, 228–29
Mamout, Yarrow, 26–27, 248n.45
Mandingo, Paul A. *See* Kaba, Lamine
Manning, Patrick, 247n.33
Mansa Muhammad (son of Mansa Qu), 19
Mansa Musa, 18, 19
Mansa Qu, 19
Mansa Uli (son of Sundiata), 18–19
al-Mansur, Yaqub, 14
Marable, Manning, 211, 212
Marke, George O., 84
Marks, Carole, 153
Marschalk, Colonel, 30
Marsh, Clifton E., 50
Marty, Martin, 72–73, 157, 170
McCall, Nathan, 239
McCloud, Aminah Beverly, 138–39, 140–41, 233, 243n.9, 256n.3, 259n.57, 260nn.59,75
McGuire, George Alexander, 83
Media: and Nation of Islam, 197; images of African-American Muslims in 1990s, 236
The Messenger (journal), 257n.22
Michener, James A., 6
Minto, Bashir Ahmad, 194
Mintz, Sidney W., 247n.39
Mississippi: FBI campaign against Moorish Americans in, 103
Modernity and modernism: and slave trade in West Africa, 21–23; colonialism and Islamic in nineteenth century, 62–63; W. D. Fard and Islamic, 170–71

Mohammad, Carrie, 161
Mohammed, Abdul, 166
Mohammed, Warith Deen, 6, 138, 164, 175, 189–90, 195, 203, 210, 213, 223–31, 276n.142
Moore, Francis, 248n.44
Moore, Richard B., 84
Moore, R. Laurence, 131
Moore, Samuel, 41, 42
Moorish Guide (newspaper), 106
Moorish Science Temple of America, 90–108, 158, 256nn.2,3, 259–60nn.57–59
Moorish Voice (magazine), 105
Moors: use of term in antebellum period, 44
Morony, Michael, 15
Morocco: conquest of Songhay empire, 21; and Noble Drew Ali's construction of identity, 96
Moses, Wilson J., 48, 49–50, 53, 54, 253nn.1,4
Moslem Sunrise/Muslim Sunrise (journal), 121–24, 126, 127, 130, 132, 135, 137
Moslem World Publishing Company, 64
Mousa, F. M., 250n.83
Mudimbe, V. Y., 53, 55, 56, 253n.1
al-Muhallabi (Arabic geographer), 16
Muhammad (Prophet): on slavery and race, 13; jihad and Islamic expansionism, 14; and Ahmadiyya movement, 112
Muhammad, Akbar, 164–65, 171, 239, 269n.53
Muhammad, Augustus, 167
Muhammad, Clara, 169
Muhammad, Elijah, 138, 151–63, 166–69, 175–76, 182, 188–214, 224
Muhammad, Emmanuel Abdullah, 168, 227
Muhammad, Herbert, 210
Muhammad, John, 227
Muhammad, Kallat, 167
Muhammad, Khallid, 193, 236, 240, 280n.9
Muhammad, Silis, 227
Muhammad, Tynetta, 230
Muhammad, Wallace. *See* Mohammed, Warith Deen
Muhammad Speaks (newspaper), 199
Mujadid: Ahmadiyya movement and orthodox Islam, 113
Mullin, Michael, 252n.110
Mullowny, Thomas, 30
Murphy, John C., 31
Music. *See* Jazz musicians; Rap musicians, and Islam in 1990s
Muslim American Community, 225–27, 229–31
Muslim Mosque, Inc., 214, 219
Muslim Student Association, 236
Muslim World League, 236
Mustafa, Fatima. *See* Sobolewski, S. W.
Myths of creation and genealogy, 95–96

NAACP, 76, 210

and future of Islam in U.S., 234–37. *See also* Racism

Race riots: and Great Migration, 75; in Detroit during 1940s, 135

Racism: Turner on Christianity and, 59–62; and military service in early 1900s, 75; Bengalee on, 133

Rahatullah, Madame, 119

al-Rahman II, Abd (ruler of Morocco), 30–31

Rahman, Amina, 201

Randolph, A. Philip, 78, 187, 257n.22

Rao, Ganesh, 128–29

Rap musicians, and Islam in 1990s, 239–40, 279n.6

Rassel, Mrs. Elias. *See* Rasul, Ghulam

Rasul, Ghulam, 125

Ray, Lamine, 26

Reconstruction: impact of failure of, 59, 66

Reed, Ishmael, 239

Reis, João, 40

Religion: and symbols of Islam in African-American popular culture, 4; and Blyden's conversion to Islam, 56–59; Garvey and black civil, 82; and Ahmadiyya movement in early 1900s, 123. *See also* Christianity; Islam; Religious history

Religious history: and historiography of Islam in America, 6–7; Ahmadiyya movement and theory of religious outsidership, 131

Resistance: and concept of signification as analytical tool, 3–4; slavery and Black Islam, 23–25; slavery and identity, 247n.37, 252n.108

The Review of Religions (journal), 262n.1

Robinson, Cedric, 96

Robinson, David, 98

Rochford, R. J. H., 116

Roosevelt, Franklin D., 187

Rudwick, Elliott M., 76

Russwurm, John, 31

Rustin, Bayard, 1

Sadiq, Muhammad, 115–31, 140, 265n.68

Said, Edward, 39

Said, Mohammed Ali Ben, 41–43, 251n.87

Said, Omar Ibn, 37–40, 51, 250n.83

Sakura, 19

Salaam, Abdus, 127

Salih Bilali, 34–36

Sam, Alfred C., 78

Samadu, 58

Sanchez, Sonia, 239

Saussure, Ferdinand de, 3

Schomburg, Arthur Alphonso, 78, 84

Schroeder, John F., 31

Scott, James C., 3–4, 252n.108

Sectarianism: Nation of Islam and tradition of in global Islam, 192

Segregation: urbanization and Great Migration, 74–75; Ahmadiyya movement on Protestant churches and, 135

Shabazz, Attallah, 177

Shabazz, Betty, 201

El-Shabazz, El Hajj Malik. *See* Malcolm X

Shabazz, Qubilah, 280n.9

Shafeek, Mursil, 140

Shah, Idries, 94

Shaku, Soyen, 62

Shakur, Sanyika, 239

Sharrief, Raymond, 210

Shawarbi, Mahmoud Yousse, 204

Sherrod, Pearl, 168

Shihab, Sahib, 139

Shiites, present status of in U.S., 234

Shklar, Judith N., 95–96

Sierra Leone: Blyden's visit to, 51; Turner's visit to, 60

Signification: concept of as analytical tool, 2–7; resistance and African Muslim slaves, 24–25; names and African Muslim slaves, 43–46; and Webb's Islamic identity, 65; Marcus Garvey and Islam, 80–90; Noble Drew Ali and Moorish Science Temple, 97–98; and Nation of Islam, 156, 158–59, 160–66; Malcolm X as model for, 214–23

Simpkins, C. O., 139

Sisei, Mohammed, 24

Sisters National Auxiliary, 105

Slave revolts: and African Muslim slaves, 23–24, 40

Slavery: and history of Islam in America, 5; Prophet Muhammad on, 13; Islam and trade in West Africa, 21–23; African Muslim slaves in America, 11–12, 23–46; Blyden on Islam and, 55; Nation of Islam on history and, 156; Malcolm X on racism in orthodox Islam and, 216–17; and Quran, 244n.6; Europe and transformation of African in modern era, 246–47n.33; identity and resistance to, 247n.37, 252n.108

Sloane, Hans, 26

Smith, Jane I., 97–98, 192, 265n.68

Smith, Leonard, 107

Smith, R. Bosworth, 52

Smyth, John Henry, 60–61

Sobolewski, S. W., 119

Songhay empire: and history of Islam in West Africa, 20–21, 246n.31

Soninke (Ghana), 16–17

Sori (king of Timbo), 28

Spalding, Thomas, 32, 33, 249n.64

Sprengling, Martin, 132

Staton, Dakota. *See* Rabia, Aliyah

Stein, Judith, 159–60

Steward, Theophilus Gould, 61, 66

Stoddard, Lothrop, 76

Stokes, Ronald, 204–206
Strickland, William, 176, 180, 183, 185, 205–206, 209, 271*n*.4
Stuckey, Sterling, 252*n*.111
Sudan, early history of Islam in, 16–17
Sufism: influence of on Noble Drew Ali, 94; present status of in U. S., 233
Sukarno, Ahmad, 204
Sullivan, Ben, 35
Sunderland, George, 117
Sundiata (c.1230–1255), 18
Sunni Ali, 20
Sunni Islamic Mission of America, 131
Sutton, Rev. *See* Salaam, Abdus

Takahashi, Satokata, 102, 168
Tappan, Arthur, 31
Tarbell, Harlan, 133
Taylor, John Louis, 39
Terrell, Mary Church, 78
Thaxton, Osborne, and Leroy Thaxton, 188
Theosophy, influence of on Noble Drew Ali, 93–94
Thind, Bhagat Singh, 117
Third World: and politics of Malcolm X, 204; and ideological identification of northern and middle Africa, 216. *See also* West Africa
Thornton, John, 246–47*n*.33
Tijaniyyah (Sufi path), 233
Trotter, William Monroe, 77, 78
Trubetskoy, Prince Nicholas, 43
Turner, Henry McNeal, 59–62, 66
Tyner, McCoy, 139
Tyson, Mike, 239

al-Umari, 18
U.S. vs. Bhagat Singh Thind (1923), 117
Unity Nation, 280*n*.9
Universal Negro Improvement Association (UNIA), 72, 79, 80–90, 127–30, 154–55, 178–79
Universal Races Congress, 83–84
University of Islam, 166, 196
Urbanization: Great Migration and Black Islamic identity, 73–80

Values: African Muslims and African-American culture, 45–46
Vivekananda, Swami, 62

Wali, Al Hajj Iba, 218

Walker, David, 31
Wallace, Mike, 197
Washington, Booker T., 71, 77
Wati (brother of Mansa Uli), 19
Webb, Mohammed Alexander Russell, 63–66, 94, 171, 255*n*.39
Weber, Max, 228–29
Webster, Noah, 11
Weller, Charles F., 133
Wells, Ida B., 66, 78
West, Cornel, 174
West Africa: slave trade and history of Islam in, 13–23; separatist community model of Islam in, 60; Garvey and Muslim communities in, 85; Ahmadiyya movement missions in, 130; Malcolm X's tour of, 217–18, 273–74*n*.46; Islam and naming practices in, 245*n*.20. *See also* Africa; *specific countries*
West Indies, African Muslim slaves in, 24
Williams, Eric, 247*n*.33
Williams, Peter, 31
Wilson, Mike, 241
Wilson, Peter Lamborn, 94, 259*nn*.55,58–59, 262*n*.93
Wirth, Louis, 163
Wolfenstein, Eugene Victor, 271*n*.4
Women: and preservation of Muslim identities during slavery, 35–36; roles of in Moorish American movement of 1940s, 104–105; Sister Clara as model for black Muslim in 1940s, 169
Women's club movement, 78
Wood, John T., 137
Works Progress Administration (Georgia Writer's Project), 33, 35
World Fellowship of Faiths, 133
World's Parliament of Religions (1893), 62–67, 95
World War I: military service and racism during, 75; and black nationalism, 78
World War II: FBI and Moorish Science Temple, 101–106; as turning point in African-American history, 174, 187; Islamic world in aftermath of, 175
Wylie, Kenneth C., 162, 253*n*.1, 254*n*.20

Yacub, Dhul Waqar, 144–46
Yaqoob, Muhammad, 125
Yearwood, James, 84

Zafr, Muzaffar Ahmad, 141, 270*n*.65

Richard Brent Turner
is an assistant professor of theology at
Xavier University in New Orleans.